THE FLASH
RACE AGAINST TIME!

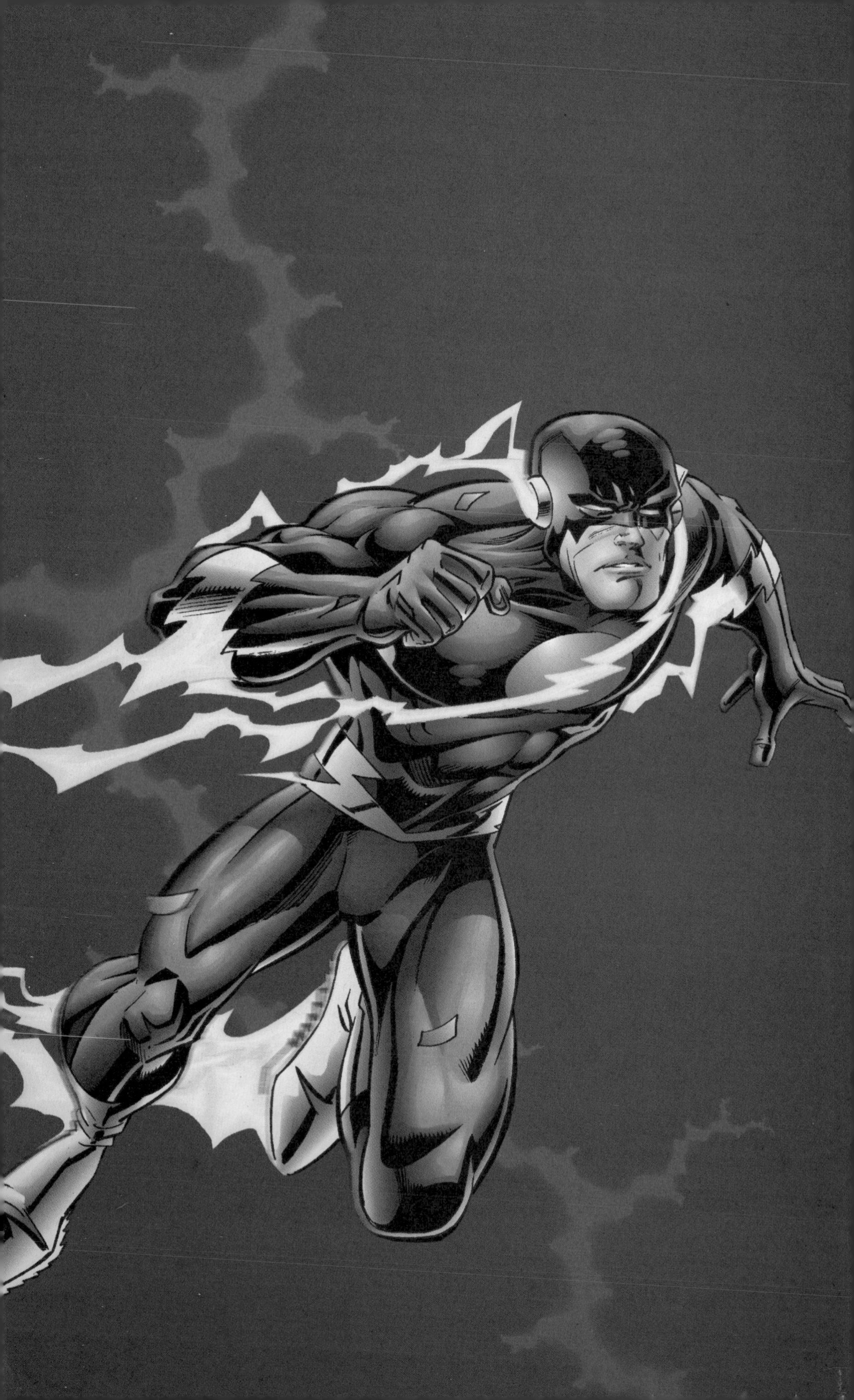

THE FLASH
RACE AGAINST TIME!

Mark Waid
Brian Augustyn
writers

Tom McCraw
colorist

Oscar Jimenez
Anthony Castrillo
Jim Cheung
Sergio Cariello
pencillers

Gaspar Saladino
Kevin Cunningham
letterers

José Marzán, Jr.
Anibal Rodriguez
John Nyberg
Brian Garvey
inkers

Oscar Jimenez
Steve Lightle
Mike Wieringo
José Marzán, Jr.
original covers

The Flash: Race Against Time!

Published by DC Comics.

DC Comics, 1700 Broadway, New York, NY 10019
A division of Warner Bros. - An AOL Time Warner Company
Printed in Canada. First Printing.
ISBN: 1-56389-721-0
Cover illustration by Mike Wieringo & José Marzán, Jr.
Cover color by Patrick Martin.

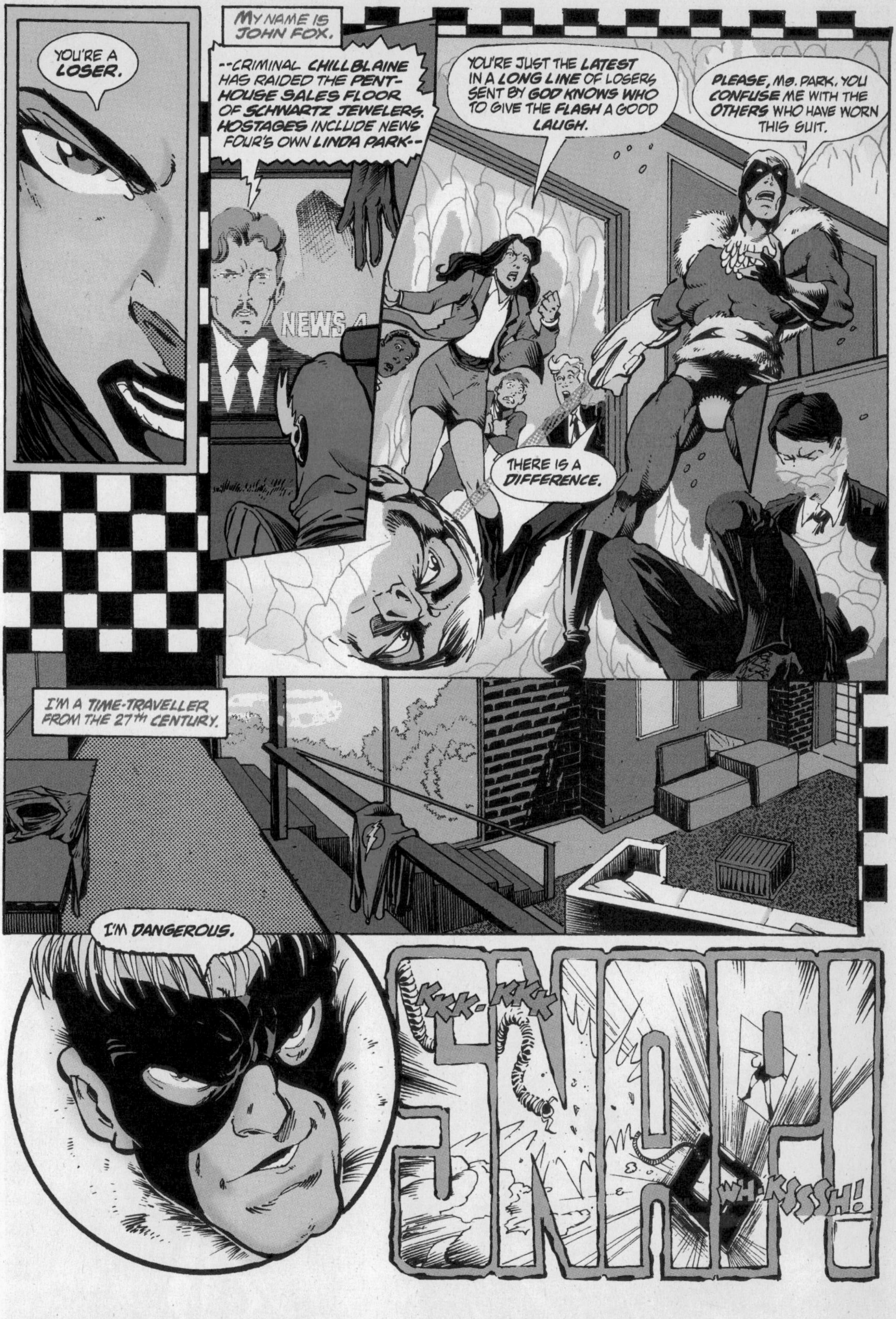

YOU'RE A LOSER.
MY NAME IS JOHN FOX.
--CRIMINAL CHILLBLAINE HAS RAIDED THE PENT-HOUSE SALES FLOOR OF SCHWARTZ JEWELERS. HOSTAGES INCLUDE NEWS FOUR'S OWN LINDA PARK--
NEWS 4
YOU'RE JUST THE LATEST IN A LONG LINE OF LOSERS SENT BY GOD KNOWS WHO TO GIVE THE FLASH A GOOD LAUGH.
PLEASE, MS. PARK, YOU CONFUSE ME WITH THE OTHERS WHO HAVE WORN THIS SUIT.
THERE IS A DIFFERENCE.
I'M A TIME-TRAVELLER FROM THE 27th CENTURY.
I'M DANGEROUS.
KKK-KKK
SNAP!
WHKISSH!

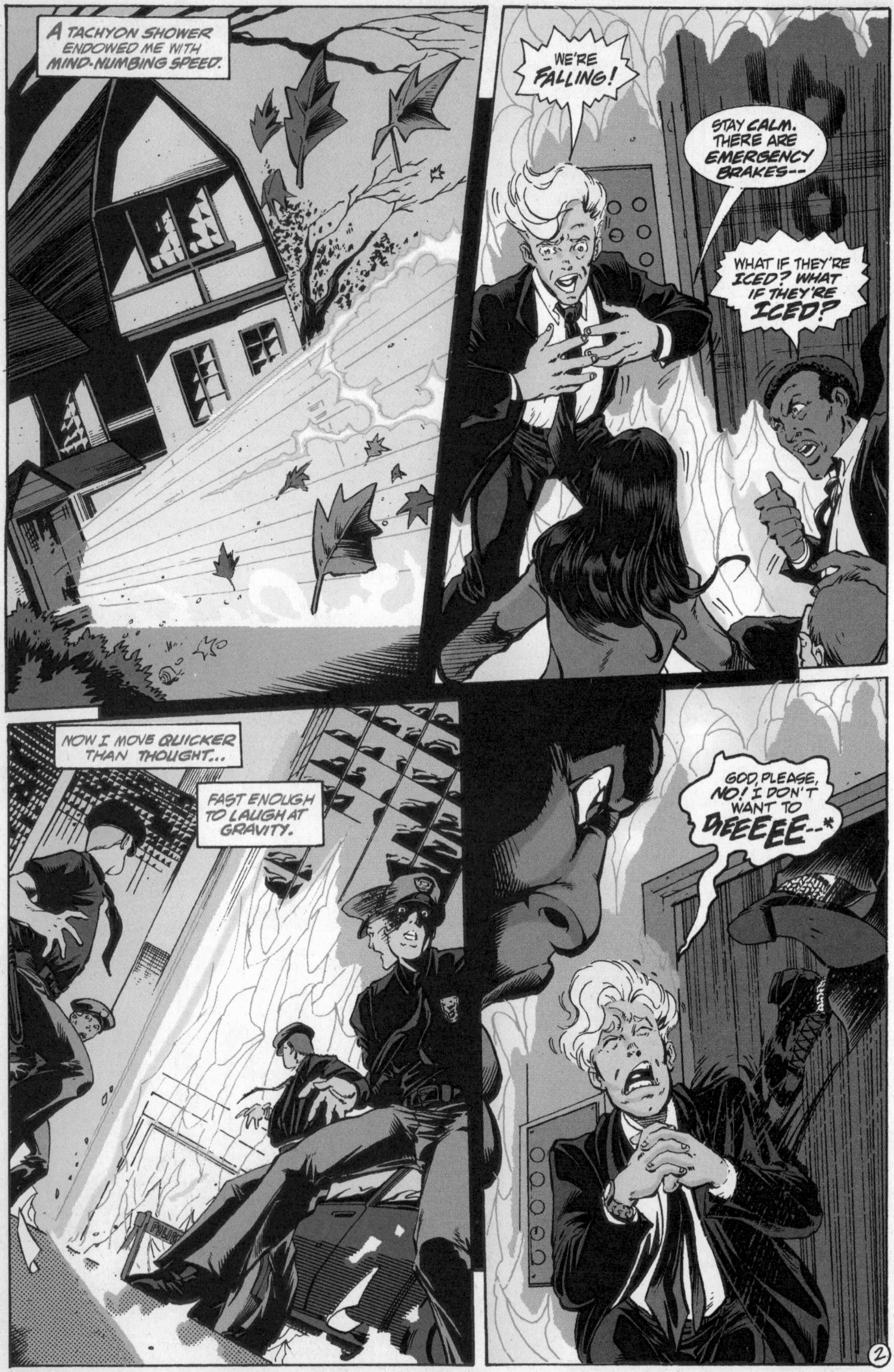
A TACHYON SHOWER ENDOWED ME WITH MIND-NUMBING SPEED.
WE'RE FALLING!
STAY CALM. THERE ARE EMERGENCY BRAKES--
WHAT IF THEY'RE ICED? WHAT IF THEY'RE ICED?
NOW I MOVE QUICKER THAN THOUGHT...
FAST ENOUGH TO LAUGH AT GRAVITY.
GOD, PLEASE, NO! I DON'T WANT TO DEEEEE--*
2

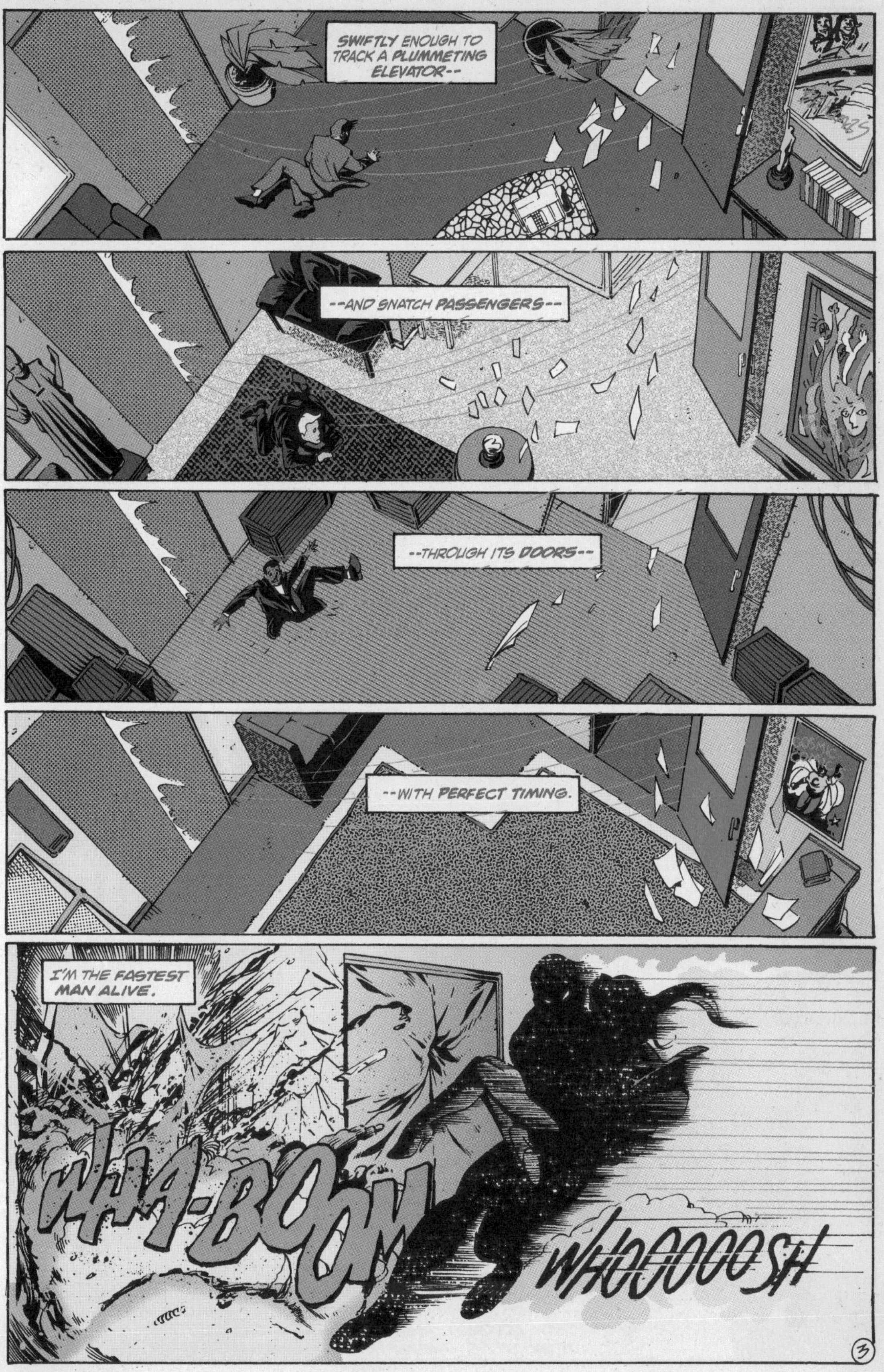
SWIFTLY ENOUGH TO TRACK A PLUMMETING ELEVATOR--
--AND SNATCH PASSENGERS--
--THROUGH ITS DOORS--
--WITH PERFECT TIMING.
COSMIC
I'M THE FASTEST MAN ALIVE.
WHA-BOOM
WHOOOOOOSH
3

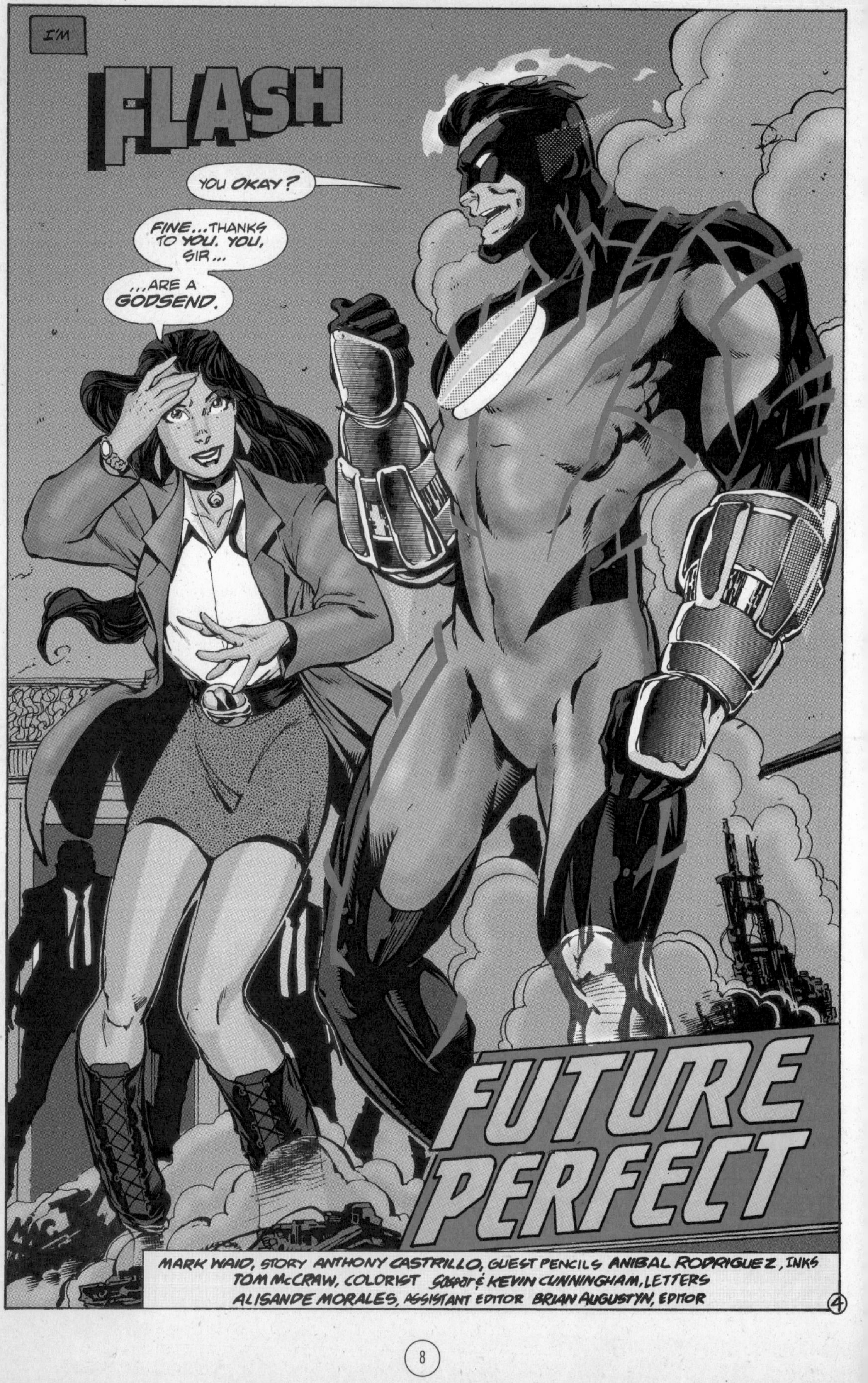
I'M
FLASH
YOU OKAY?
FINE... THANKS TO YOU. YOU, SIR...
...ARE A GODSEND.
FUTURE PERFECT
MARK WAID, STORY ANTHONY CASTRILLO, GUEST PENCILS ANIBAL RODRIGUEZ, INKS
TOM McCRAW, COLORIST Gaspar & KEVIN CUNNINGHAM, LETTERS
ALISANDE MORALES, ASSISTANT EDITOR BRIAN AUGUSTYN, EDITOR
4

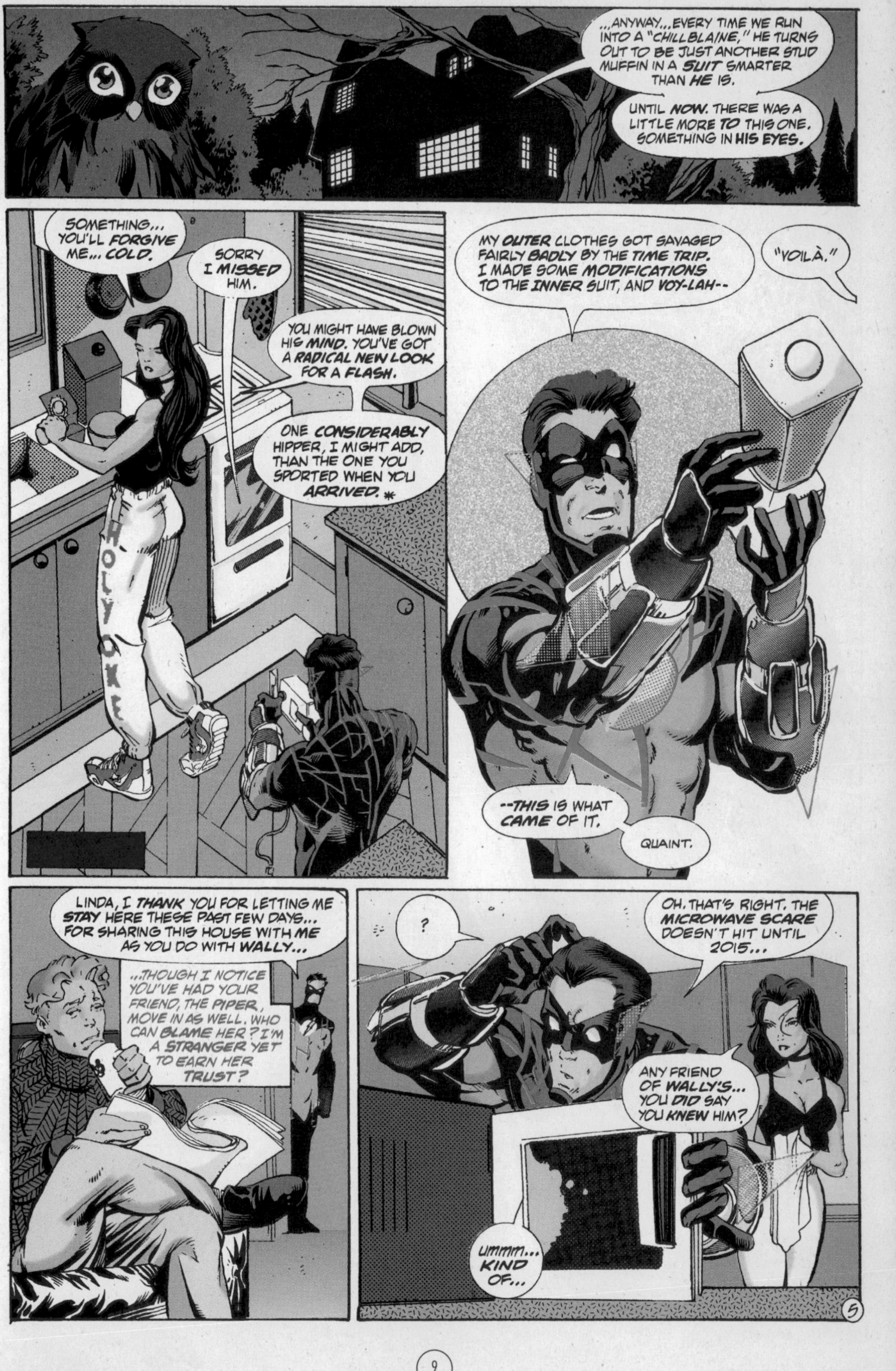
...ANYWAY... EVERY TIME WE RUN INTO A "CHILLBLAINE," HE TURNS OUT TO BE JUST ANOTHER STUD MUFFIN IN A SUIT SMARTER THAN HE IS.
UNTIL NOW. THERE WAS A LITTLE MORE TO THIS ONE. SOMETHING IN HIS EYES.
SOMETHING... YOU'LL FORGIVE ME... COLD.
SORRY I MISSED HIM.
YOU MIGHT HAVE BLOWN HIS MIND. YOU'VE GOT A RADICAL NEW LOOK FOR A FLASH.
ONE CONSIDERABLY HIPPER, I MIGHT ADD, THAN THE ONE YOU SPORTED WHEN YOU ARRIVED.*
[redacted]
MY OUTER CLOTHES GOT SAVAGED FAIRLY BADLY BY THE TIME TRIP. I MADE SOME MODIFICATIONS TO THE INNER SUIT, AND VOY-LAH--
"VOILÀ."
--THIS IS WHAT CAME OF IT.
QUAINT.
LINDA, I THANK YOU FOR LETTING ME STAY HERE THESE PAST FEW DAYS... FOR SHARING THIS HOUSE WITH ME AS YOU DO WITH WALLY...
...THOUGH I NOTICE YOU'VE HAD YOUR FRIEND, THE PIPER, MOVE IN AS WELL. WHO CAN BLAME HER? I'M A STRANGER YET TO EARN HER TRUST?
?
OH, THAT'S RIGHT. THE MICROWAVE SCARE DOESN'T HIT UNTIL 2015...
ANY FRIEND OF WALLY'S... YOU DID SAY YOU KNEW HIM?
UMMM... KIND OF...
5

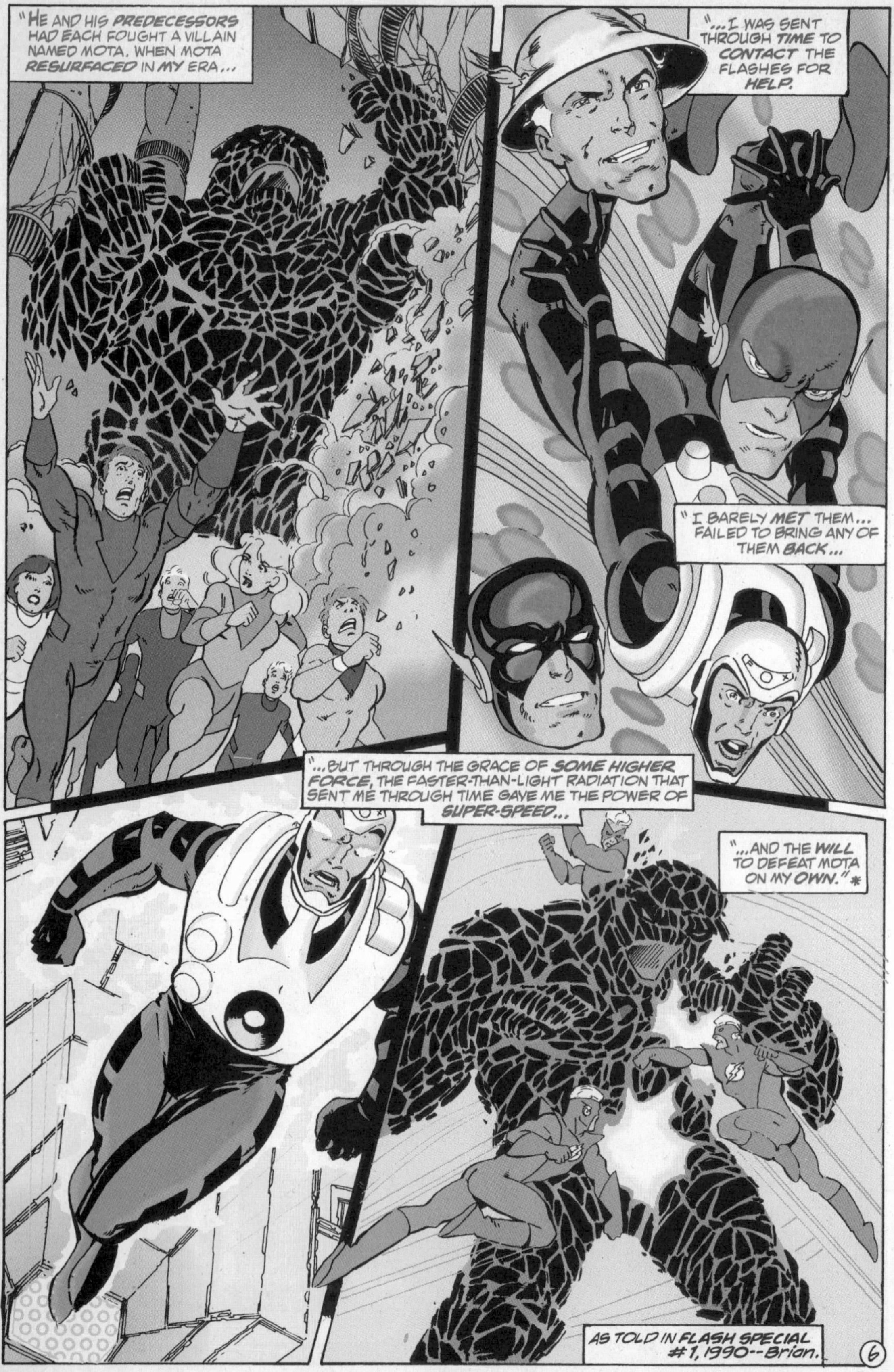
"HE AND HIS PREDECESSORS HAD EACH FOUGHT A VILLAIN NAMED MOTA. WHEN MOTA RESURFACED IN MY ERA...
"...I WAS SENT THROUGH TIME TO CONTACT THE FLASHES FOR HELP.
"I BARELY MET THEM... FAILED TO BRING ANY OF THEM BACK...
"...BUT THROUGH THE GRACE OF SOME HIGHER FORCE, THE FASTER-THAN-LIGHT RADIATION THAT SENT ME THROUGH TIME GAVE ME THE POWER OF SUPER-SPEED...
"...AND THE WILL TO DEFEAT MOTA ON MY OWN." *
AS TOLD IN FLASH SPECIAL #1, 1990--Brian.
6

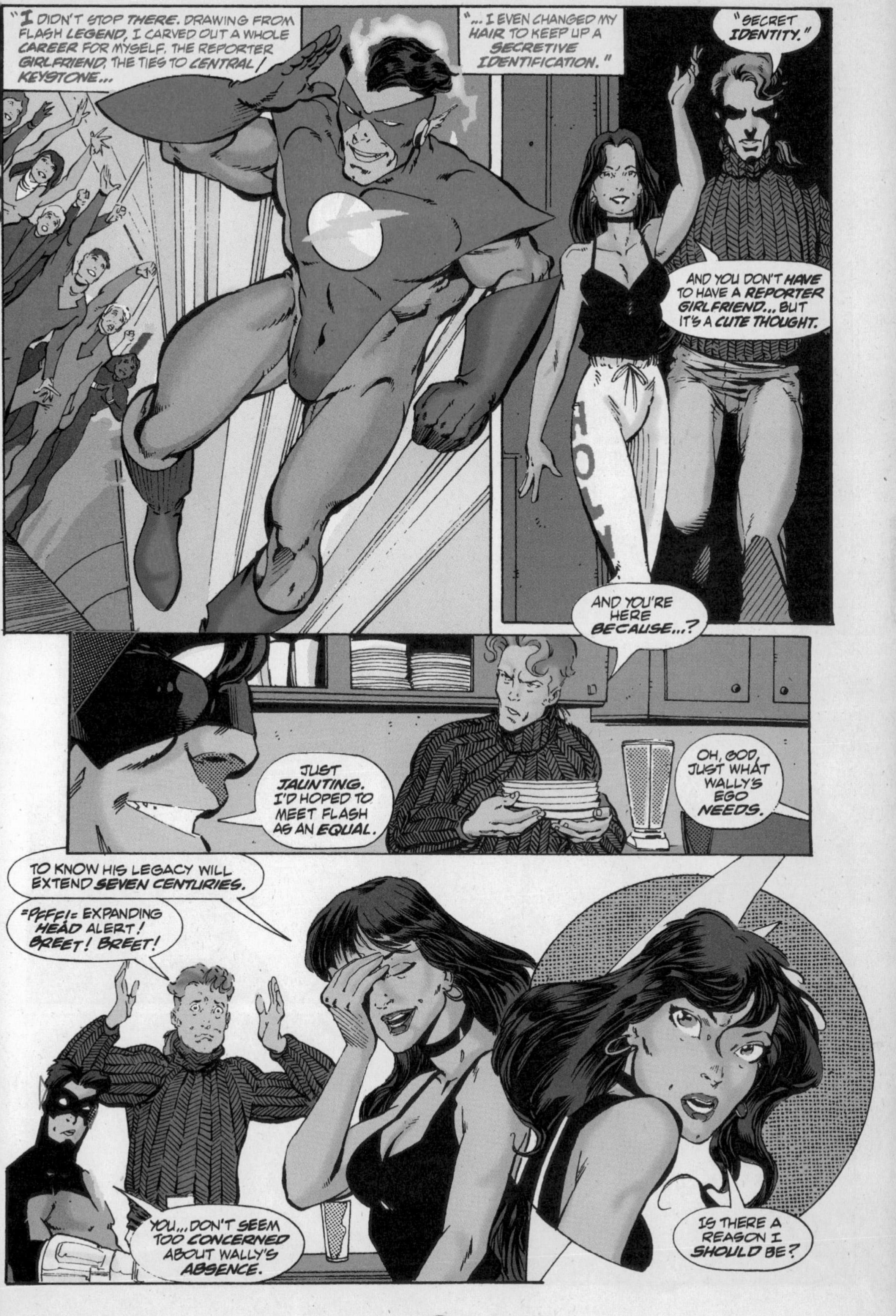
"I DIDN'T STOP THERE. DRAWING FROM FLASH LEGEND, I CARVED OUT A WHOLE CAREER FOR MYSELF. THE REPORTER GIRLFRIEND, THE TIES TO CENTRAL/ KEYSTONE...
"...I EVEN CHANGED MY HAIR TO KEEP UP A SECRETIVE IDENTIFICATION."
"SECRET IDENTITY."
AND YOU DON'T HAVE TO HAVE A REPORTER GIRLFRIEND... BUT IT'S A CUTE THOUGHT.
AND YOU'RE HERE BECAUSE...?
JUST JAUNTING. I'D HOPED TO MEET FLASH AS AN EQUAL.
OH, GOD, JUST WHAT WALLY'S EGO NEEDS.
TO KNOW HIS LEGACY WILL EXTEND SEVEN CENTURIES.
=PFFF!= EXPANDING HEAD ALERT! BREET! BREET!
YOU... DON'T SEEM TOO CONCERNED ABOUT WALLY'S ABSENCE.
IS THERE A REASON I SHOULD BE?

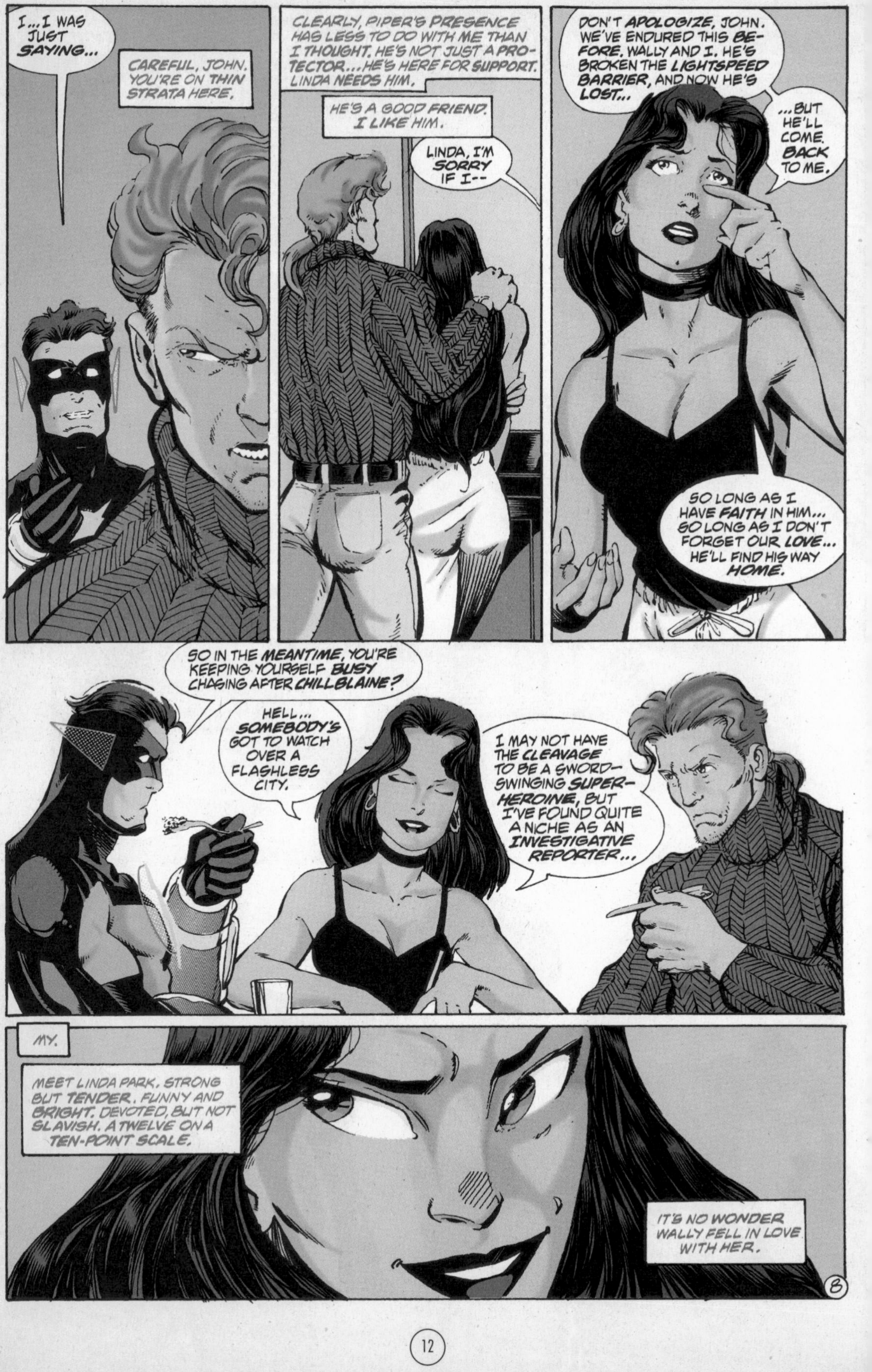
I... I WAS JUST SAYING...
CAREFUL, JOHN. YOU'RE ON THIN STRATA HERE.
CLEARLY, PIPER'S PRESENCE HAS LESS TO DO WITH ME THAN I THOUGHT. HE'S NOT JUST A PROTECTOR... HE'S HERE FOR SUPPORT. LINDA NEEDS HIM.
HE'S A GOOD FRIEND. I LIKE HIM.
LINDA, I'M SORRY IF I--
DON'T APOLOGIZE, JOHN. WE'VE ENDURED THIS BEFORE, WALLY AND I. HE'S BROKEN THE LIGHTSPEED BARRIER, AND NOW HE'S LOST...
...BUT HE'LL COME BACK TO ME.
SO LONG AS I HAVE FAITH IN HIM... SO LONG AS I DON'T FORGET OUR LOVE... HE'LL FIND HIS WAY HOME.
SO IN THE MEANTIME, YOU'RE KEEPING YOURSELF BUSY CHASING AFTER CHILLBLAINE?
HELL... SOMEBODY'S GOT TO WATCH OVER A FLASHLESS CITY.
I MAY NOT HAVE THE CLEAVAGE TO BE A SWORD-SWINGING SUPER-HEROINE, BUT I'VE FOUND QUITE A NICHE AS AN INVESTIGATIVE REPORTER...
MY.
MEET LINDA PARK. STRONG BUT TENDER. FUNNY AND BRIGHT. DEVOTED, BUT NOT SLAVISH. A TWELVE ON A TEN-POINT SCALE.
IT'S NO WONDER WALLY FELL IN LOVE WITH HER.
8

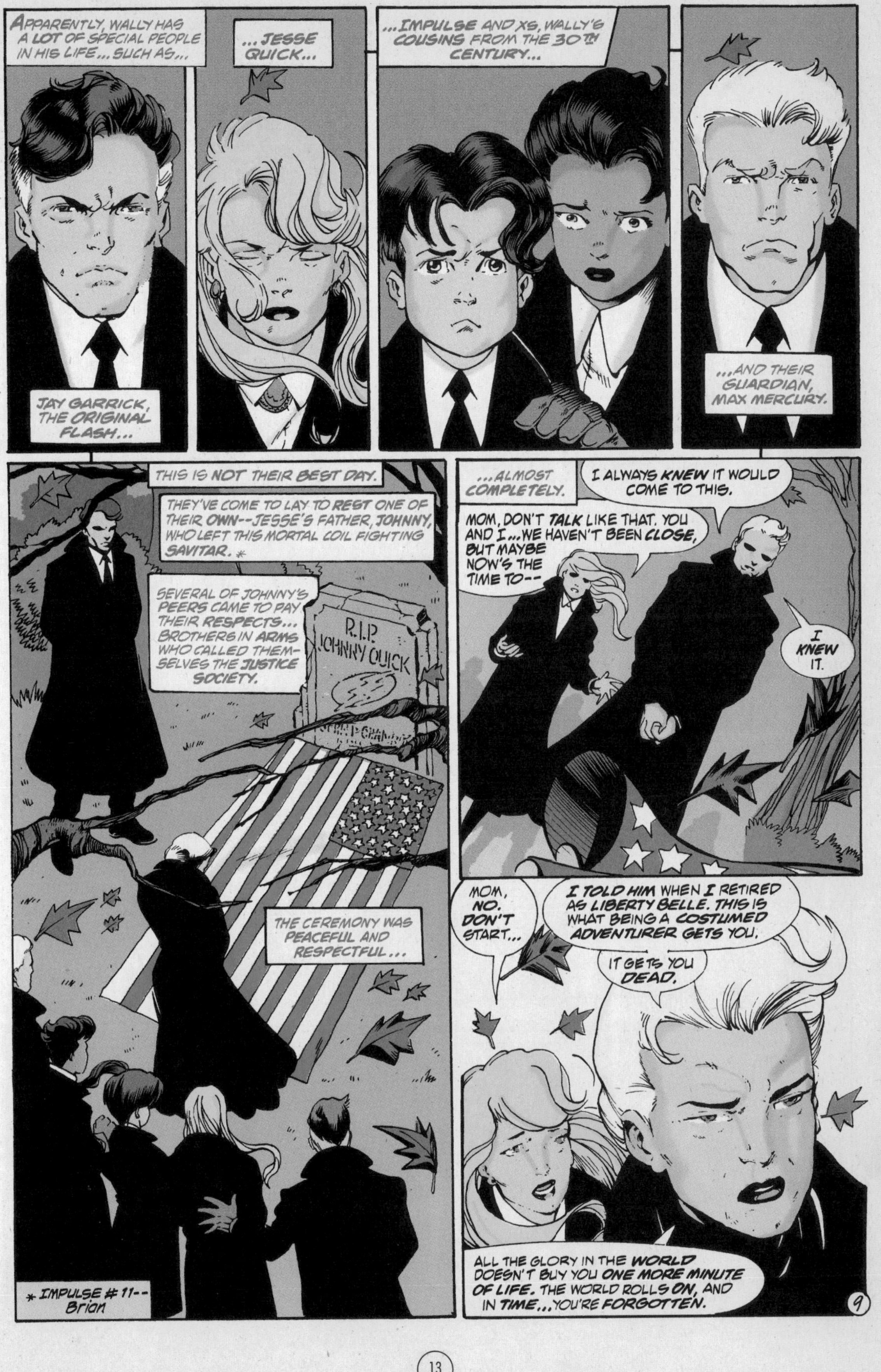
APPARENTLY, WALLY HAS A LOT OF SPECIAL PEOPLE IN HIS LIFE... SUCH AS...
JAY GARRICK, THE ORIGINAL FLASH...
...JESSE QUICK...
...IMPULSE AND XS, WALLY'S COUSINS FROM THE 30TH CENTURY...
...AND THEIR GUARDIAN, MAX MERCURY.
THIS IS NOT THEIR BEST DAY.
THEY'VE COME TO LAY TO REST ONE OF THEIR OWN--JESSE'S FATHER, JOHNNY, WHO LEFT THIS MORTAL COIL FIGHTING SAVITAR. *
SEVERAL OF JOHNNY'S PEERS CAME TO PAY THEIR RESPECTS... BROTHERS IN ARMS WHO CALLED THEMSELVES THE JUSTICE SOCIETY.
R.I.P. JOHNNY QUICK
THE CEREMONY WAS PEACEFUL AND RESPECTFUL...
* IMPULSE #11-- Brian
...ALMOST COMPLETELY.
I ALWAYS KNEW IT WOULD COME TO THIS.
MOM, DON'T TALK LIKE THAT. YOU AND I... WE HAVEN'T BEEN CLOSE, BUT MAYBE NOW'S THE TIME TO--
I KNEW IT.
MOM, NO. DON'T START...
I TOLD HIM WHEN I RETIRED AS LIBERTY BELLE. THIS IS WHAT BEING A COSTUMED ADVENTURER GETS YOU.
IT GETS YOU DEAD.
ALL THE GLORY IN THE WORLD DOESN'T BUY YOU ONE MORE MINUTE OF LIFE. THE WORLD ROLLS ON, AND IN TIME... YOU'RE FORGOTTEN.
9

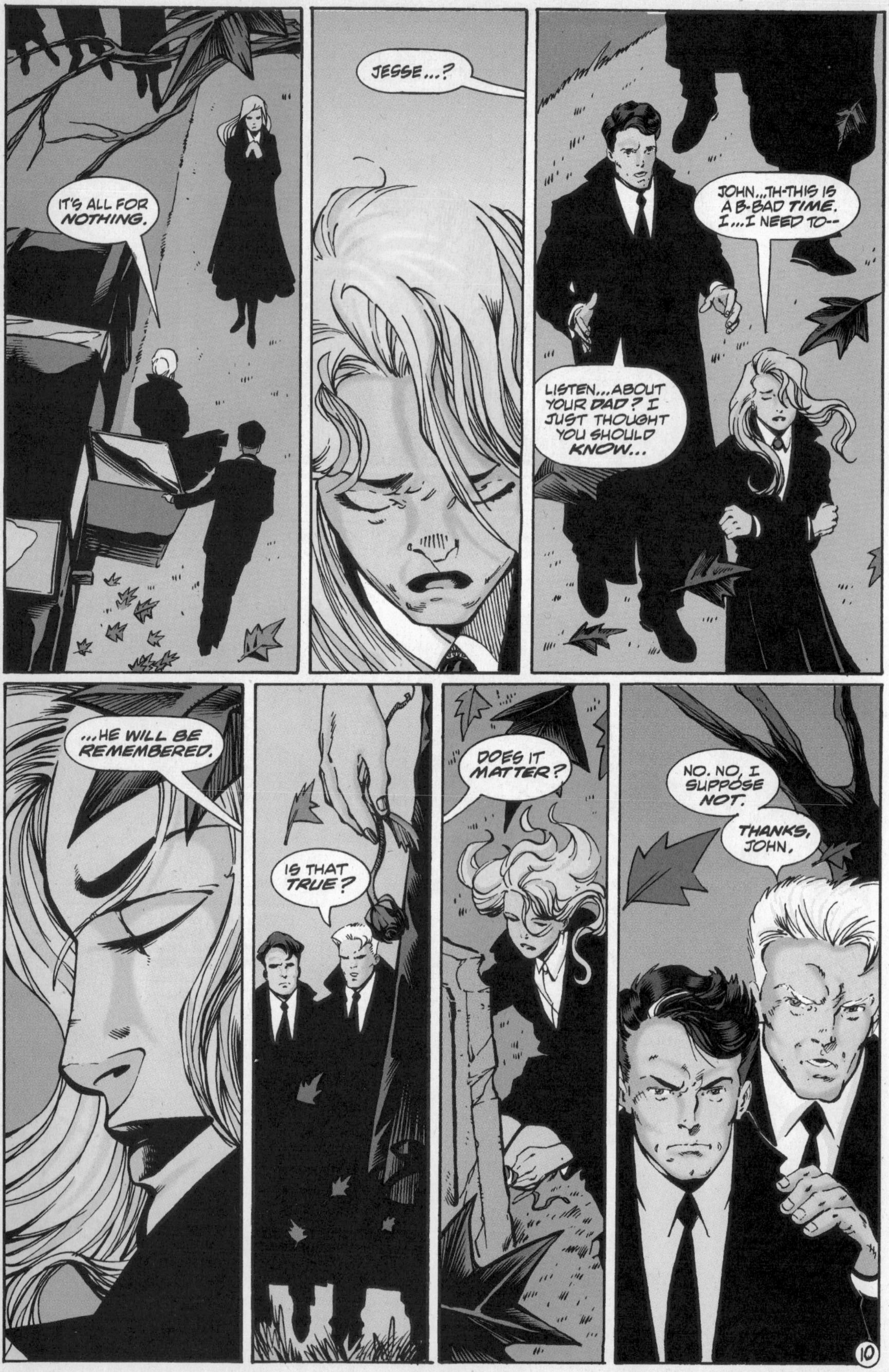
IT'S ALL FOR NOTHING.
JESSE...?
JOHN...TH-THIS IS A B-BAD TIME. I...I NEED TO--
LISTEN...ABOUT YOUR DAD? I JUST THOUGHT YOU SHOULD KNOW...
...HE WILL BE REMEMBERED.
IS THAT TRUE?
DOES IT MATTER?
NO. NO, I SUPPOSE NOT.
THANKS, JOHN.
10

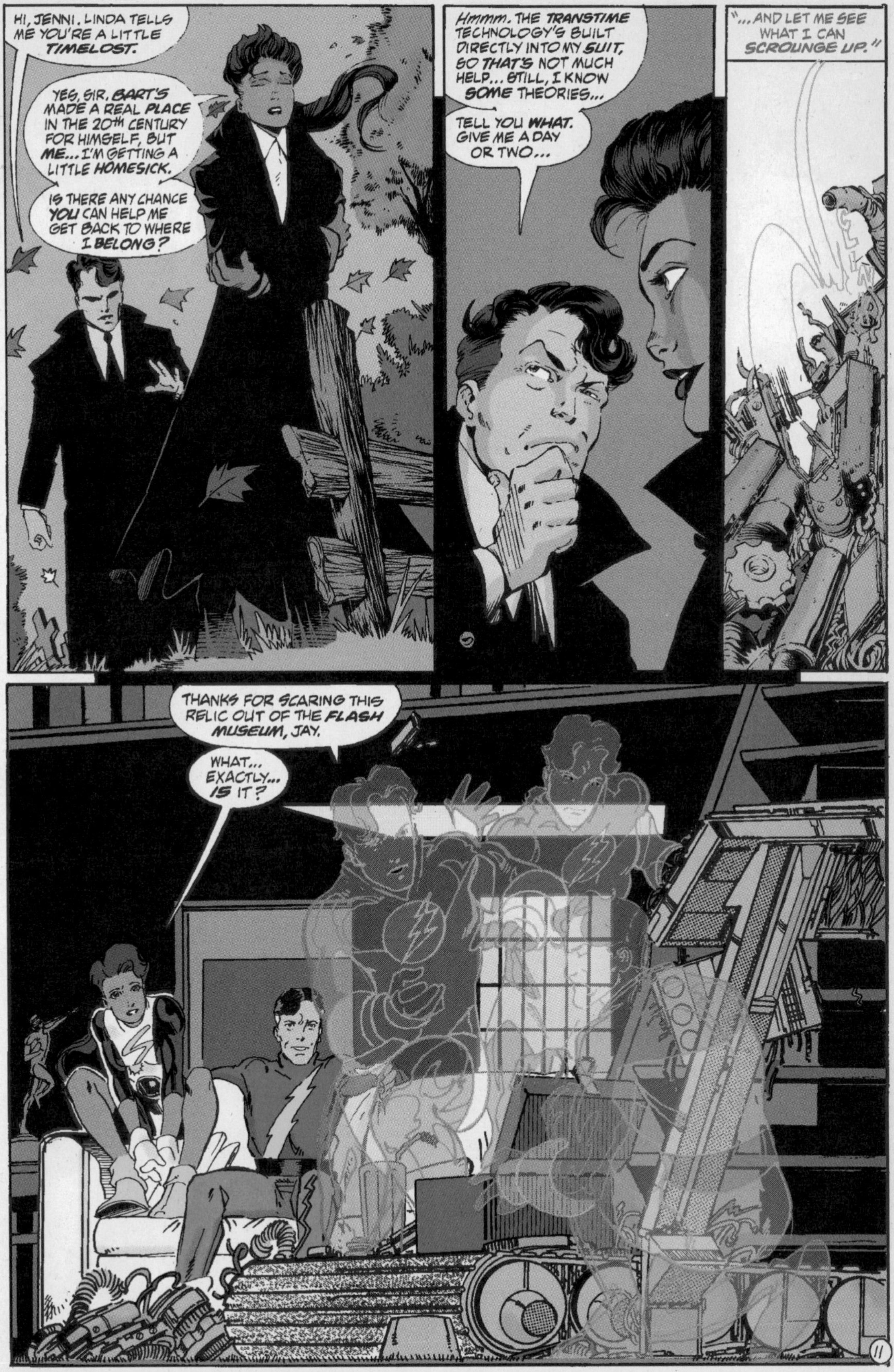
HI, JENNI. LINDA TELLS ME YOU'RE A LITTLE TIMELOST.
YES, SIR. BART'S MADE A REAL PLACE IN THE 20TH CENTURY FOR HIMSELF, BUT ME... I'M GETTING A LITTLE HOMESICK.
IS THERE ANY CHANCE YOU CAN HELP ME GET BACK TO WHERE I BELONG?
Hmmm. THE TRANSTIME TECHNOLOGY'S BUILT DIRECTLY INTO MY SUIT, SO THAT'S NOT MUCH HELP... STILL, I KNOW SOME THEORIES...
TELL YOU WHAT. GIVE ME A DAY OR TWO...
"...AND LET ME SEE WHAT I CAN SCROUNGE UP."
THANKS FOR SCARING THIS RELIC OUT OF THE FLASH MUSEUM, JAY.
WHAT... EXACTLY... IS IT?
11

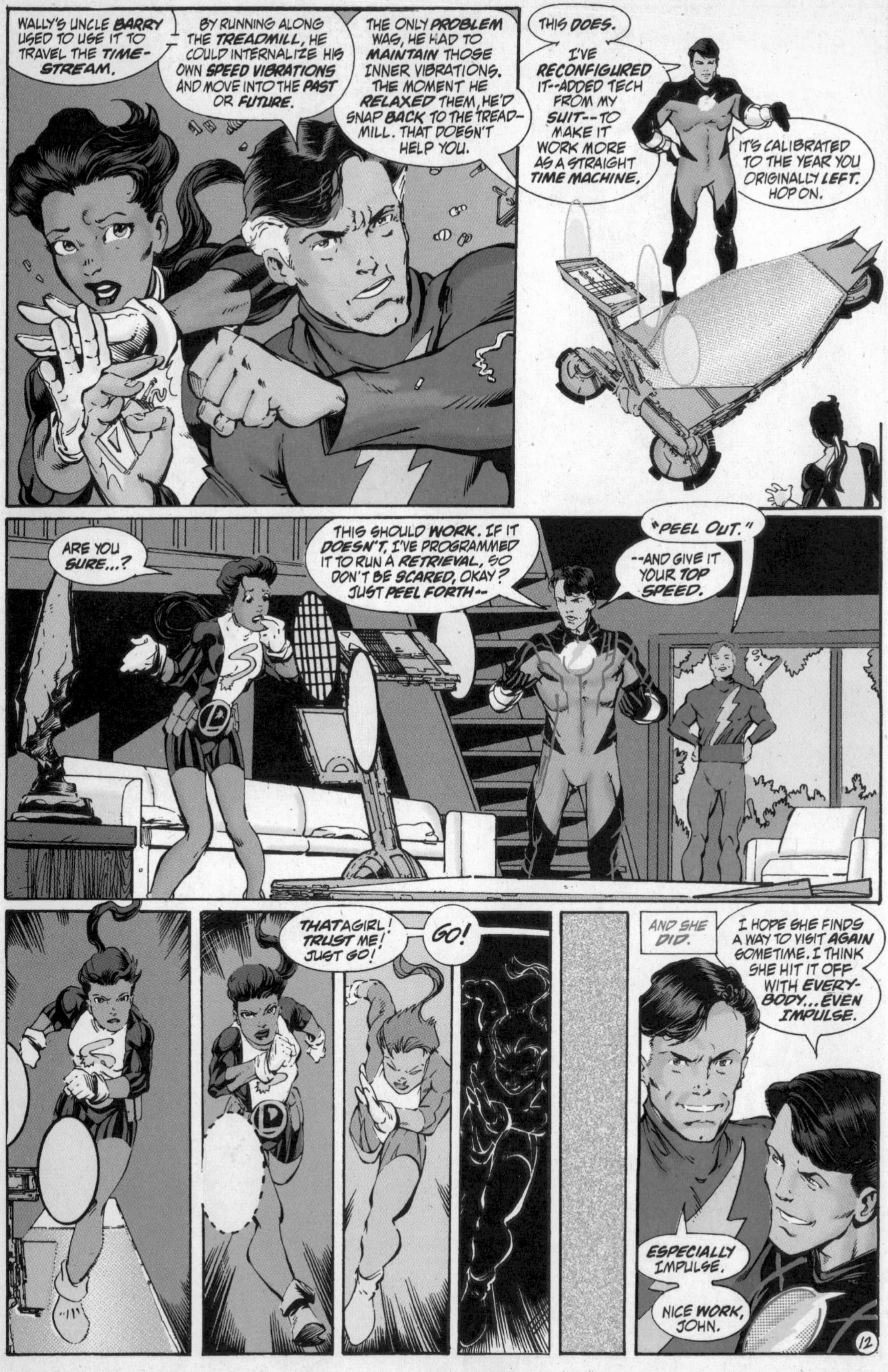
WALLY'S UNCLE BARRY USED TO USE IT TO TRAVEL THE TIME-STREAM.
BY RUNNING ALONG THE TREADMILL, HE COULD INTERNALIZE HIS OWN SPEED VIBRATIONS AND MOVE INTO THE PAST OR FUTURE.
THE ONLY PROBLEM WAS, HE HAD TO MAINTAIN THOSE INNER VIBRATIONS. THE MOMENT HE RELAXED THEM, HE'D SNAP BACK TO THE TREAD-MILL. THAT DOESN'T HELP YOU.
THIS DOES.
I'VE RECONFIGURED IT--ADDED TECH FROM MY SUIT--TO MAKE IT WORK MORE AS A STRAIGHT TIME MACHINE.
IT'S CALIBRATED TO THE YEAR YOU ORIGINALLY LEFT. HOP ON.
ARE YOU SURE...?
THIS SHOULD WORK. IF IT DOESN'T, I'VE PROGRAMMED IT TO RUN A RETRIEVAL, SO DON'T BE SCARED, OKAY? JUST PEEL FORTH--
"PEEL OUT."
--AND GIVE IT YOUR TOP SPEED.
THATAGIRL! TRUST ME! JUST GO!
GO!
AND SHE DID.
I HOPE SHE FINDS A WAY TO VISIT AGAIN SOMETIME. I THINK SHE HIT IT OFF WITH EVERY-BODY... EVEN IMPULSE.
ESPECIALLY IMPULSE.
NICE WORK, JOHN.
12

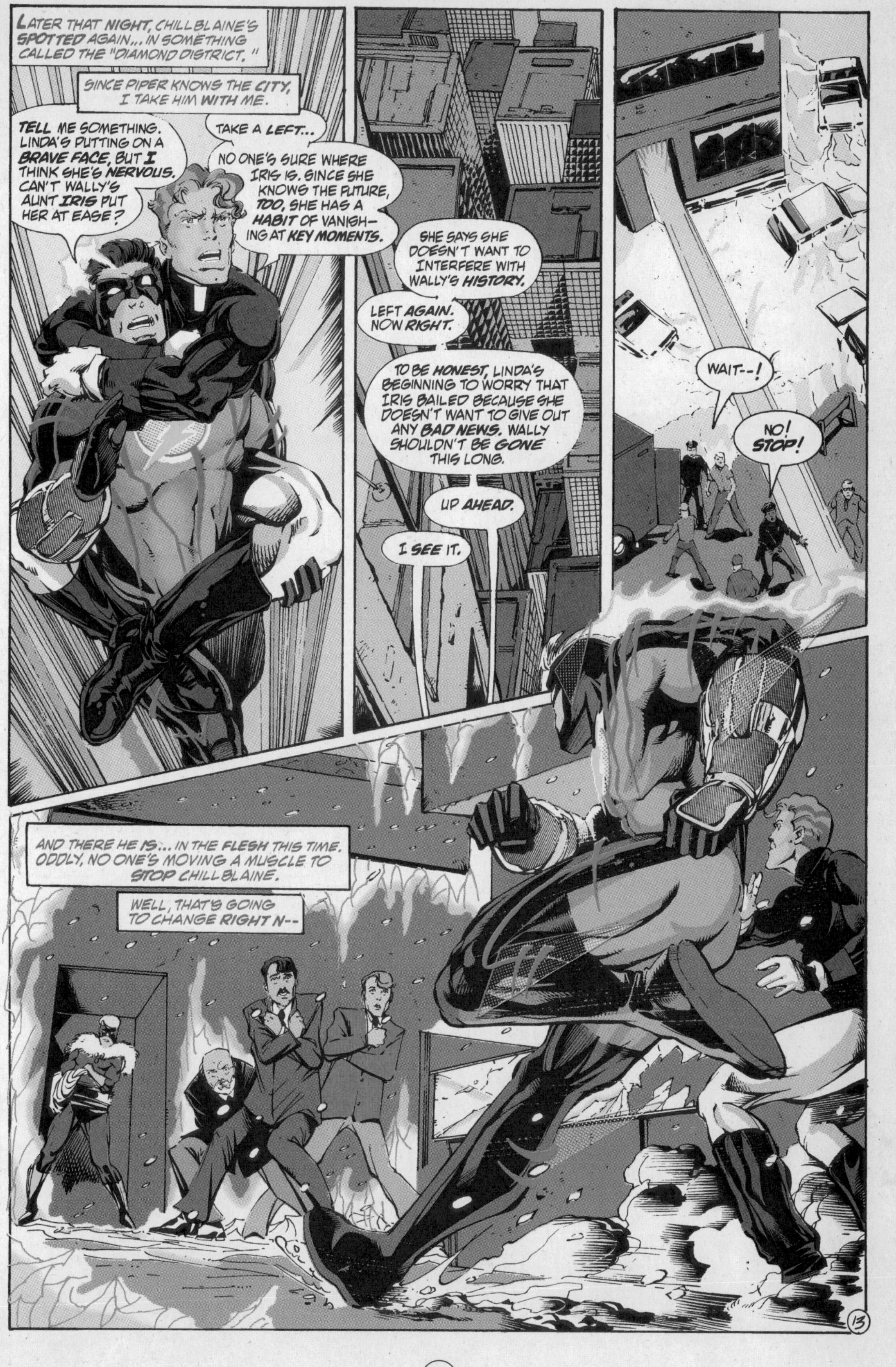
LATER THAT NIGHT, CHILLBLAINE'S SPOTTED AGAIN... IN SOMETHING CALLED THE "DIAMOND DISTRICT."
SINCE PIPER KNOWS THE CITY, I TAKE HIM WITH ME.
TELL ME SOMETHING. LINDA'S PUTTING ON A BRAVE FACE, BUT I THINK SHE'S NERVOUS. CAN'T WALLY'S AUNT IRIS PUT HER AT EASE?
TAKE A LEFT...
NO ONE'S SURE WHERE IRIS IS. SINCE SHE KNOWS THE FUTURE, TOO, SHE HAS A HABIT OF VANISHING AT KEY MOMENTS.
SHE SAYS SHE DOESN'T WANT TO INTERFERE WITH WALLY'S HISTORY.
LEFT AGAIN. NOW RIGHT.
TO BE HONEST, LINDA'S BEGINNING TO WORRY THAT IRIS BAILED BECAUSE SHE DOESN'T WANT TO GIVE OUT ANY BAD NEWS. WALLY SHOULDN'T BE GONE THIS LONG.
UP AHEAD.
I SEE IT.
WAIT--!
NO! STOP!
AND THERE HE IS... IN THE FLESH THIS TIME. ODDLY, NO ONE'S MOVING A MUSCLE TO STOP CHILLBLAINE.
WELL, THAT'S GOING TO CHANGE RIGHT N--
13

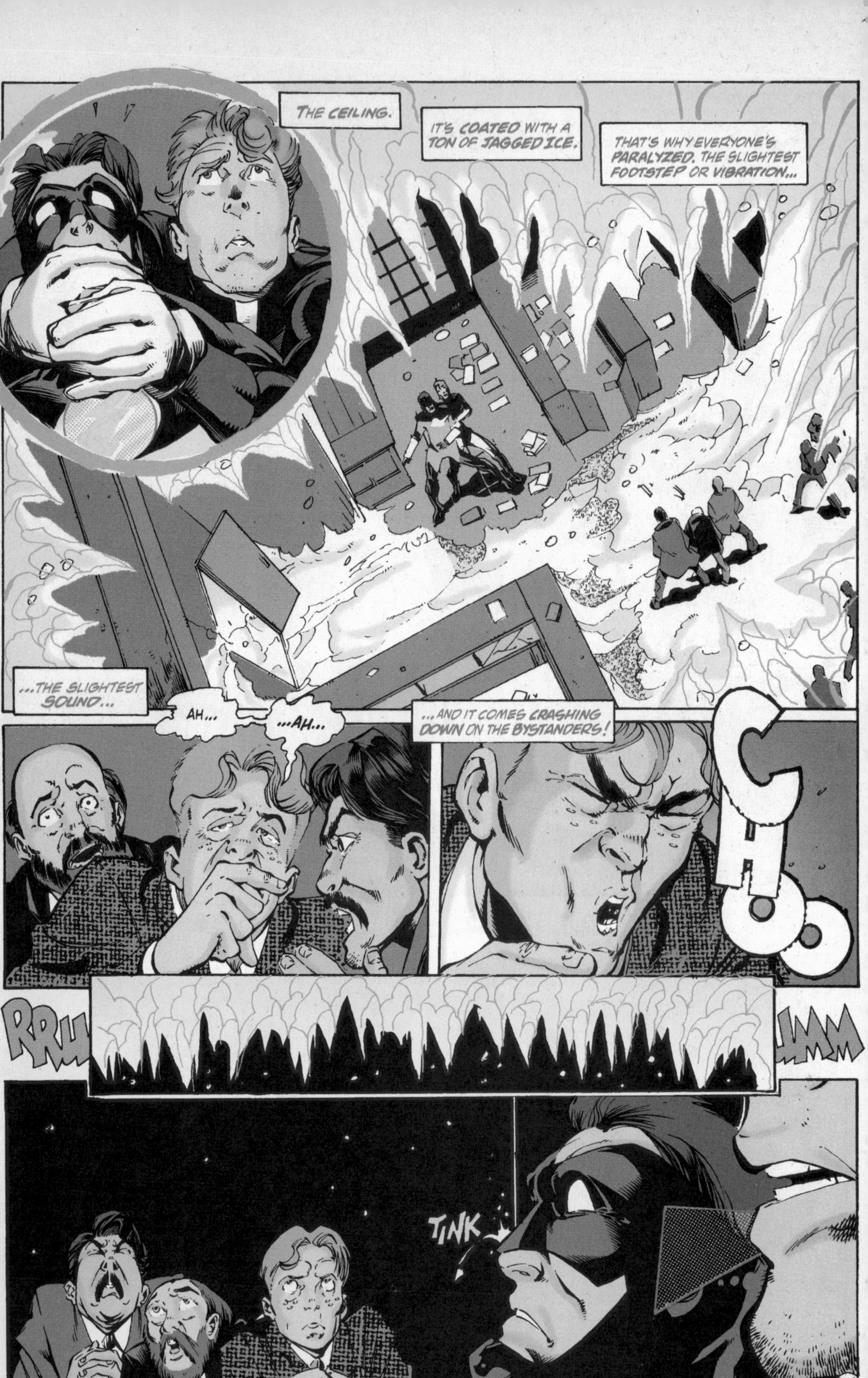
THE CEILING.
IT'S COATED WITH A TON OF JAGGED ICE.
THAT'S WHY EVERYONE'S PARALYZED. THE SLIGHTEST FOOTSTEP OR VIBRATION...
...THE SLIGHTEST SOUND...
AH...
...AH...
...AND IT COMES CRASHING DOWN ON THE BYSTANDERS!
CHOO
RRUMM
TINK
14

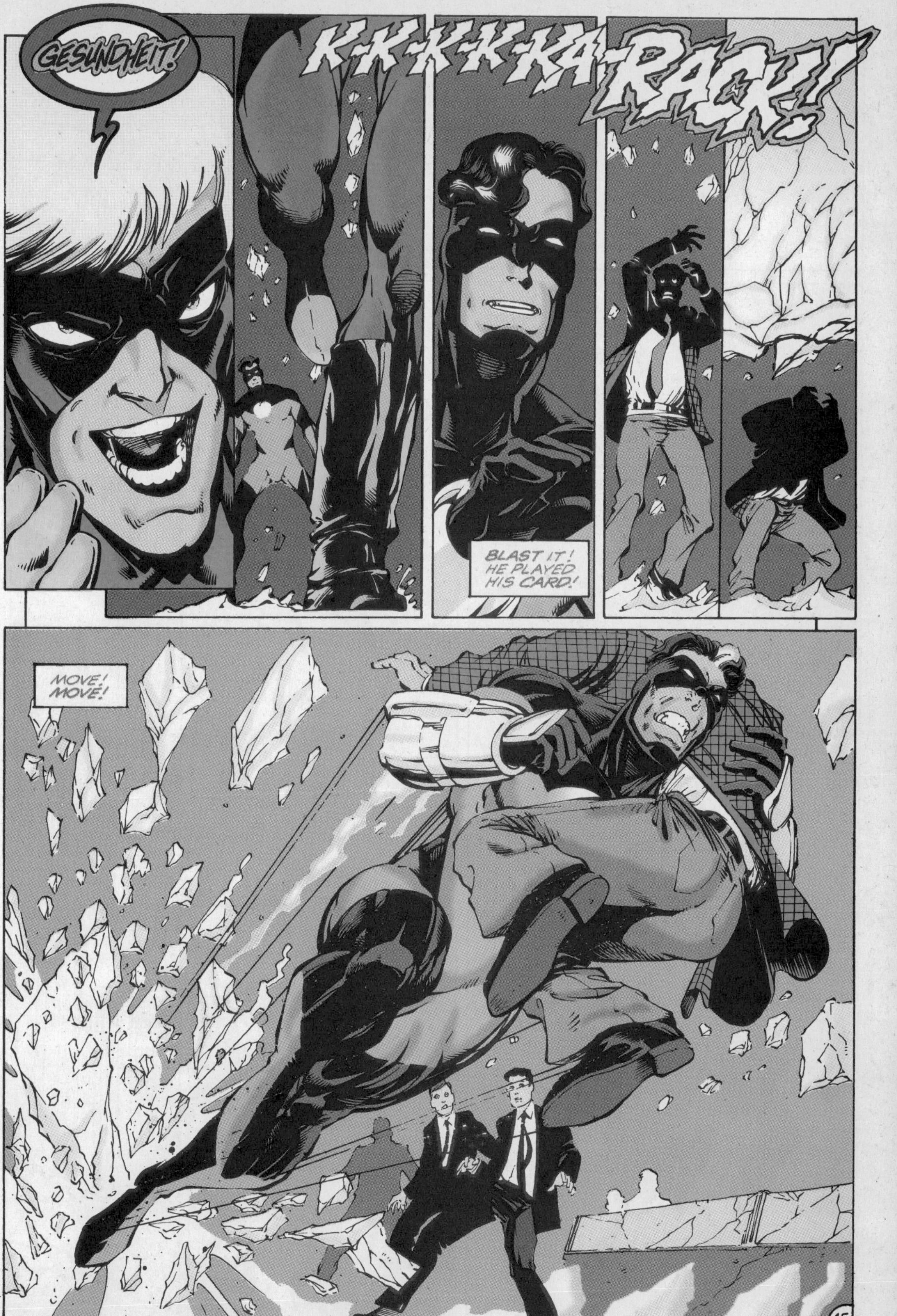
GESUNDHEIT!
K-K-K-K-KA-RACK!
BLAST IT! HE PLAYED HIS CARD!
MOVE! MOVE!
15

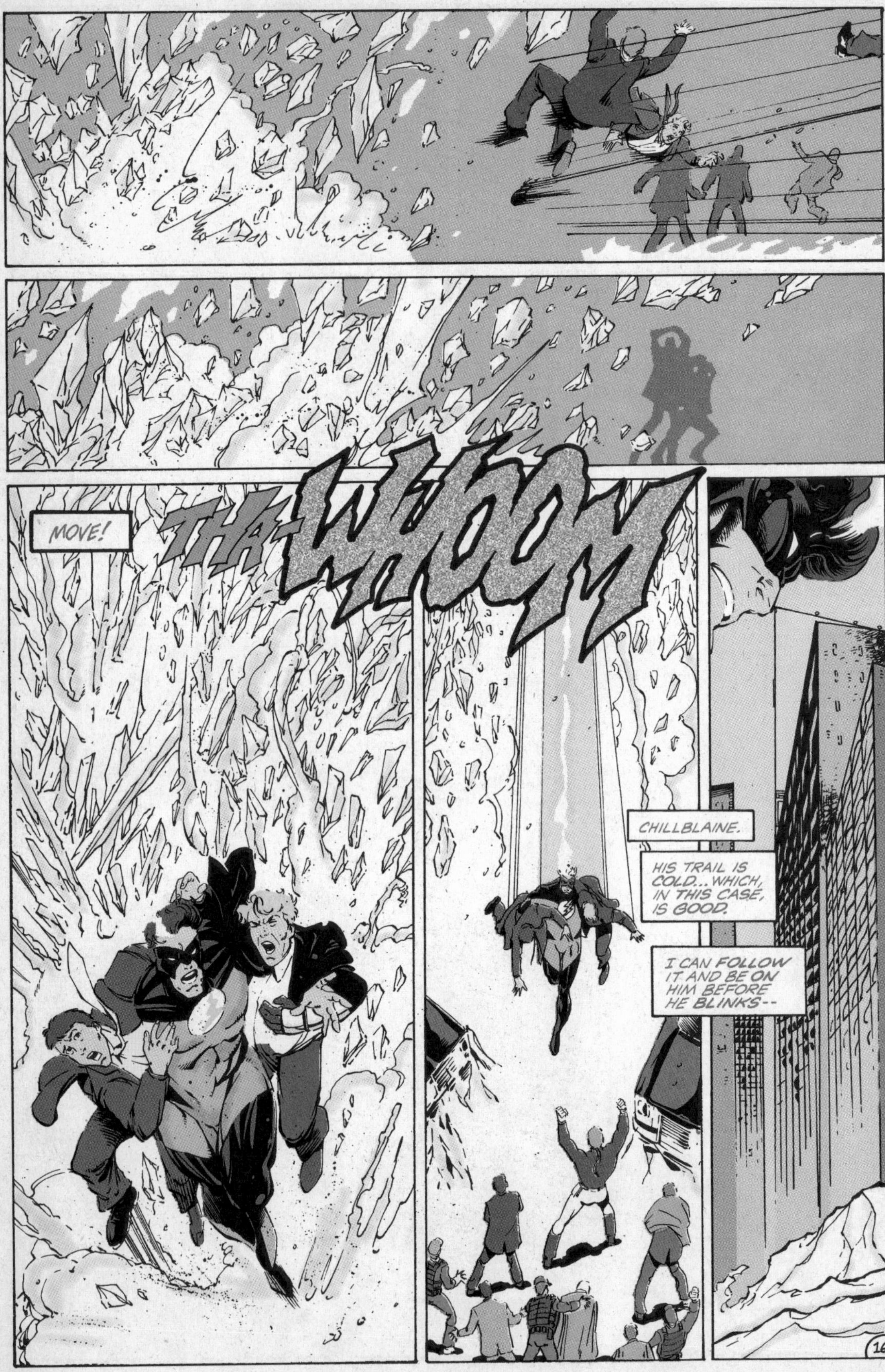
MOVE!
THA-WHOOM
CHILLBLAINE.
HIS TRAIL IS COLD... WHICH, IN THIS CASE, IS GOOD.
I CAN FOLLOW IT AND BE ON HIM BEFORE HE BLINKS--
16

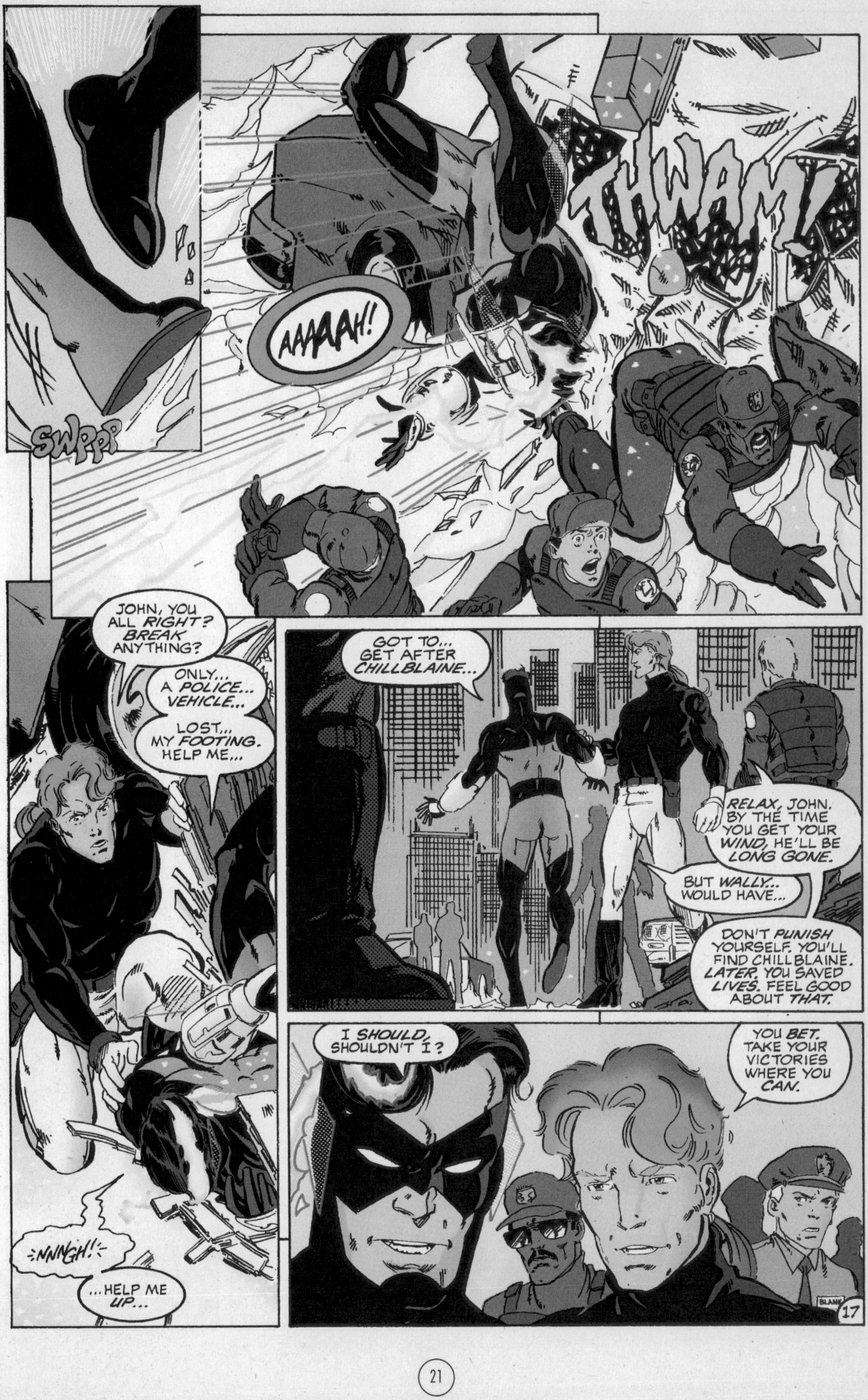
SWPPP
AAAAAH!
THWAM!
JOHN, YOU ALL RIGHT? BREAK ANYTHING?
ONLY... A POLICE... VEHICLE...
LOST... MY FOOTING. HELP ME...
NNNGH!
...HELP ME UP...
GOT TO... GET AFTER CHILLBLAINE...
RELAX, JOHN. BY THE TIME YOU GET YOUR WIND, HE'LL BE LONG GONE.
BUT WALLY... WOULD HAVE...
DON'T PUNISH YOURSELF. YOU'LL FIND CHILLBLAINE. LATER. YOU SAVED LIVES. FEEL GOOD ABOUT THAT.
I SHOULD, SHOULDN'T I?
YOU BET. TAKE YOUR VICTORIES WHERE YOU CAN.
BLANK
17

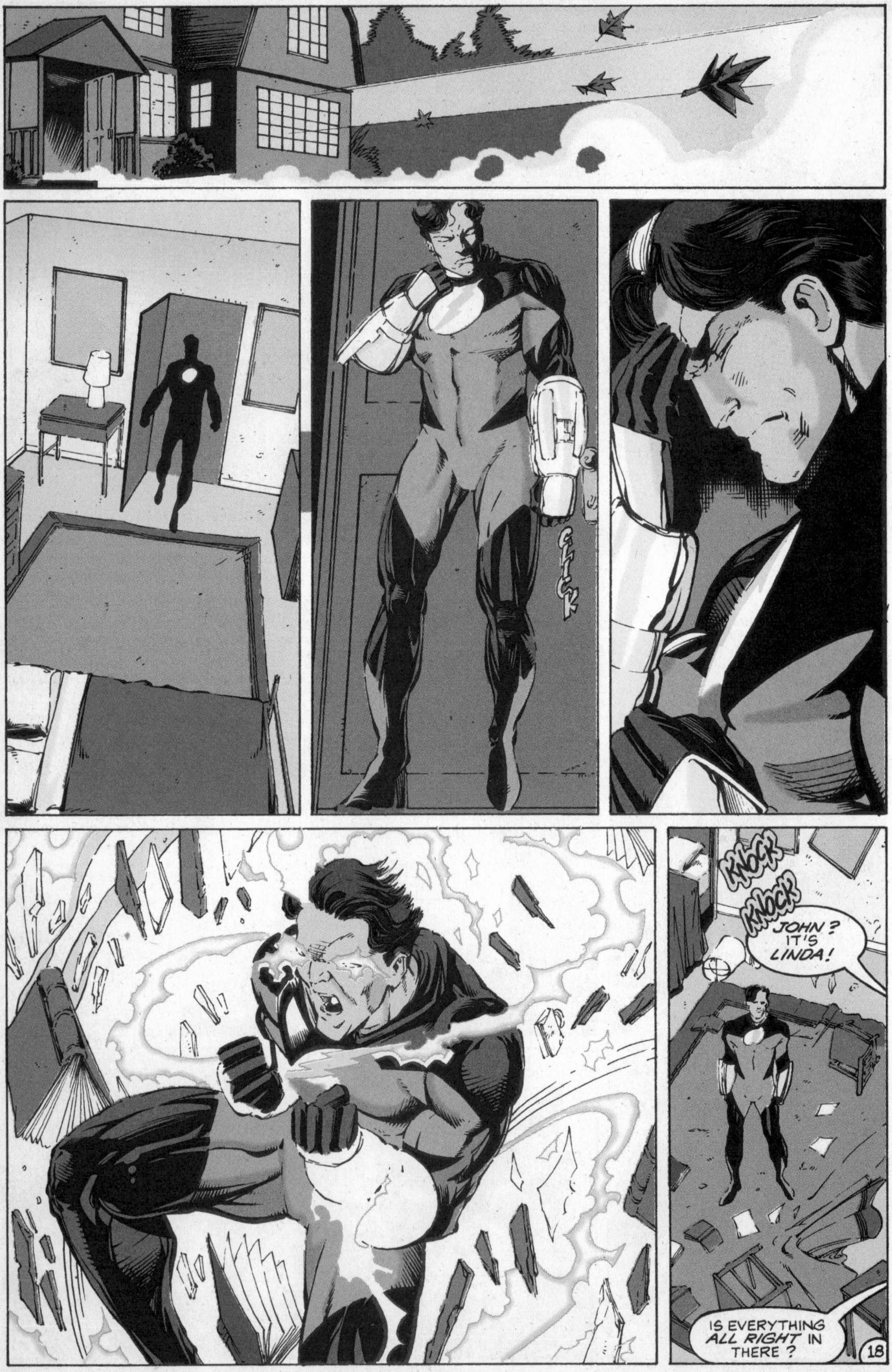
CLICK
KNOCK
KNOCK
JOHN? IT'S LINDA!
IS EVERYTHING ALL RIGHT IN THERE?
18

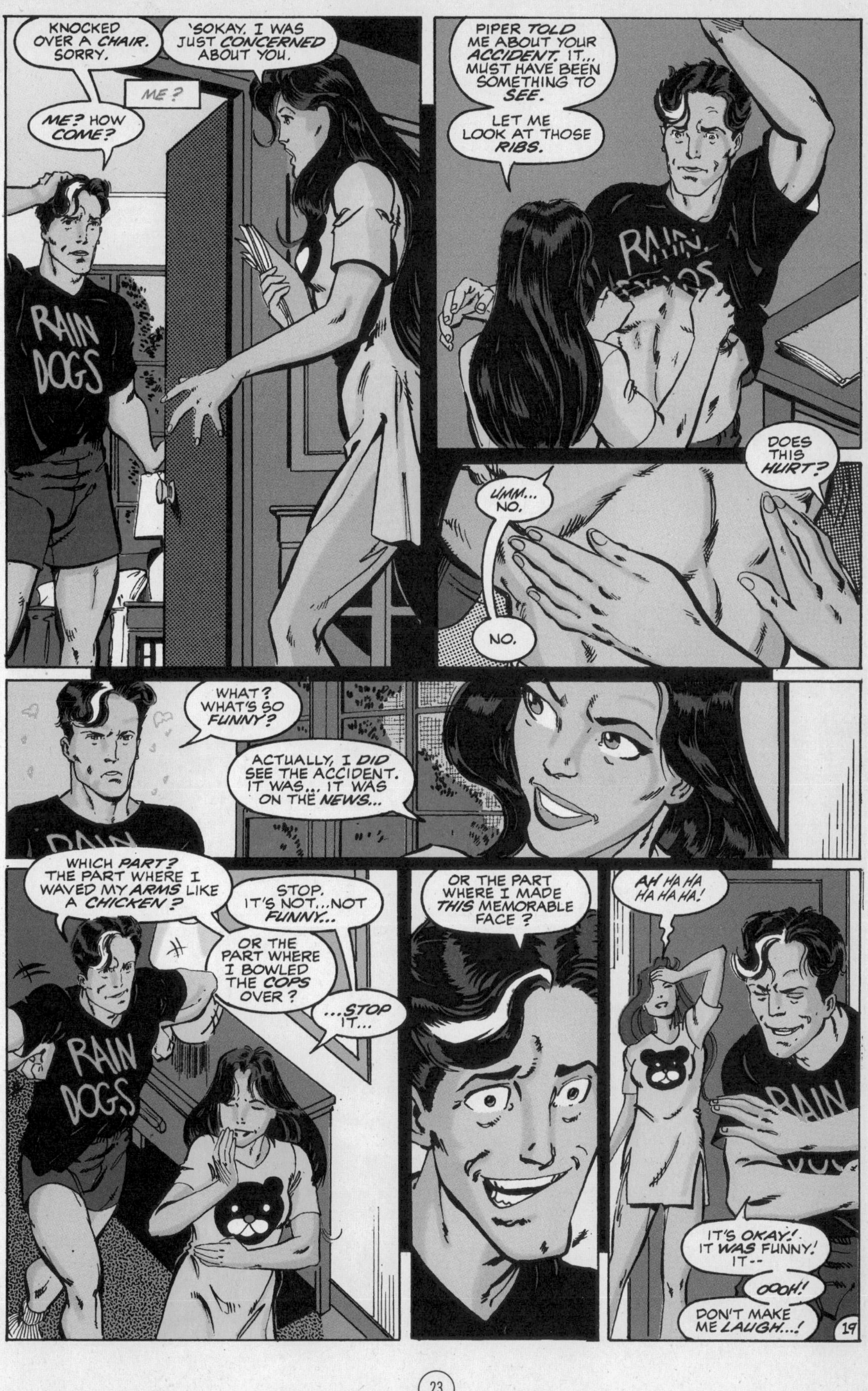
KNOCKED OVER A CHAIR. SORRY.
'SOKAY. I WAS JUST CONCERNED ABOUT YOU.
ME?
ME? HOW COME?
PIPER TOLD ME ABOUT YOUR ACCIDENT. IT... MUST HAVE BEEN SOMETHING TO SEE.
LET ME LOOK AT THOSE RIBS.
RAIN DOGS
DOES THIS HURT?
UMM... NO.
NO.
WHAT? WHAT'S SO FUNNY?
ACTUALLY, I DID SEE THE ACCIDENT. IT WAS... IT WAS ON THE NEWS...
WHICH PART? THE PART WHERE I WAVED MY ARMS LIKE A CHICKEN?
STOP. IT'S NOT...NOT FUNNY...
OR THE PART WHERE I BOWLED THE COPS OVER?
...STOP IT...
OR THE PART WHERE I MADE THIS MEMORABLE FACE?
AH HA HA HA HA HA!
IT'S OKAY! IT WAS FUNNY! IT--
OOOH!
DON'T MAKE ME LAUGH...!
19

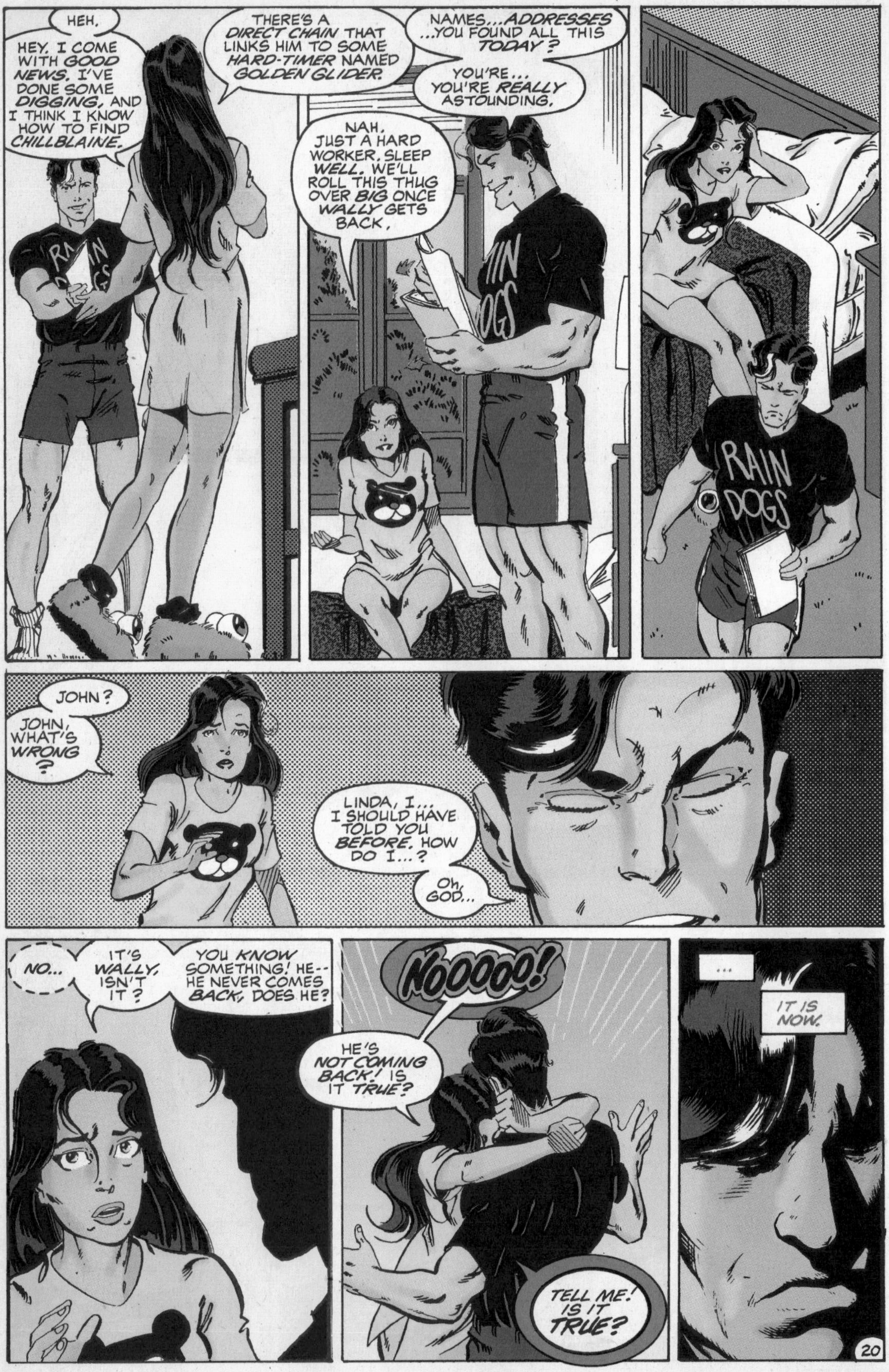
HEH.
HEY. I COME WITH GOOD NEWS. I'VE DONE SOME DIGGING, AND I THINK I KNOW HOW TO FIND CHILLBLAINE.
THERE'S A DIRECT CHAIN THAT LINKS HIM TO SOME HARD-TIMER NAMED GOLDEN GLIDER.
NAMES...ADDRESSES ...YOU FOUND ALL THIS TODAY?
YOU'RE... YOU'RE REALLY ASTOUNDING.
NAH. JUST A HARD WORKER. SLEEP WELL. WE'LL ROLL THIS THUG OVER BIG ONCE WALLY GETS BACK.
RAIN DOGS
JOHN?
JOHN, WHAT'S WRONG?
LINDA, I... I SHOULD HAVE TOLD YOU BEFORE. HOW DO I...?
OH, GOD...
NO...
IT'S WALLY, ISN'T IT?
YOU KNOW SOMETHING! HE--HE NEVER COMES BACK, DOES HE?
NOOOOO!
HE'S NOT COMING BACK! IS IT TRUE?
TELL ME! IS IT TRUE?
...
IT IS NOW.
20

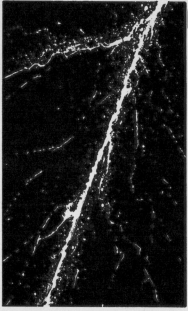

UHHHH.

MY NAME IS WALLY WEST.

THE LAST MEMORY I HAVE IS BOUNCING OUT OF THE EXTRA-DIMENSIONAL FORCE KNOWN AS THE SPEED FIELD.

ACTUALLY, THAT'S NOT TRUE. THE LAST MEMORY I HAVE IS CAREENING THROUGH TIME AND SPACE LIKE A HOMER BATTED OUT OF YANKEE STADIUM.

FORTUNATELY, I SEEM TO BE ON SOLID GROUND ONCE MORE. WHAT A RELIEF. IN THE WORDS OF THE KID WITH THE RUBY SLIPPERS, THERE'S NO PLACE LIKE...

...HOME...

21

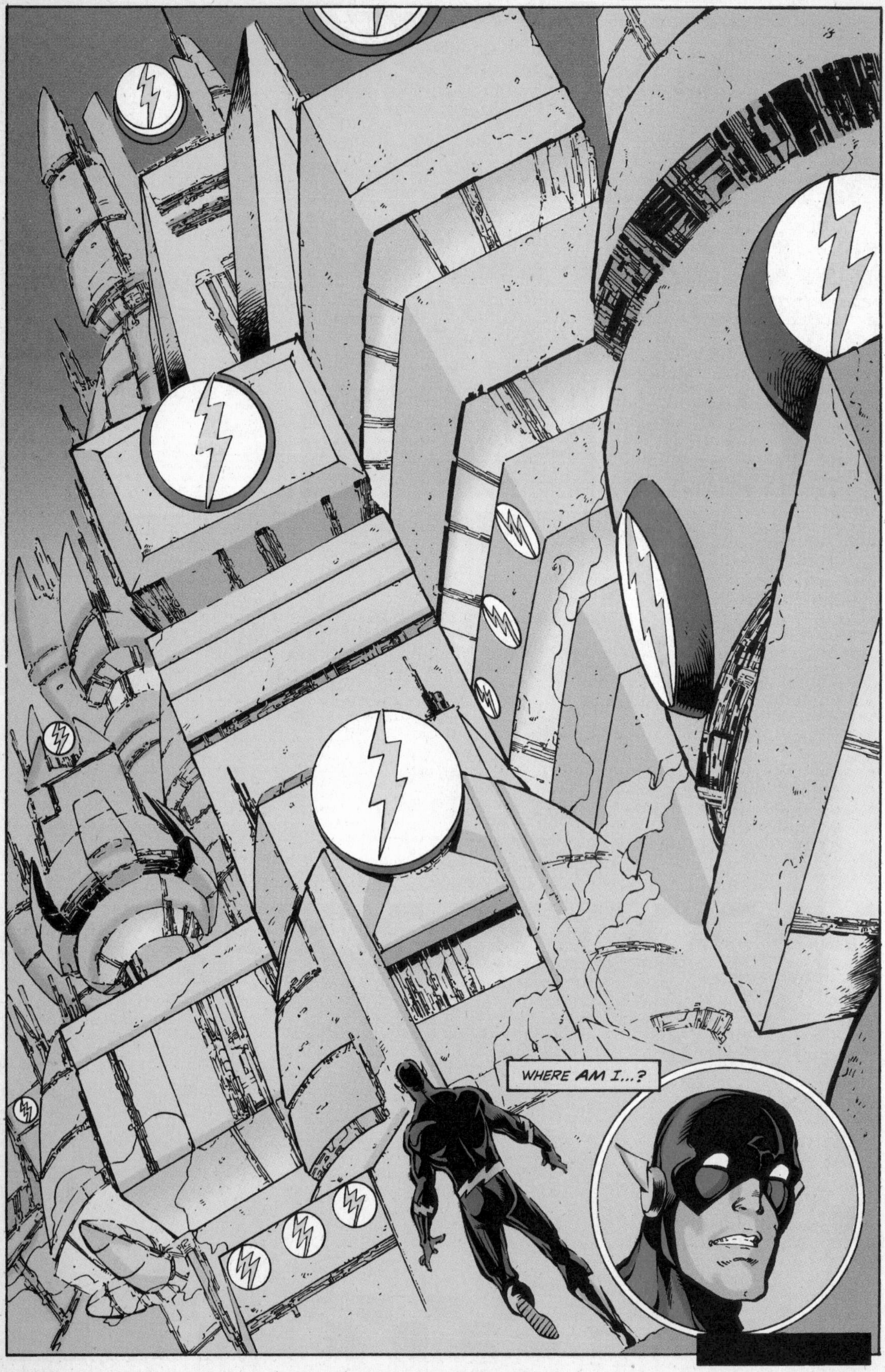
WHERE AM I...?

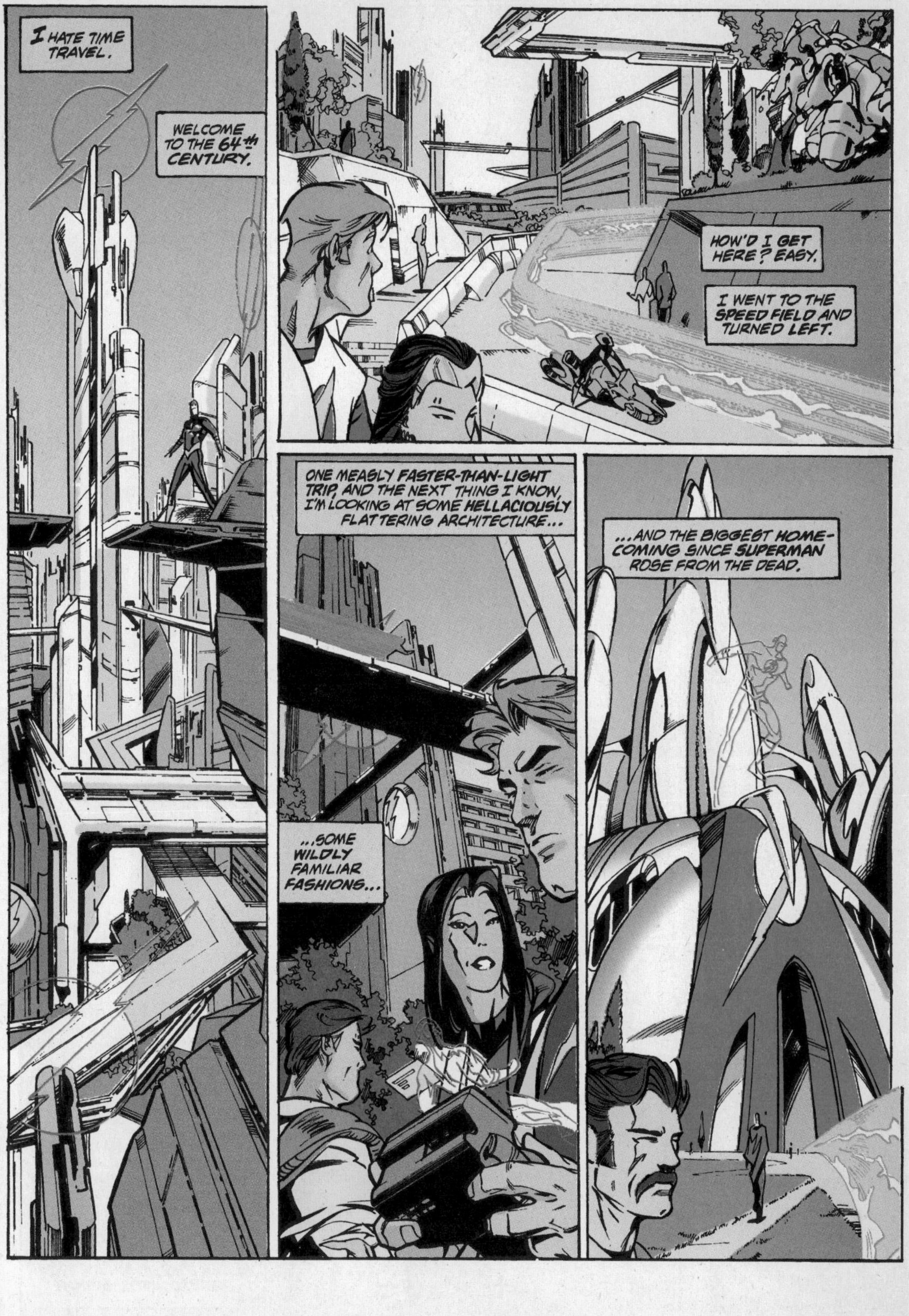
I HATE TIME TRAVEL.
WELCOME TO THE 64th CENTURY.
HOW'D I GET HERE? EASY.
I WENT TO THE SPEED FIELD AND TURNED LEFT.
ONE MEASLY FASTER-THAN-LIGHT TRIP, AND THE NEXT THING I KNOW, I'M LOOKING AT SOME HELLACIOUSLY FLATTERING ARCHITECTURE...
...SOME WILDLY FAMILIAR FASHIONS...
...AND THE BIGGEST HOME-COMING SINCE SUPERMAN ROSE FROM THE DEAD.

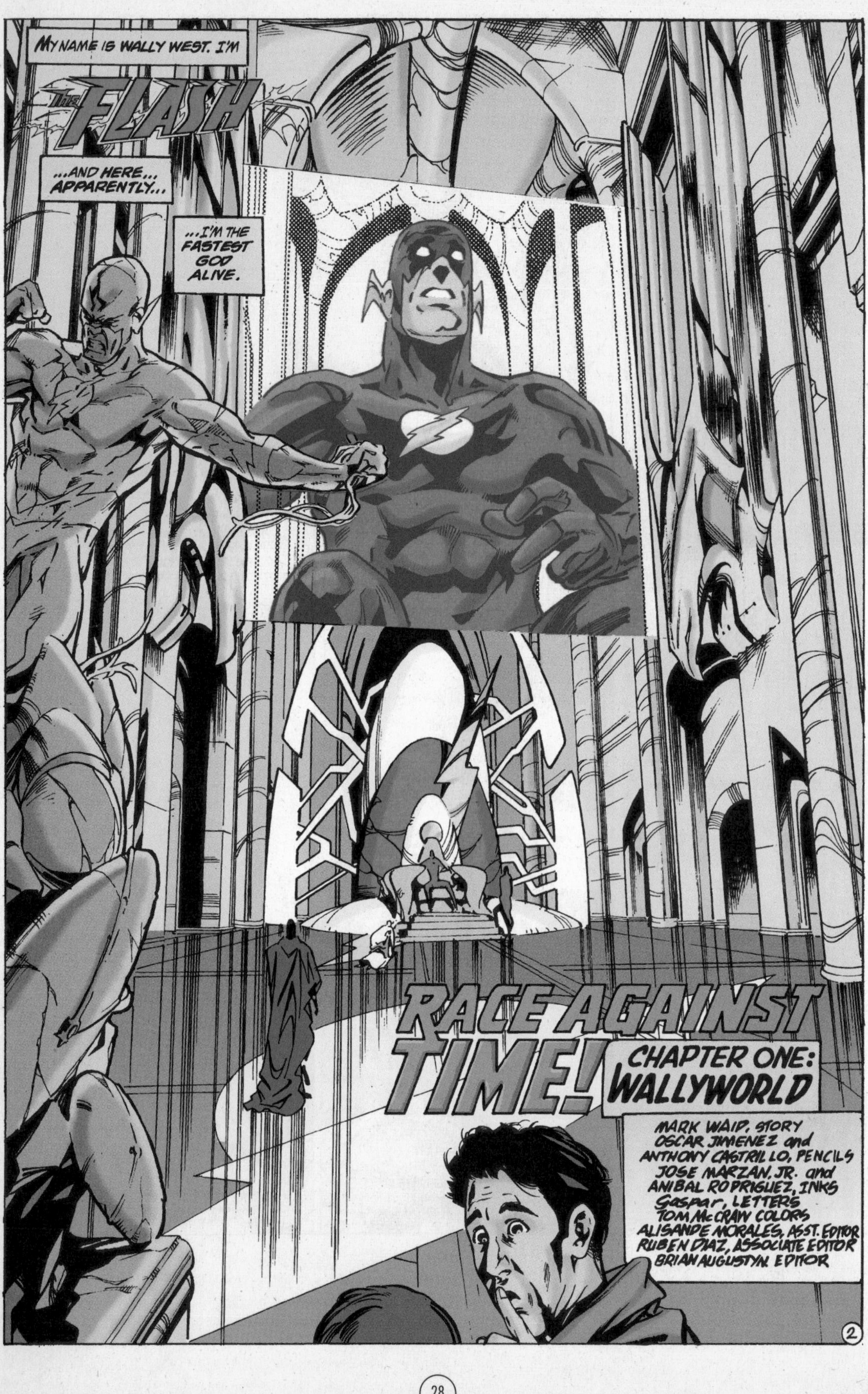
MY NAME IS WALLY WEST. I'M
THE FLASH
...AND HERE... APPARENTLY...
...I'M THE FASTEST GOD ALIVE.
RACE AGAINST TIME!
CHAPTER ONE: WALLYWORLD
MARK WAID, STORY
OSCAR JIMENEZ and ANTHONY CASTRILLO, PENCILS
JOSE MARZAN, JR. and ANIBAL RODRIGUEZ, INKS
Gaspar, LETTERS
TOM McCRAW COLORS
ALISANDE MORALES, ASST. EDITOR
RUBEN DIAZ, ASSOCIATE EDITOR
BRIAN AUGUSTYN, EDITOR
2

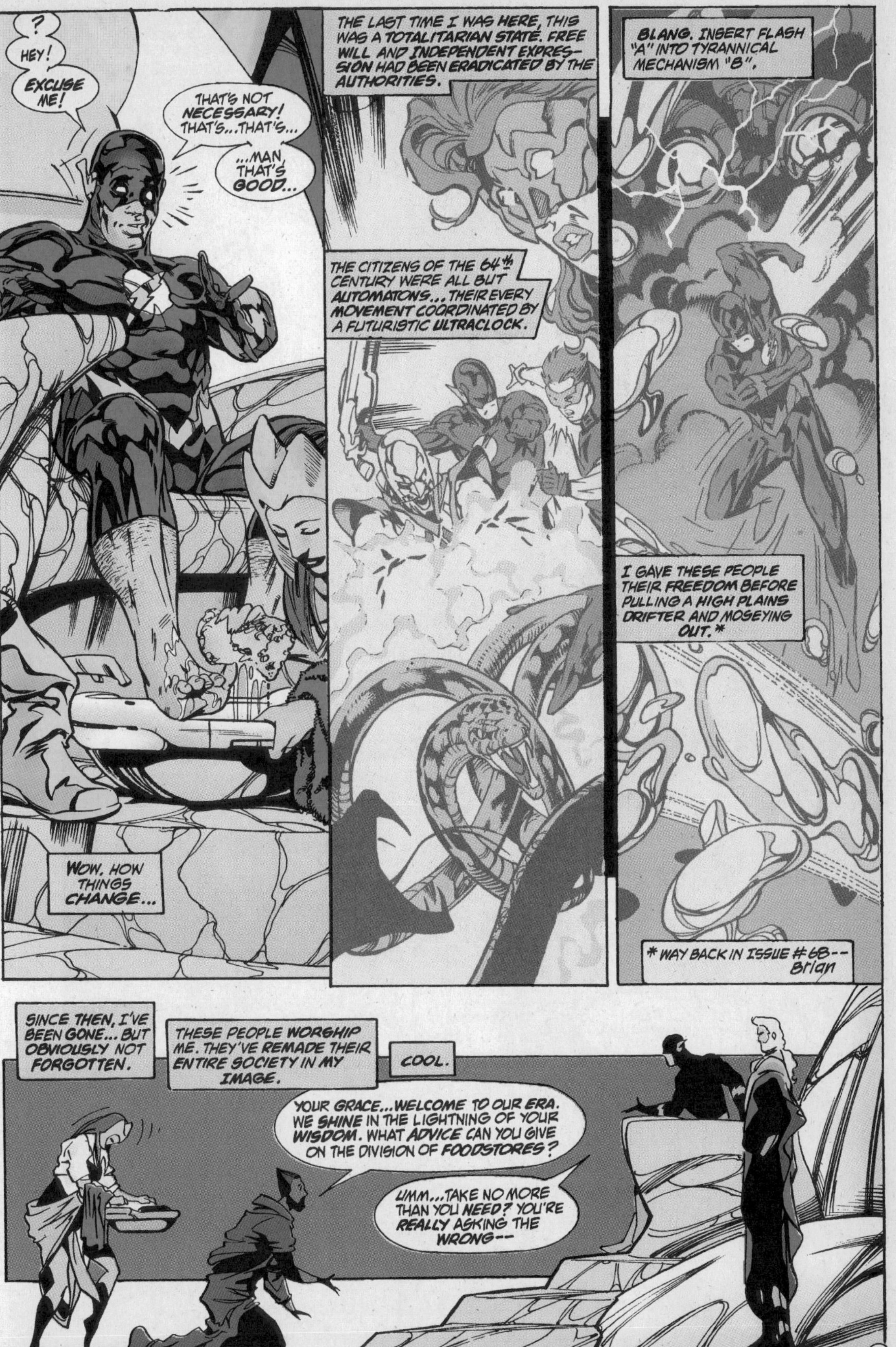
?
HEY!
EXCUSE ME!
THAT'S NOT NECESSARY! THAT'S...THAT'S...
...MAN, THAT'S GOOD...
WOW. HOW THINGS CHANGE...
THE LAST TIME I WAS HERE, THIS WAS A TOTALITARIAN STATE. FREE WILL AND INDEPENDENT EXPRESSION HAD BEEN ERADICATED BY THE AUTHORITIES.
THE CITIZENS OF THE 64TH CENTURY WERE ALL BUT AUTOMATONS... THEIR EVERY MOVEMENT COORDINATED BY A FUTURISTIC ULTRACLOCK.
BLANG. INSERT FLASH "A" INTO TYRANNICAL MECHANISM "B".
I GAVE THESE PEOPLE THEIR FREEDOM BEFORE PULLING A HIGH PLAINS DRIFTER AND MOSEYING OUT.*
* WAY BACK IN ISSUE #68-- Brian
SINCE THEN, I'VE BEEN GONE... BUT OBVIOUSLY NOT FORGOTTEN.
THESE PEOPLE WORSHIP ME. THEY'VE REMADE THEIR ENTIRE SOCIETY IN MY IMAGE.
COOL.
YOUR GRACE... WELCOME TO OUR ERA. WE SHINE IN THE LIGHTNING OF YOUR WISDOM. WHAT ADVICE CAN YOU GIVE ON THE DIVISION OF FOODSTORES?
UMM... TAKE NO MORE THAN YOU NEED? YOU'RE REALLY ASKING THE WRONG--
3

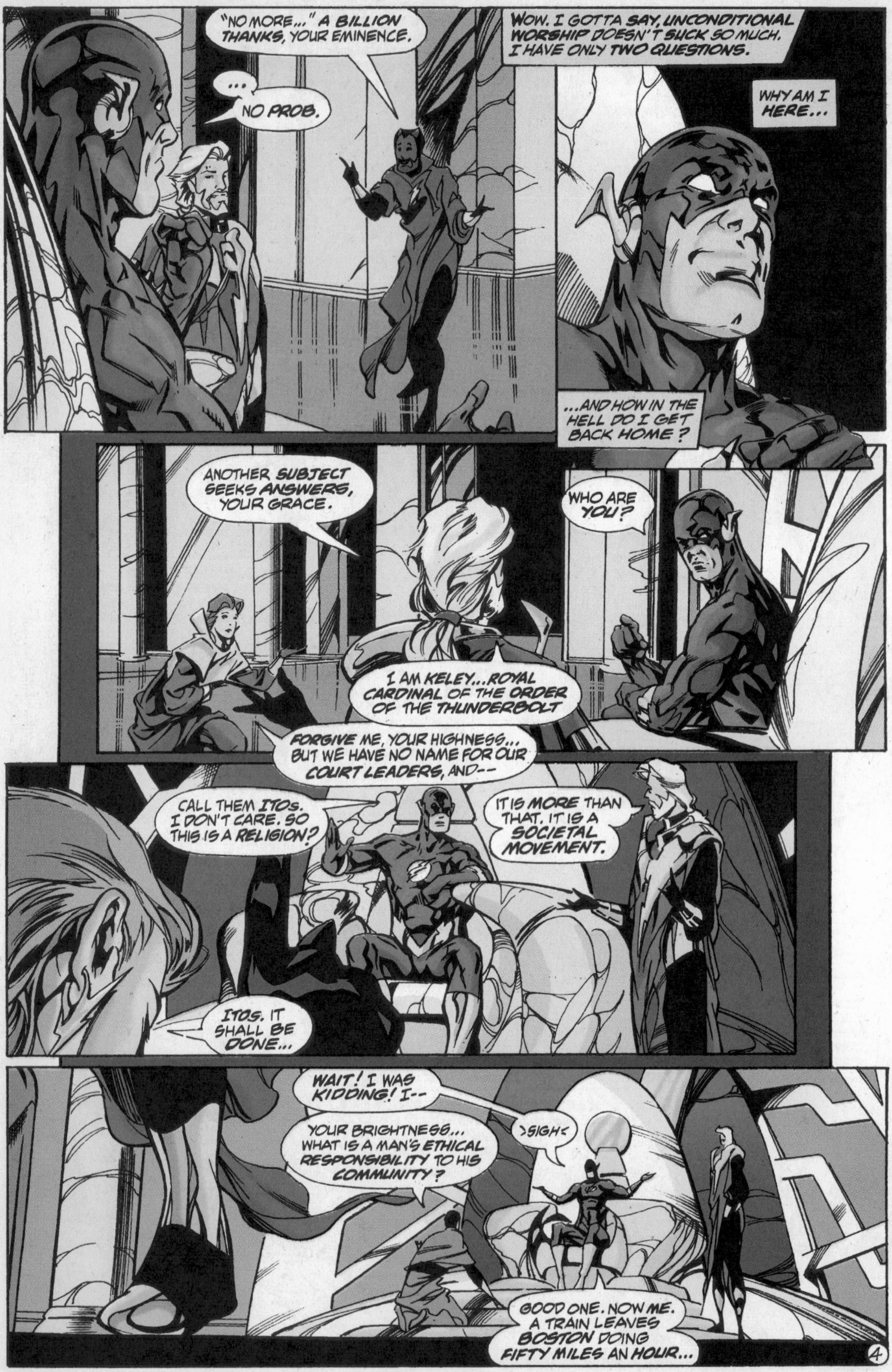

"NO MORE..." A BILLION THANKS, YOUR EMINENCE.
... NO PROB.
WOW. I GOTTA SAY, UNCONDITIONAL WORSHIP DOESN'T SUCK SO MUCH. I HAVE ONLY TWO QUESTIONS.
WHY AM I HERE...
...AND HOW IN THE HELL DO I GET BACK HOME?
ANOTHER SUBJECT SEEKS ANSWERS, YOUR GRACE.
WHO ARE YOU?
I AM KELEY...ROYAL CARDINAL OF THE ORDER OF THE THUNDERBOLT
FORGIVE ME, YOUR HIGHNESS... BUT WE HAVE NO NAME FOR OUR COURT LEADERS, AND--
CALL THEM ITOS. I DON'T CARE. SO THIS IS A RELIGION?
IT IS MORE THAN THAT. IT IS A SOCIETAL MOVEMENT.
ITOS. IT SHALL BE DONE...
WAIT! I WAS KIDDING! I--
YOUR BRIGHTNESS... WHAT IS A MAN'S ETHICAL RESPONSIBILITY TO HIS COMMUNITY?
>SIGH<
GOOD ONE. NOW ME. A TRAIN LEAVES BOSTON DOING FIFTY MILES AN HOUR...
4

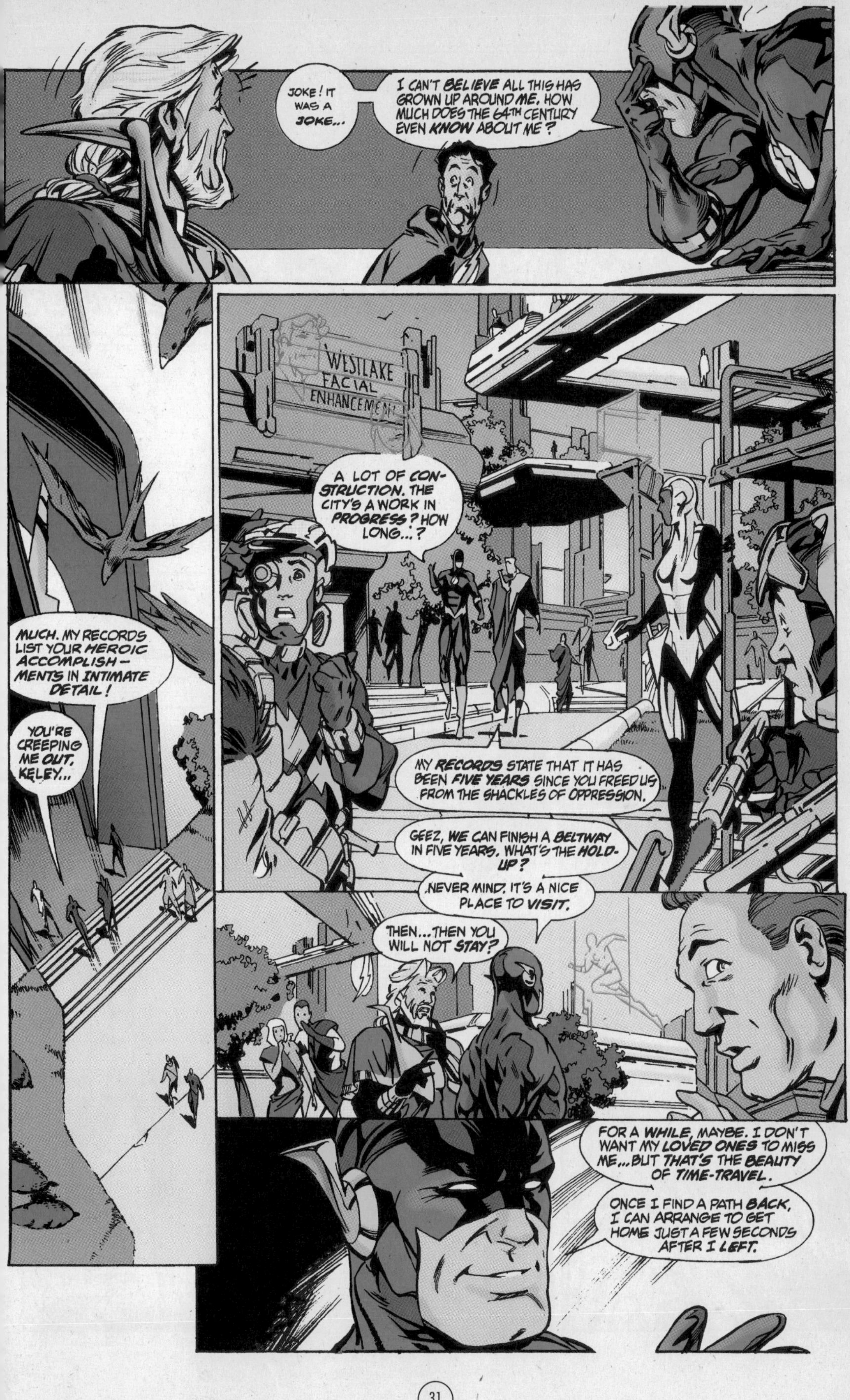
JOKE! IT WAS A JOKE...
I CAN'T BELIEVE ALL THIS HAS GROWN UP AROUND ME. HOW MUCH DOES THE 64TH CENTURY EVEN KNOW ABOUT ME?
WESTLAKE FACIAL ENHANCEMENT
A LOT OF CONSTRUCTION. THE CITY'S A WORK IN PROGRESS? HOW LONG...?
MUCH. MY RECORDS LIST YOUR HEROIC ACCOMPLISHMENTS IN INTIMATE DETAIL!
YOU'RE CREEPING ME OUT, KELEY...
MY RECORDS STATE THAT IT HAS BEEN FIVE YEARS SINCE YOU FREED US FROM THE SHACKLES OF OPPRESSION.
GEEZ, WE CAN FINISH A BELTWAY IN FIVE YEARS. WHAT'S THE HOLD-UP?
NEVER MIND. IT'S A NICE PLACE TO VISIT.
THEN...THEN YOU WILL NOT STAY?
FOR A WHILE, MAYBE. I DON'T WANT MY LOVED ONES TO MISS ME...BUT THAT'S THE BEAUTY OF TIME-TRAVEL.
ONCE I FIND A PATH BACK, I CAN ARRANGE TO GET HOME JUST A FEW SECONDS AFTER I LEFT.

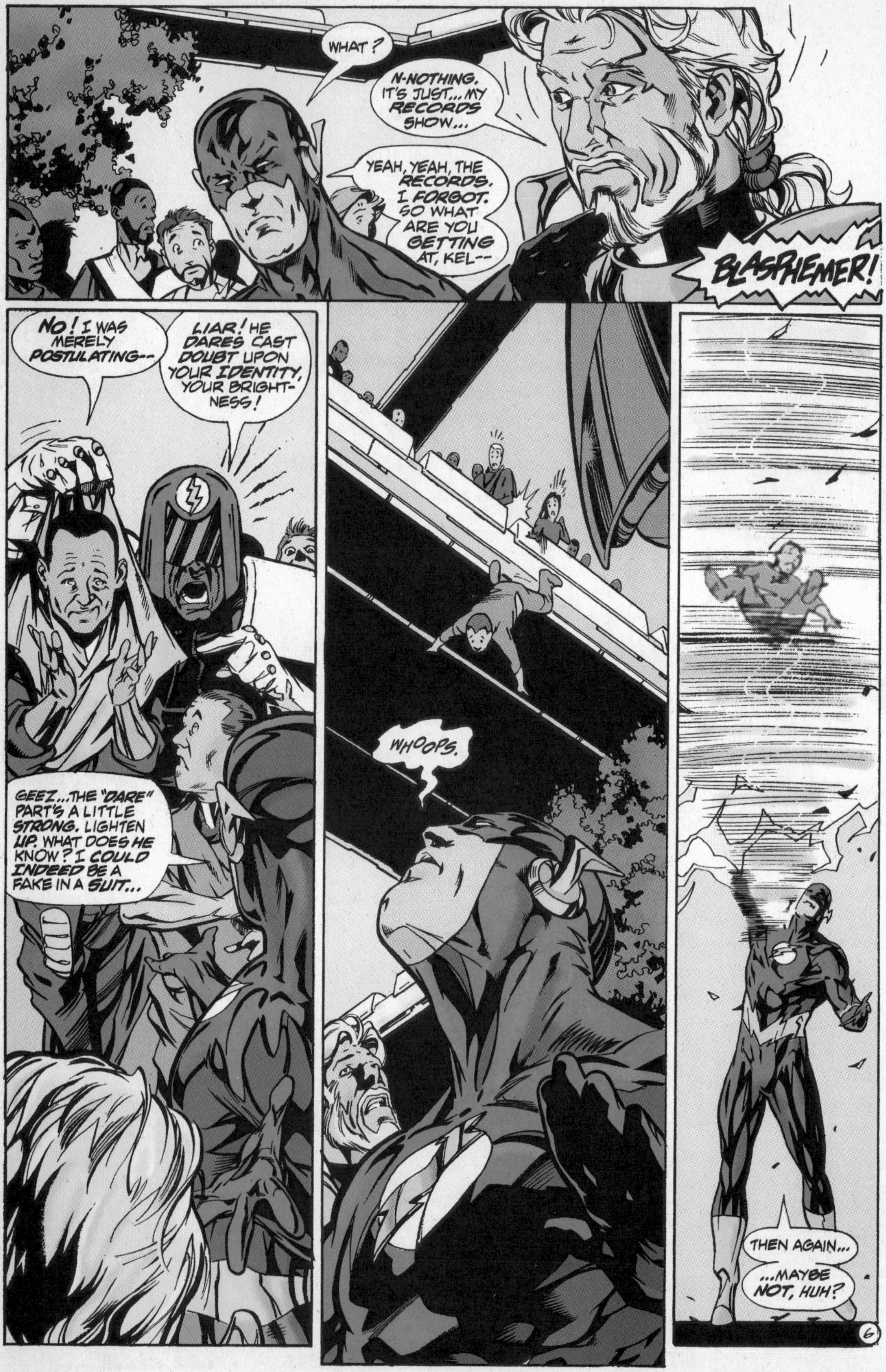
WHAT?
N-NOTHING. IT'S JUST... MY RECORDS SHOW...
YEAH, YEAH, THE RECORDS. I FORGOT. SO WHAT ARE YOU GETTING AT, KEL--
BLASPHEMER!
NO! I WAS MERELY POSTULATING--
LIAR! HE DARES CAST DOUBT UPON YOUR IDENTITY, YOUR BRIGHTNESS!
GEEZ... THE "DARE" PART'S A LITTLE STRONG. LIGHTEN UP. WHAT DOES HE KNOW? I COULD INDEED BE A FAKE IN A SUIT...
WHOOPS.
THEN AGAIN...
...MAYBE NOT, HUH?
6

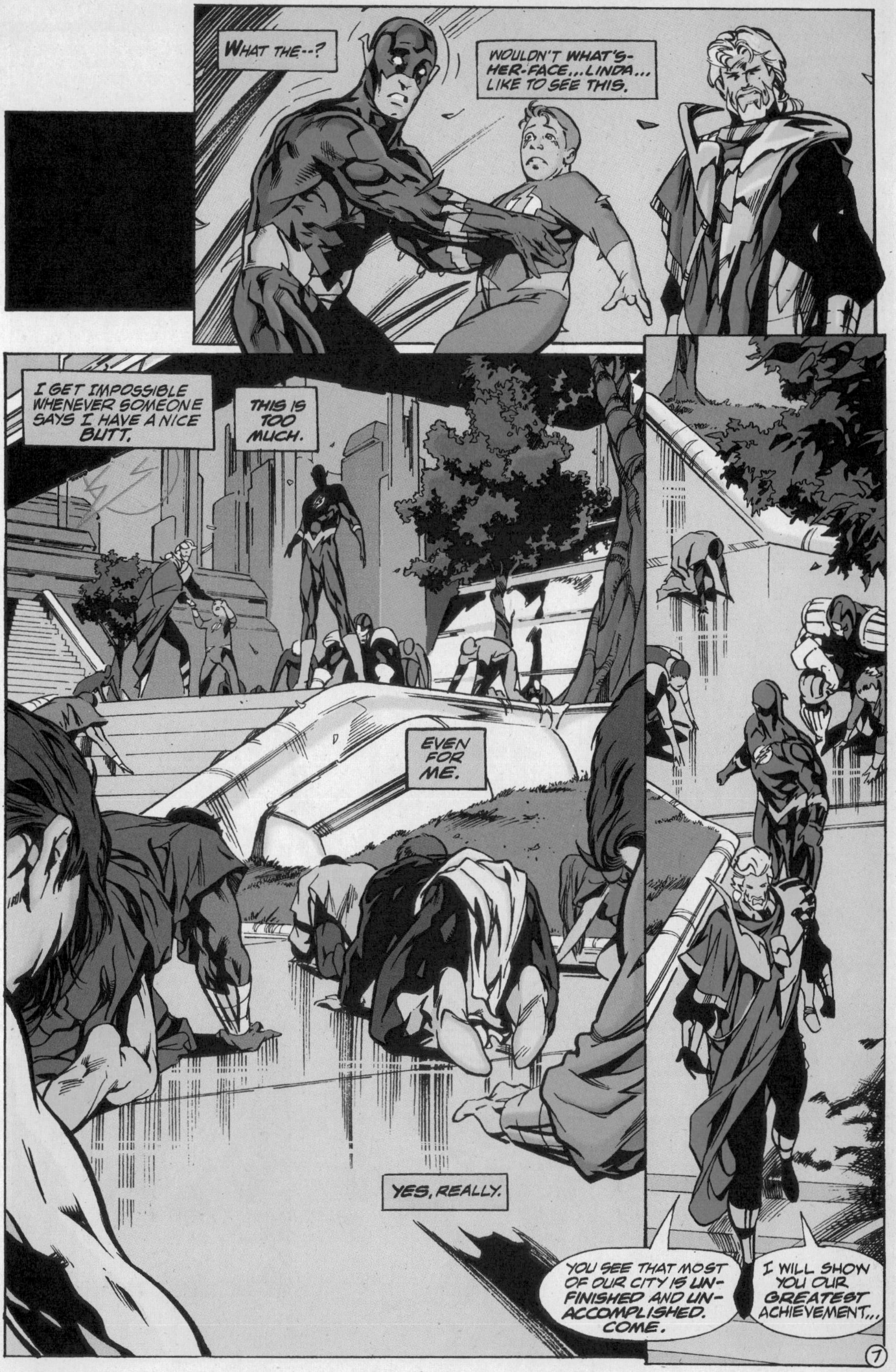
WHAT THE--?
WOULDN'T WHAT'S-HER-FACE...LINDA... LIKE TO SEE THIS.
I GET IMPOSSIBLE WHENEVER SOMEONE SAYS I HAVE A NICE BUTT.
THIS IS TOO MUCH.
EVEN FOR ME.
YES, REALLY.
YOU SEE THAT MOST OF OUR CITY IS UN-FINISHED AND UN-ACCOMPLISHED. COME.
I WILL SHOW YOU OUR GREATEST ACHIEVEMENT...
7

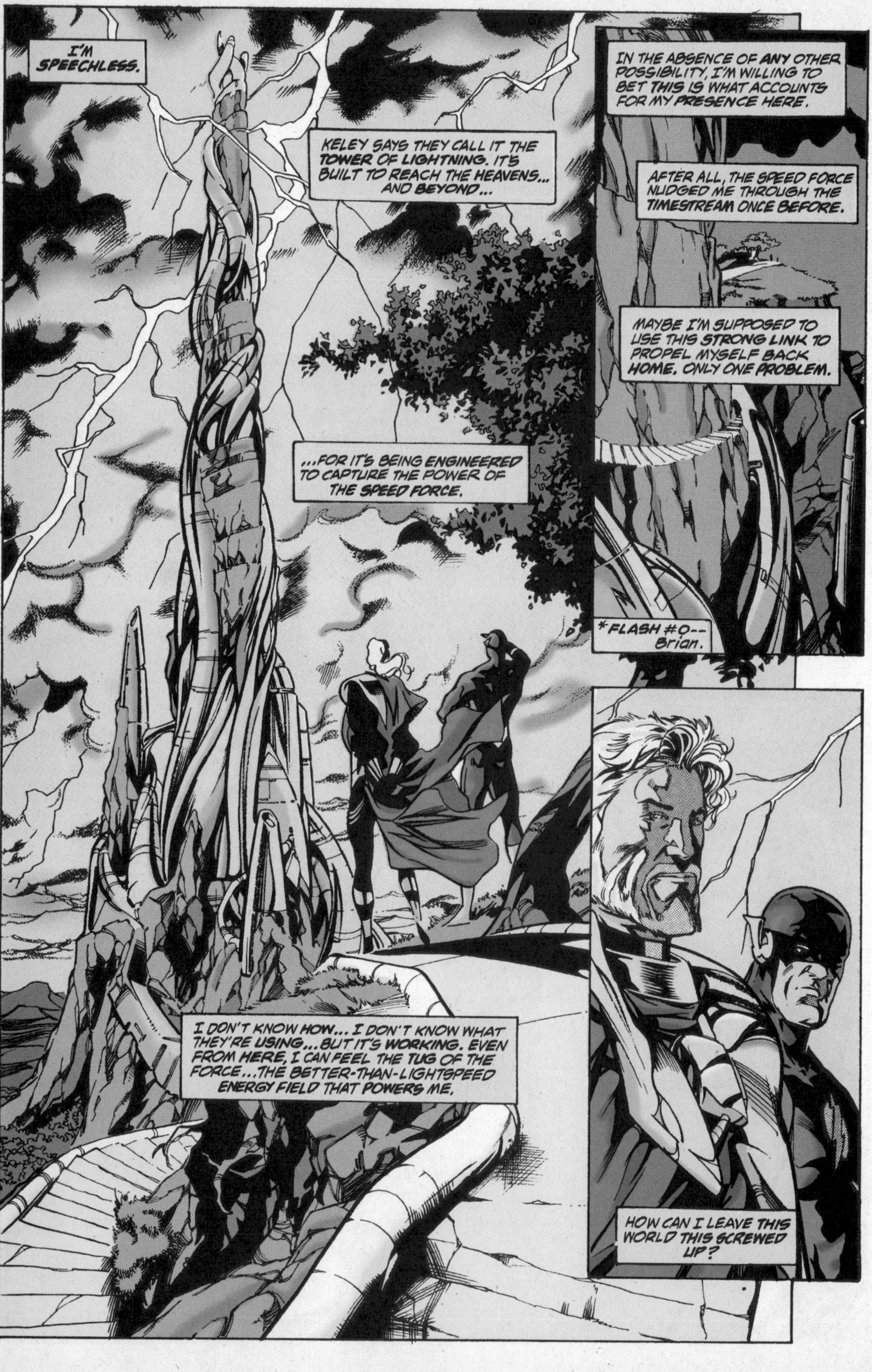
I'M SPEECHLESS.
KELEY SAYS THEY CALL IT THE TOWER OF LIGHTNING. IT'S BUILT TO REACH THE HEAVENS... AND BEYOND...
...FOR IT'S BEING ENGINEERED TO CAPTURE THE POWER OF THE SPEED FORCE.
I DON'T KNOW HOW... I DON'T KNOW WHAT THEY'RE USING... BUT IT'S WORKING. EVEN FROM HERE, I CAN FEEL THE TUG OF THE FORCE... THE BETTER-THAN-LIGHTSPEED ENERGY FIELD THAT POWERS ME.
IN THE ABSENCE OF ANY OTHER POSSIBILITY, I'M WILLING TO BET THIS IS WHAT ACCOUNTS FOR MY PRESENCE HERE.
AFTER ALL, THE SPEED FORCE NUDGED ME THROUGH THE TIMESTREAM ONCE BEFORE.
MAYBE I'M SUPPOSED TO USE THIS STRONG LINK TO PROPEL MYSELF BACK HOME. ONLY ONE PROBLEM.
*FLASH #0-- Brian.
HOW CAN I LEAVE THIS WORLD THIS SCREWED UP?

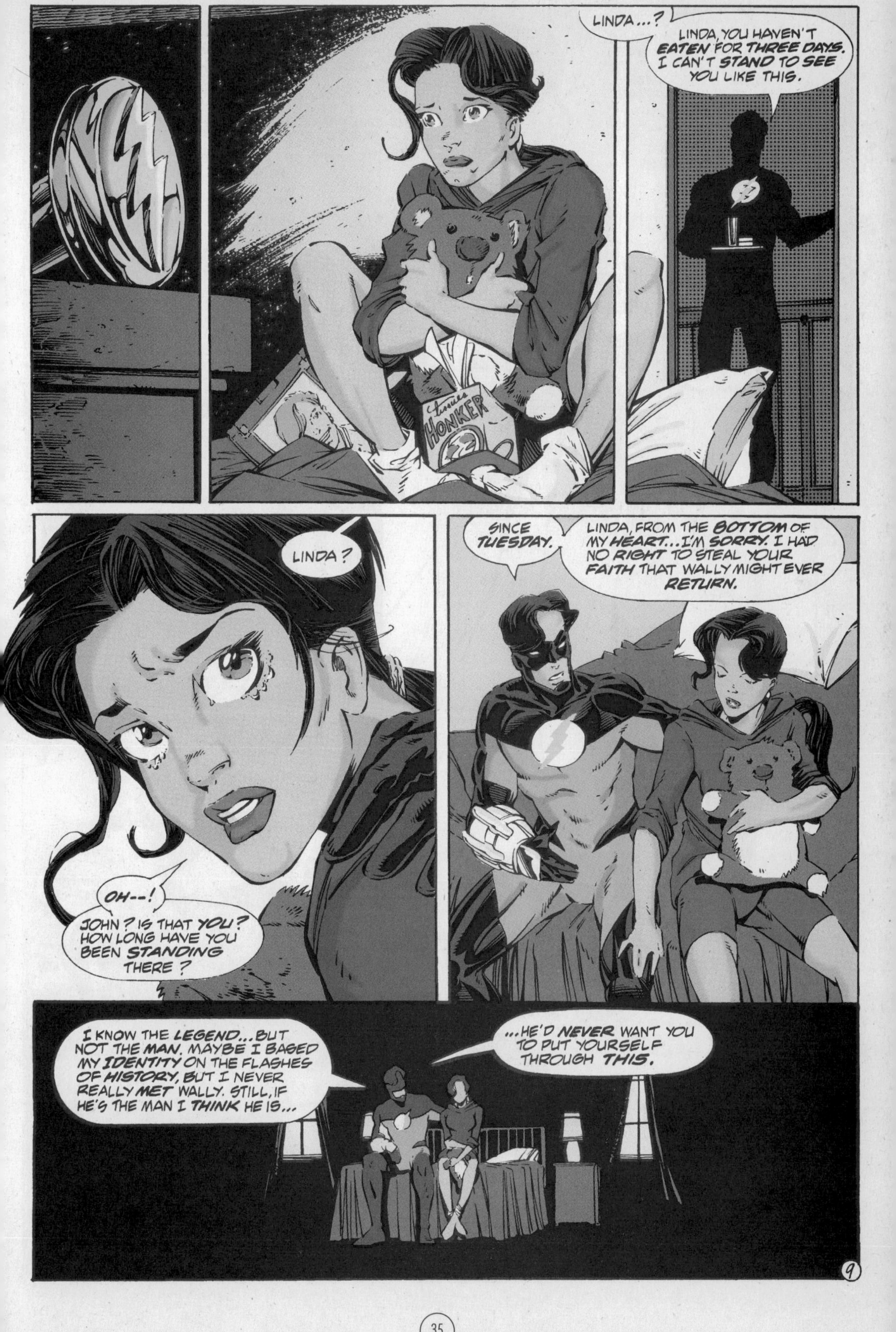
LINDA...?
LINDA, YOU HAVEN'T EATEN FOR THREE DAYS. I CAN'T STAND TO SEE YOU LIKE THIS.
HONKER
LINDA?
OH--!
JOHN? IS THAT YOU? HOW LONG HAVE YOU BEEN STANDING THERE?
SINCE TUESDAY.
LINDA, FROM THE BOTTOM OF MY HEART... I'M SORRY. I HAD NO RIGHT TO STEAL YOUR FAITH THAT WALLY MIGHT EVER RETURN.
I KNOW THE LEGEND... BUT NOT THE MAN. MAYBE I BASED MY IDENTITY ON THE FLASHES OF HISTORY, BUT I NEVER REALLY MET WALLY. STILL, IF HE'S THE MAN I THINK HE IS...
...HE'D NEVER WANT YOU TO PUT YOURSELF THROUGH THIS.
9

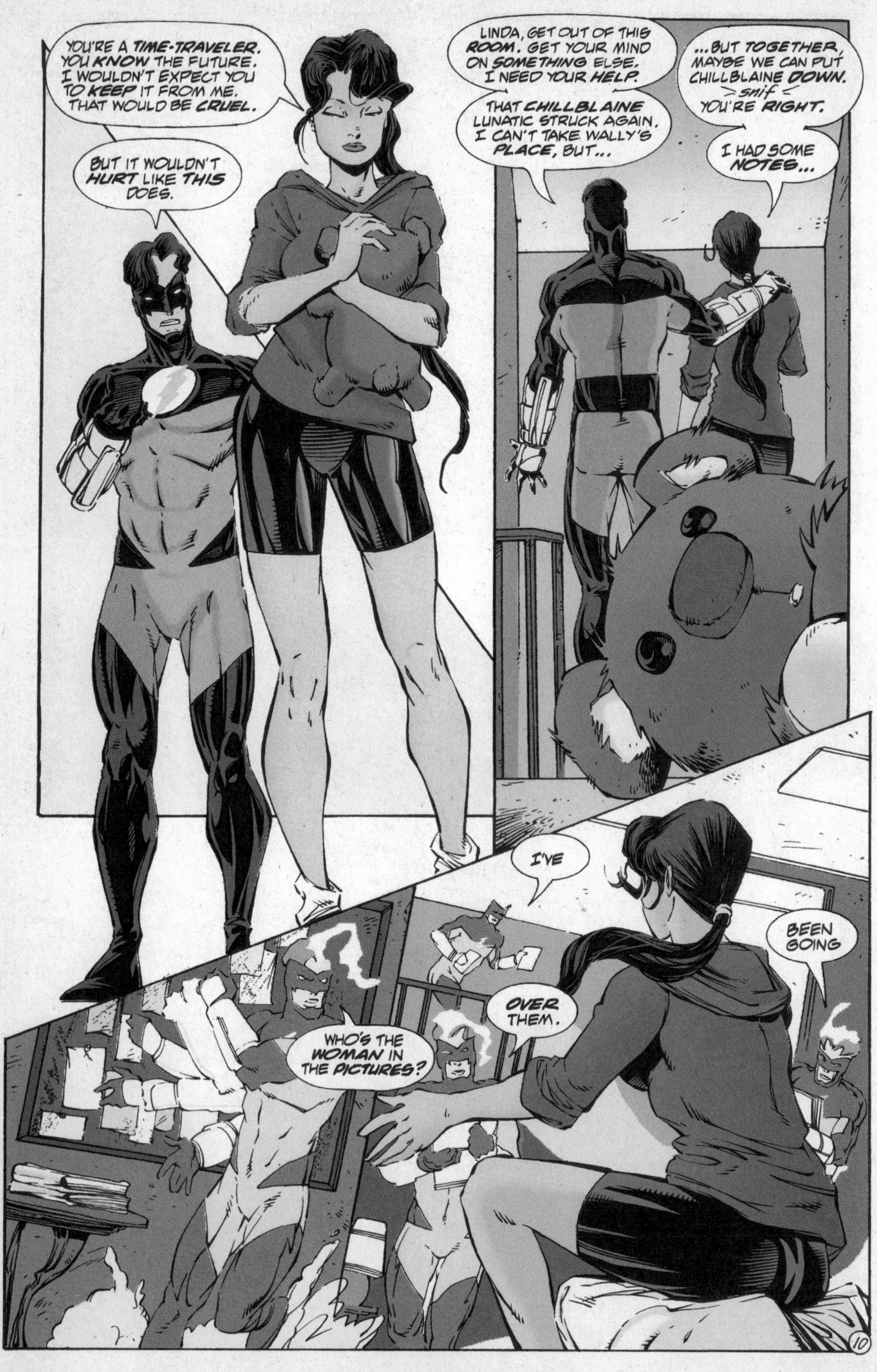

YOU'RE A TIME-TRAVELER. YOU KNOW THE FUTURE. I WOULDN'T EXPECT YOU TO KEEP IT FROM ME. THAT WOULD BE CRUEL.
BUT IT WOULDN'T HURT LIKE THIS DOES.
LINDA, GET OUT OF THIS ROOM. GET YOUR MIND ON SOMETHING ELSE. I NEED YOUR HELP.
THAT CHILLBLAINE LUNATIC STRUCK AGAIN. I CAN'T TAKE WALLY'S PLACE, BUT...
...BUT TOGETHER, MAYBE WE CAN PUT CHILLBLAINE DOWN.
>snif< YOU'RE RIGHT.
I HAD SOME NOTES...
I'VE
BEEN GOING
OVER THEM.
WHO'S THE WOMAN IN THE PICTURES?
10

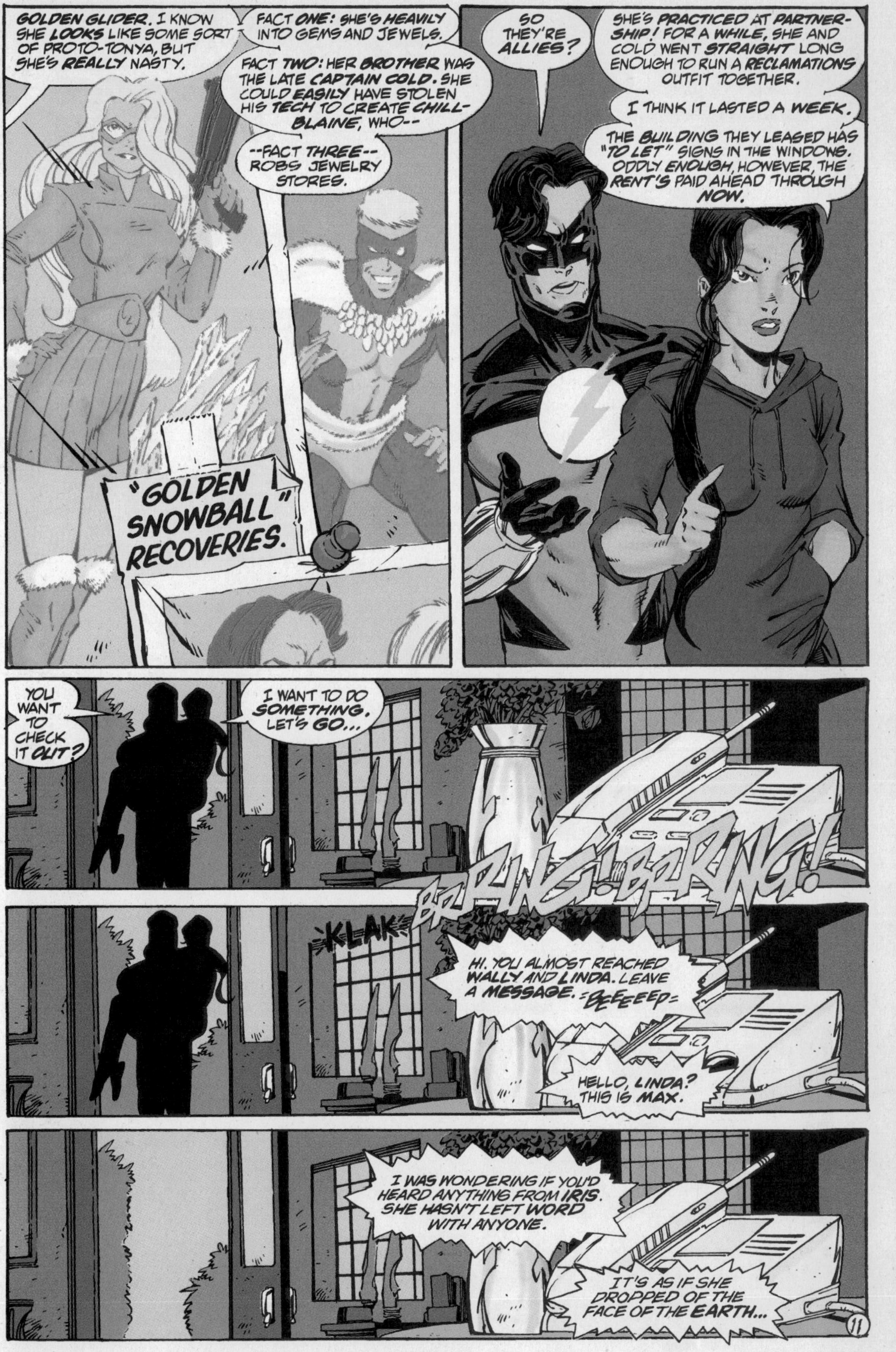
GOLDEN GLIDER. I KNOW SHE LOOKS LIKE SOME SORT OF PROTO-TONYA, BUT SHE'S REALLY NASTY.
FACT ONE: SHE'S HEAVILY INTO GEMS AND JEWELS.
FACT TWO: HER BROTHER WAS THE LATE CAPTAIN COLD. SHE COULD EASILY HAVE STOLEN HIS TECH TO CREATE CHILL-BLAINE, WHO--
--FACT THREE-- ROBS JEWELRY STORES.
"GOLDEN SNOWBALL" RECOVERIES.
SO THEY'RE ALLIES?
SHE'S PRACTICED AT PARTNERSHIP! FOR A WHILE, SHE AND COLD WENT STRAIGHT LONG ENOUGH TO RUN A RECLAMATIONS OUTFIT TOGETHER.
I THINK IT LASTED A WEEK.
THE BUILDING THEY LEASED HAS "TO LET" SIGNS IN THE WINDOWS. ODDLY ENOUGH, HOWEVER, THE RENT'S PAID AHEAD THROUGH NOW.
YOU WANT TO CHECK IT OUT?
I WANT TO DO SOMETHING. LET'S GO...
BRRING! BRRING!
KLAK
HI. YOU ALMOST REACHED WALLY AND LINDA. LEAVE A MESSAGE. BEEEEEP
HELLO, LINDA? THIS IS MAX.
I WAS WONDERING IF YOU'D HEARD ANYTHING FROM IRIS. SHE HASN'T LEFT WORD WITH ANYONE.
IT'S AS IF SHE DROPPED OF THE FACE OF THE EARTH...
11

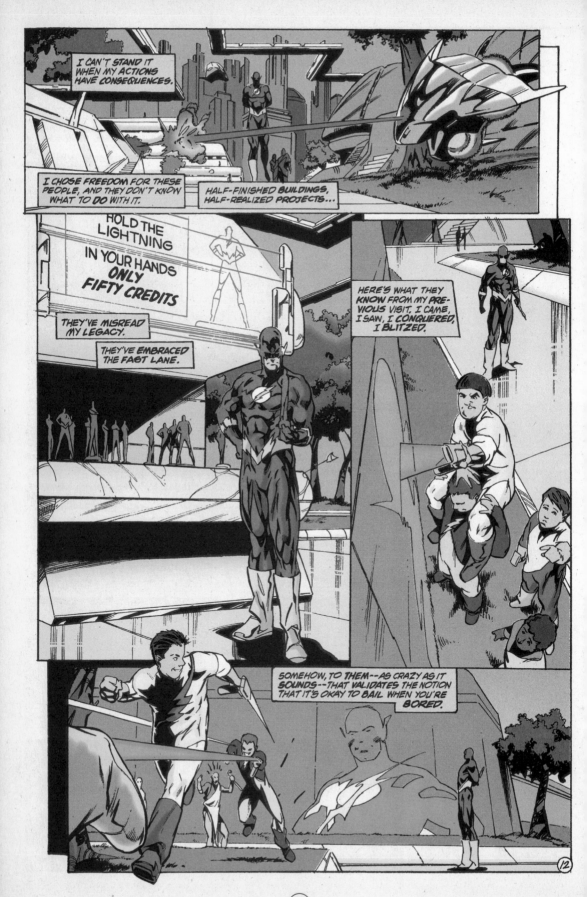

I CAN'T STAND IT WHEN MY ACTIONS HAVE CONSEQUENCES.

I CHOSE FREEDOM FOR THESE PEOPLE, AND THEY DON'T KNOW WHAT TO DO WITH IT.

HALF-FINISHED BUILDINGS, HALF-REALIZED PROJECTS...

HOLD THE LIGHTNING IN YOUR HANDS ONLY FIFTY CREDITS

THEY'VE MISREAD MY LEGACY.

THEY'VE EMBRACED THE FAST LANE.

HERE'S WHAT THEY KNOW FROM MY PREVIOUS VISIT. I CAME, I SAW, I CONQUERED, I BLITZED.

SOMEHOW, TO THEM--AS CRAZY AS IT SOUNDS--THAT VALIDATES THE NOTION THAT IT'S OKAY TO BAIL WHEN YOU'RE BORED.

12

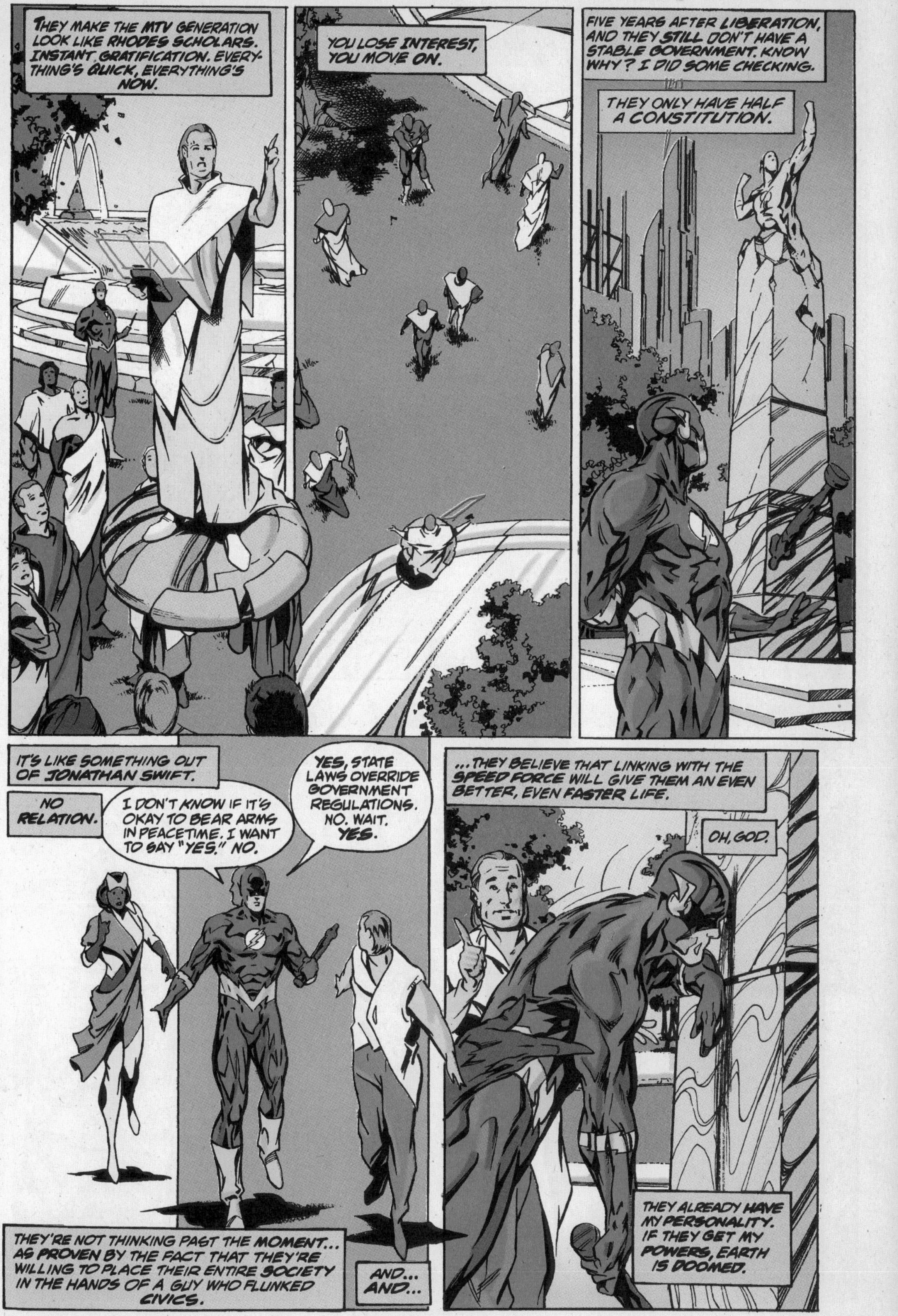

THEY MAKE THE MTV GENERATION LOOK LIKE RHODES SCHOLARS. INSTANT GRATIFICATION. EVERYTHING'S QUICK, EVERYTHING'S NOW.
YOU LOSE INTEREST, YOU MOVE ON.
FIVE YEARS AFTER LIBERATION, AND THEY STILL DON'T HAVE A STABLE GOVERNMENT. KNOW WHY? I DID SOME CHECKING.
THEY ONLY HAVE HALF A CONSTITUTION.
IT'S LIKE SOMETHING OUT OF JONATHAN SWIFT.
NO RELATION.
I DON'T KNOW IF IT'S OKAY TO BEAR ARMS IN PEACETIME. I WANT TO SAY "YES." NO.
YES, STATE LAWS OVERRIDE GOVERNMENT REGULATIONS. NO. WAIT. YES.
THEY'RE NOT THINKING PAST THE MOMENT... AS PROVEN BY THE FACT THAT THEY'RE WILLING TO PLACE THEIR ENTIRE SOCIETY IN THE HANDS OF A GUY WHO FLUNKED CIVICS.
AND... AND...
...THEY BELIEVE THAT LINKING WITH THE SPEED FORCE WILL GIVE THEM AN EVEN BETTER, EVEN FASTER LIFE.
OH, GOD.
THEY ALREADY HAVE MY PERSONALITY. IF THEY GET MY POWERS, EARTH IS DOOMED.

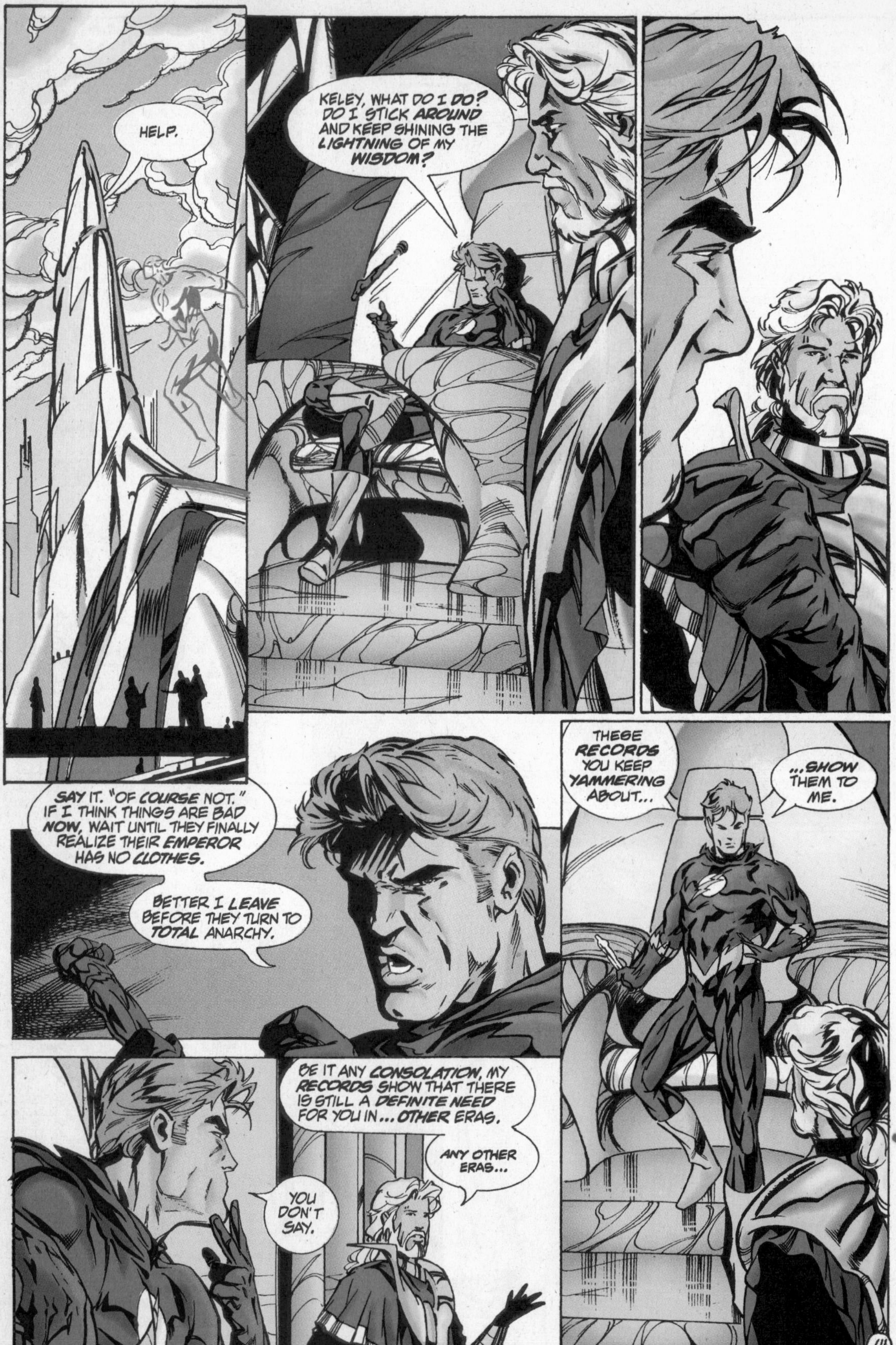
HELP.
KELEY, WHAT DO I DO? DO I STICK AROUND AND KEEP SHINING THE LIGHTNING OF MY WISDOM?
SAY IT. "OF COURSE NOT." IF I THINK THINGS ARE BAD NOW, WAIT UNTIL THEY FINALLY REALIZE THEIR EMPEROR HAS NO CLOTHES.
BETTER I LEAVE BEFORE THEY TURN TO TOTAL ANARCHY.
BE IT ANY CONSOLATION, MY RECORDS SHOW THAT THERE IS STILL A DEFINITE NEED FOR YOU IN... OTHER ERAS.
ANY OTHER ERAS...
YOU DON'T SAY.
THESE RECORDS YOU KEEP YAMMERING ABOUT...
...SHOW THEM TO ME.
14

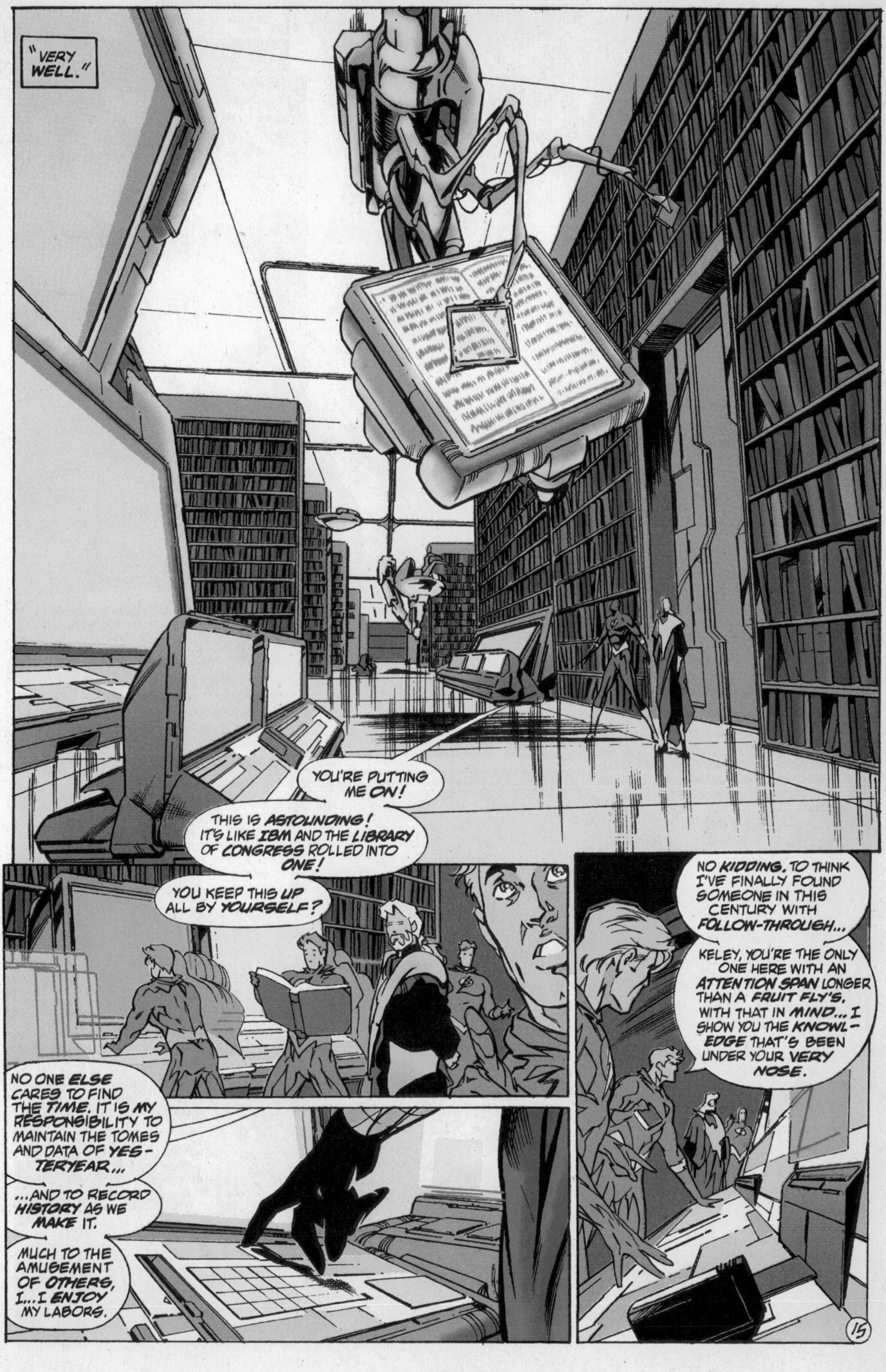
"VERY WELL."
YOU'RE PUTTING ME ON!
THIS IS ASTOUNDING! IT'S LIKE IBM AND THE LIBRARY OF CONGRESS ROLLED INTO ONE!
YOU KEEP THIS UP ALL BY YOURSELF?
NO ONE ELSE CARES TO FIND THE TIME. IT IS MY RESPONSIBILITY TO MAINTAIN THE TOMES AND DATA OF YES-TERYEAR...
...AND TO RECORD HISTORY AS WE MAKE IT.
MUCH TO THE AMUSEMENT OF OTHERS, I...I ENJOY MY LABORS.
NO KIDDING. TO THINK I'VE FINALLY FOUND SOMEONE IN THIS CENTURY WITH FOLLOW-THROUGH...
KELEY, YOU'RE THE ONLY ONE HERE WITH AN ATTENTION SPAN LONGER THAN A FRUIT FLY'S. WITH THAT IN MIND... I SHOW YOU THE KNOWL-EDGE THAT'S BEEN UNDER YOUR VERY NOSE.
15

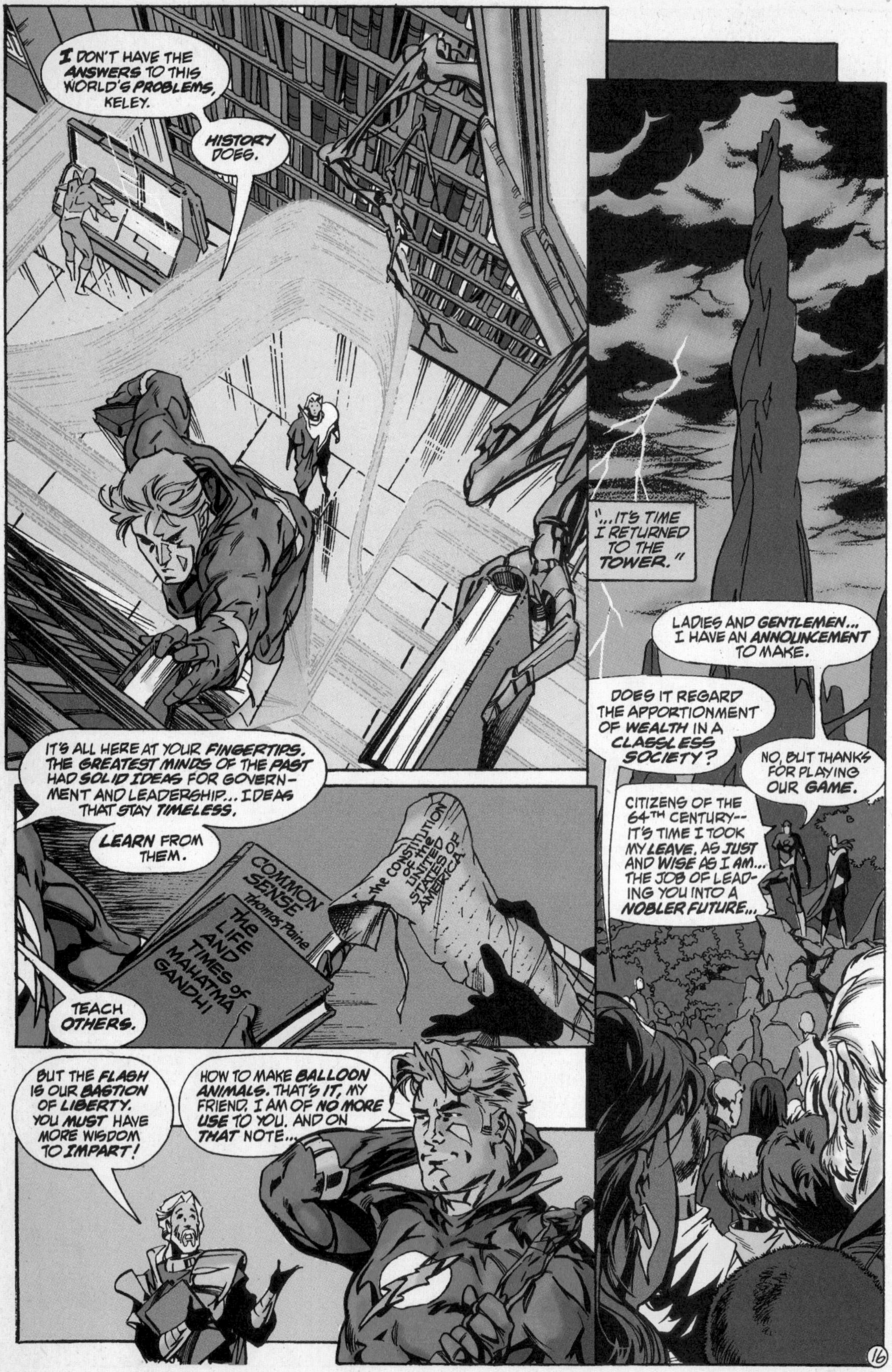

I DON'T HAVE THE ANSWERS TO THIS WORLD'S PROBLEMS, KELEY.
HISTORY DOES.
IT'S ALL HERE AT YOUR FINGERTIPS. THE GREATEST MINDS OF THE PAST HAD SOLID IDEAS FOR GOVERNMENT AND LEADERSHIP... IDEAS THAT STAY TIMELESS.
LEARN FROM THEM.
COMMON SENSE Thomas Paine
THE LIFE AND TIMES of MAHATMA GANDHI
the CONSTITUTION of the UNITED STATES of AMERICA
TEACH OTHERS.
BUT THE FLASH IS OUR BASTION OF LIBERTY. YOU MUST HAVE MORE WISDOM TO IMPART!
HOW TO MAKE BALLOON ANIMALS. THAT'S IT, MY FRIEND. I AM OF NO MORE USE TO YOU. AND ON THAT NOTE...
"...IT'S TIME I RETURNED TO THE TOWER."
LADIES AND GENTLEMEN... I HAVE AN ANNOUNCEMENT TO MAKE.
DOES IT REGARD THE APPORTIONMENT OF WEALTH IN A CLASSLESS SOCIETY?
NO, BUT THANKS FOR PLAYING OUR GAME.
CITIZENS OF THE 64TH CENTURY-- IT'S TIME I TOOK MY LEAVE. AS JUST AND WISE AS I AM... THE JOB OF LEADING YOU INTO A NOBLER FUTURE...
16

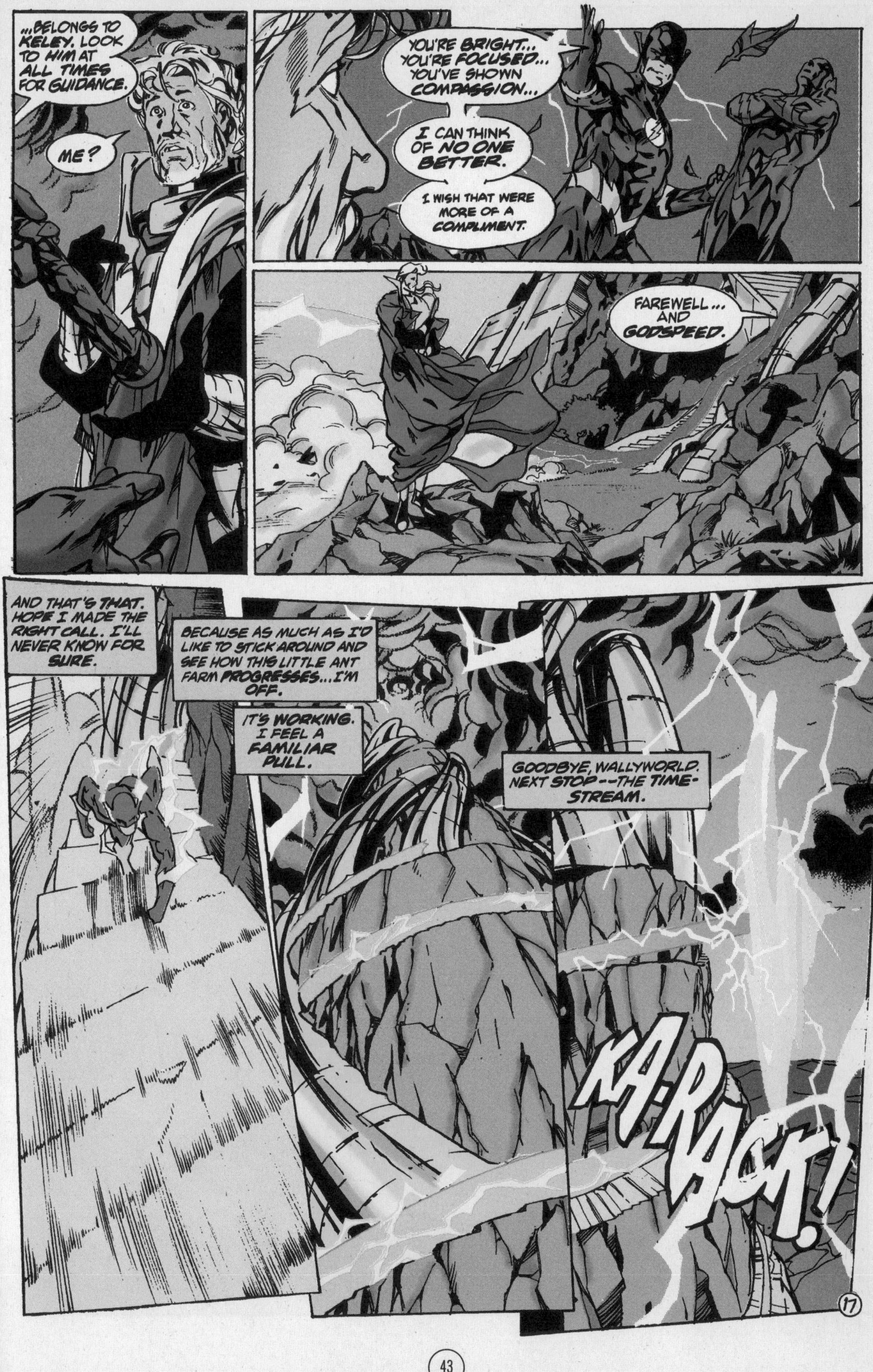
...BELONGS TO KELEY. LOOK TO HIM AT ALL TIMES FOR GUIDANCE.
ME?
YOU'RE BRIGHT... YOU'RE FOCUSED... YOU'VE SHOWN COMPASSION...
I CAN THINK OF NO ONE BETTER.
I WISH THAT WERE MORE OF A COMPLIMENT.
FAREWELL... AND GODSPEED.
AND THAT'S THAT. HOPE I MADE THE RIGHT CALL. I'LL NEVER KNOW FOR SURE.
BECAUSE AS MUCH AS I'D LIKE TO STICK AROUND AND SEE HOW THIS LITTLE ANT FARM PROGRESSES...I'M OFF.
IT'S WORKING. I FEEL A FAMILIAR PULL.
GOODBYE, WALLYWORLD. NEXT STOP--THE TIME-STREAM.
KA-RACK!
17

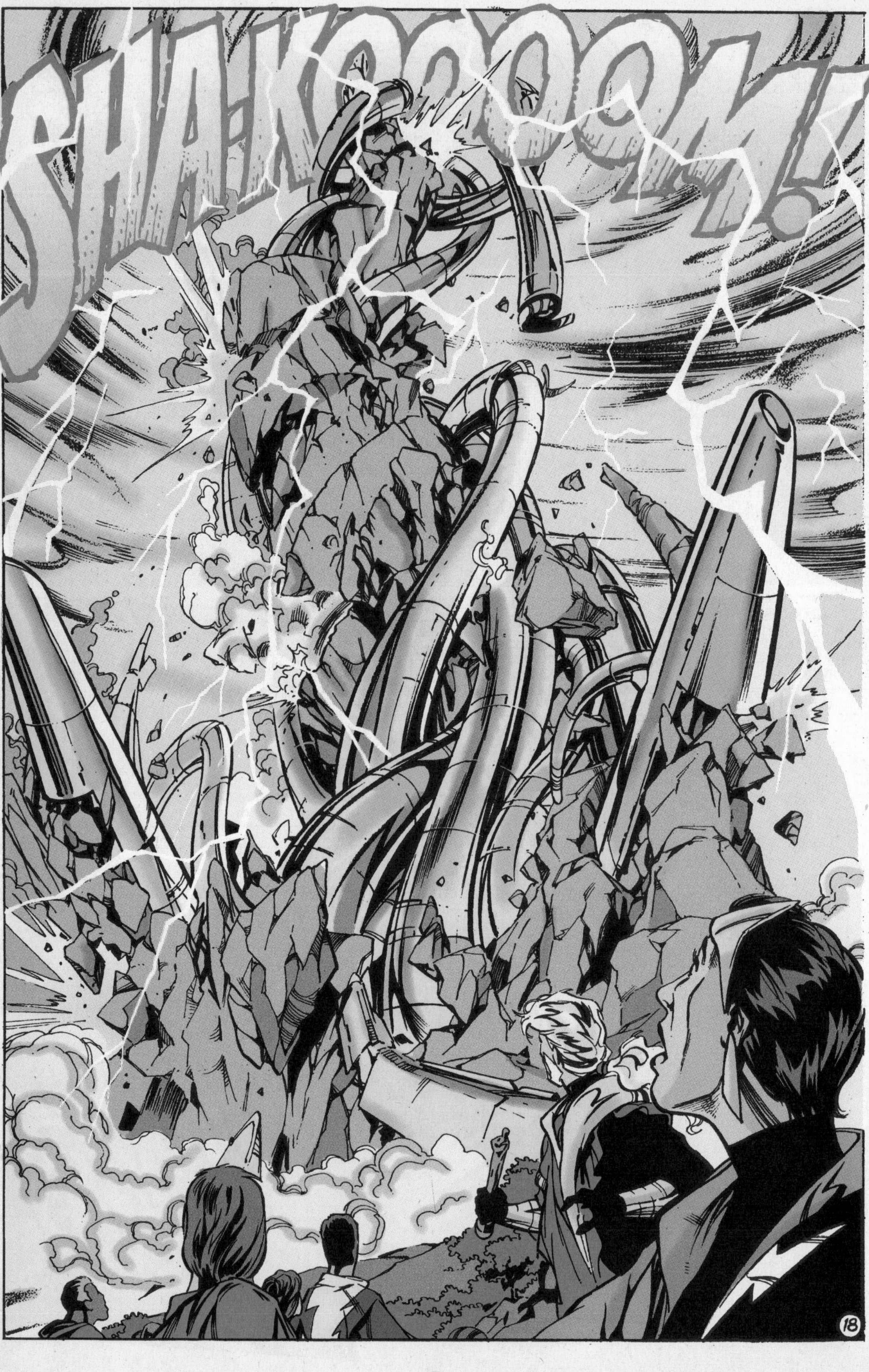
SHAKOOOOM!
18

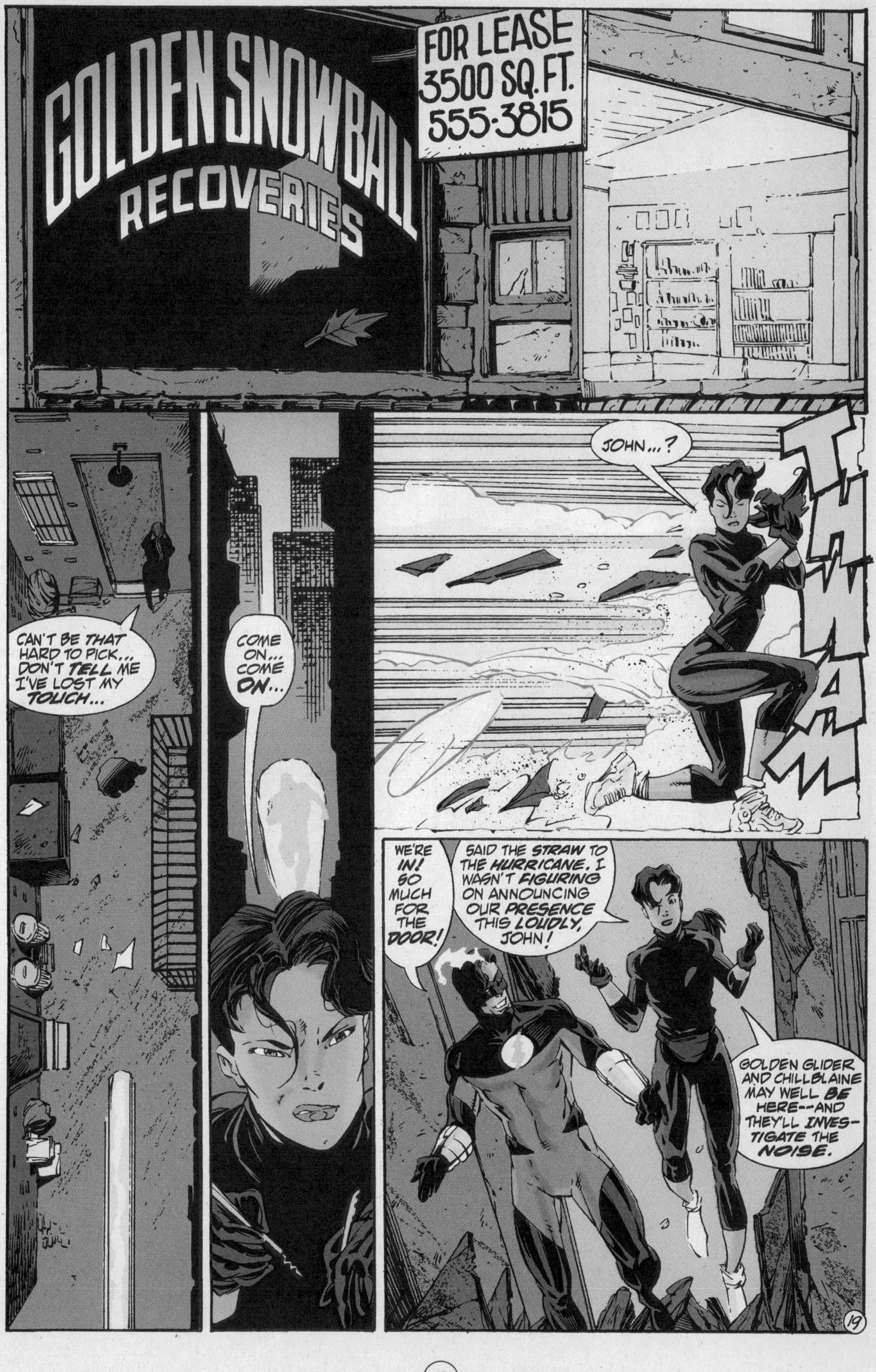
GOLDEN SNOWBALL RECOVERIES
FOR LEASE 3500 SQ. FT. 555-3815
CAN'T BE THAT HARD TO PICK... DON'T TELL ME I'VE LOST MY TOUCH...
COME ON... COME ON...
JOHN...?
THWAM
WE'RE IN! SO MUCH FOR THE DOOR!
SAID THE STRAW TO THE HURRICANE. I WASN'T FIGURING ON ANNOUNCING OUR PRESENCE THIS LOUDLY, JOHN!
GOLDEN GLIDER AND CHILLBLAINE MAY WELL BE HERE--AND THEY'LL INVESTIGATE THE NOISE.
19

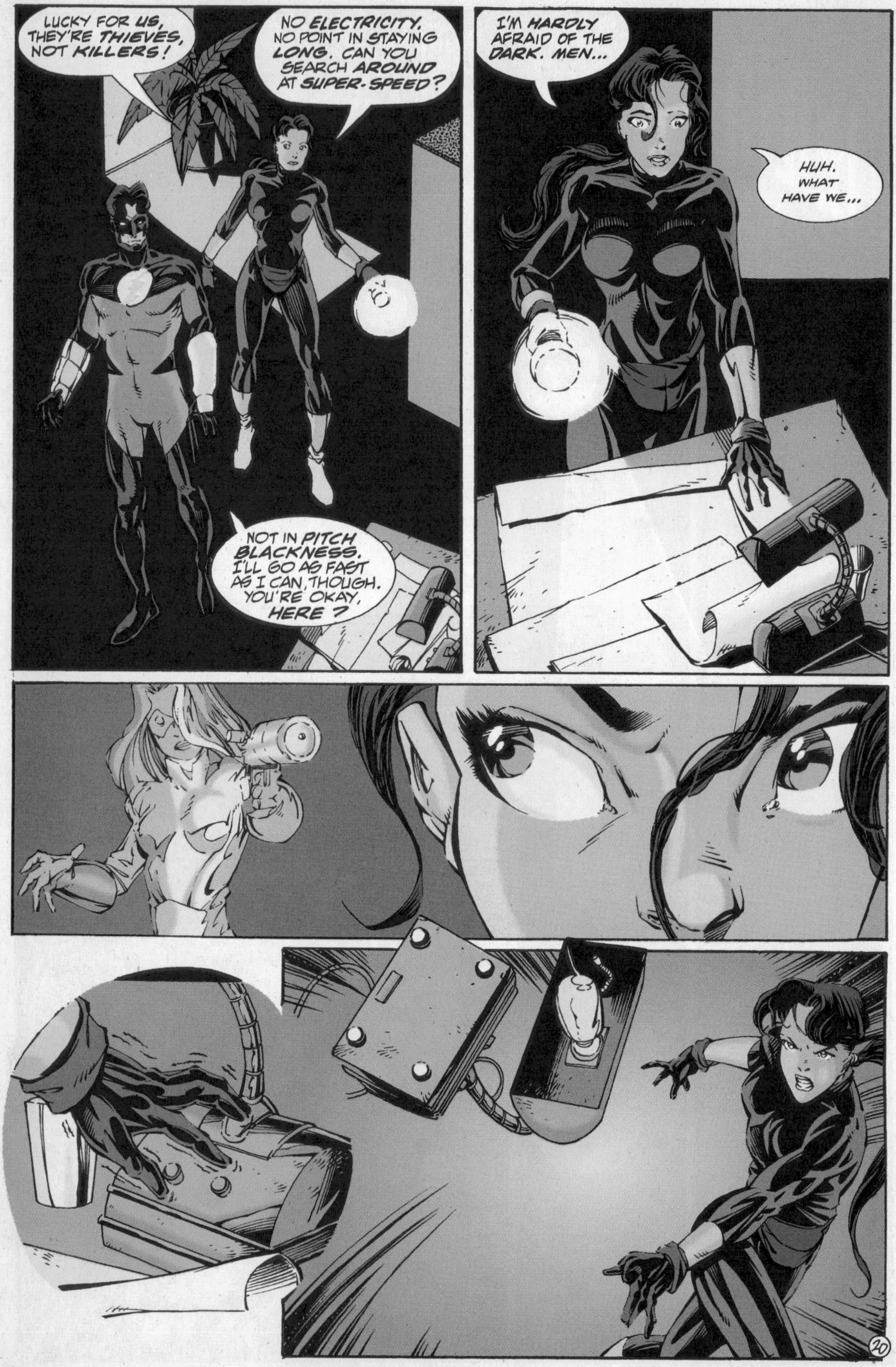
LUCKY FOR US, THEY'RE THIEVES, NOT KILLERS!
NO ELECTRICITY. NO POINT IN STAYING LONG. CAN YOU SEARCH AROUND AT SUPER-SPEED?
NOT IN PITCH BLACKNESS. I'LL GO AS FAST AS I CAN, THOUGH. YOU'RE OKAY, HERE ?
I'M HARDLY AFRAID OF THE DARK. MEN...
HUH. WHAT HAVE WE...
20

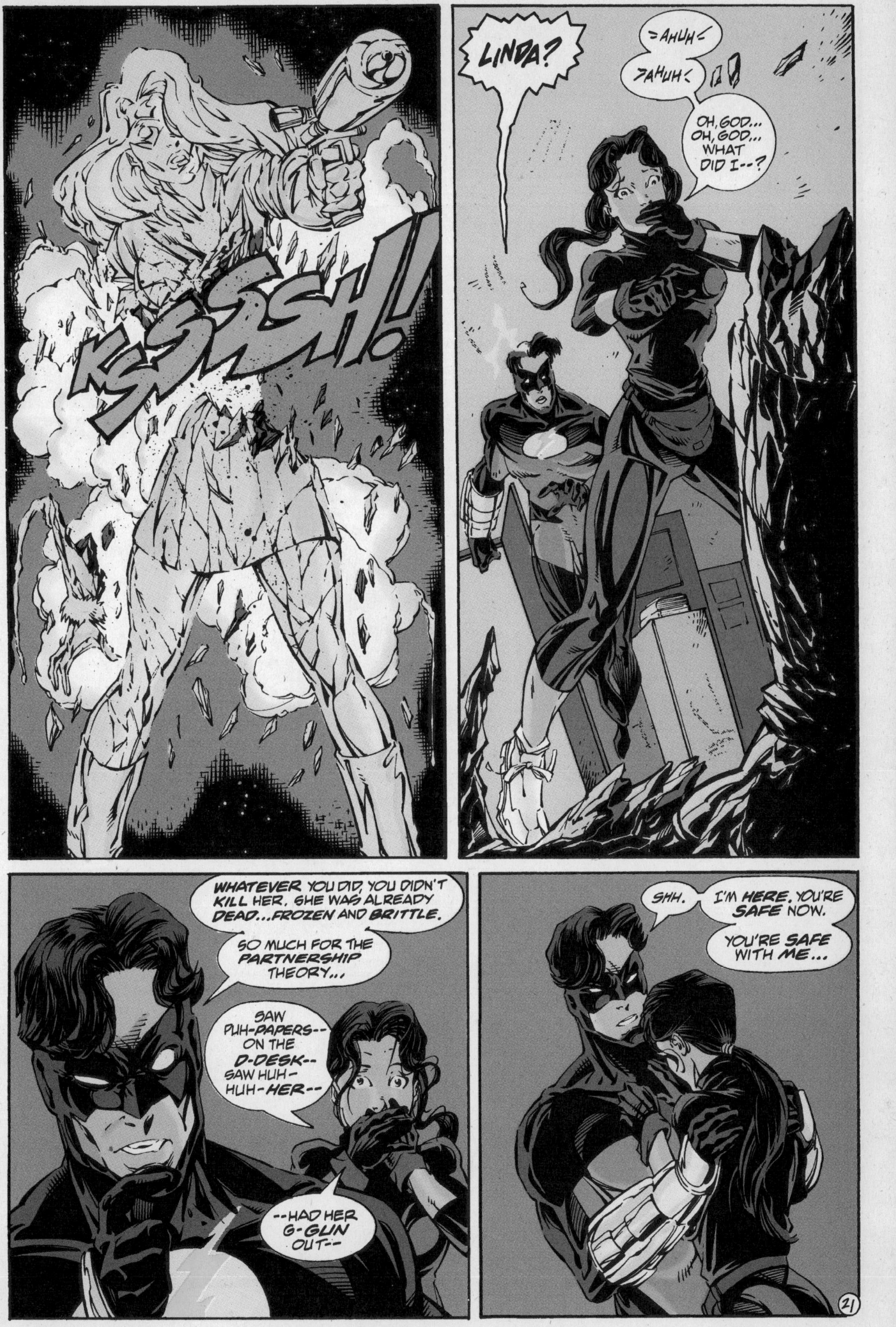
KSSSH!
LINDA?
=AHUH=
=AHUH=
OH, GOD... OH, GOD... WHAT DID I--?
WHATEVER YOU DID, YOU DIDN'T KILL HER. SHE WAS ALREADY DEAD...FROZEN AND BRITTLE.
SO MUCH FOR THE PARTNERSHIP THEORY...
SAW PUH-PAPERS-- ON THE D-DESK-- SAW HUH-HUH-HER--
--HAD HER G-GUN OUT--
SHH.
I'M HERE. YOU'RE SAFE NOW.
YOU'RE SAFE WITH ME...
21

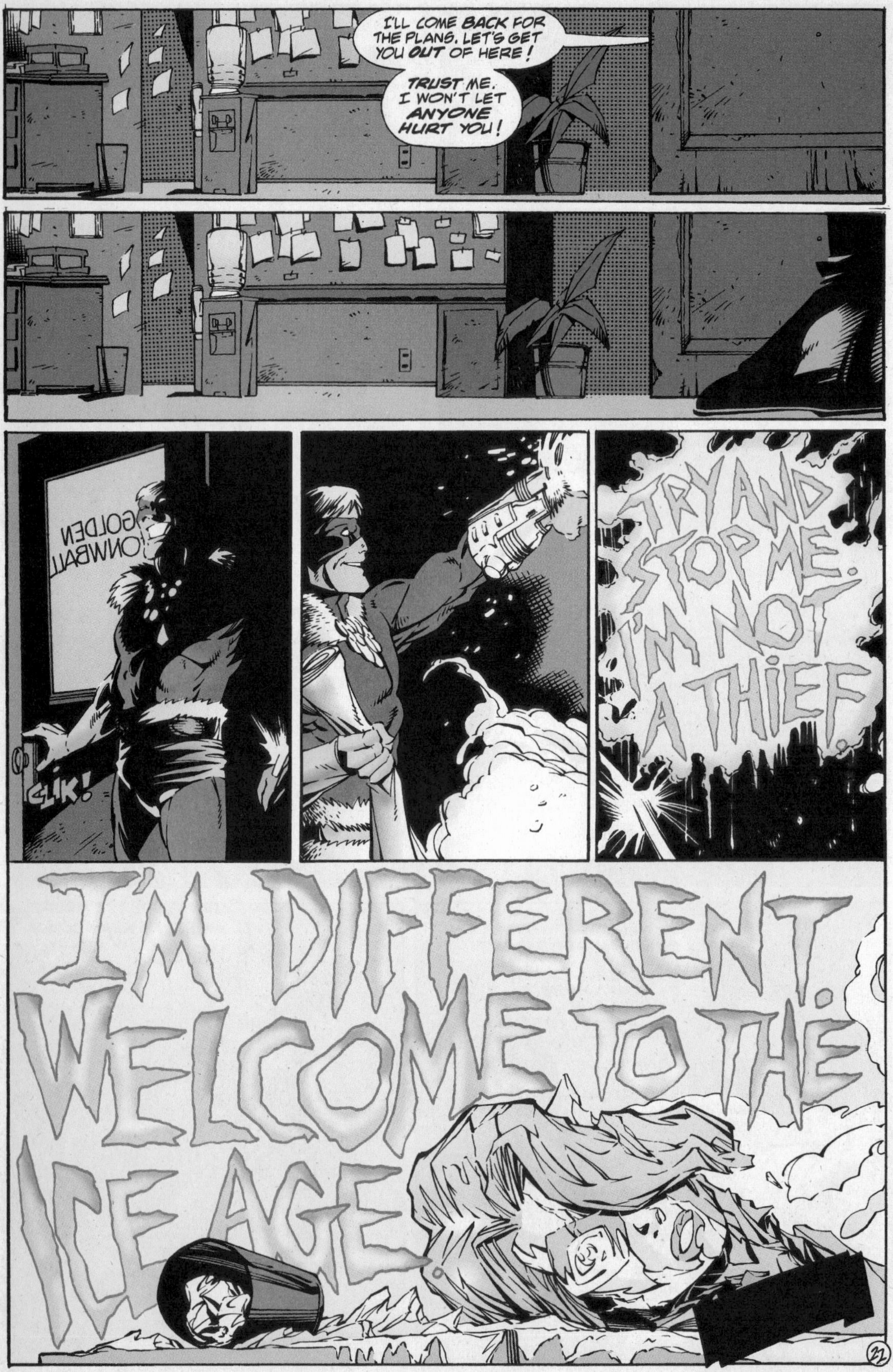
I'LL COME BACK FOR THE PLANS. LET'S GET YOU OUT OF HERE!
TRUST ME. I WON'T LET ANYONE HURT YOU!
CLIK!
TRY AND STOP ME. I'M NOT A THIEF.
I'M DIFFERENT. WELCOME TO THE ICE AGE

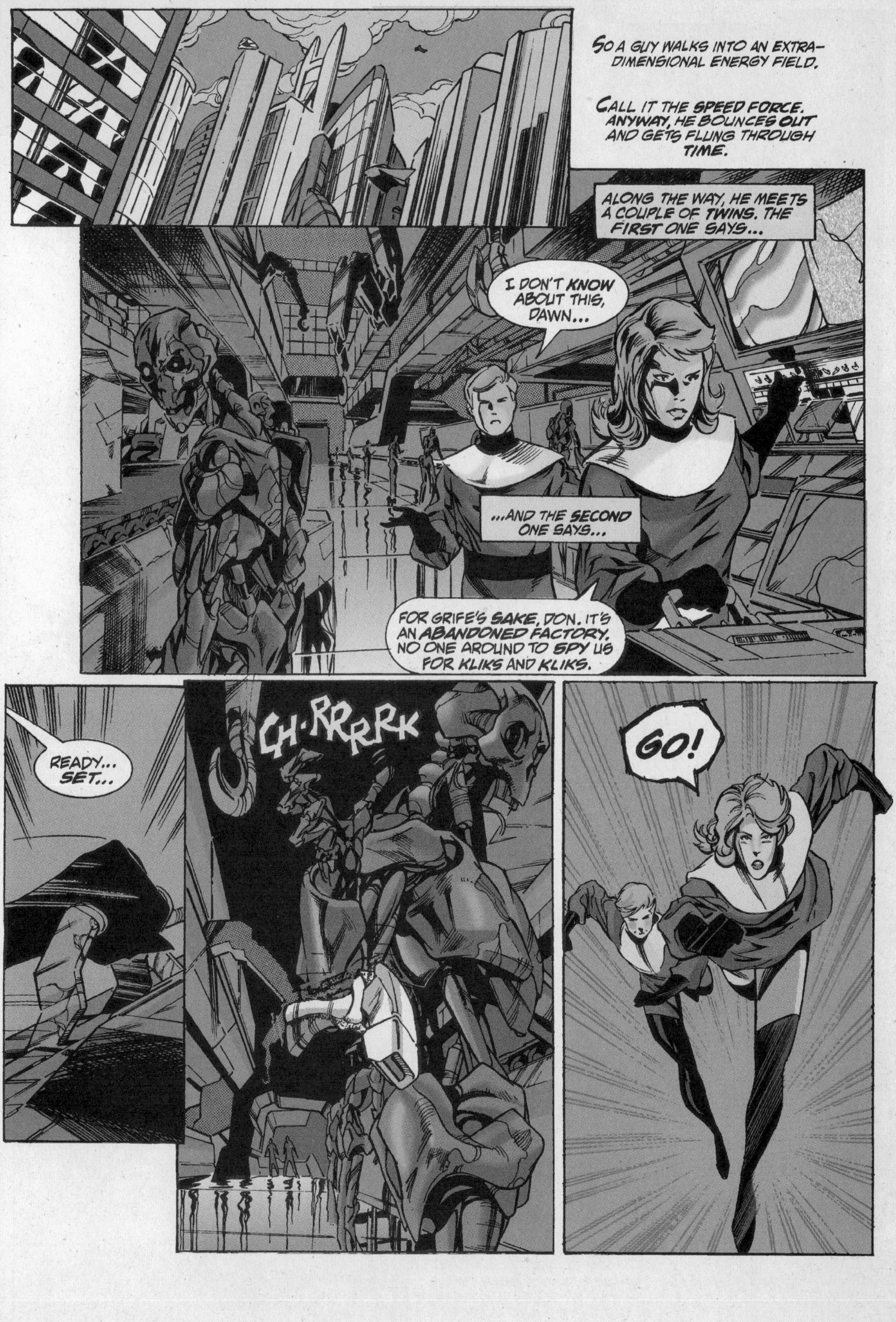
SO A GUY WALKS INTO AN EXTRA-DIMENSIONAL ENERGY FIELD.
CALL IT THE SPEED FORCE. ANYWAY, HE BOUNCES OUT AND GETS FLUNG THROUGH TIME.
ALONG THE WAY, HE MEETS A COUPLE OF TWINS. THE FIRST ONE SAYS...
I DON'T KNOW ABOUT THIS, DAWN...
...AND THE SECOND ONE SAYS...
FOR GRIFE'S SAKE, DON. IT'S AN ABANDONED FACTORY. NO ONE AROUND TO SPY US FOR KLIKS AND KLIKS.
READY... SET...
CH-RRRRK
GO!

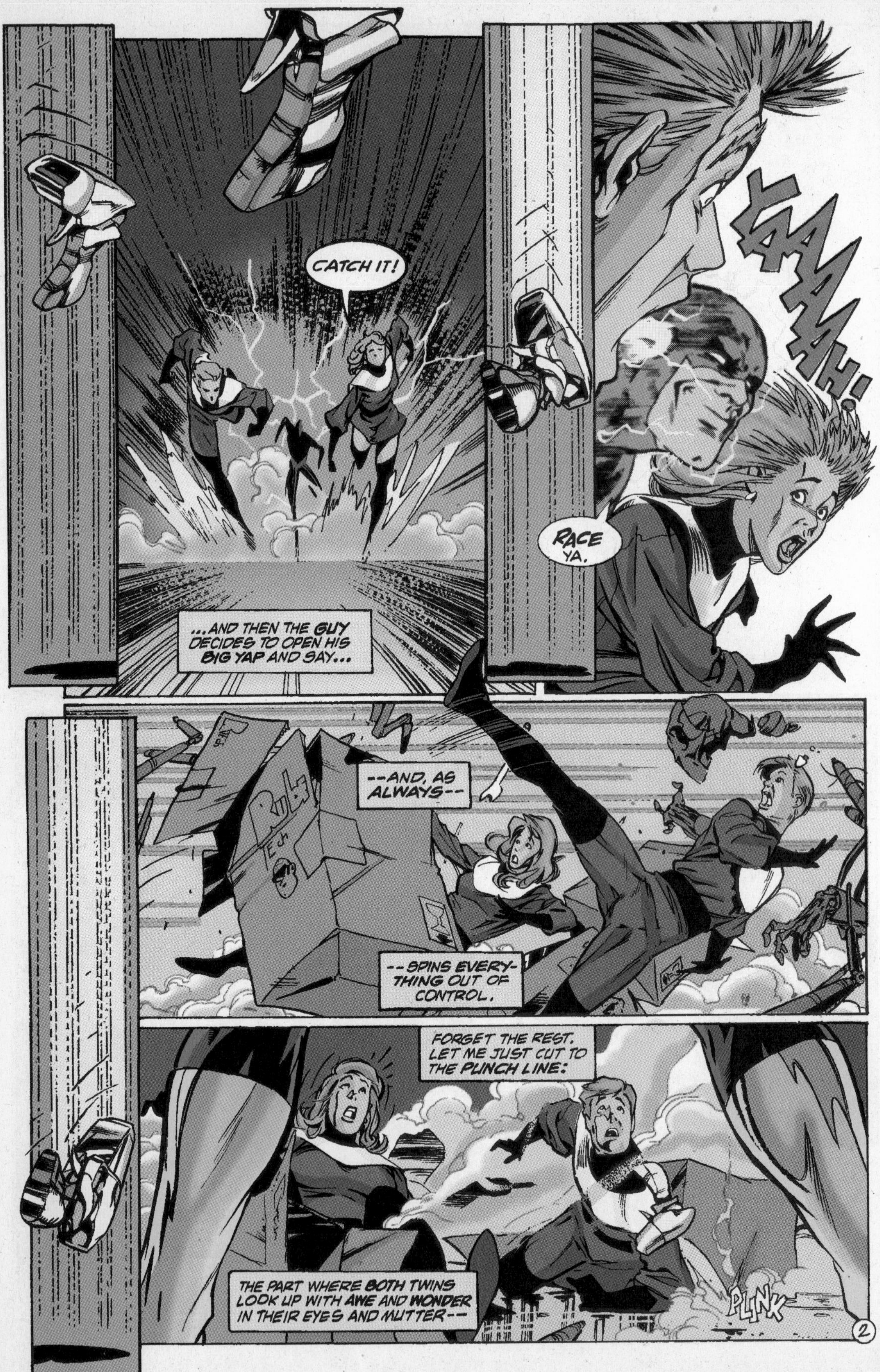
CATCH IT!
...AND THEN THE GUY DECIDES TO OPEN HIS BIG YAP AND SAY...
YAAAAAH!
RACE YA.
--AND, AS ALWAYS--
--SPINS EVERYTHING OUT OF CONTROL.
FORGET THE REST. LET ME JUST CUT TO THE PUNCH LINE:
THE PART WHERE BOTH TWINS LOOK UP WITH AWE AND WONDER IN THEIR EYES AND MUTTER--
PLINK
2

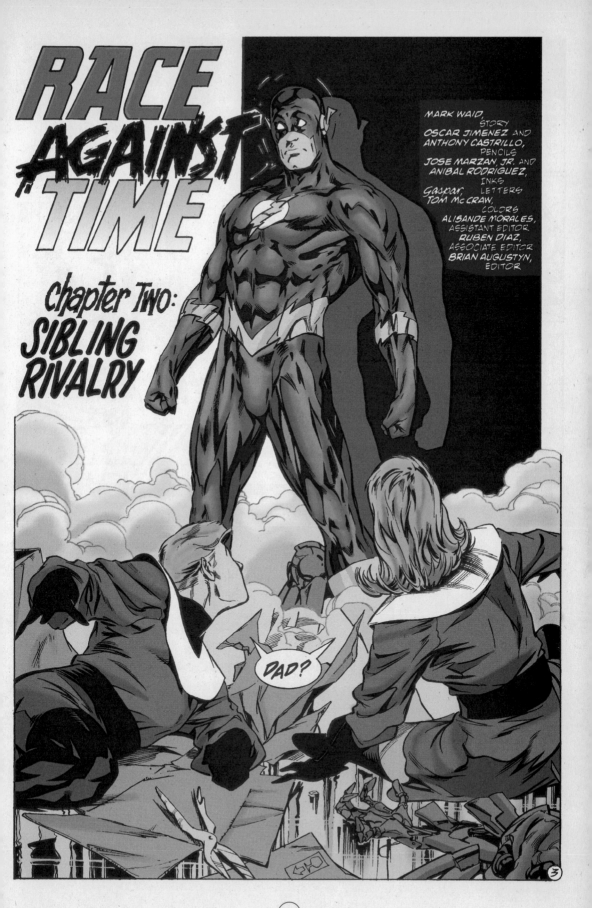

RACE AGAINST TIME

Chapter Two: SIBLING RIVALRY

MARK WAID,
STORY
OSCAR JIMENEZ AND
ANTHONY CASTRILLO,
PENCILS
JOSE MARZAN, JR. AND
ANIBAL RODRIGUEZ,
INKS
Gaspar,
LETTERS
TOM McCRAW,
COLORS
ALISANDE MORALES,
ASSISTANT EDITOR
RUBEN DIAZ,
ASSOCIATE EDITOR
BRIAN AUGUSTYN,
EDITOR

DAD?

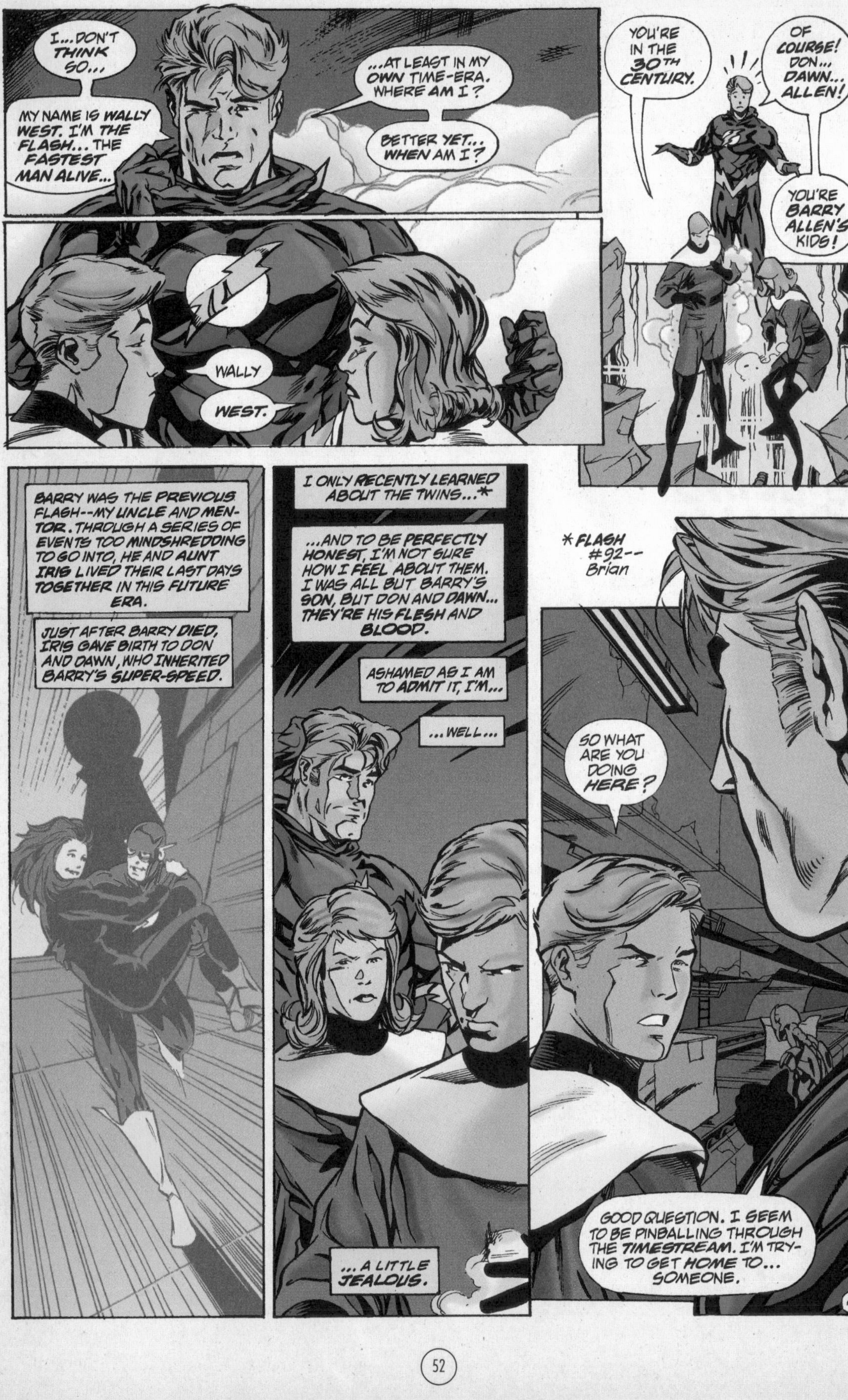
I... DON'T THINK SO...
MY NAME IS WALLY WEST. I'M THE FLASH... THE FASTEST MAN ALIVE...
...AT LEAST IN MY OWN TIME-ERA. WHERE AM I?
BETTER YET... WHEN AM I?
YOU'RE IN THE 30TH CENTURY.
OF COURSE! DON... DAWN... ALLEN!
YOU'RE BARRY ALLEN'S KIDS!
WALLY
WEST.
BARRY WAS THE PREVIOUS FLASH--MY UNCLE AND MENTOR. THROUGH A SERIES OF EVENTS TOO MINDSHREDDING TO GO INTO, HE AND AUNT IRIS LIVED THEIR LAST DAYS TOGETHER IN THIS FUTURE ERA.
JUST AFTER BARRY DIED, IRIS GAVE BIRTH TO DON AND DAWN, WHO INHERITED BARRY'S SUPER-SPEED.
I ONLY RECENTLY LEARNED ABOUT THE TWINS...*
...AND TO BE PERFECTLY HONEST, I'M NOT SURE HOW I FEEL ABOUT THEM. I WAS ALL BUT BARRY'S SON, BUT DON AND DAWN... THEY'RE HIS FLESH AND BLOOD.
ASHAMED AS I AM TO ADMIT IT, I'M...
...WELL...
...A LITTLE JEALOUS.
*FLASH #92-- Brian
SO WHAT ARE YOU DOING HERE?
GOOD QUESTION. I SEEM TO BE PINBALLING THROUGH THE TIMESTREAM. I'M TRYING TO GET HOME TO... SOMEONE.
4

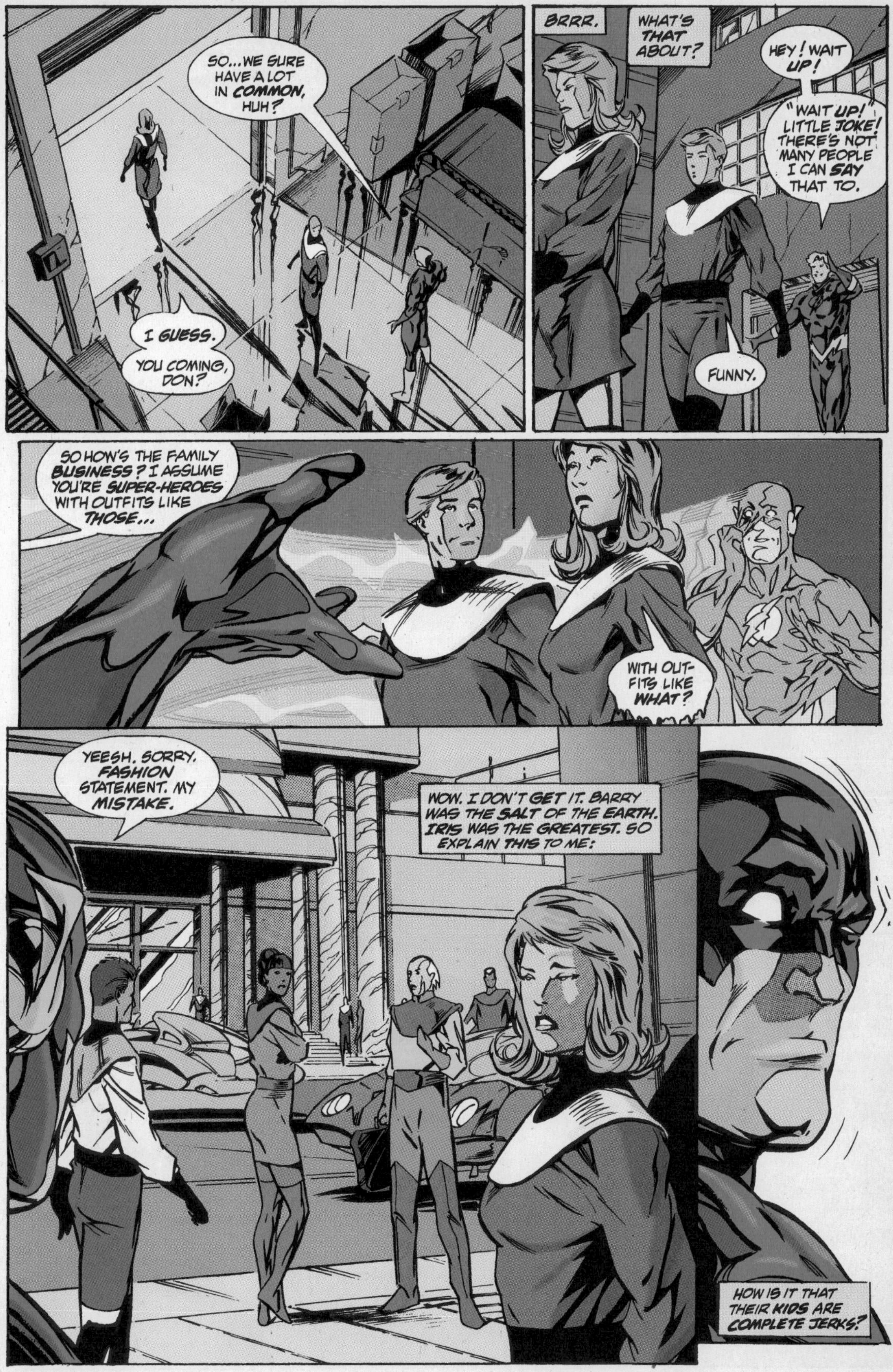
SO...WE SURE HAVE A LOT IN COMMON, HUH?
I GUESS.
YOU COMING, DON?
BRRR.
WHAT'S THAT ABOUT?
HEY! WAIT UP!
"WAIT UP!" LITTLE JOKE! THERE'S NOT MANY PEOPLE I CAN SAY THAT TO.
FUNNY.
SO HOW'S THE FAMILY BUSINESS? I ASSUME YOU'RE SUPER-HEROES WITH OUTFITS LIKE THOSE...
WITH OUT-FITS LIKE WHAT?
YEESH. SORRY. FASHION STATEMENT. MY MISTAKE.
WOW. I DON'T GET IT. BARRY WAS THE SALT OF THE EARTH. IRIS WAS THE GREATEST. SO EXPLAIN THIS TO ME:
HOW IS IT THAT THEIR KIDS ARE COMPLETE JERKS?

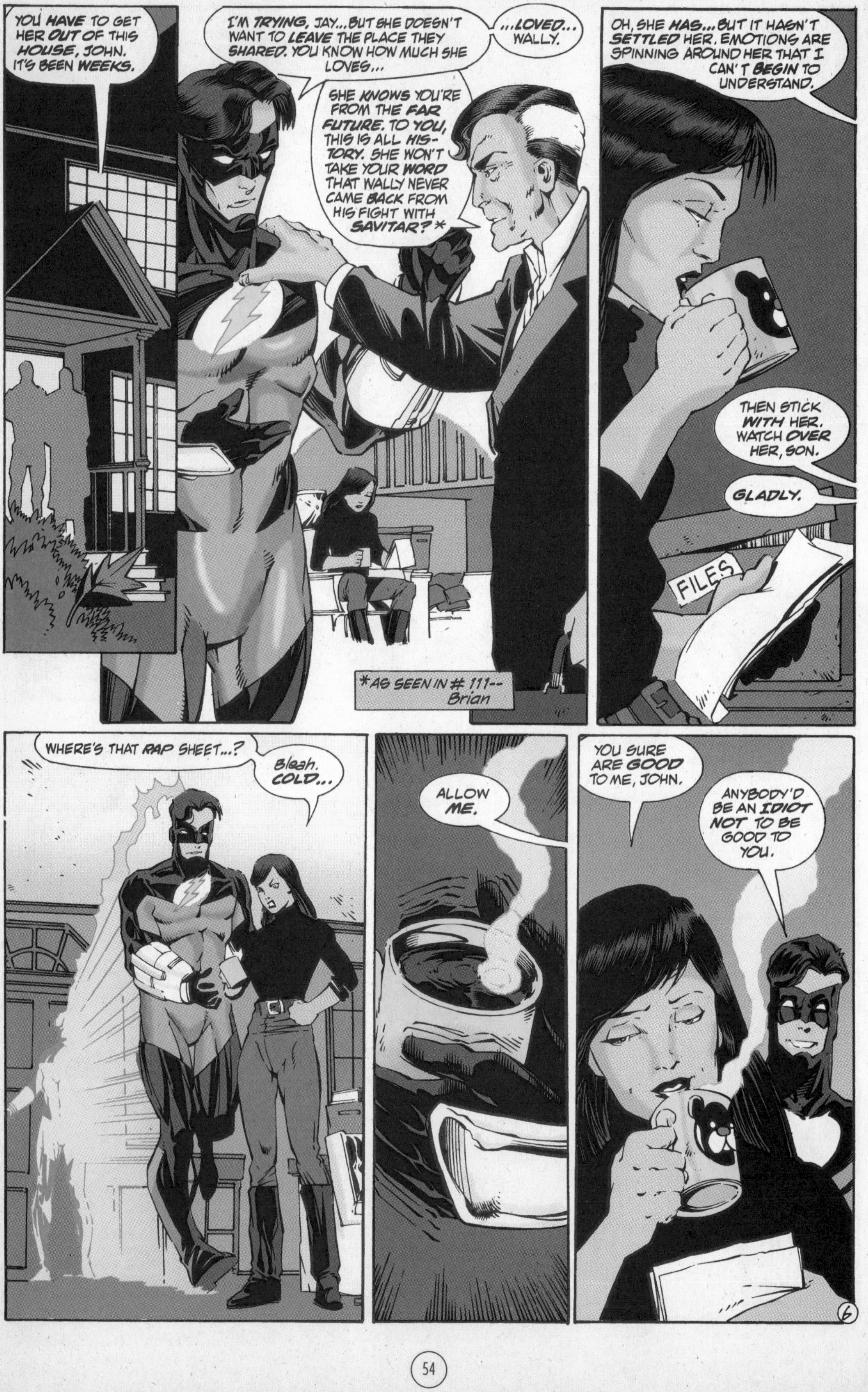
YOU HAVE TO GET HER OUT OF THIS HOUSE, JOHN. IT'S BEEN WEEKS.
I'M TRYING, JAY...BUT SHE DOESN'T WANT TO LEAVE THE PLACE THEY SHARED. YOU KNOW HOW MUCH SHE LOVES...
...LOVED... WALLY.
SHE KNOWS YOU'RE FROM THE FAR FUTURE. TO YOU, THIS IS ALL HISTORY. SHE WON'T TAKE YOUR WORD THAT WALLY NEVER CAME BACK FROM HIS FIGHT WITH SAVITAR?*
*AS SEEN IN #111-- Brian
OH, SHE HAS...BUT IT HASN'T SETTLED HER. EMOTIONS ARE SPINNING AROUND HER THAT I CAN'T BEGIN TO UNDERSTAND.
THEN STICK WITH HER. WATCH OVER HER, SON.
GLADLY.
FILES
WHERE'S THAT RAP SHEET...?
Bleah. COLD...
ALLOW ME.
YOU SURE ARE GOOD TO ME, JOHN.
ANYBODY'D BE AN IDIOT NOT TO BE GOOD TO YOU.
6

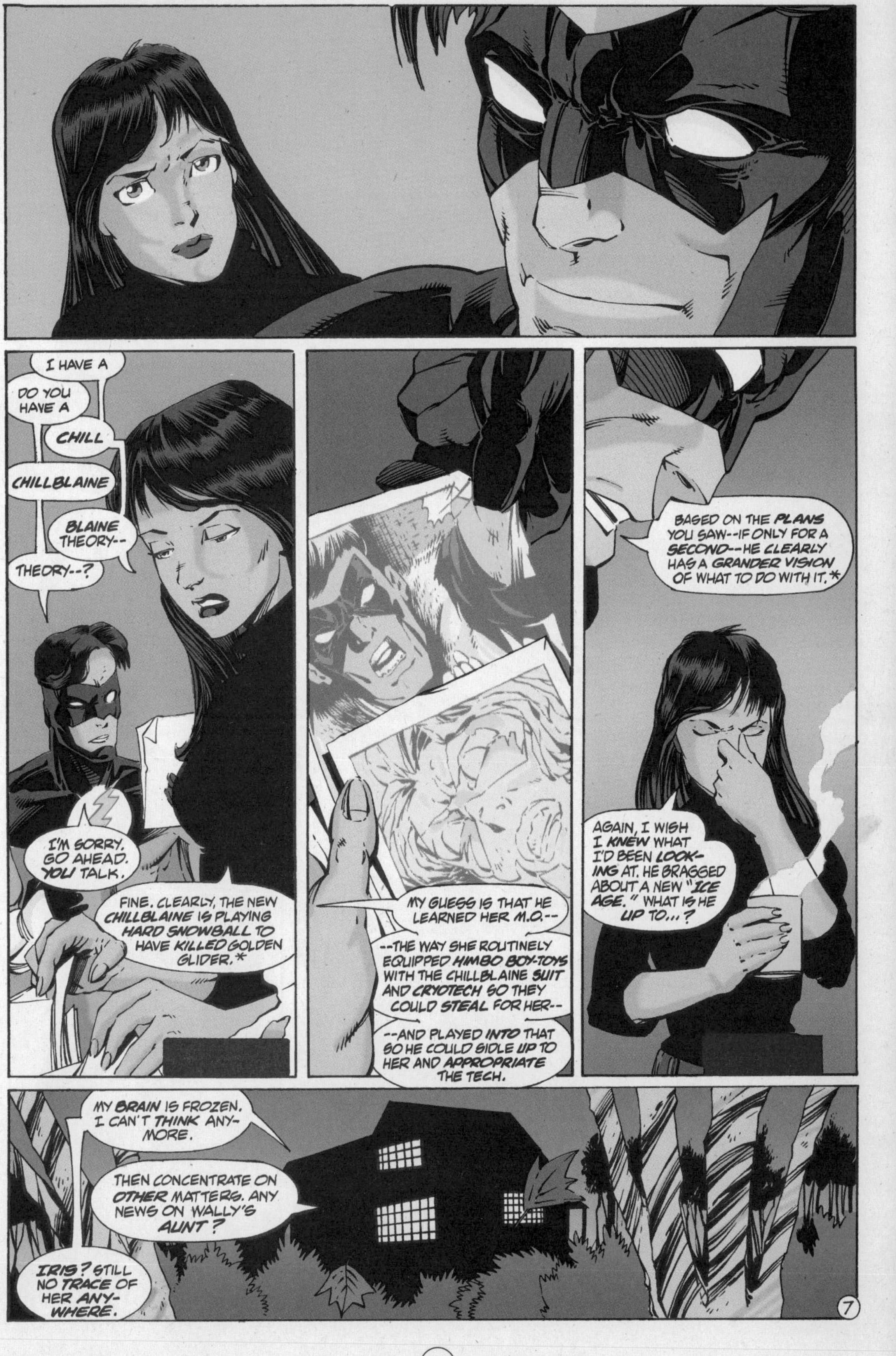
I HAVE A
DO YOU HAVE A
CHILL
CHILLBLAINE
BLAINE THEORY--
THEORY--?
I'M SORRY. GO AHEAD. YOU TALK.
FINE. CLEARLY, THE NEW CHILLBLAINE IS PLAYING HARD SNOWBALL TO HAVE KILLED GOLDEN GLIDER.*
MY GUESS IS THAT HE LEARNED HER M.O.--
--THE WAY SHE ROUTINELY EQUIPPED HIMBO BOY-TOYS WITH THE CHILLBLAINE SUIT AND CRYOTECH SO THEY COULD STEAL FOR HER--
--AND PLAYED INTO THAT SO HE COULD SIDLE UP TO HER AND APPROPRIATE THE TECH.
BASED ON THE PLANS YOU SAW--IF ONLY FOR A SECOND--HE CLEARLY HAS A GRANDER VISION OF WHAT TO DO WITH IT.*
AGAIN, I WISH I KNEW WHAT I'D BEEN LOOKING AT. HE BRAGGED ABOUT A NEW "ICE AGE." WHAT IS HE UP TO...?
MY BRAIN IS FROZEN. I CAN'T THINK ANYMORE.
THEN CONCENTRATE ON OTHER MATTERS. ANY NEWS ON WALLY'S AUNT?
IRIS? STILL NO TRACE OF HER ANYWHERE.
7

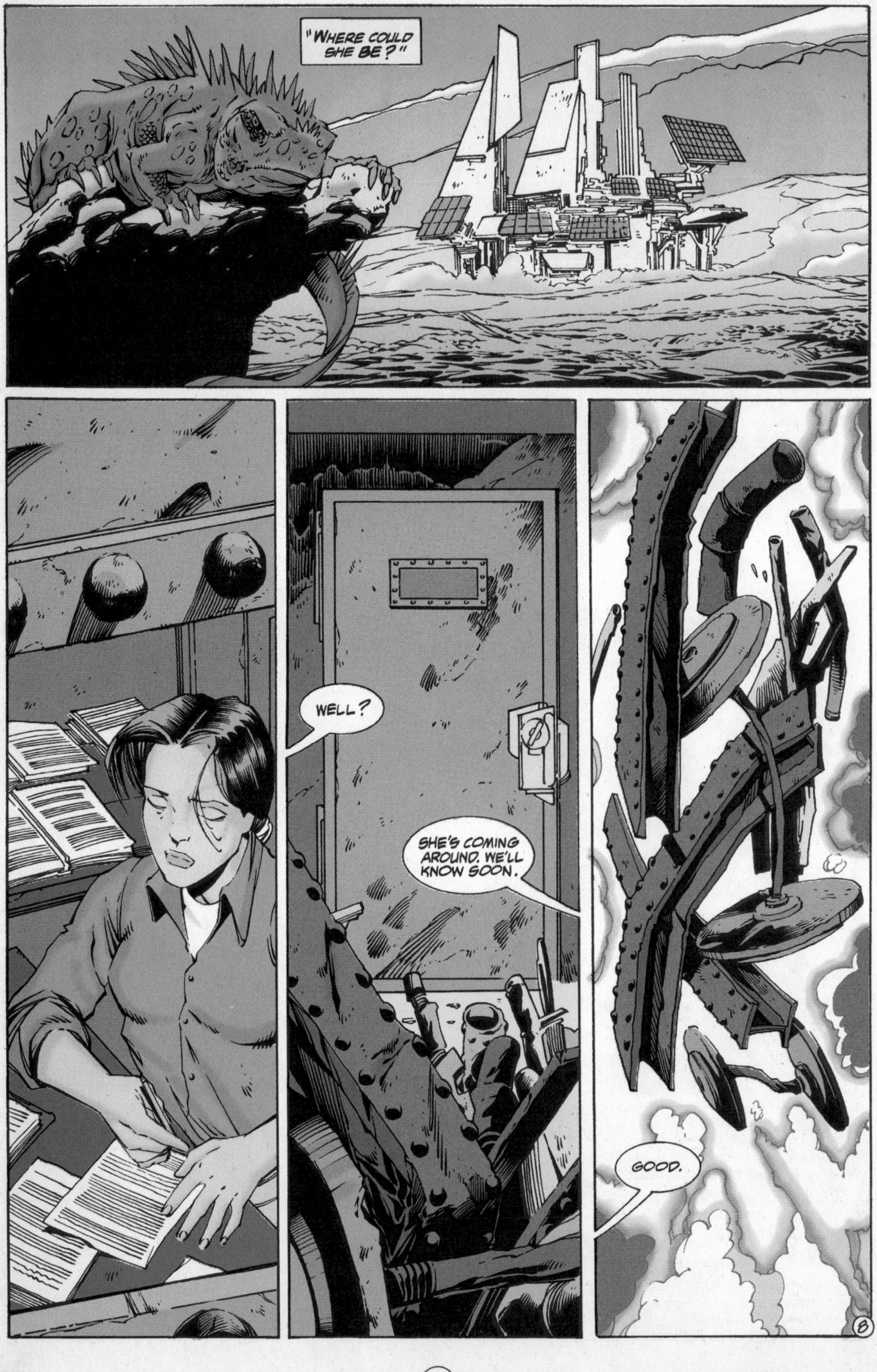
"WHERE COULD SHE BE?"
WELL?
SHE'S COMING AROUND. WE'LL KNOW SOON.
GOOD.
8

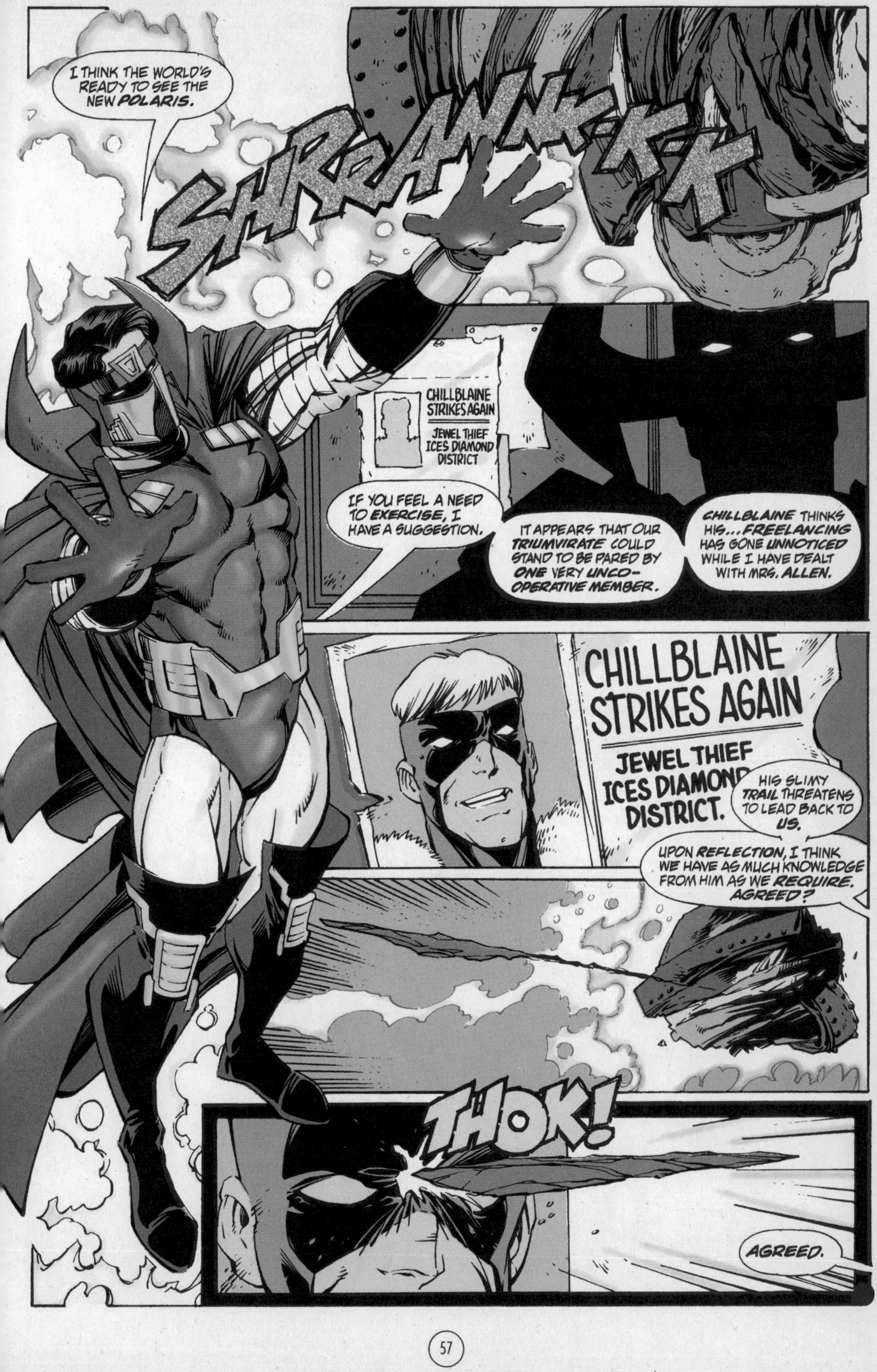
I THINK THE WORLD'S READY TO SEE THE NEW POLARIS.
SHRRAWNK-K-K
CHILLBLAINE STRIKES AGAIN
JEWEL THIEF ICES DIAMOND DISTRICT
IF YOU FEEL A NEED TO EXERCISE, I HAVE A SUGGESTION.
IT APPEARS THAT OUR TRIUMVIRATE COULD STAND TO BE PARED BY ONE VERY UNCO-OPERATIVE MEMBER.
CHILLBLAINE THINKS HIS... FREELANCING HAS GONE UNNOTICED WHILE I HAVE DEALT WITH MRS. ALLEN.
CHILLBLAINE STRIKES AGAIN
JEWEL THIEF ICES DIAMOND DISTRICT.
HIS SLIMY TRAIL THREATENS TO LEAD BACK TO US.
UPON REFLECTION, I THINK WE HAVE AS MUCH KNOWLEDGE FROM HIM AS WE REQUIRE. AGREED?
THOK!
AGREED.

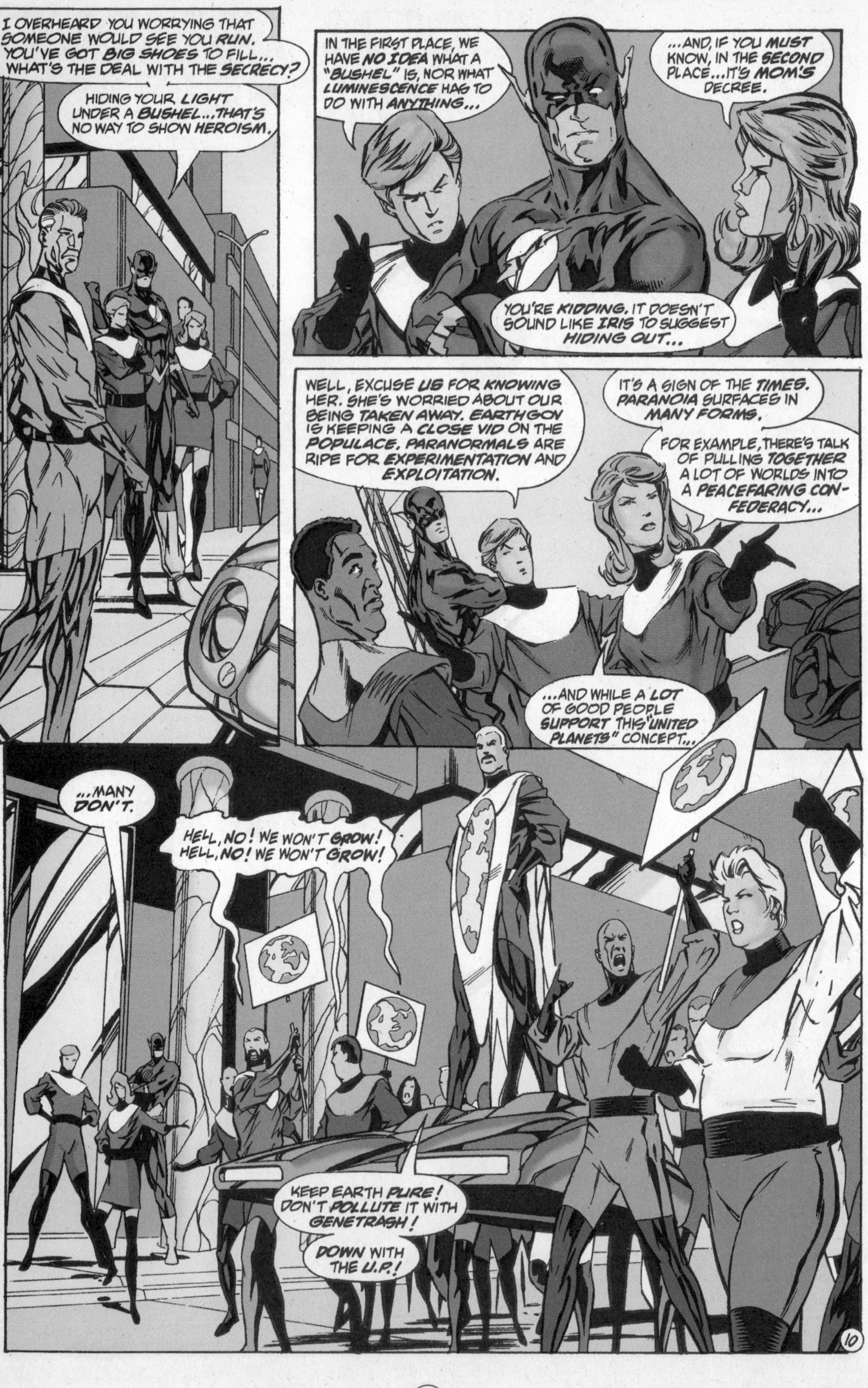

I OVERHEARD YOU WORRYING THAT SOMEONE WOULD SEE YOU RUN. YOU'VE GOT BIG SHOES TO FILL... WHAT'S THE DEAL WITH THE SECRECY?
HIDING YOUR LIGHT UNDER A BUSHEL...THAT'S NO WAY TO SHOW HEROISM.
IN THE FIRST PLACE, WE HAVE NO IDEA WHAT A "BUSHEL" IS, NOR WHAT LUMINESCENCE HAS TO DO WITH ANYTHING...
...AND, IF YOU MUST KNOW, IN THE SECOND PLACE...IT'S MOM'S DECREE.
YOU'RE KIDDING. IT DOESN'T SOUND LIKE IRIS TO SUGGEST HIDING OUT...
WELL, EXCUSE US FOR KNOWING HER. SHE'S WORRIED ABOUT OUR BEING TAKEN AWAY. EARTHGOV IS KEEPING A CLOSE VID ON THE POPULACE. PARANORMALS ARE RIPE FOR EXPERIMENTATION AND EXPLOITATION.
IT'S A SIGN OF THE TIMES. PARANOIA SURFACES IN MANY FORMS.
FOR EXAMPLE, THERE'S TALK OF PULLING TOGETHER A LOT OF WORLDS INTO A PEACEFARING CON-FEDERACY...
...AND WHILE A LOT OF GOOD PEOPLE SUPPORT THIS "UNITED PLANETS" CONCEPT...
...MANY DON'T.
HELL, NO! WE WON'T GROW! HELL, NO! WE WON'T GROW!
KEEP EARTH PURE! DON'T POLLUTE IT WITH GENETRASH!
DOWN WITH THE U.P.!
10

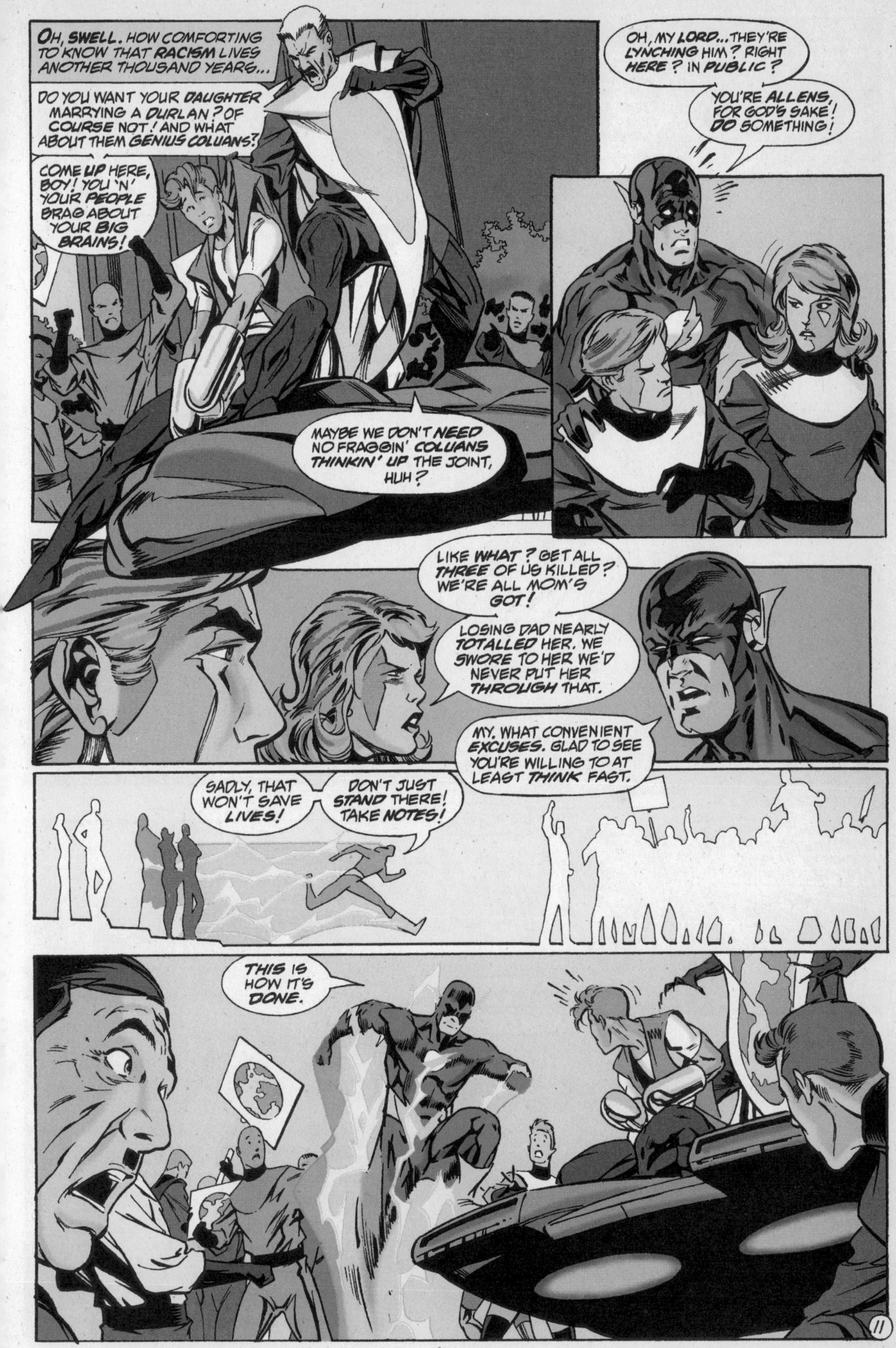
OH, SWELL. HOW COMFORTING TO KNOW THAT RACISM LIVES ANOTHER THOUSAND YEARS...
DO YOU WANT YOUR DAUGHTER MARRYING A DURLAN? OF COURSE NOT! AND WHAT ABOUT THEM GENIUS COLUANS?
COME UP HERE, BOY! YOU 'N' YOUR PEOPLE BRAG ABOUT YOUR BIG BRAINS!
MAYBE WE DON'T NEED NO FRAGGIN' COLUANS THINKIN' UP THE JOINT, HUH?
OH, MY LORD... THEY'RE LYNCHING HIM? RIGHT HERE? IN PUBLIC?
YOU'RE ALLENS, FOR GOD'S SAKE! DO SOMETHING!
LIKE WHAT? GET ALL THREE OF US KILLED? WE'RE ALL MOM'S GOT!
LOSING DAD NEARLY TOTALLED HER. WE SWORE TO HER WE'D NEVER PUT HER THROUGH THAT.
MY. WHAT CONVENIENT EXCUSES. GLAD TO SEE YOU'RE WILLING TO AT LEAST THINK FAST.
SADLY, THAT WON'T SAVE LIVES!
DON'T JUST STAND THERE! TAKE NOTES!
THIS IS HOW IT'S DONE.
11

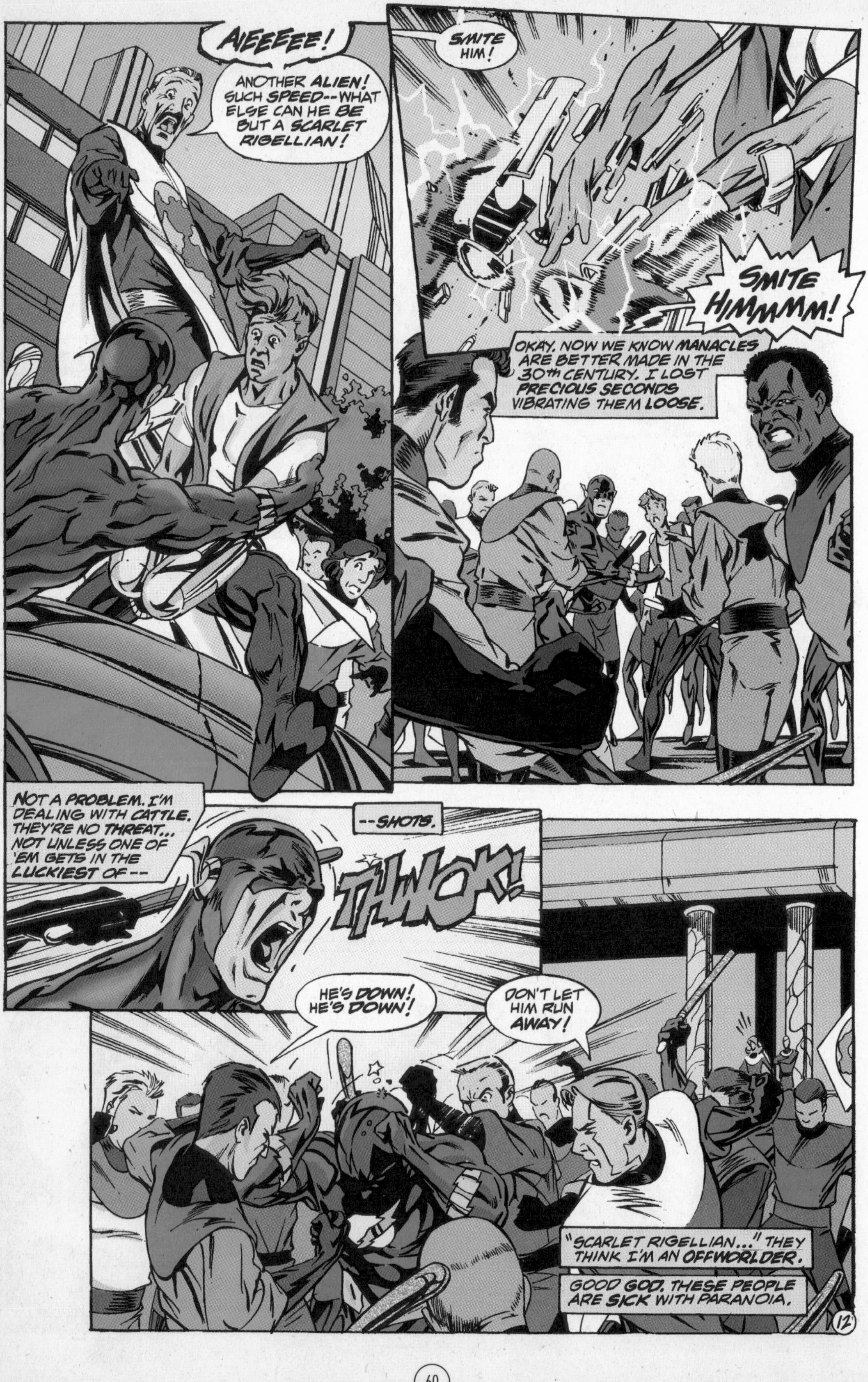
AIEEEEEE!
ANOTHER ALIEN! SUCH SPEED--WHAT ELSE CAN HE BE BUT A SCARLET RIGELLIAN!
SMITE HIM!
SMITE HIMMMM!
OKAY. NOW WE KNOW MANACLES ARE BETTER MADE IN THE 30th CENTURY. I LOST PRECIOUS SECONDS VIBRATING THEM LOOSE.
NOT A PROBLEM. I'M DEALING WITH CATTLE. THEY'RE NO THREAT... NOT UNLESS ONE OF 'EM GETS IN THE LUCKIEST OF--
--SHOTS.
THWOK!
HE'S DOWN! HE'S DOWN!
DON'T LET HIM RUN AWAY!
"SCARLET RIGELLIAN..." THEY THINK I'M AN OFFWORLDER.
GOOD GOD. THESE PEOPLE ARE SICK WITH PARANOIA.
12

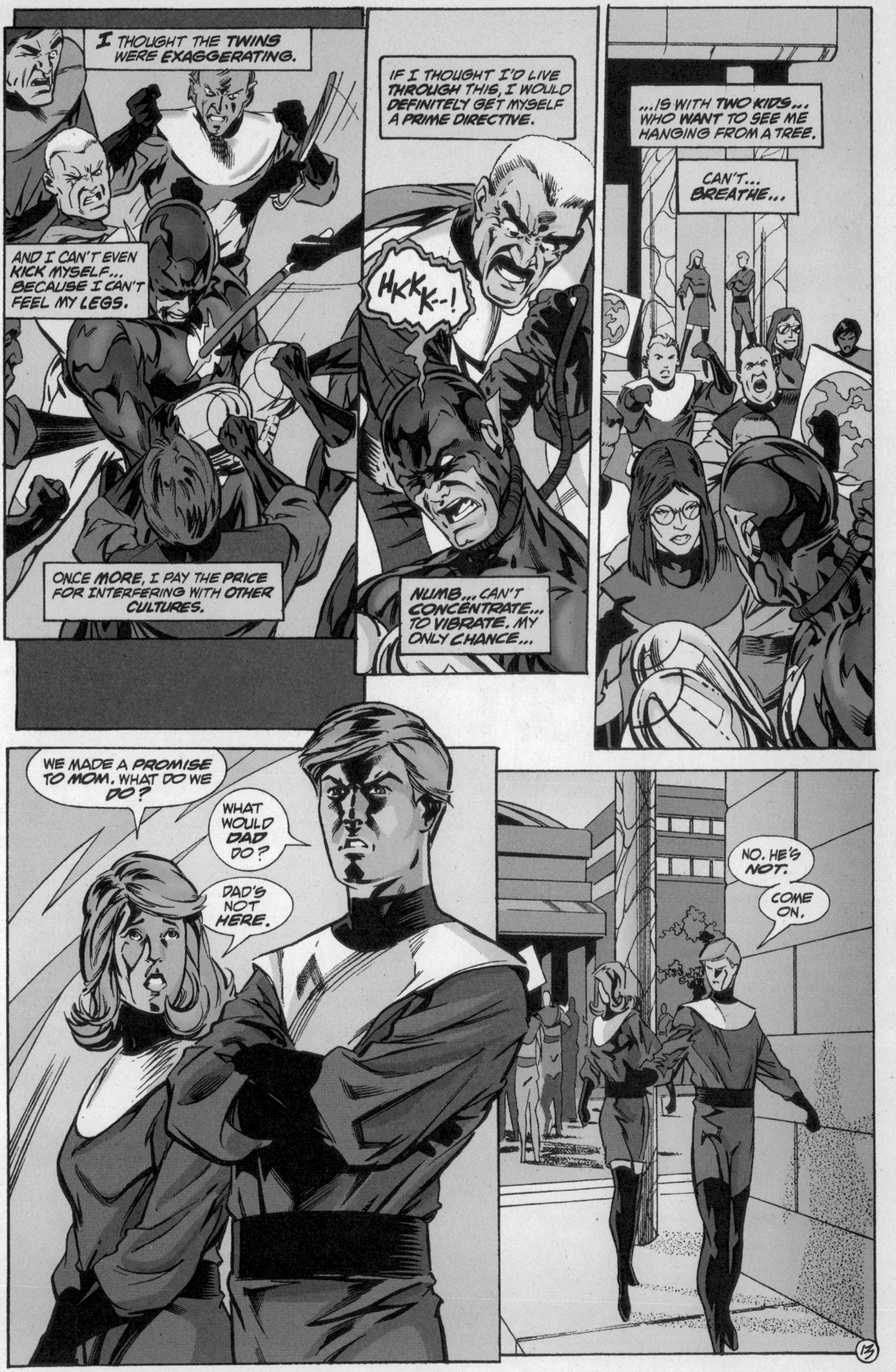

I THOUGHT THE TWINS WERE EXAGGERATING.
AND I CAN'T EVEN KICK MYSELF... BECAUSE I CAN'T FEEL MY LEGS.
ONCE MORE, I PAY THE PRICE FOR INTERFERING WITH OTHER CULTURES.
IF I THOUGHT I'D LIVE THROUGH THIS, I WOULD DEFINITELY GET MYSELF A PRIME DIRECTIVE.
HKKK--!
NUMB... CAN'T CONCENTRATE... TO VIBRATE. MY ONLY CHANCE...
...IS WITH TWO KIDS... WHO WANT TO SEE ME HANGING FROM A TREE.
CAN'T... BREATHE...
WE MADE A PROMISE TO MOM. WHAT DO WE DO?
WHAT WOULD DAD DO?
DAD'S NOT HERE.
NO. HE'S NOT.
COME ON.
13

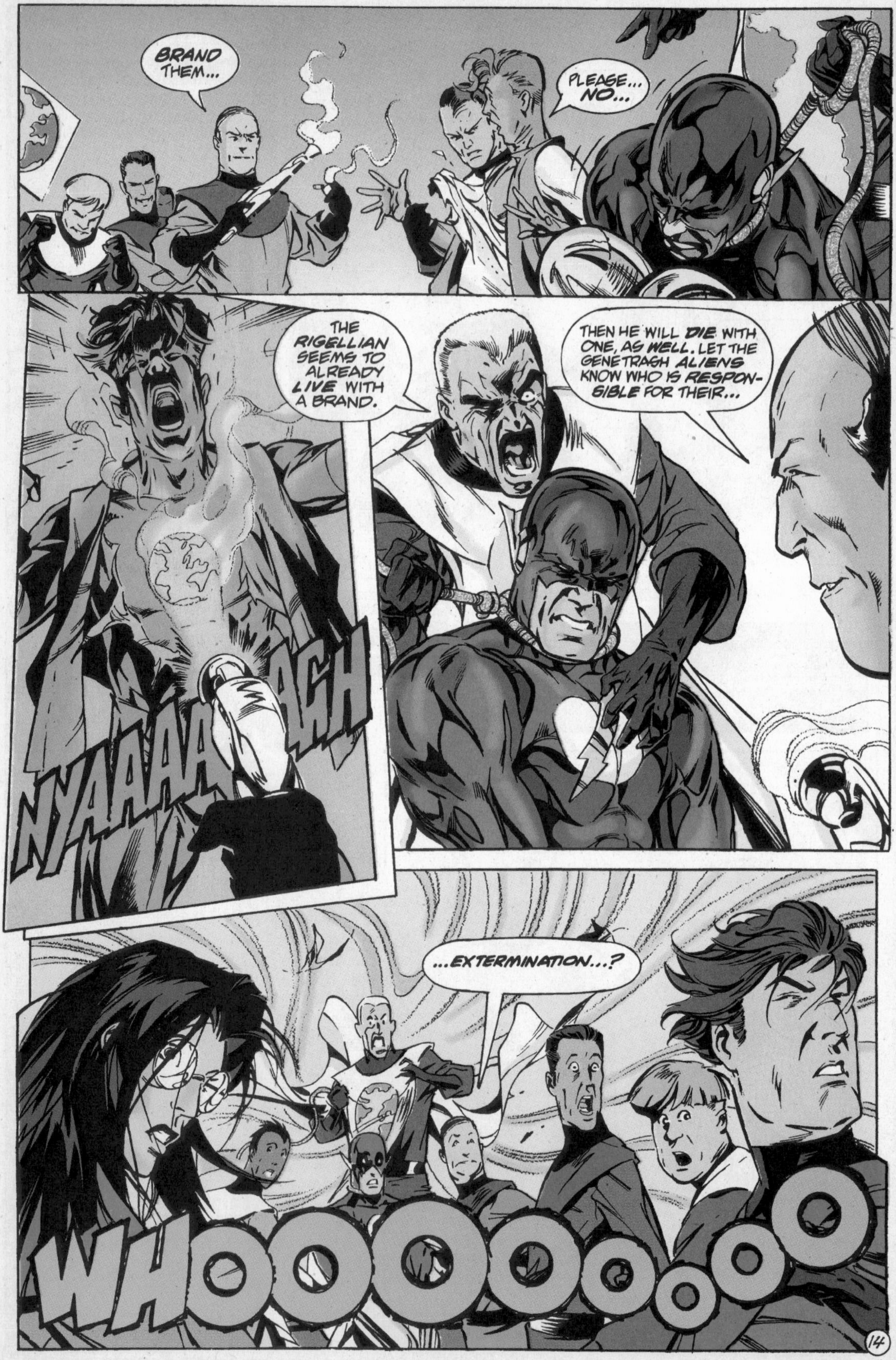
BRAND THEM...
PLEASE... NO...
THE RIGELLIAN SEEMS TO ALREADY LIVE WITH A BRAND.
THEN HE WILL DIE WITH ONE, AS WELL. LET THE GENETRAGH ALIENS KNOW WHO IS RESPONSIBLE FOR THEIR...
NYAAAAAAGH
...EXTERMINATION...?
WHOOOOOO...OOO
14

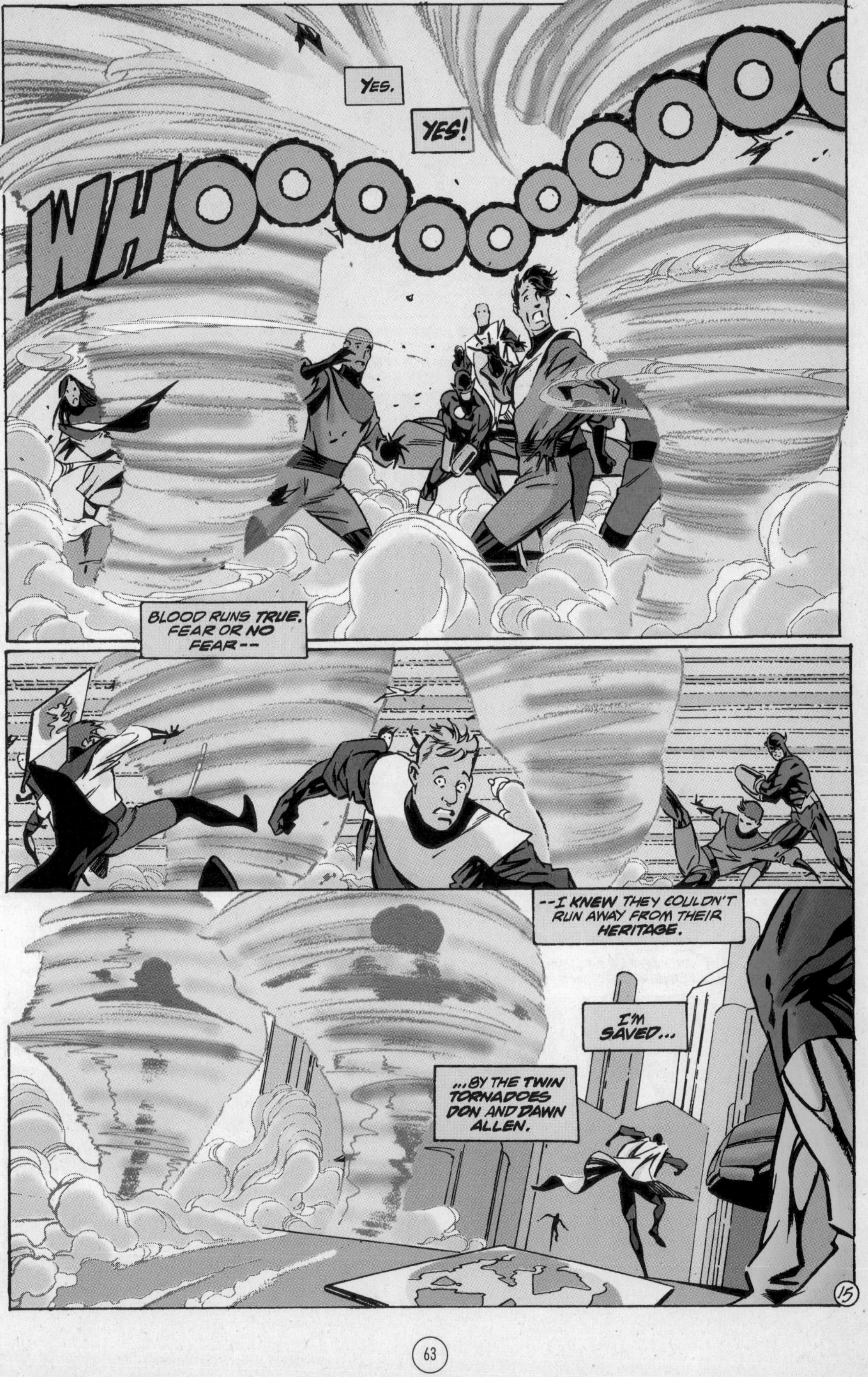
YES.
YES!
WHOOOOOOOOOOOOO
BLOOD RUNS TRUE. FEAR OR NO FEAR--
--I KNEW THEY COULDN'T RUN AWAY FROM THEIR HERITAGE.
I'M SAVED...
...BY THE TWIN TORNADOES DON AND DAWN ALLEN.
15

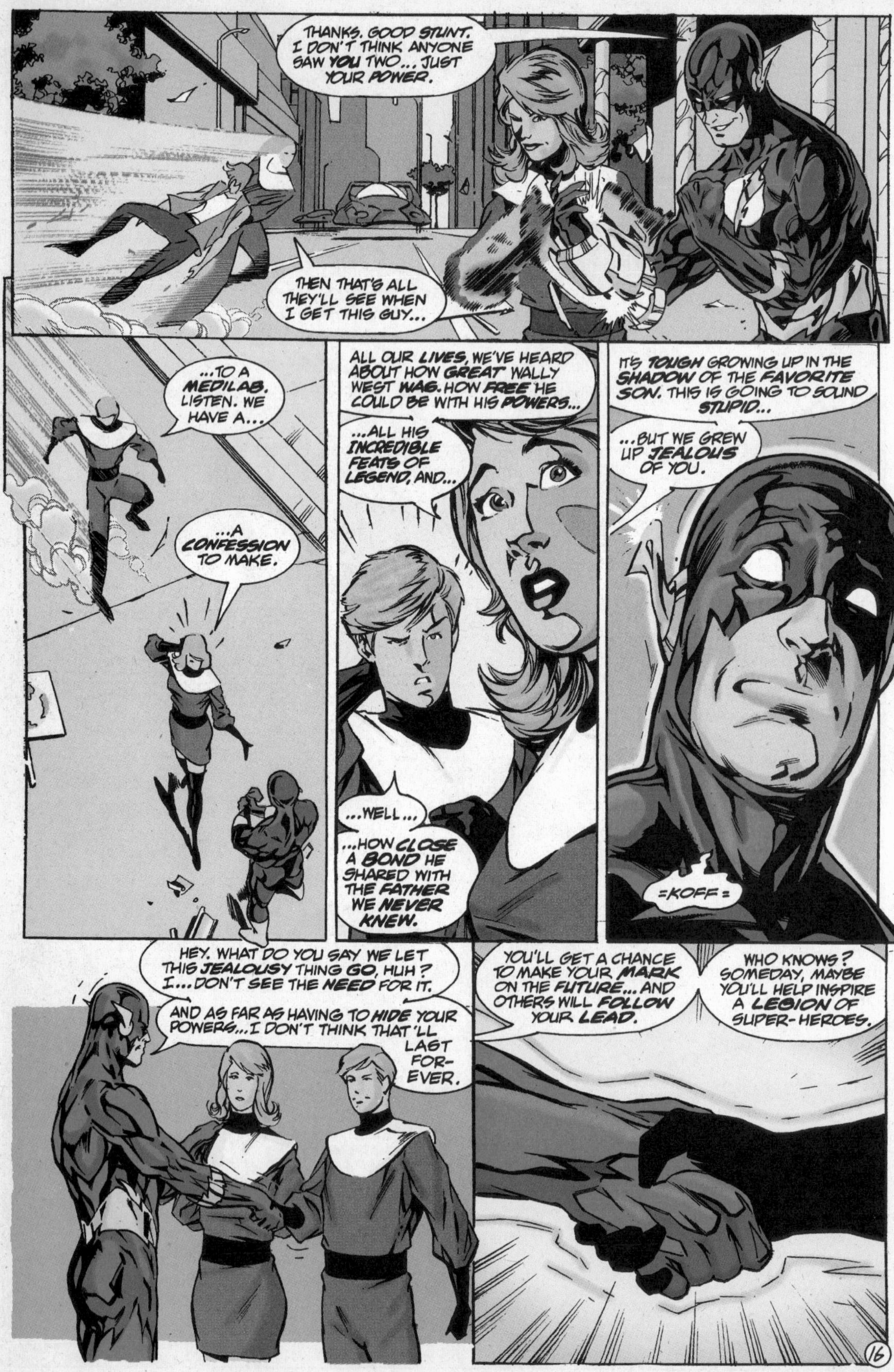
THANKS. GOOD STUNT. I DON'T THINK ANYONE SAW YOU TWO... JUST YOUR POWER.
THEN THAT'S ALL THEY'LL SEE WHEN I GET THIS GUY...
...TO A MEDILAB. LISTEN. WE HAVE A...
...A CONFESSION TO MAKE.
ALL OUR LIVES, WE'VE HEARD ABOUT HOW GREAT WALLY WEST WAS. HOW FREE HE COULD BE WITH HIS POWERS...
...ALL HIS INCREDIBLE FEATS OF LEGEND, AND...
...WELL...
...HOW CLOSE A BOND HE SHARED WITH THE FATHER WE NEVER KNEW.
IT'S TOUGH GROWING UP IN THE SHADOW OF THE FAVORITE SON. THIS IS GOING TO SOUND STUPID...
...BUT WE GREW UP JEALOUS OF YOU.
=KOFF=
HEY. WHAT DO YOU SAY WE LET THIS JEALOUSY THING GO, HUH? I... DON'T SEE THE NEED FOR IT.
AND AS FAR AS HAVING TO HIDE YOUR POWERS... I DON'T THINK THAT'LL LAST FOREVER.
YOU'LL GET A CHANCE TO MAKE YOUR MARK ON THE FUTURE... AND OTHERS WILL FOLLOW YOUR LEAD.
WHO KNOWS? SOMEDAY, MAYBE YOU'LL HELP INSPIRE A LEGION OF SUPER-HEROES.
16

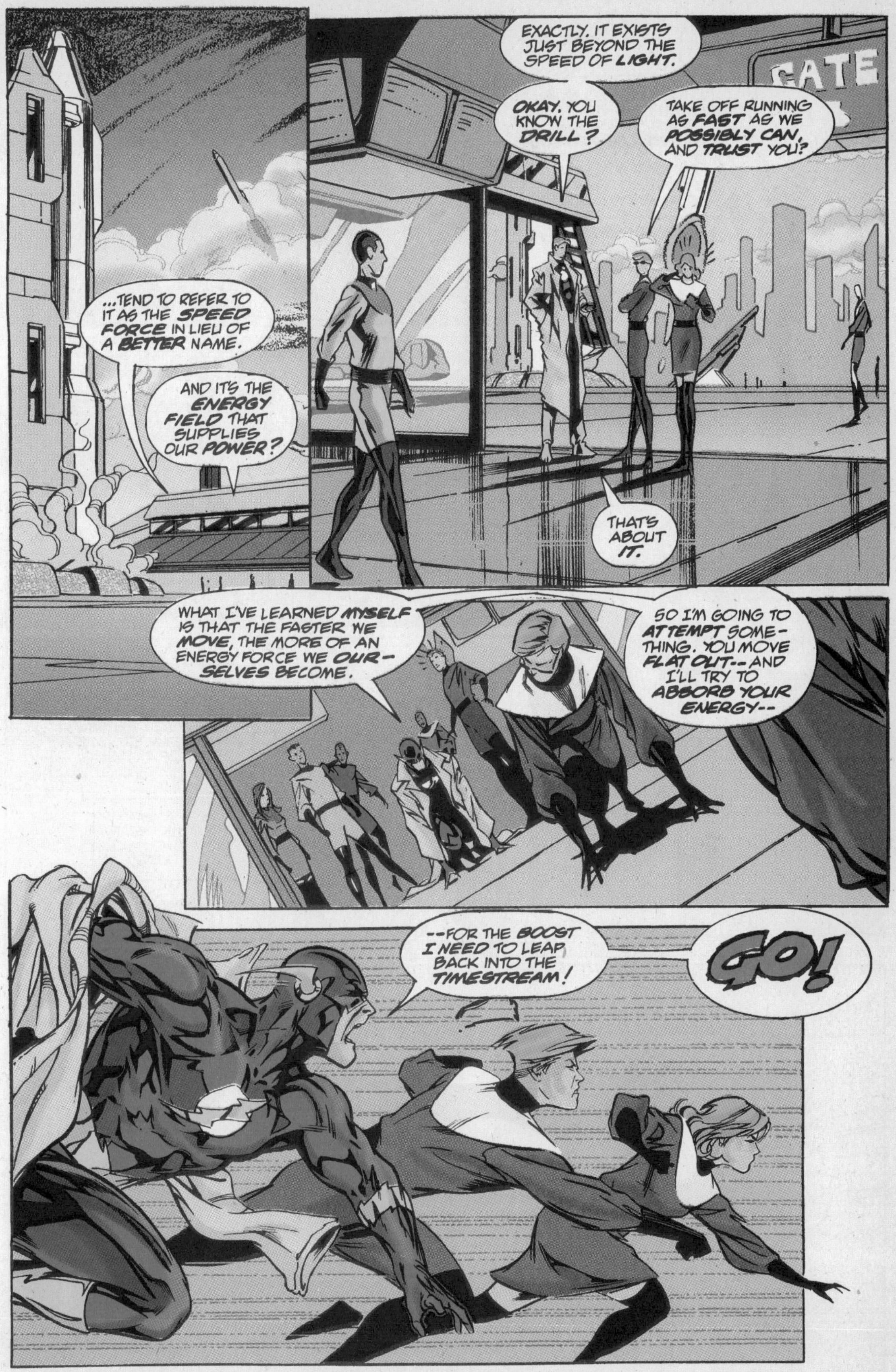
...TEND TO REFER TO IT AS THE SPEED FORCE IN LIEU OF A BETTER NAME.
AND IT'S THE ENERGY FIELD THAT SUPPLIES OUR POWER?
EXACTLY. IT EXISTS JUST BEYOND THE SPEED OF LIGHT.
OKAY. YOU KNOW THE DRILL?
TAKE OFF RUNNING AS FAST AS WE POSSIBLY CAN, AND TRUST YOU?
THAT'S ABOUT IT.
GATE
WHAT I'VE LEARNED MYSELF IS THAT THE FASTER WE MOVE, THE MORE OF AN ENERGY FORCE WE OURSELVES BECOME.
SO I'M GOING TO ATTEMPT SOMETHING. YOU MOVE FLAT OUT-- AND I'LL TRY TO ABSORB YOUR ENERGY--
--FOR THE BOOST I NEED TO LEAP BACK INTO THE TIMESTREAM!
GO!

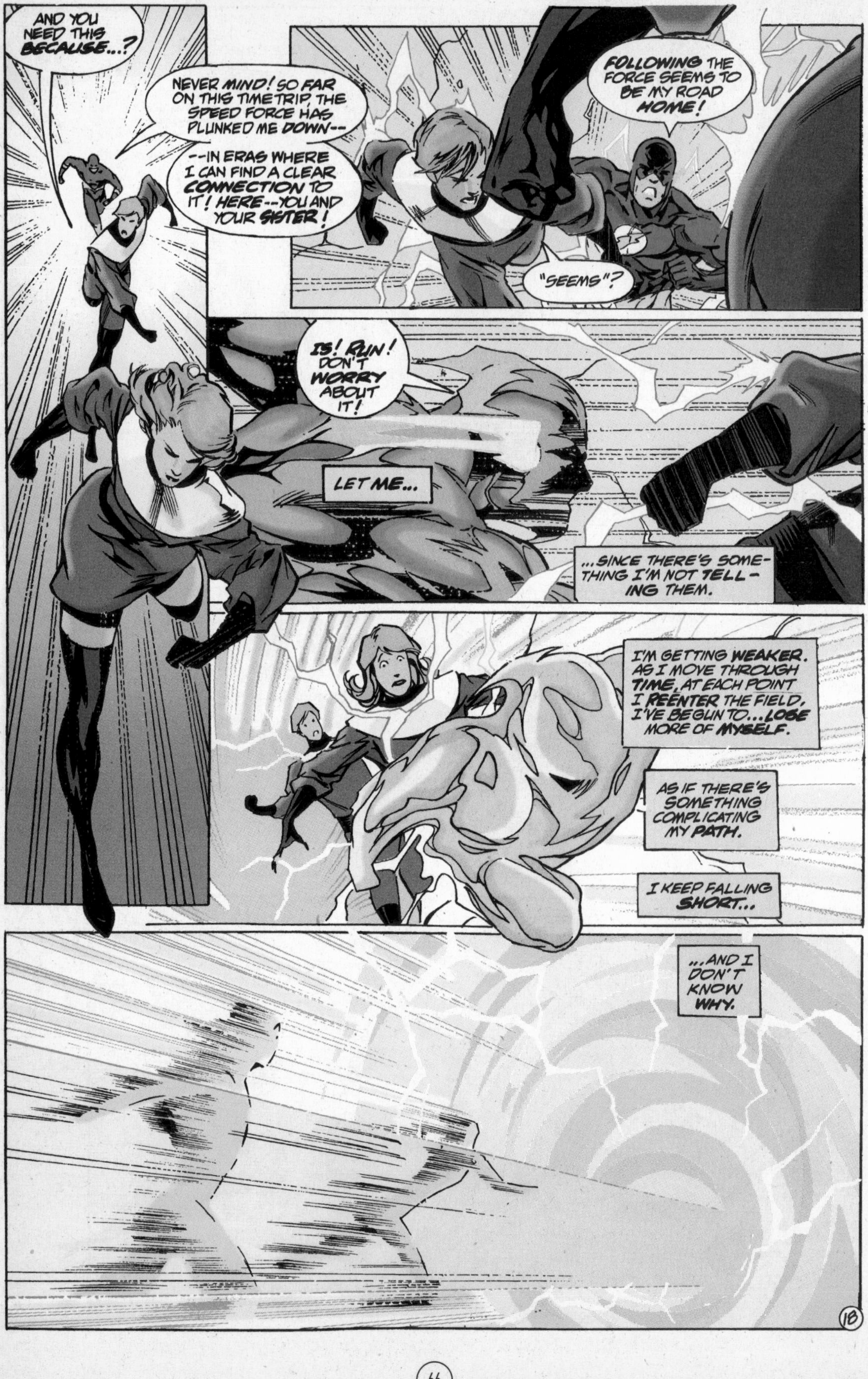
AND YOU NEED THIS BECAUSE...?
NEVER MIND! SO FAR ON THIS TIME TRIP, THE SPEED FORCE HAS PLUNKED ME DOWN--
--IN ERAS WHERE I CAN FIND A CLEAR CONNECTION TO IT! HERE--YOU AND YOUR SISTER!
FOLLOWING THE FORCE SEEMS TO BE MY ROAD HOME!
"SEEMS"?
IS! RUN! DON'T WORRY ABOUT IT!
LET ME...
...SINCE THERE'S SOMETHING I'M NOT TELLING THEM.
I'M GETTING WEAKER. AS I MOVE THROUGH TIME, AT EACH POINT I REENTER THE FIELD, I'VE BEGUN TO...LOSE MORE OF MYSELF.
AS IF THERE'S SOMETHING COMPLICATING MY PATH.
I KEEP FALLING SHORT...
...AND I DON'T KNOW WHY.
18

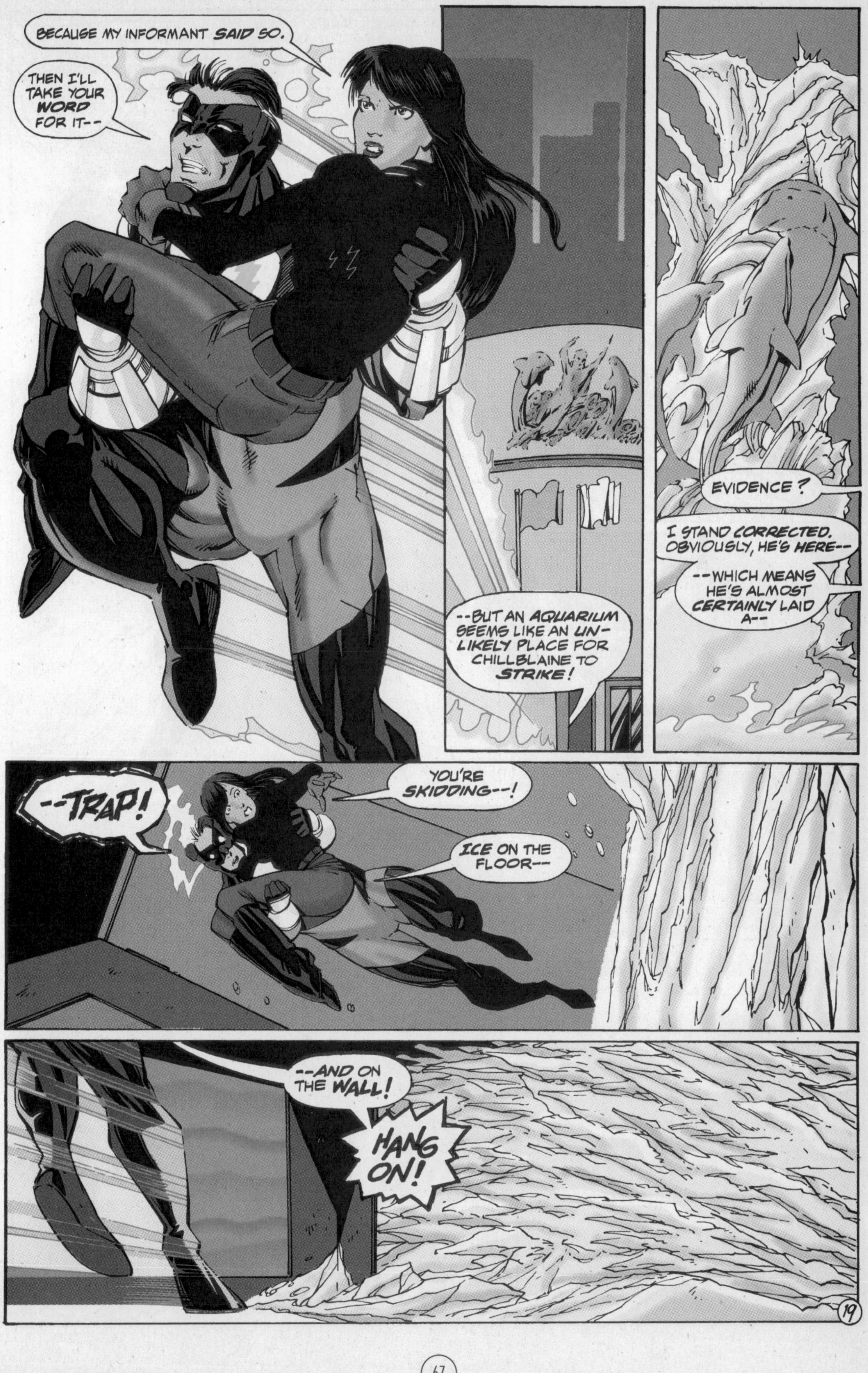
BECAUSE MY INFORMANT SAID SO.
THEN I'LL TAKE YOUR WORD FOR IT--
--BUT AN AQUARIUM SEEMS LIKE AN UNLIKELY PLACE FOR CHILLBLAINE TO STRIKE!
EVIDENCE?
I STAND CORRECTED. OBVIOUSLY, HE'S HERE--
--WHICH MEANS HE'S ALMOST CERTAINLY LAID A--
--TRAP!
YOU'RE SKIDDING--!
ICE ON THE FLOOR--
--AND ON THE WALL!
HANG ON!
19

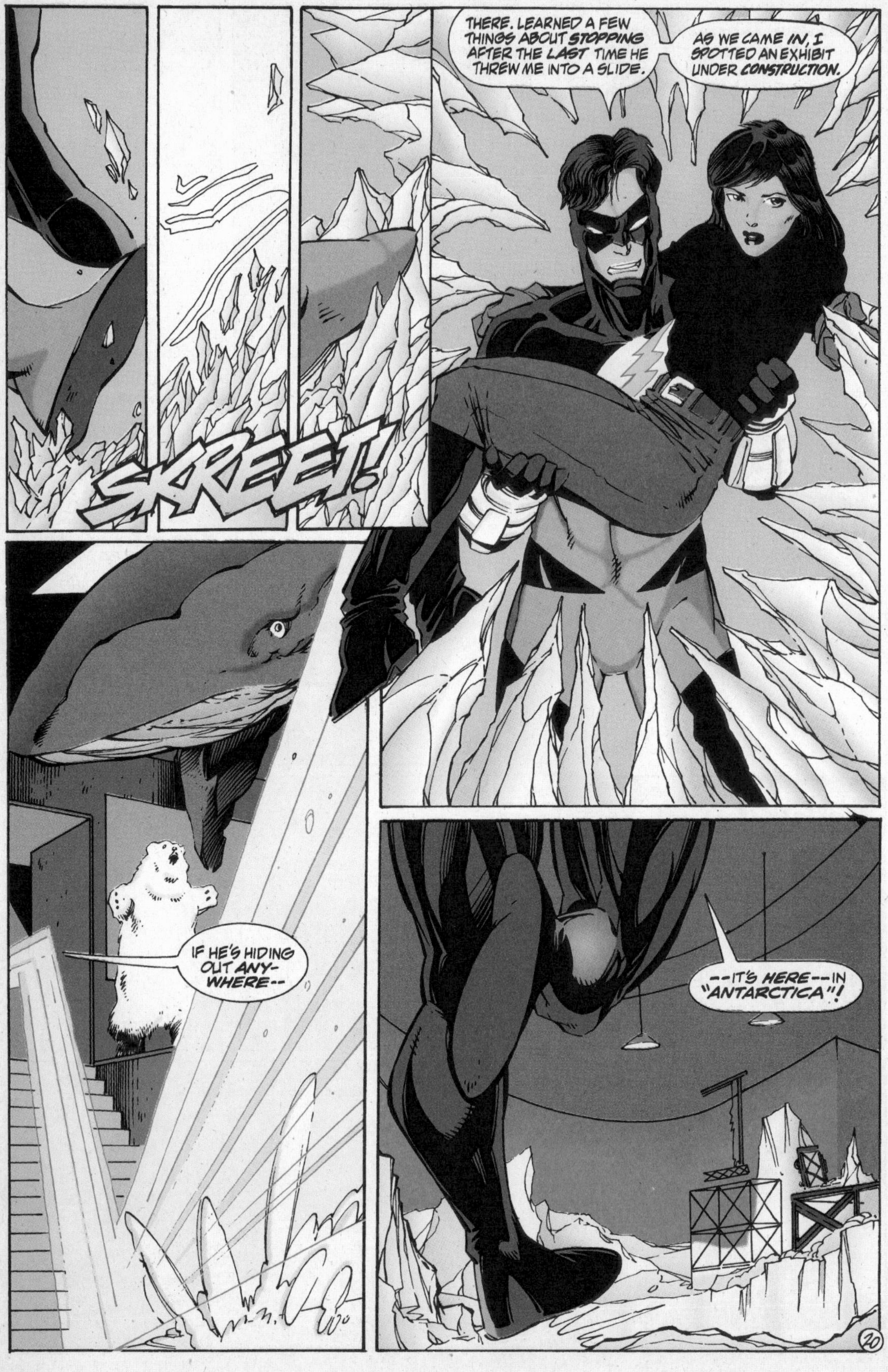
SKREET!
THERE. LEARNED A FEW THINGS ABOUT STOPPING AFTER THE LAST TIME HE THREW ME INTO A SLIDE.
AS WE CAME IN, I SPOTTED AN EXHIBIT UNDER CONSTRUCTION.
IF HE'S HIDING OUT ANY-WHERE--
--IT'S HERE--IN "ANTARCTICA"!
20

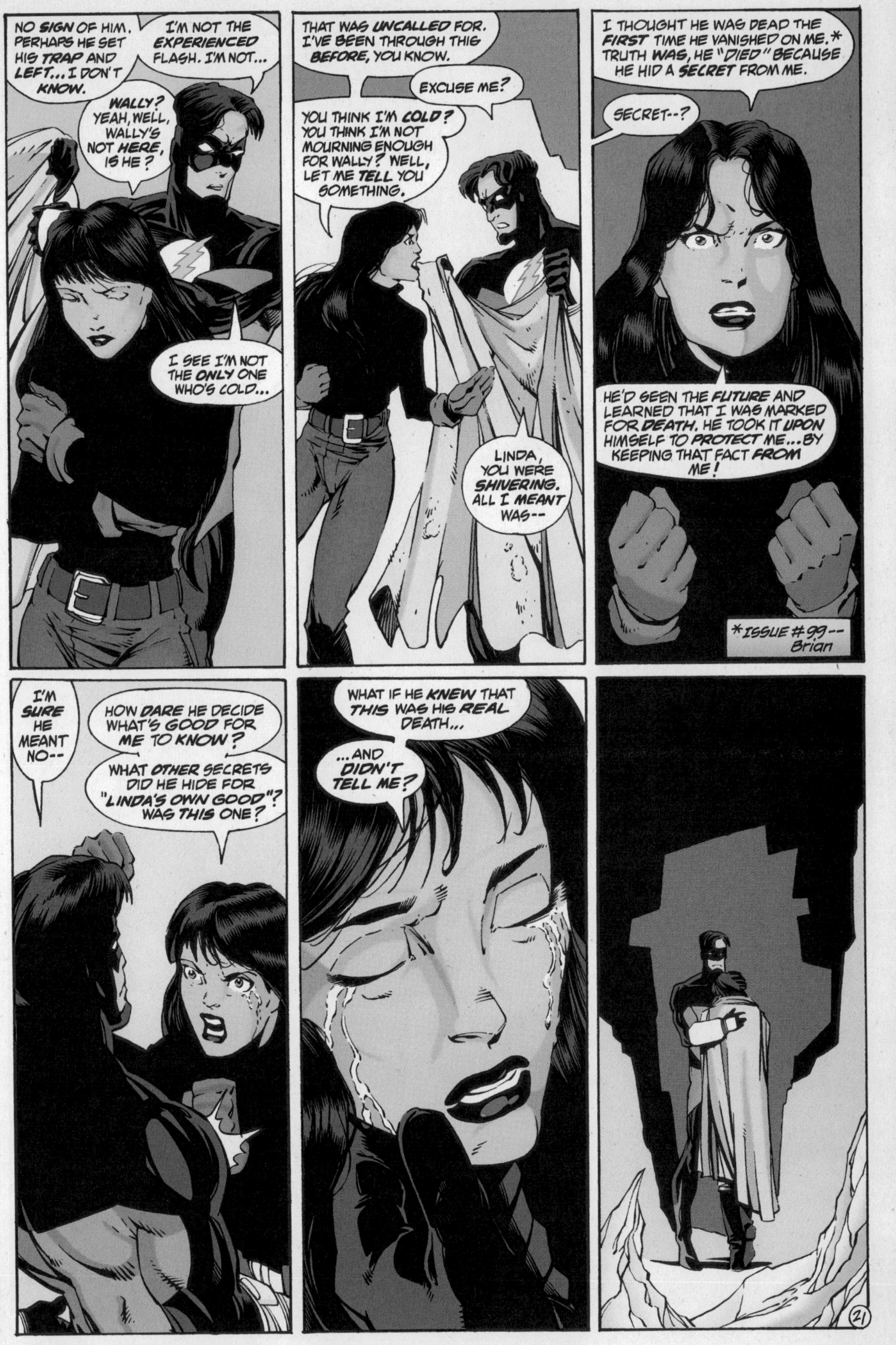
NO SIGN OF HIM. PERHAPS HE SET HIS TRAP AND LEFT... I DON'T KNOW.
I'M NOT THE EXPERIENCED FLASH. I'M NOT...
WALLY? YEAH, WELL, WALLY'S NOT HERE, IS HE?
I SEE I'M NOT THE ONLY ONE WHO'S COLD...
THAT WAS UNCALLED FOR. I'VE BEEN THROUGH THIS BEFORE, YOU KNOW.
EXCUSE ME?
YOU THINK I'M COLD? YOU THINK I'M NOT MOURNING ENOUGH FOR WALLY? WELL, LET ME TELL YOU SOMETHING.
LINDA, YOU WERE SHIVERING. ALL I MEANT WAS--
I THOUGHT HE WAS DEAD THE FIRST TIME HE VANISHED ON ME.* TRUTH WAS, HE "DIED" BECAUSE HE HID A SECRET FROM ME.
SECRET--?
HE'D SEEN THE FUTURE AND LEARNED THAT I WAS MARKED FOR DEATH. HE TOOK IT UPON HIMSELF TO PROTECT ME...BY KEEPING THAT FACT FROM ME!
*ISSUE #99-- Brian
I'M SURE HE MEANT NO--
HOW DARE HE DECIDE WHAT'S GOOD FOR ME TO KNOW?
WHAT OTHER SECRETS DID HE HIDE FOR "LINDA'S OWN GOOD"? WAS THIS ONE?
WHAT IF HE KNEW THAT THIS WAS HIS REAL DEATH...
...AND DIDN'T TELL ME?
21

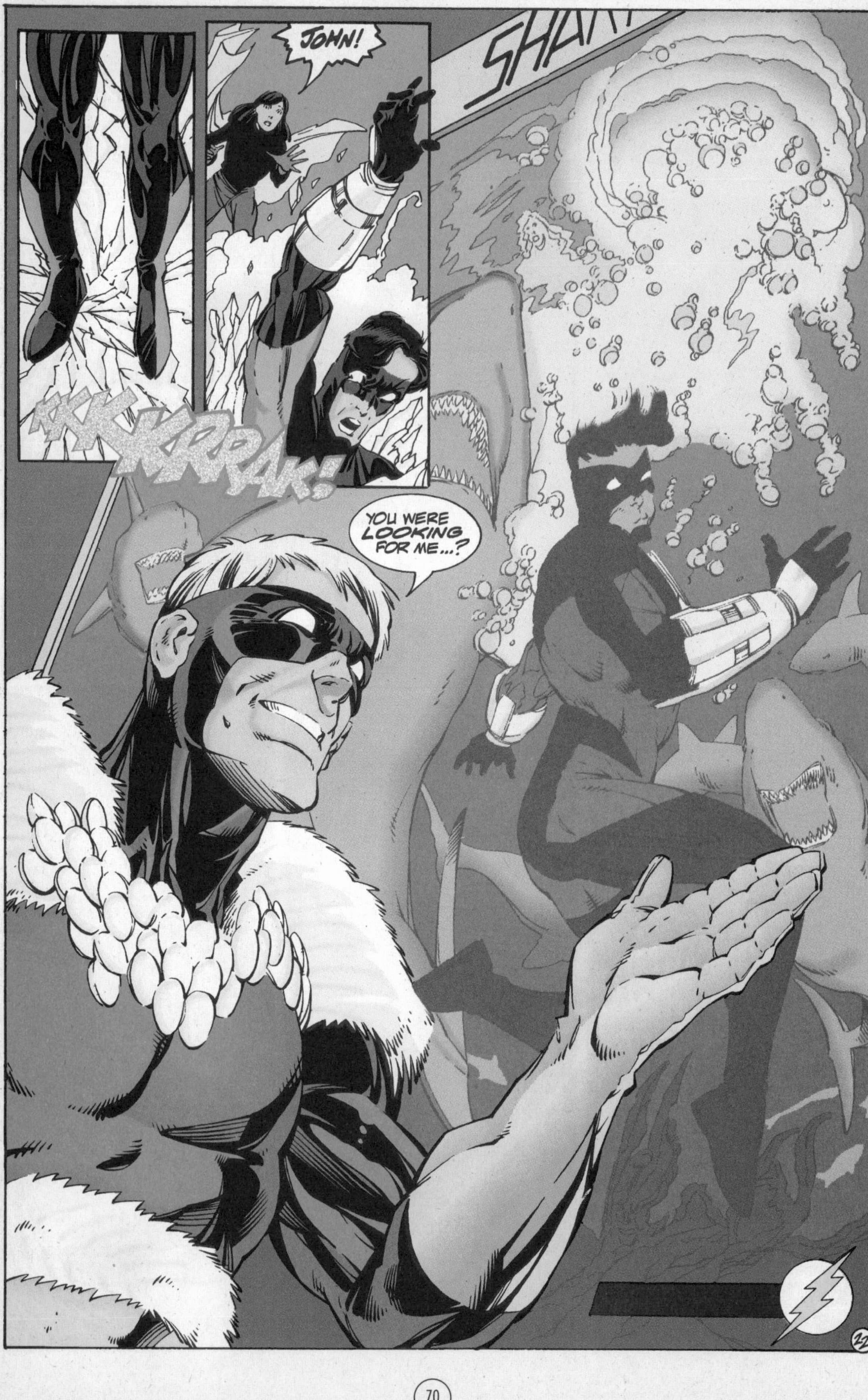
JOHN!
SHAK
KKKKRRRAK!
YOU WERE LOOKING FOR ME...?
22

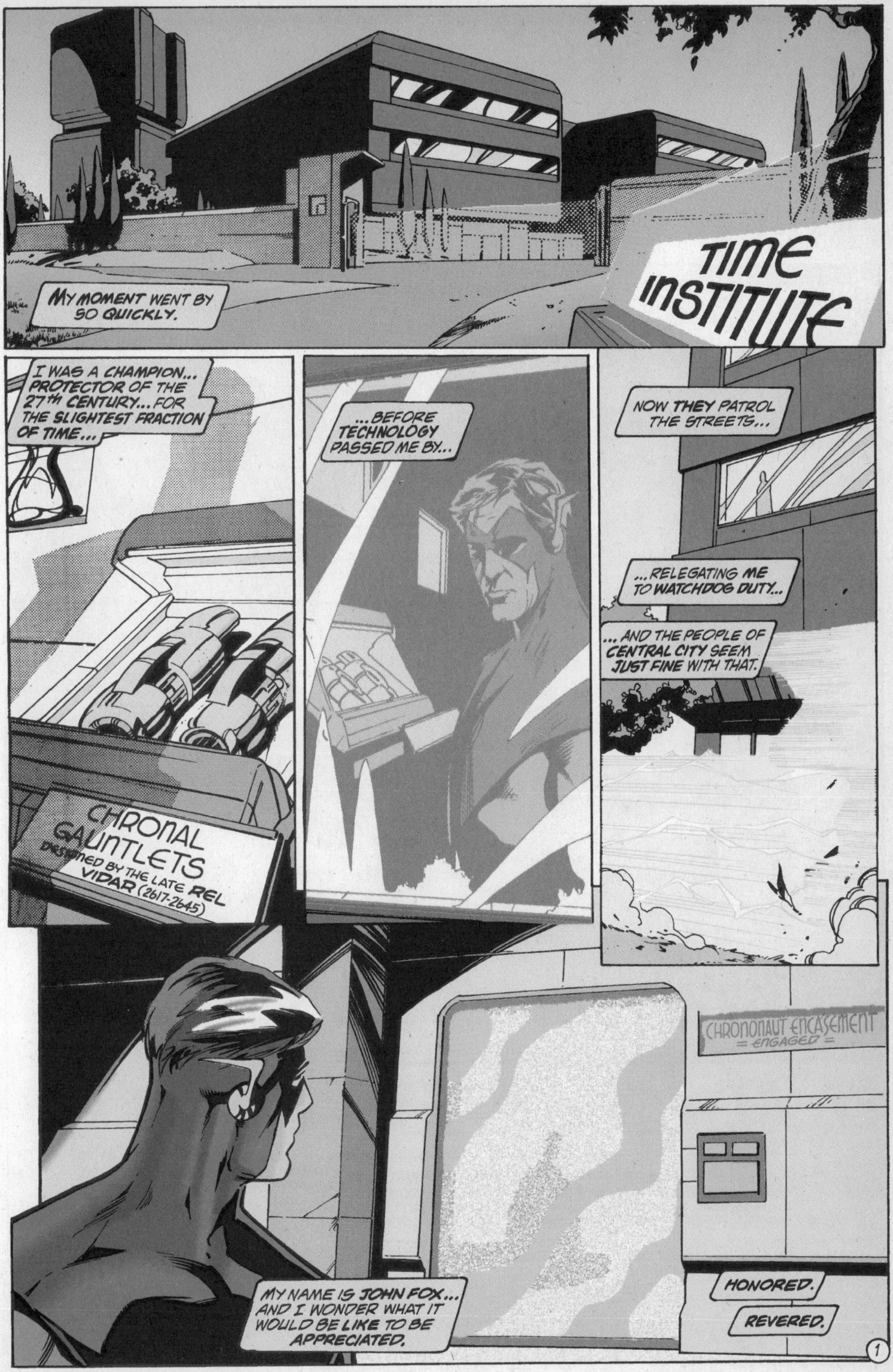
TIME INSTITUTE
MY MOMENT WENT BY SO QUICKLY.
I WAS A CHAMPION... PROTECTOR OF THE 27th CENTURY... FOR THE SLIGHTEST FRACTION OF TIME...
CHRONAL GAUNTLETS DESIGNED BY THE LATE REL VIDAR (2617-2645)
...BEFORE TECHNOLOGY PASSED ME BY...
NOW THEY PATROL THE STREETS...
...RELEGATING ME TO WATCHDOG DUTY...
...AND THE PEOPLE OF CENTRAL CITY SEEM JUST FINE WITH THAT.
CHRONONAUT ENCASEMENT = ENGAGED =
MY NAME IS JOHN FOX... AND I WONDER WHAT IT WOULD BE LIKE TO BE APPRECIATED.
HONORED.
REVERED.
1

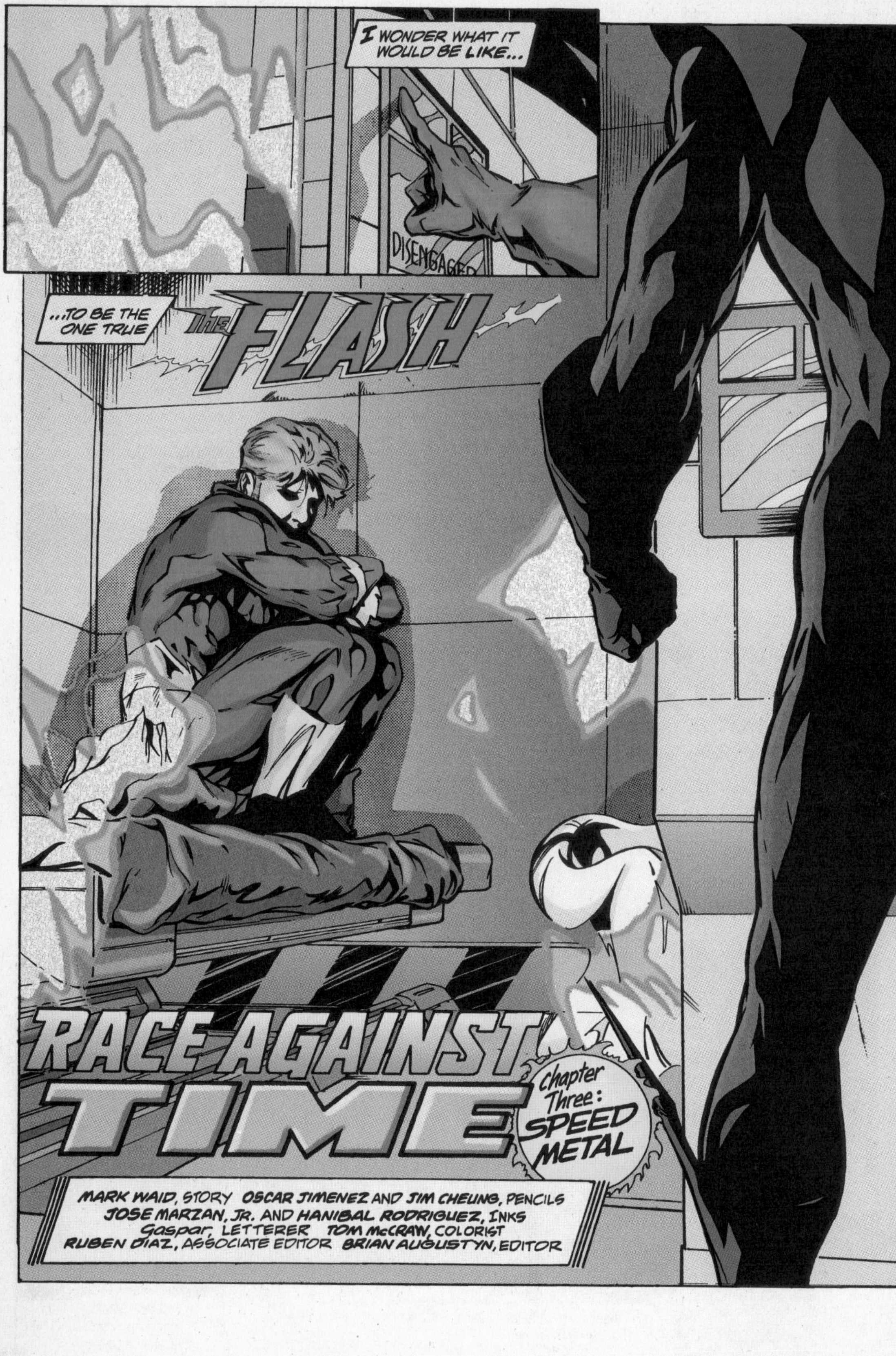
I WONDER WHAT IT WOULD BE LIKE...
DISENGAGED
...TO BE THE ONE TRUE
THE FLASH
RACE AGAINST TIME
Chapter Three: SPEED METAL
MARK WAID, STORY OSCAR JIMENEZ AND JIM CHEUNG, PENCILS
JOSE MARZAN, JR. AND HANIBAL RODRIGUEZ, INKS
Gaspar, LETTERER TOM McCRAW, COLORIST
RUBEN DIAZ, ASSOCIATE EDITOR BRIAN AUGUSTYN, EDITOR

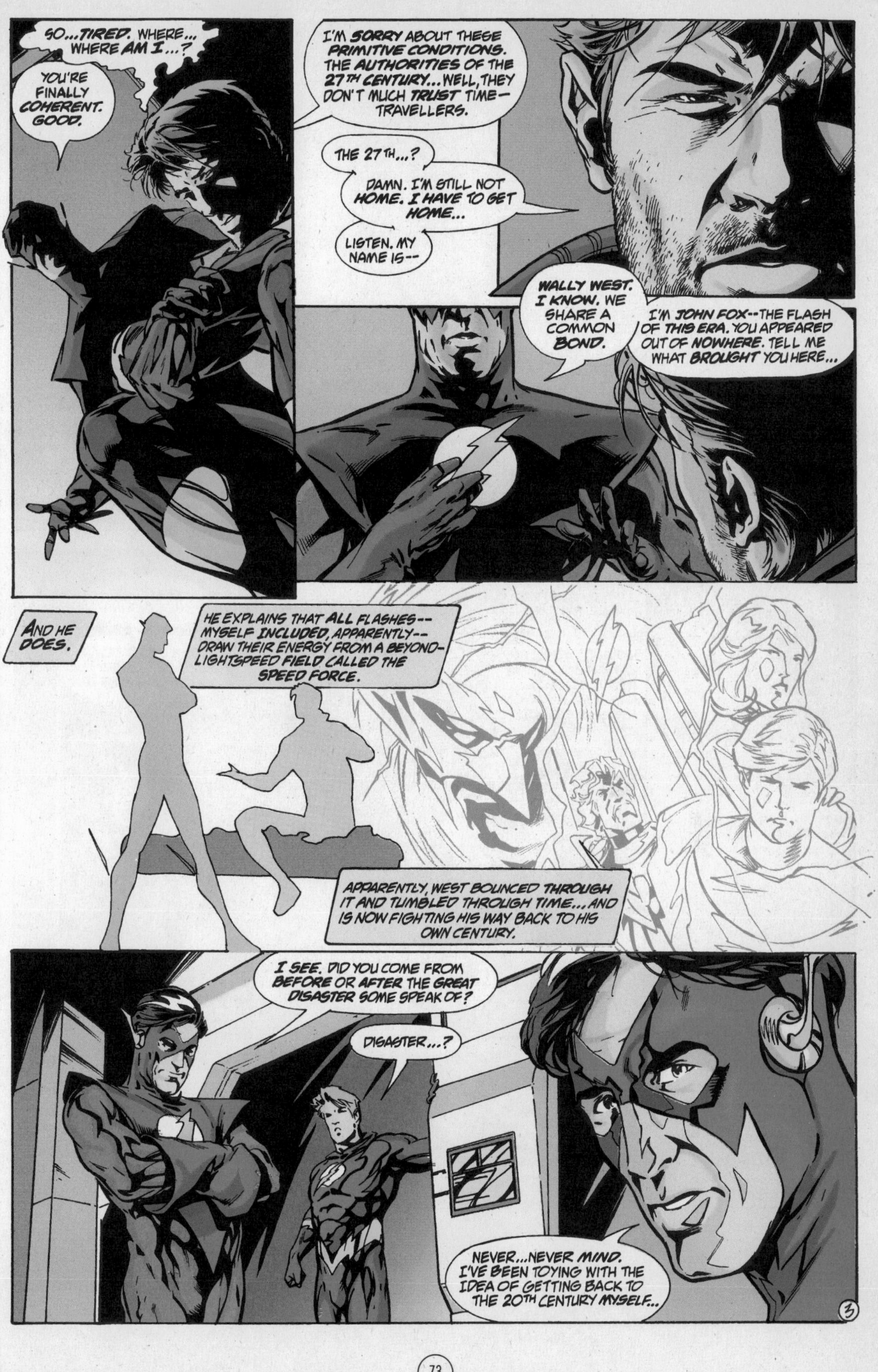

SO...TIRED. WHERE... WHERE AM I...?
YOU'RE FINALLY COHERENT. GOOD.
I'M SORRY ABOUT THESE PRIMITIVE CONDITIONS. THE AUTHORITIES OF THE 27TH CENTURY... WELL, THEY DON'T MUCH TRUST TIME-TRAVELLERS.
THE 27TH...?
DAMN. I'M STILL NOT HOME. I HAVE TO GET HOME...
LISTEN. MY NAME IS--
WALLY WEST. I KNOW. WE SHARE A COMMON BOND.
I'M JOHN FOX--THE FLASH OF THIS ERA. YOU APPEARED OUT OF NOWHERE. TELL ME WHAT BROUGHT YOU HERE...
AND HE DOES.
HE EXPLAINS THAT ALL FLASHES--MYSELF INCLUDED, APPARENTLY--DRAW THEIR ENERGY FROM A BEYOND-LIGHTSPEED FIELD CALLED THE SPEED FORCE.
APPARENTLY, WEST BOUNCED THROUGH IT AND TUMBLED THROUGH TIME... AND IS NOW FIGHTING HIS WAY BACK TO HIS OWN CENTURY.
I SEE. DID YOU COME FROM BEFORE OR AFTER THE GREAT DISASTER SOME SPEAK OF?
DISASTER...?
NEVER...NEVER MIND. I'VE BEEN TOYING WITH THE IDEA OF GETTING BACK TO THE 20TH CENTURY MYSELF...
3

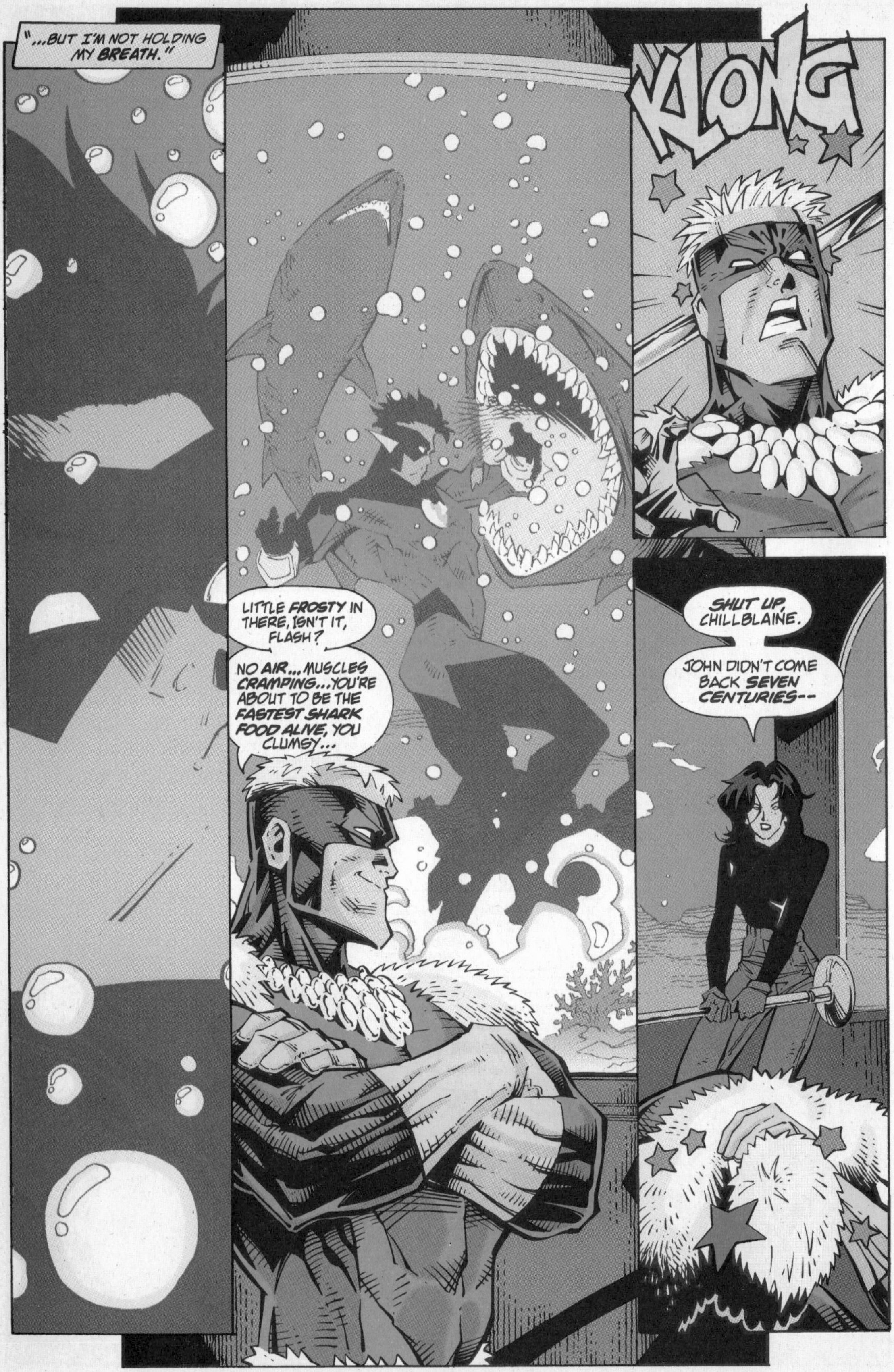
"...BUT I'M NOT HOLDING MY BREATH."
KLONG
LITTLE FROSTY IN THERE, ISN'T IT, FLASH?
NO AIR... MUSCLES CRAMPING... YOU'RE ABOUT TO BE THE FASTEST SHARK FOOD ALIVE, YOU CLUMSY...
SHUT UP, CHILLBLAINE.
JOHN DIDN'T COME BACK SEVEN CENTURIES--

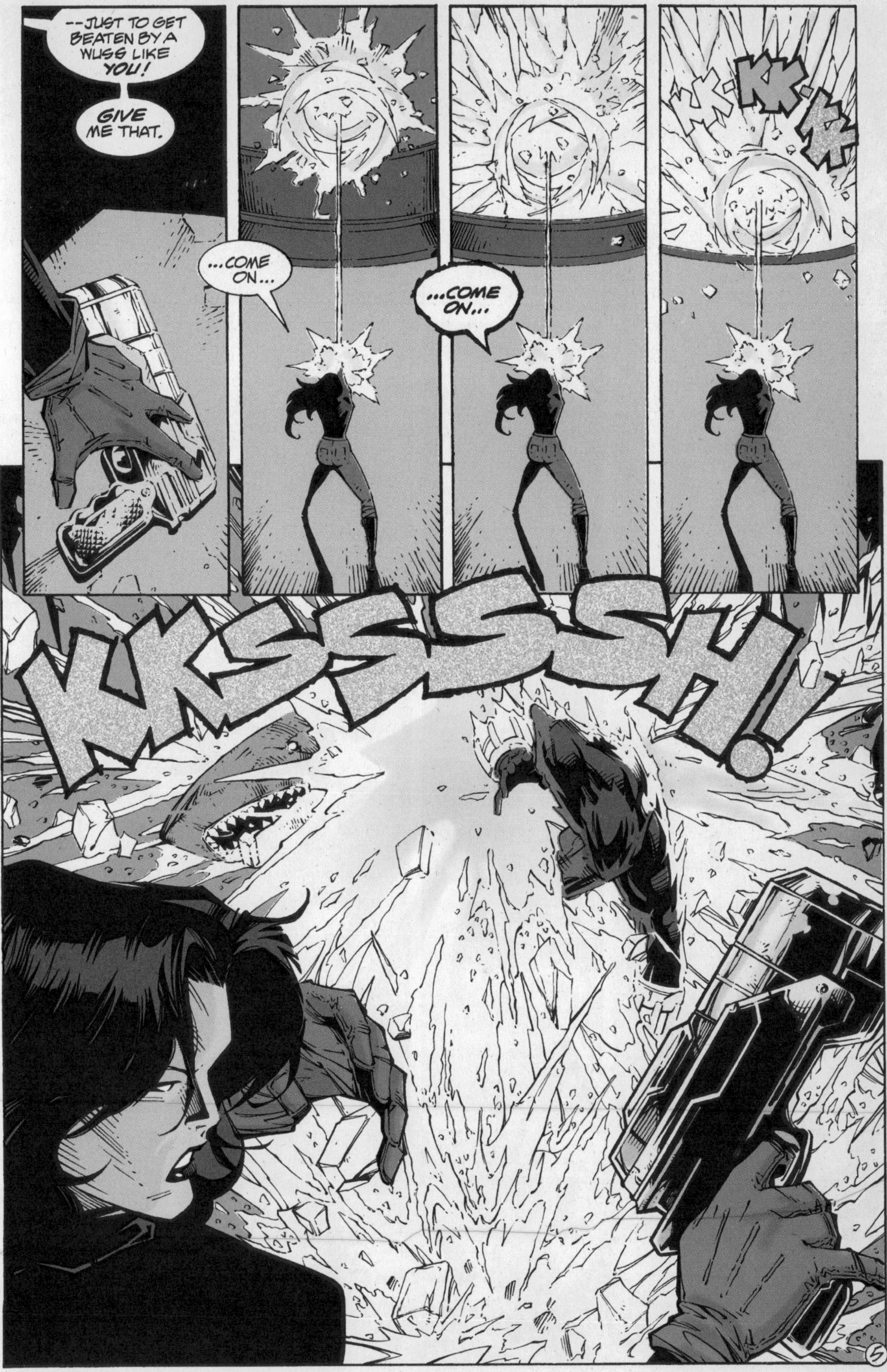
--JUST TO GET BEATEN BY A WUSS LIKE YOU!
GIVE ME THAT.
...COME ON...
...COME ON...
K-K-KK-K
KKSSSSH!!
5

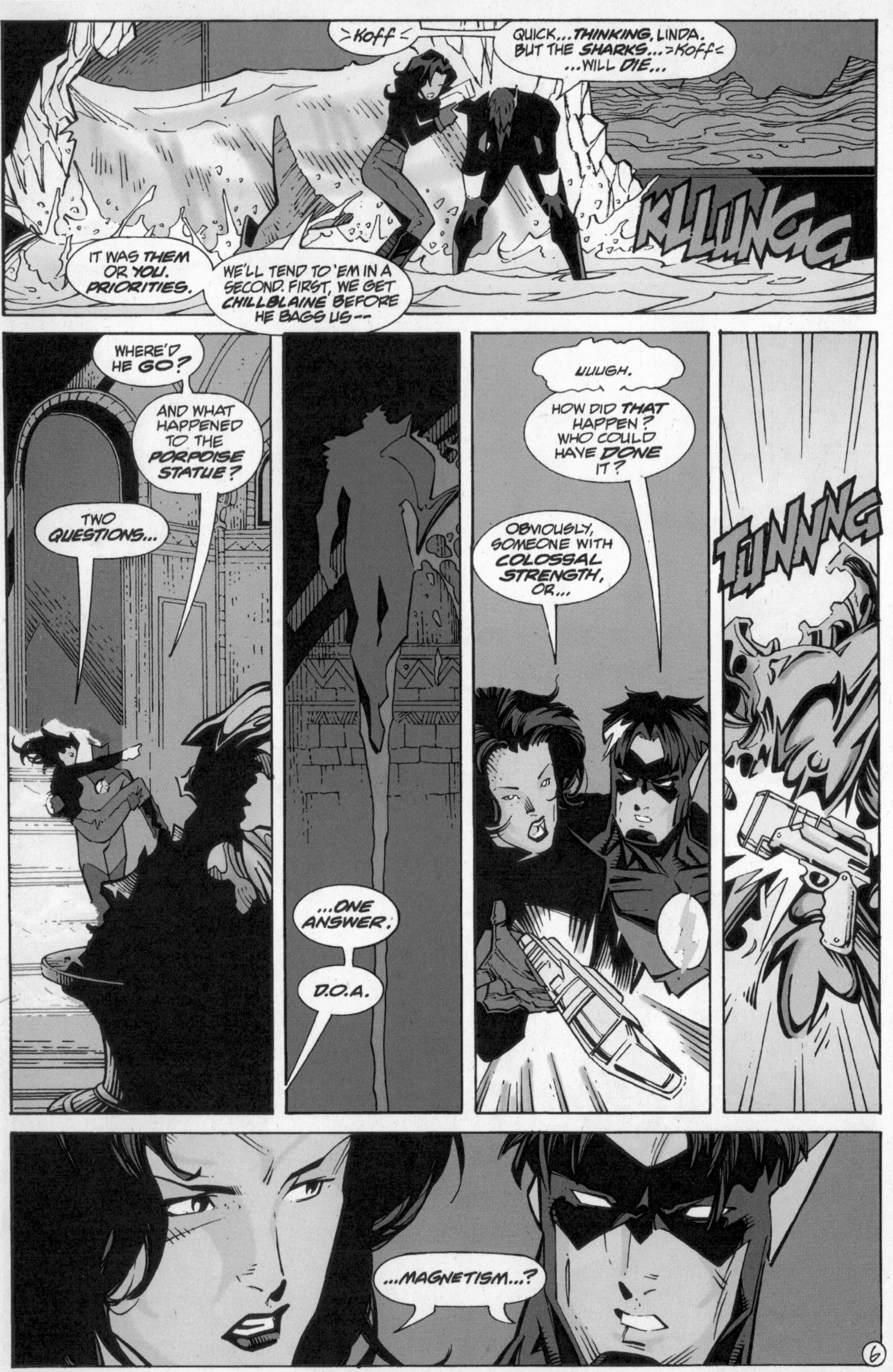
>KOFF<
QUICK... THINKING, LINDA. BUT THE SHARKS... >KOFF< ...WILL DIE...
KLLUNGG
IT WAS THEM OR YOU. PRIORITIES.
WE'LL TEND TO 'EM IN A SECOND. FIRST, WE GET CHILLBLAINE BEFORE HE BAGS US--
WHERE'D HE GO?
AND WHAT HAPPENED TO THE PORPOISE STATUE?
TWO QUESTIONS...
...ONE ANSWER.
D.O.A.
UUUGH.
HOW DID THAT HAPPEN? WHO COULD HAVE DONE IT?
OBVIOUSLY, SOMEONE WITH COLOSSAL STRENGTH, OR...
TUNNNG
...MAGNETISM...?
6

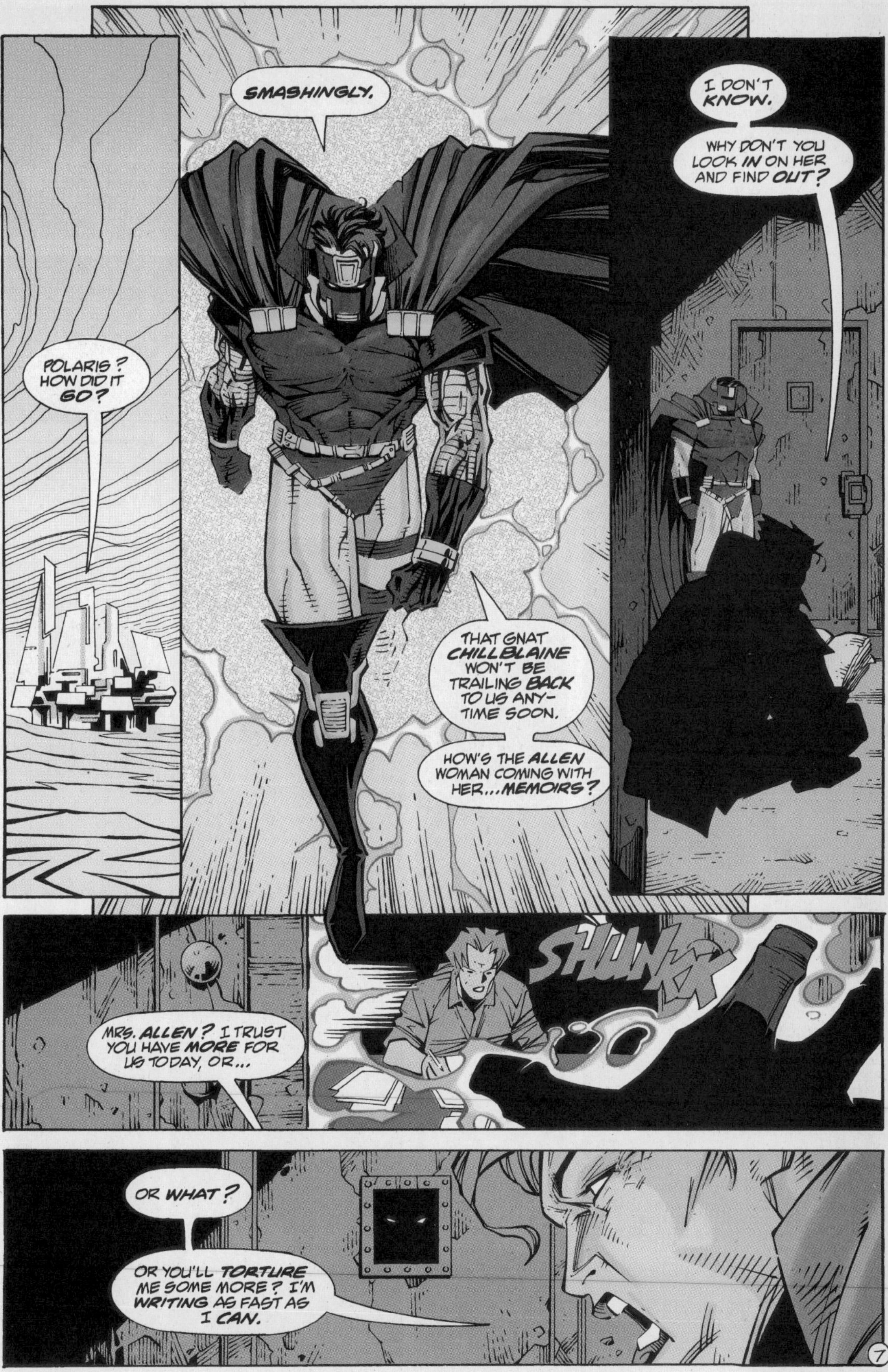
POLARIS? HOW DID IT GO?
SMASHINGLY.
THAT GNAT CHILLBLAINE WON'T BE TRAILING BACK TO US ANY-TIME SOON.
HOW'S THE ALLEN WOMAN COMING WITH HER...MEMOIRS?
I DON'T KNOW.
WHY DON'T YOU LOOK IN ON HER AND FIND OUT?
SHUNKK
MRS. ALLEN? I TRUST YOU HAVE MORE FOR US TODAY, OR...
OR WHAT?
OR YOU'LL TORTURE ME SOME MORE? I'M WRITING AS FAST AS I CAN.
7

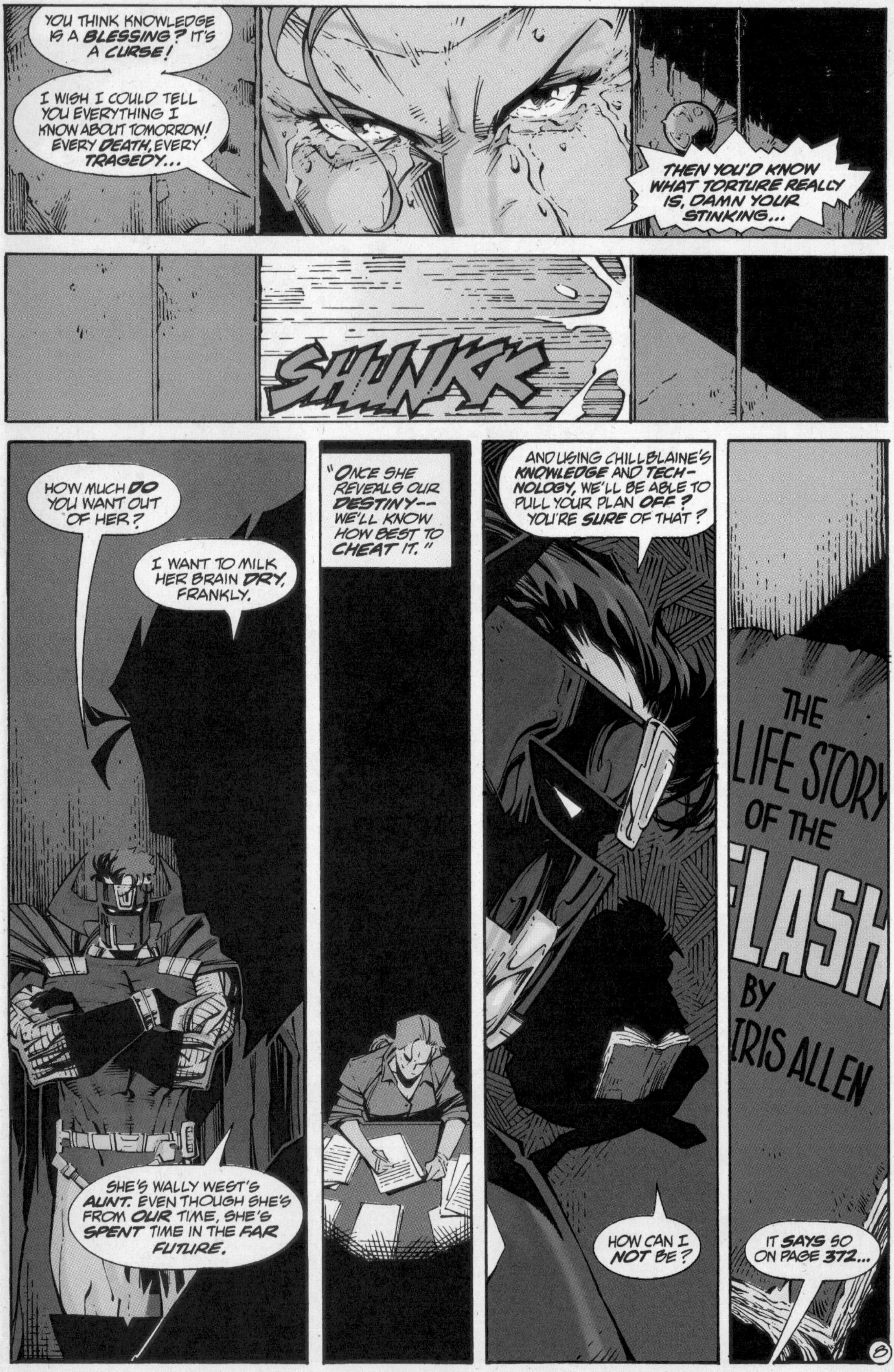

YOU THINK KNOWLEDGE IS A BLESSING? IT'S A CURSE!
I WISH I COULD TELL YOU EVERYTHING I KNOW ABOUT TOMORROW! EVERY DEATH, EVERY TRAGEDY...
THEN YOU'D KNOW WHAT TORTURE REALLY IS, DAMN YOUR STINKING...
SHUNKK
HOW MUCH DO YOU WANT OUT OF HER?
I WANT TO MILK HER BRAIN DRY, FRANKLY.
SHE'S WALLY WEST'S AUNT. EVEN THOUGH SHE'S FROM OUR TIME, SHE'S SPENT TIME IN THE FAR FUTURE.
"ONCE SHE REVEALS OUR DESTINY-- WE'LL KNOW HOW BEST TO CHEAT IT."
AND USING CHILLBLAINE'S KNOWLEDGE AND TECHNOLOGY, WE'LL BE ABLE TO PULL YOUR PLAN OFF? YOU'RE SURE OF THAT?
HOW CAN I NOT BE?
THE LIFE STORY OF THE FLASH BY IRIS ALLEN
IT SAYS SO ON PAGE 372...
8

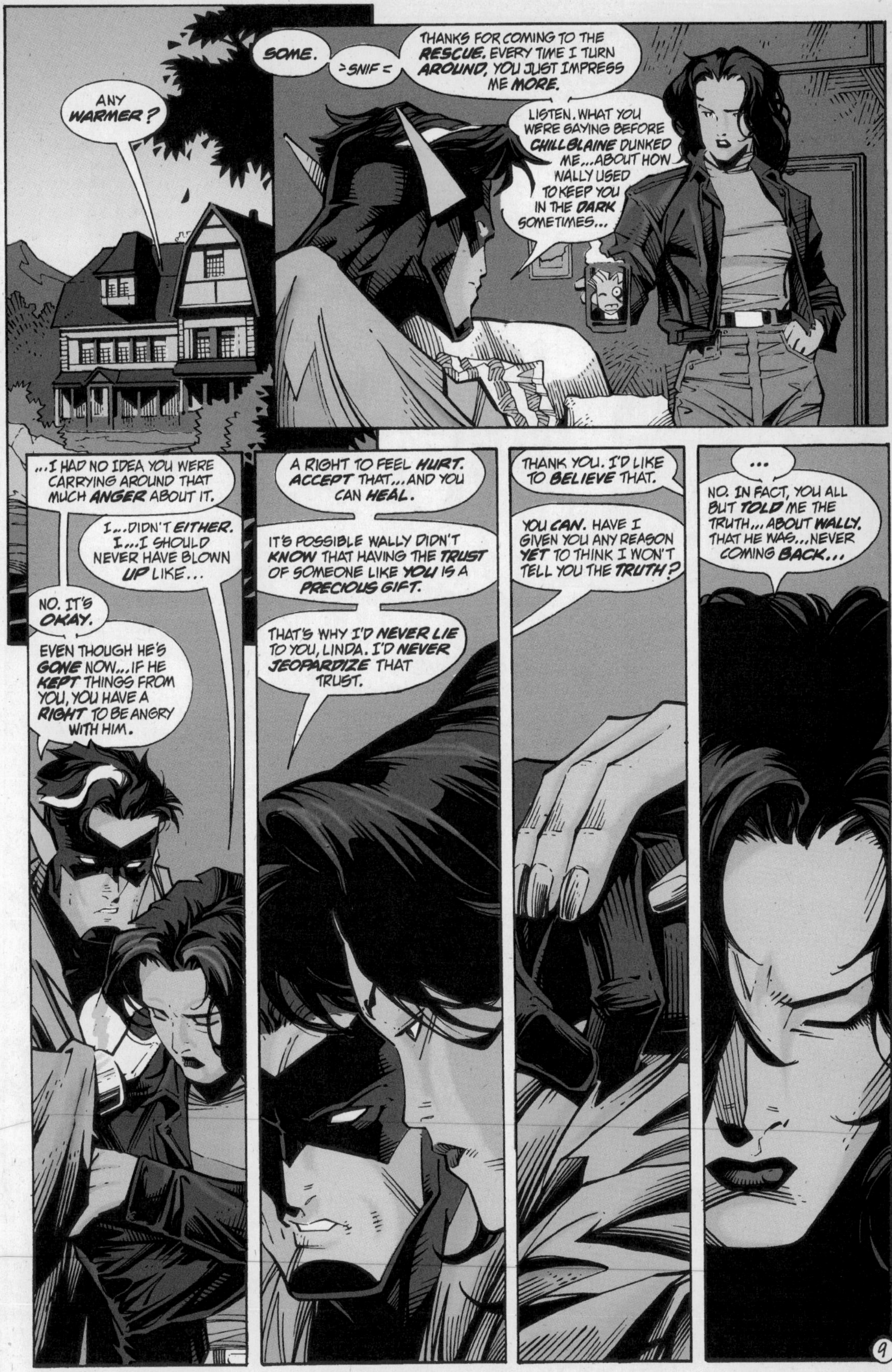
ANY WARMER?
SOME.
>SNIF<
THANKS FOR COMING TO THE RESCUE. EVERY TIME I TURN AROUND, YOU JUST IMPRESS ME MORE.
LISTEN. WHAT YOU WERE SAYING BEFORE CHILLBLAINE DUNKED ME...ABOUT HOW WALLY USED TO KEEP YOU IN THE DARK SOMETIMES...
...I HAD NO IDEA YOU WERE CARRYING AROUND THAT MUCH ANGER ABOUT IT.
I...DIDN'T EITHER. I...I SHOULD NEVER HAVE BLOWN UP LIKE...
NO. IT'S OKAY.
EVEN THOUGH HE'S GONE NOW...IF HE KEPT THINGS FROM YOU, YOU HAVE A RIGHT TO BE ANGRY WITH HIM.
A RIGHT TO FEEL HURT. ACCEPT THAT...AND YOU CAN HEAL.
IT'S POSSIBLE WALLY DIDN'T KNOW THAT HAVING THE TRUST OF SOMEONE LIKE YOU IS A PRECIOUS GIFT.
THAT'S WHY I'D NEVER LIE TO YOU, LINDA. I'D NEVER JEOPARDIZE THAT TRUST.
THANK YOU. I'D LIKE TO BELIEVE THAT.
YOU CAN. HAVE I GIVEN YOU ANY REASON YET TO THINK I WON'T TELL YOU THE TRUTH?
...
NO. IN FACT, YOU ALL BUT TOLD ME THE TRUTH...ABOUT WALLY. THAT HE WAS...NEVER COMING BACK...
9

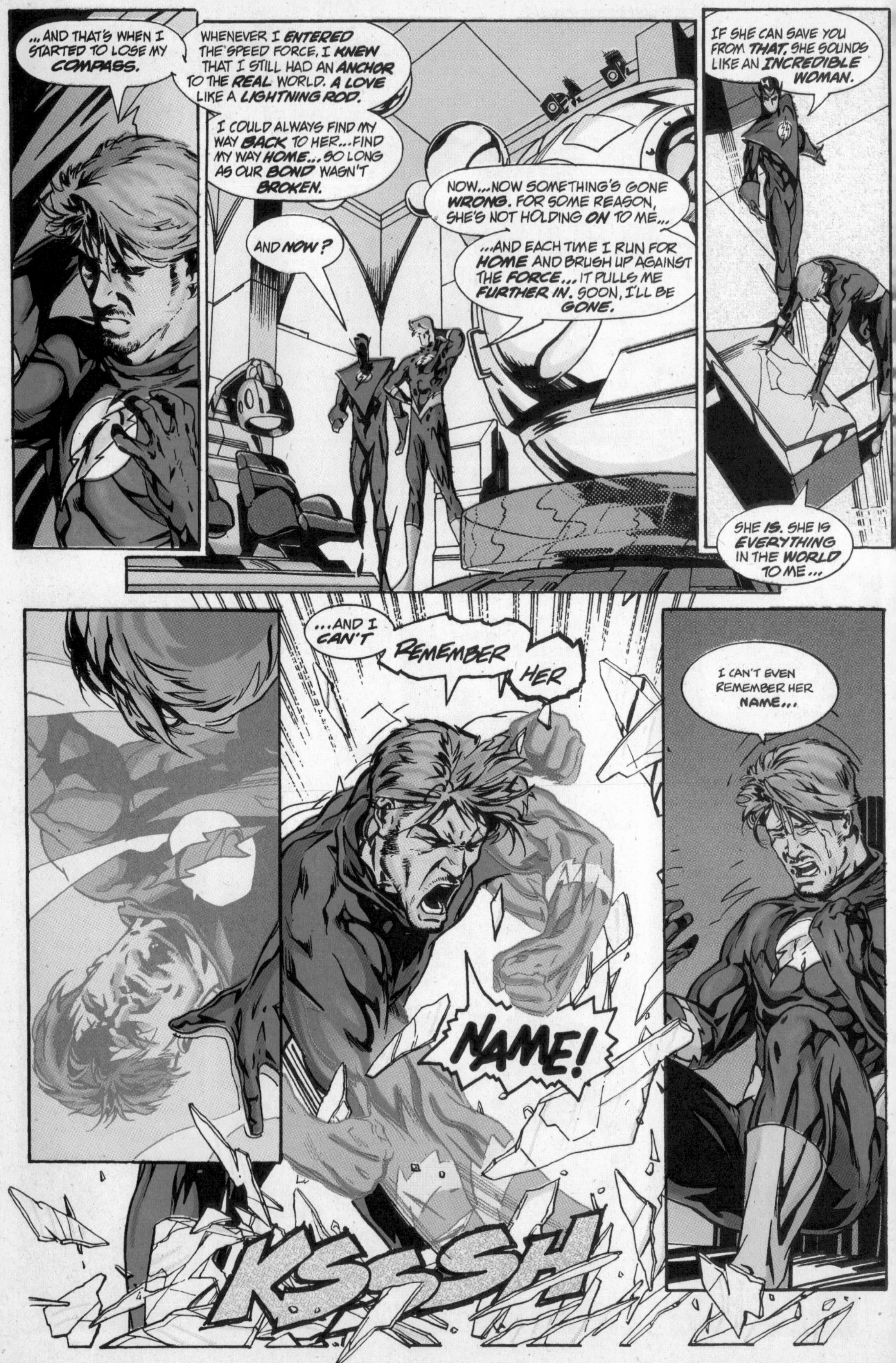
...AND THAT'S WHEN I STARTED TO LOSE MY COMPASS.
WHENEVER I ENTERED THE SPEED FORCE, I KNEW THAT I STILL HAD AN ANCHOR TO THE REAL WORLD. A LOVE LIKE A LIGHTNING ROD.
I COULD ALWAYS FIND MY WAY BACK TO HER... FIND MY WAY HOME... SO LONG AS OUR BOND WASN'T BROKEN.
AND NOW?
NOW... NOW SOMETHING'S GONE WRONG. FOR SOME REASON, SHE'S NOT HOLDING ON TO ME...
...AND EACH TIME I RUN FOR HOME AND BRUSH UP AGAINST THE FORCE... IT PULLS ME FURTHER IN. SOON, I'LL BE GONE.
IF SHE CAN SAVE YOU FROM THAT, SHE SOUNDS LIKE AN INCREDIBLE WOMAN.
SHE IS. SHE IS EVERYTHING IN THE WORLD TO ME...
...AND I CAN'T
REMEMBER
HER
NAME!
KSSSH
I CAN'T EVEN REMEMBER HER NAME...

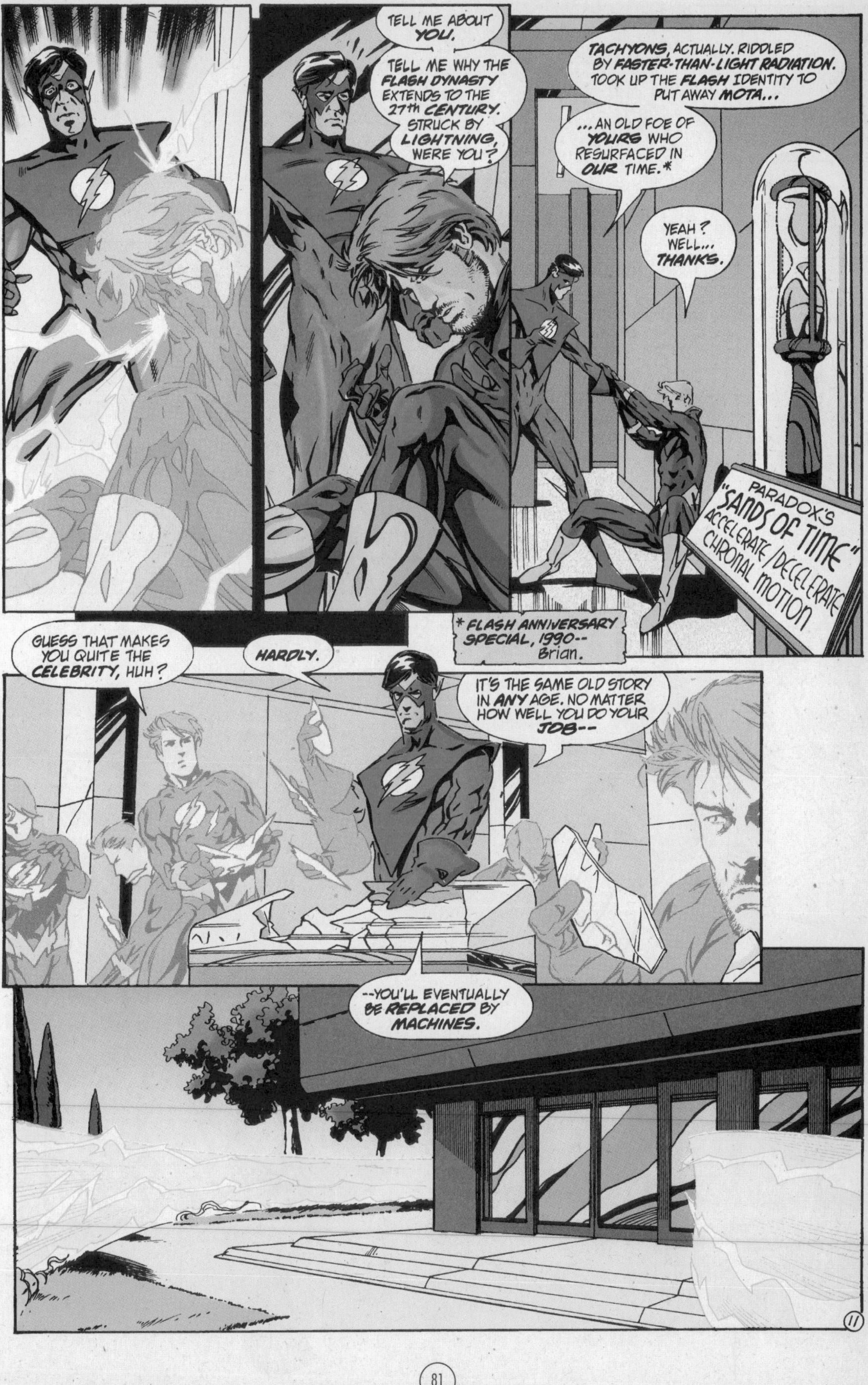
TELL ME ABOUT YOU.
TELL ME WHY THE FLASH DYNASTY EXTENDS TO THE 27th CENTURY. STRUCK BY LIGHTNING, WERE YOU?
TACHYONS, ACTUALLY. RIDDLED BY FASTER-THAN-LIGHT RADIATION. TOOK UP THE FLASH IDENTITY TO PUT AWAY MOTA...
...AN OLD FOE OF YOURS WHO RESURFACED IN OUR TIME.*
YEAH? WELL... THANKS.
PARADOX'S "SANDS OF TIME" ACCELERATE/DECELERATE CHRONAL MOTION
* FLASH ANNIVERSARY SPECIAL, 1990-- Brian.
GUESS THAT MAKES YOU QUITE THE CELEBRITY, HUH?
HARDLY.
IT'S THE SAME OLD STORY IN ANY AGE. NO MATTER HOW WELL YOU DO YOUR JOB--
--YOU'LL EVENTUALLY BE REPLACED BY MACHINES.
11

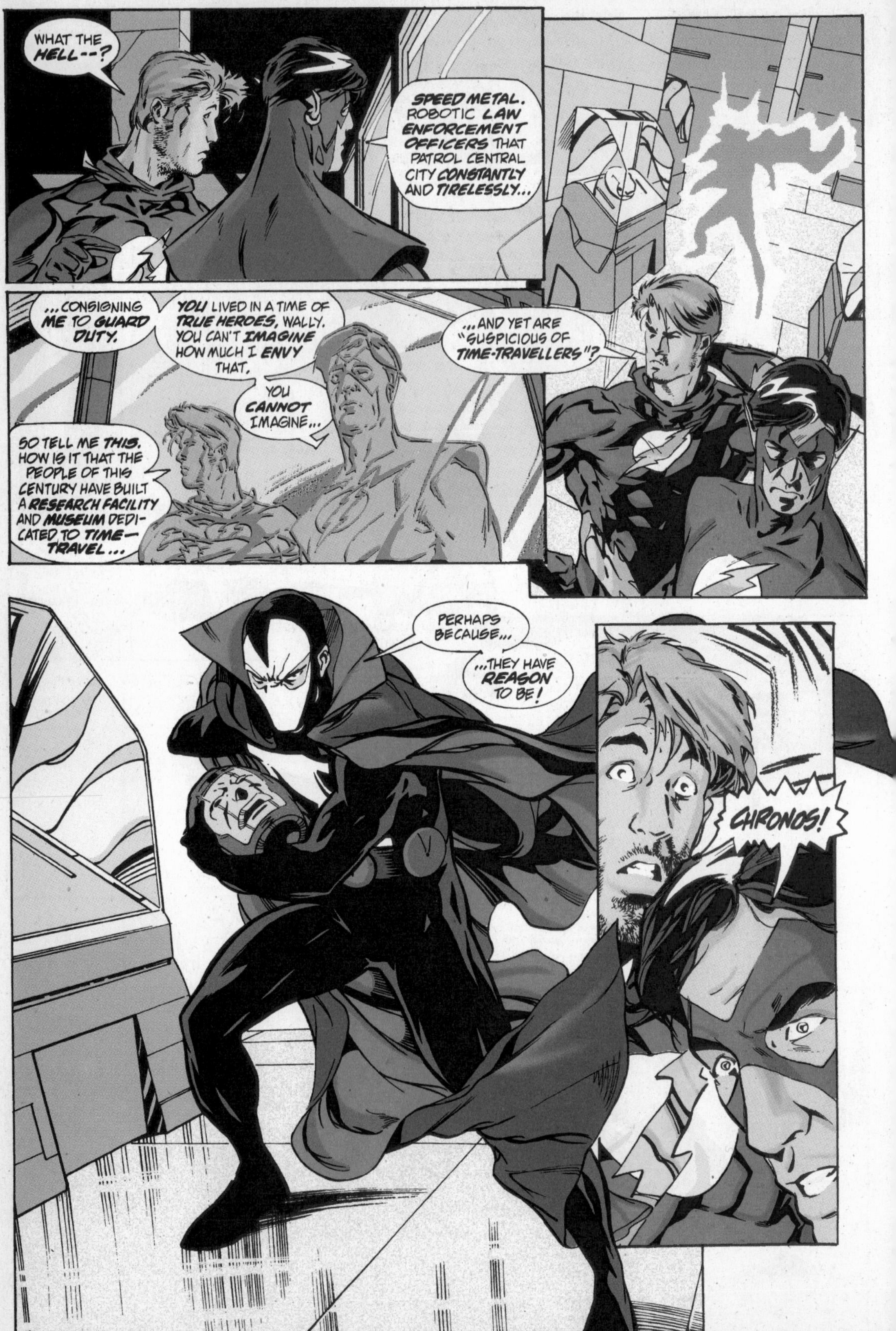
WHAT THE HELL--?
SPEED METAL. ROBOTIC LAW ENFORCEMENT OFFICERS THAT PATROL CENTRAL CITY CONSTANTLY AND TIRELESSLY...
...CONSIGNING ME TO GUARD DUTY.
YOU LIVED IN A TIME OF TRUE HEROES, WALLY. YOU CAN'T IMAGINE HOW MUCH I ENVY THAT.
YOU CANNOT IMAGINE...
SO TELL ME THIS. HOW IS IT THAT THE PEOPLE OF THIS CENTURY HAVE BUILT A RESEARCH FACILITY AND MUSEUM DEDICATED TO TIME-TRAVEL...
...AND YET ARE "SUSPICIOUS OF TIME-TRAVELLERS"?
PERHAPS BECAUSE...
...THEY HAVE REASON TO BE!
CHRONOS!

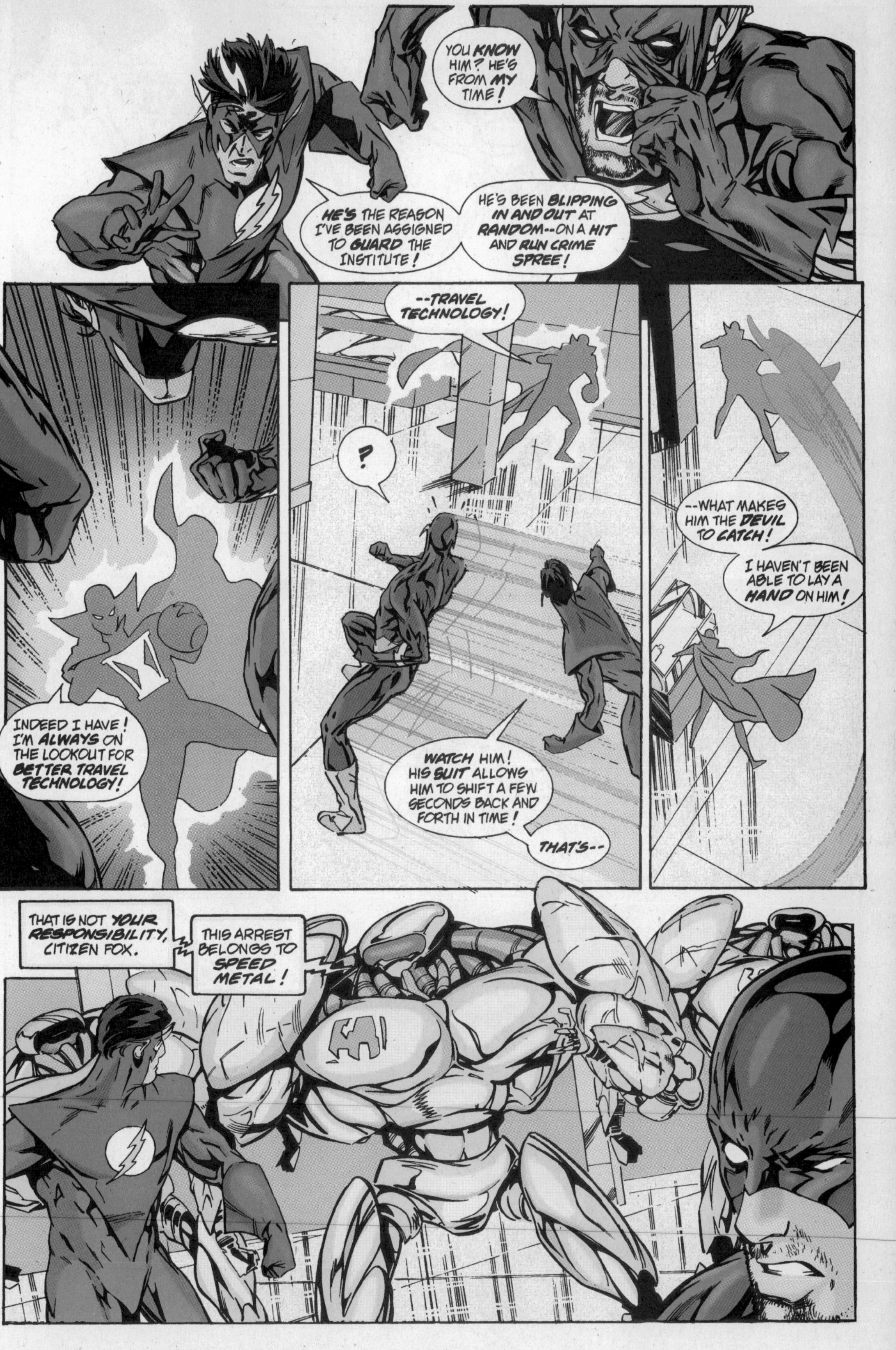
YOU KNOW HIM? HE'S FROM MY TIME!
HE'S THE REASON I'VE BEEN ASSIGNED TO GUARD THE INSTITUTE!
HE'S BEEN SLIPPING IN AND OUT AT RANDOM--ON A HIT AND RUN CRIME SPREE!
INDEED I HAVE! I'M ALWAYS ON THE LOOKOUT FOR BETTER TRAVEL TECHNOLOGY!
--TRAVEL TECHNOLOGY!
?
WATCH HIM! HIS SUIT ALLOWS HIM TO SHIFT A FEW SECONDS BACK AND FORTH IN TIME!
THAT'S--
--WHAT MAKES HIM THE DEVIL TO CATCH!
I HAVEN'T BEEN ABLE TO LAY A HAND ON HIM!
THAT IS NOT YOUR RESPONSIBILITY, CITIZEN FOX.
THIS ARREST BELONGS TO SPEED METAL!

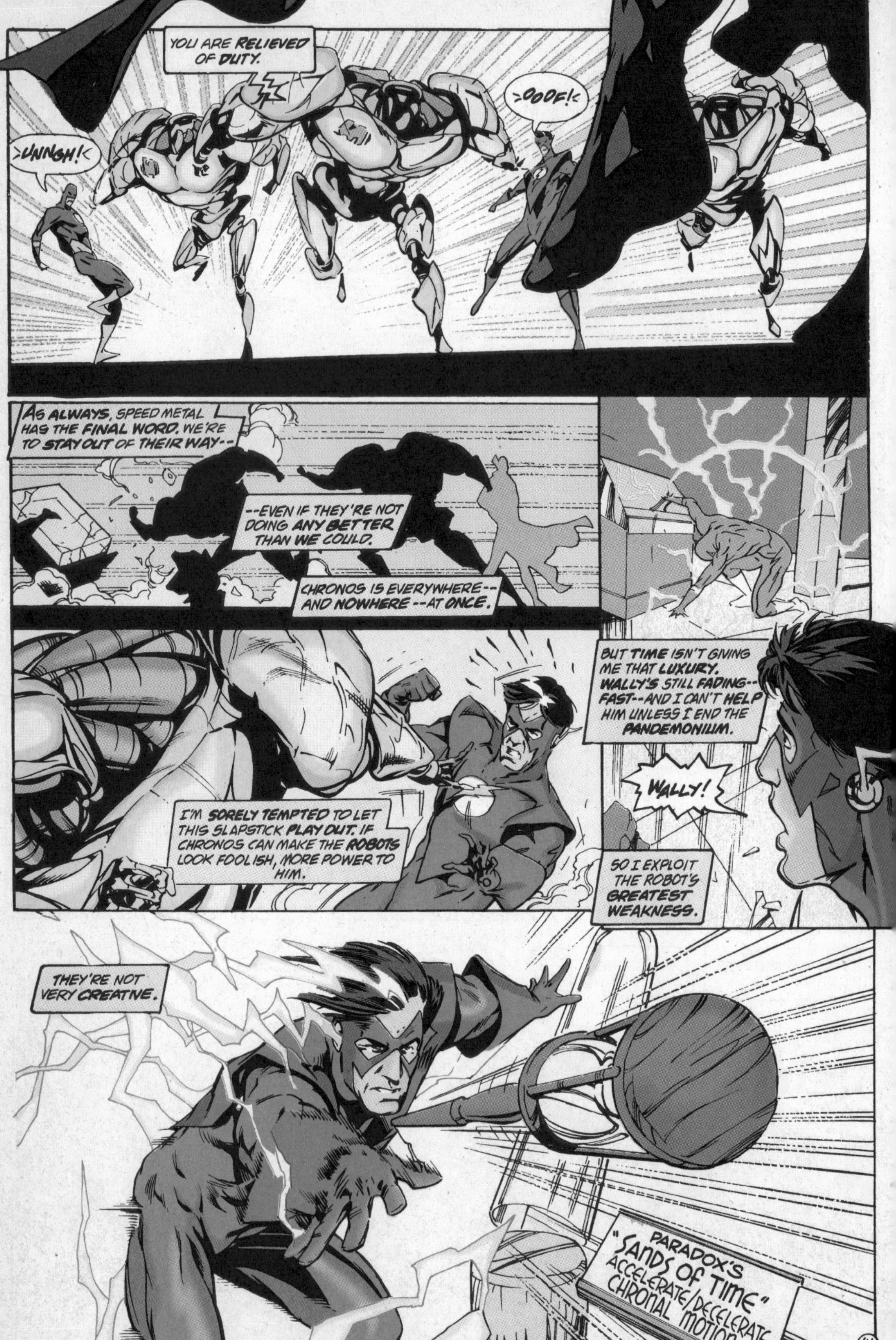

YOU ARE RELIEVED OF DUTY.
>UNNGH!<
>OOOF!<
AS ALWAYS, SPEED METAL HAS THE FINAL WORD. WE'RE TO STAY OUT OF THEIR WAY--
--EVEN IF THEY'RE NOT DOING ANY BETTER THAN WE COULD.
CHRONOS IS EVERYWHERE-- AND NOWHERE --AT ONCE.
I'M SORELY TEMPTED TO LET THIS SLAPSTICK PLAY OUT. IF CHRONOS CAN MAKE THE ROBOTS LOOK FOOLISH, MORE POWER TO HIM.
BUT TIME ISN'T GIVING ME THAT LUXURY. WALLY'S STILL FADING-- FAST--AND I CAN'T HELP HIM UNLESS I END THE PANDEMONIUM.
WALLY!
SO I EXPLOIT THE ROBOT'S GREATEST WEAKNESS.
THEY'RE NOT VERY CREATIVE.
PARADOX'S "SANDS OF TIME" ACCELERATE/DECELERATE CHRONAL MOTION
14

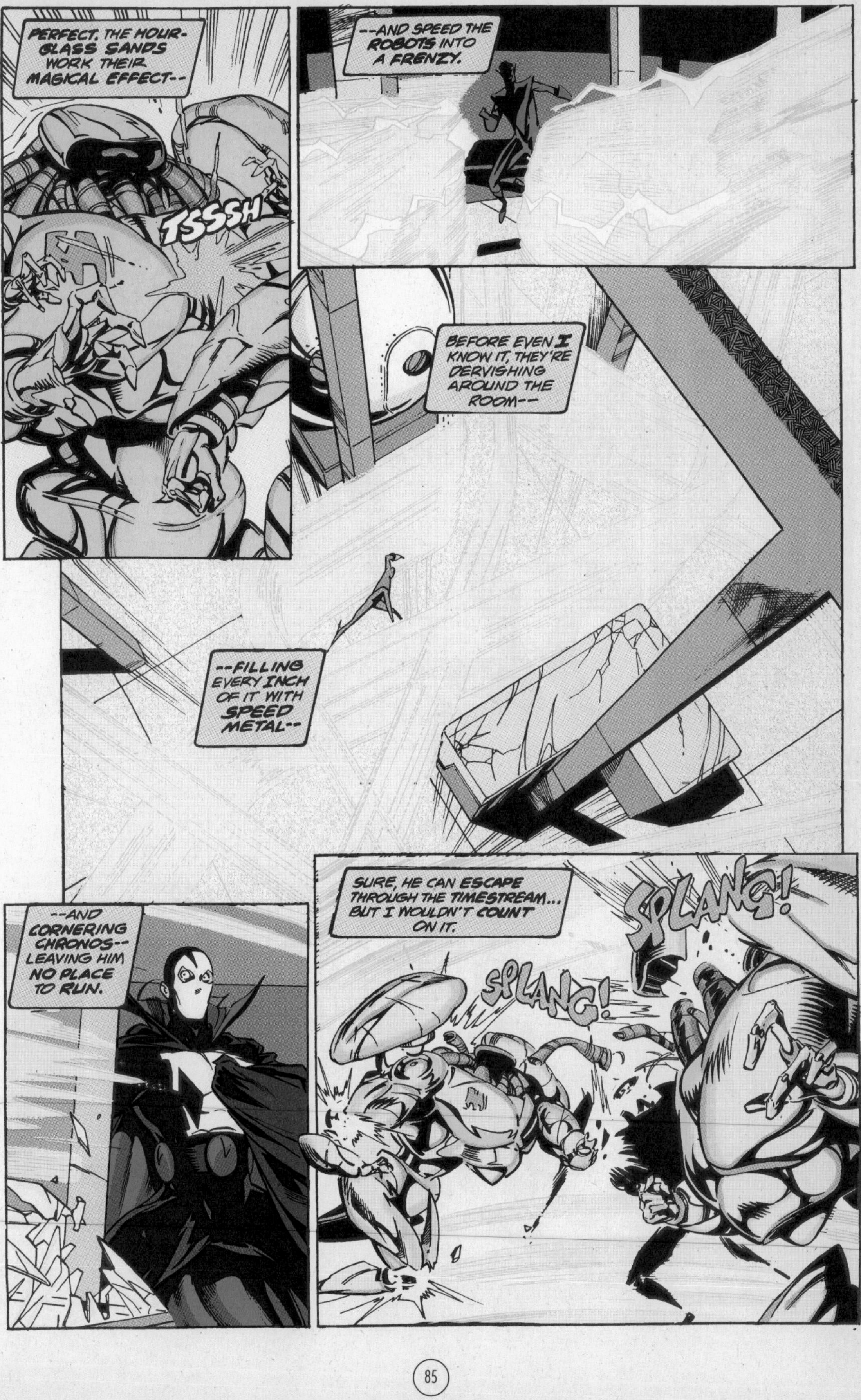
PERFECT. THE HOUR-GLASS SANDS WORK THEIR MAGICAL EFFECT--
TSSSH
--AND SPEED THE ROBOTS INTO A FRENZY.
BEFORE EVEN I KNOW IT, THEY'RE DERVISHING AROUND THE ROOM--
--FILLING EVERY INCH OF IT WITH SPEED METAL--
--AND CORNERING CHRONOS--LEAVING HIM NO PLACE TO RUN.
SURE, HE CAN ESCAPE THROUGH THE TIMESTREAM... BUT I WOULDN'T COUNT ON IT.
SPLANG!
SPLANG!

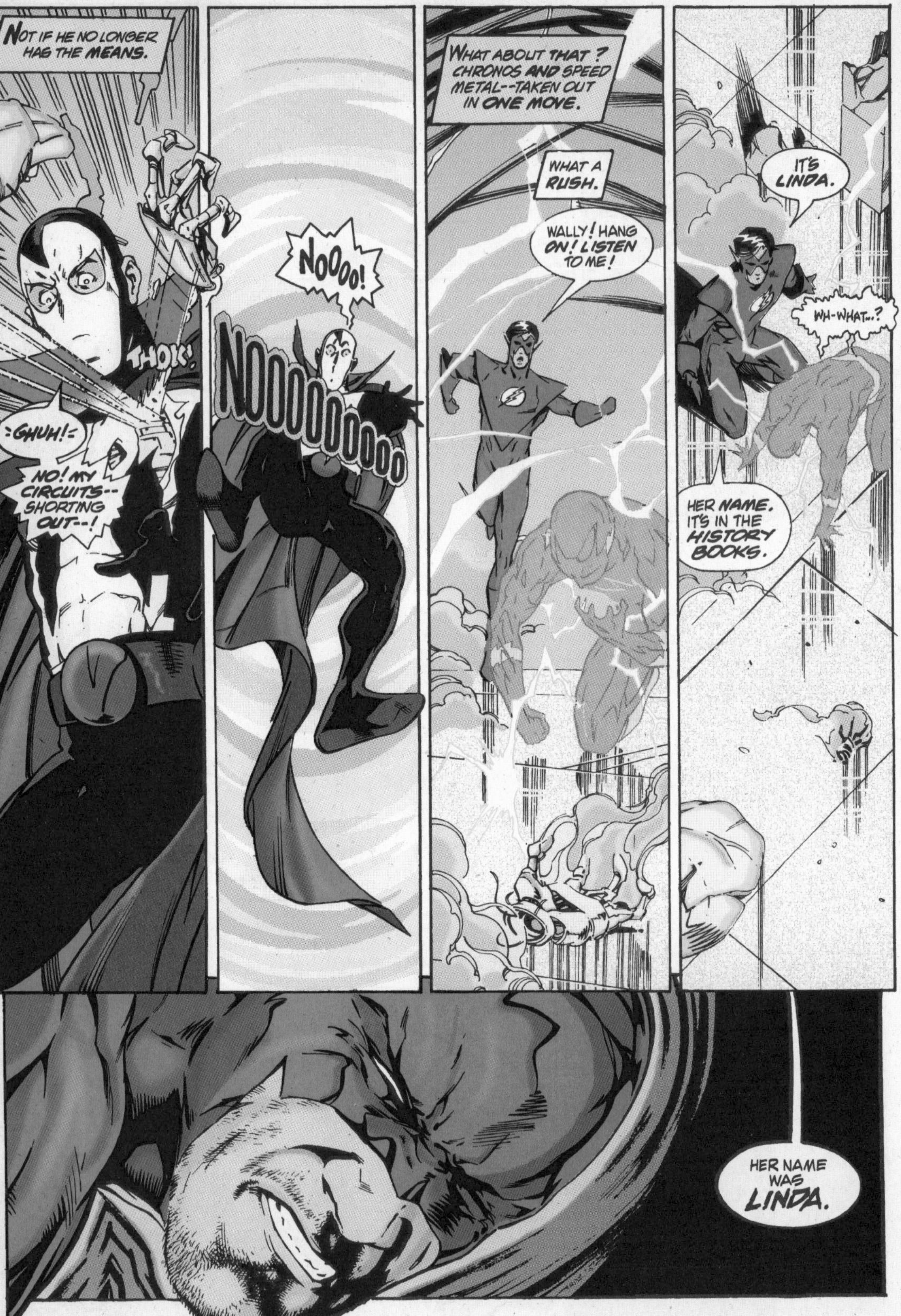
NOT IF HE NO LONGER HAS THE MEANS.
THOK!
:GHUH!:
NO! MY CIRCUITS--SHORTING OUT--!
NOOOO!
NOOOOOOOOOO
WHAT ABOUT THAT? CHRONOS AND SPEED METAL--TAKEN OUT IN ONE MOVE.
WHAT A RUSH.
WALLY! HANG ON! LISTEN TO ME!
IT'S LINDA.
WH-WHAT...?
HER NAME. IT'S IN THE HISTORY BOOKS.
HER NAME WAS LINDA.

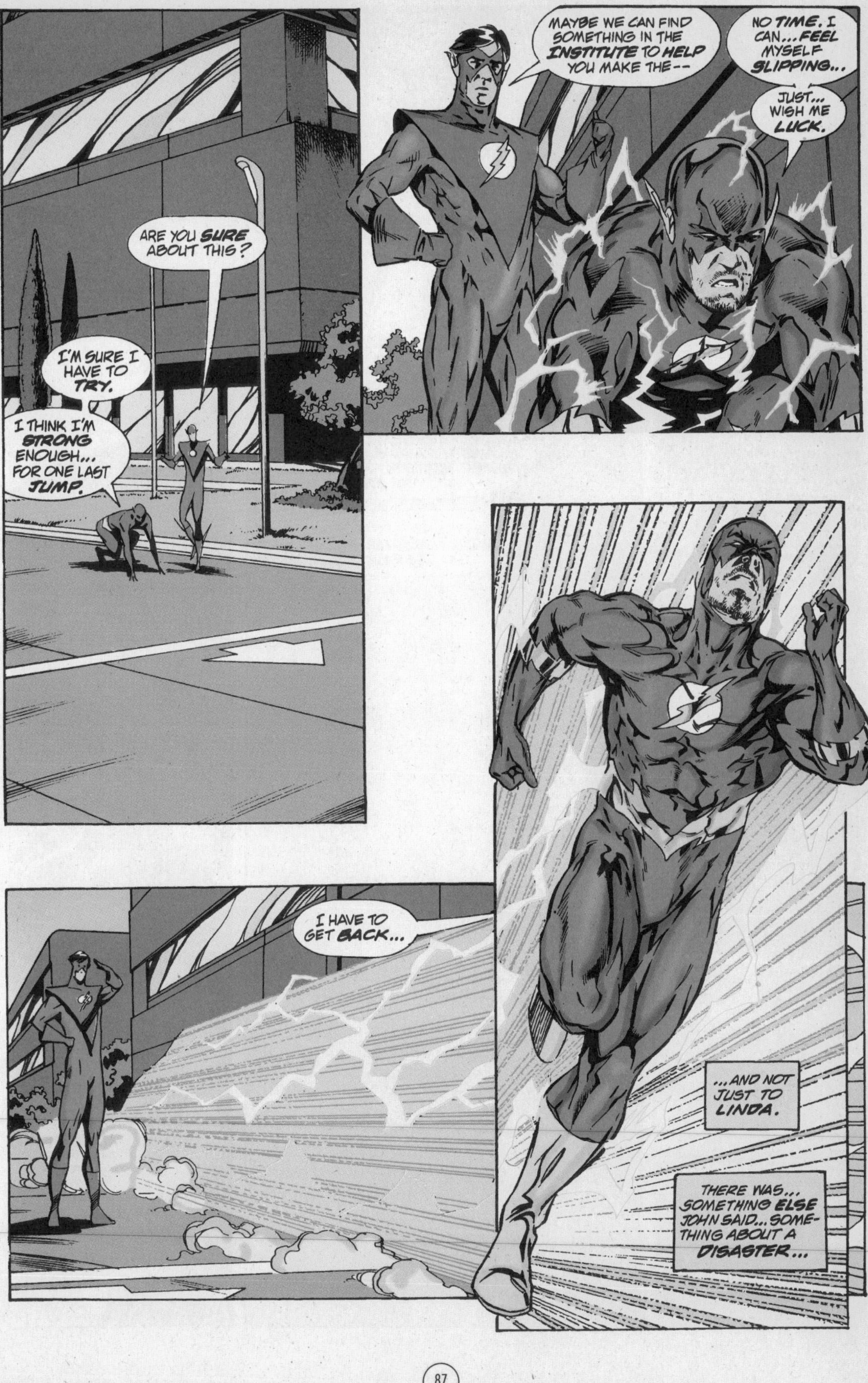
ARE YOU SURE ABOUT THIS?
I'M SURE I HAVE TO TRY.
I THINK I'M STRONG ENOUGH... FOR ONE LAST JUMP.
MAYBE WE CAN FIND SOMETHING IN THE INSTITUTE TO HELP YOU MAKE THE--
NO TIME. I CAN... FEEL MYSELF SLIPPING...
JUST... WISH ME LUCK.
I HAVE TO GET BACK...
...AND NOT JUST TO LINDA.
THERE WAS... SOMETHING ELSE JOHN SAID... SOMETHING ABOUT A DISASTER...

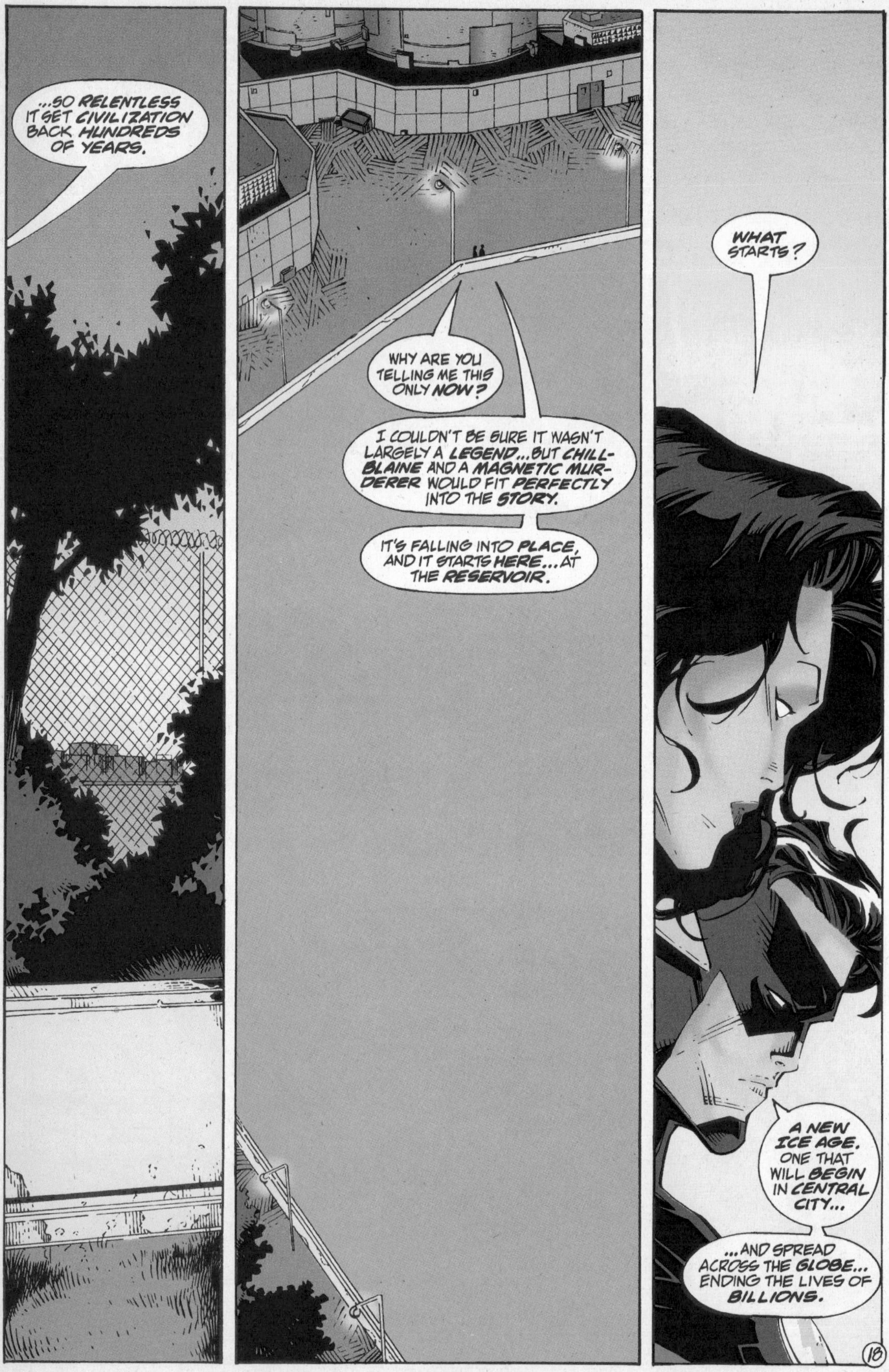
...SO RELENTLESS IT SET CIVILIZATION BACK HUNDREDS OF YEARS.
WHY ARE YOU TELLING ME THIS ONLY NOW?
I COULDN'T BE SURE IT WASN'T LARGELY A LEGEND...BUT CHILL-BLAINE AND A MAGNETIC MURDERER WOULD FIT PERFECTLY INTO THE STORY.
IT'S FALLING INTO PLACE, AND IT STARTS HERE...AT THE RESERVOIR.
WHAT STARTS?
A NEW ICE AGE. ONE THAT WILL BEGIN IN CENTRAL CITY...
...AND SPREAD ACROSS THE GLOBE... ENDING THE LIVES OF BILLIONS.
18

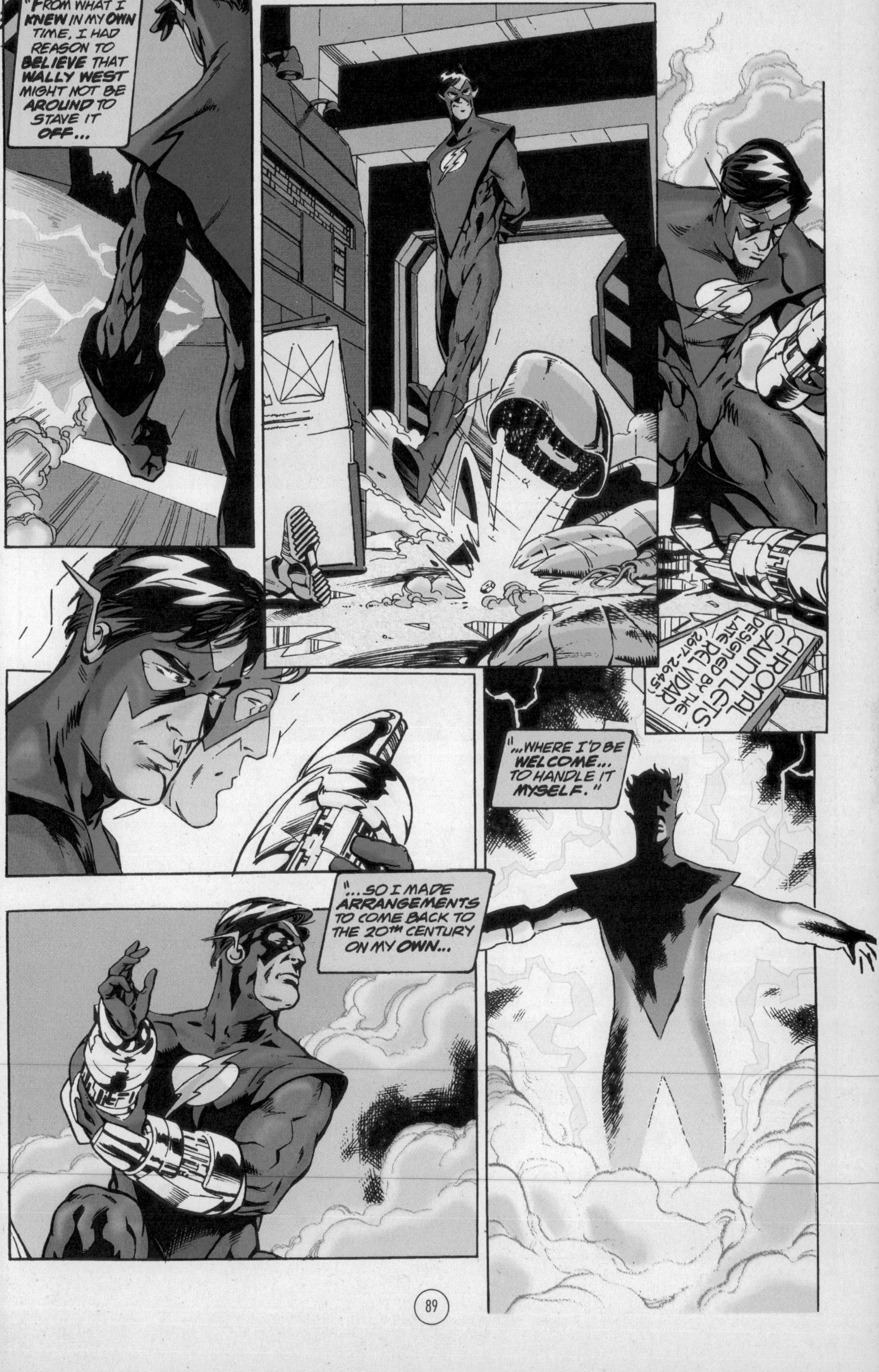

"FROM WHAT I KNEW IN MY OWN TIME, I HAD REASON TO BELIEVE THAT WALLY WEST MIGHT NOT BE AROUND TO STAVE IT OFF...
CHRONAL GAUNTLETS DESIGNED BY THE LATE RELVIDAR (2617-2645)
"...SO I MADE ARRANGEMENTS TO COME BACK TO THE 20TH CENTURY ON MY OWN...
"...WHERE I'D BE WELCOME... TO HANDLE IT MYSELF."

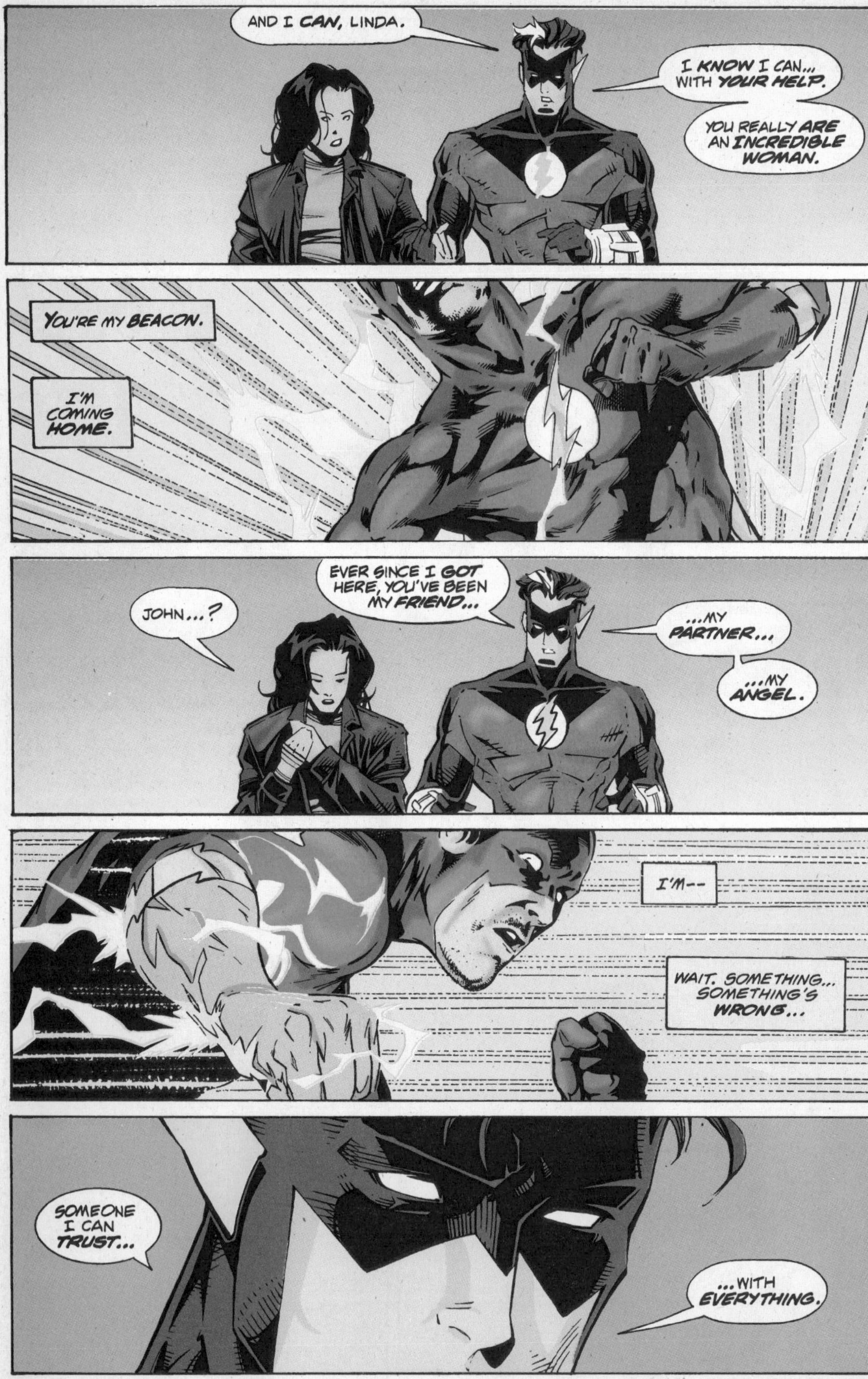
AND I CAN, LINDA.
I KNOW I CAN... WITH YOUR HELP.
YOU REALLY ARE AN INCREDIBLE WOMAN.
YOU'RE MY BEACON.
I'M COMING HOME.
JOHN...?
EVER SINCE I GOT HERE, YOU'VE BEEN MY FRIEND...
...MY PARTNER...
...MY ANGEL.
I'M--
WAIT. SOMETHING... SOMETHING'S WRONG...
SOMEONE I CAN TRUST...
...WITH EVERYTHING.

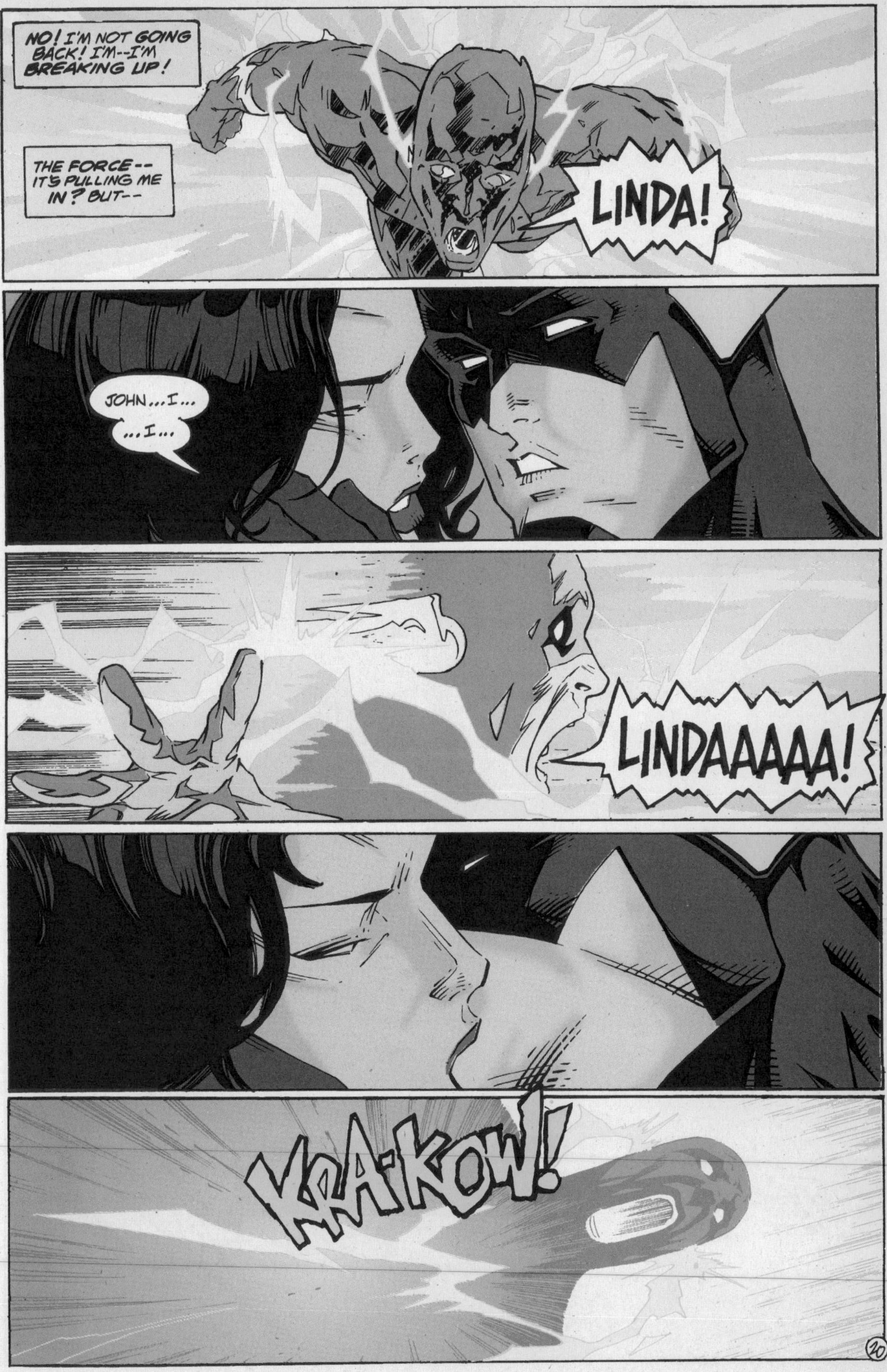
NO! I'M NOT GOING BACK! I'M--I'M BREAKING UP!
THE FORCE-- IT'S PULLING ME IN? BUT--
LINDA!
JOHN...I... ...I...
LINDAAAAA!
KRA-KOW!
20

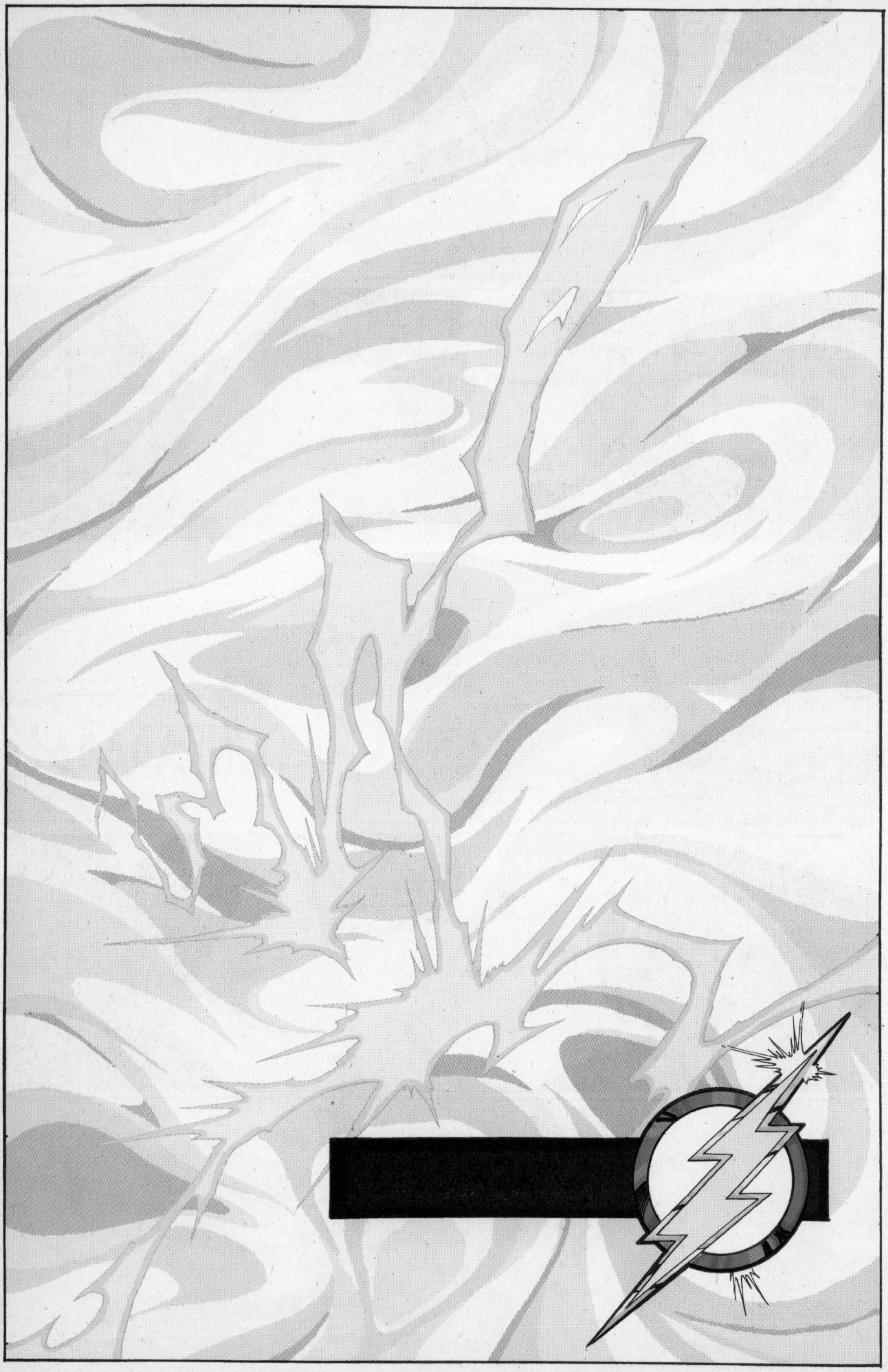

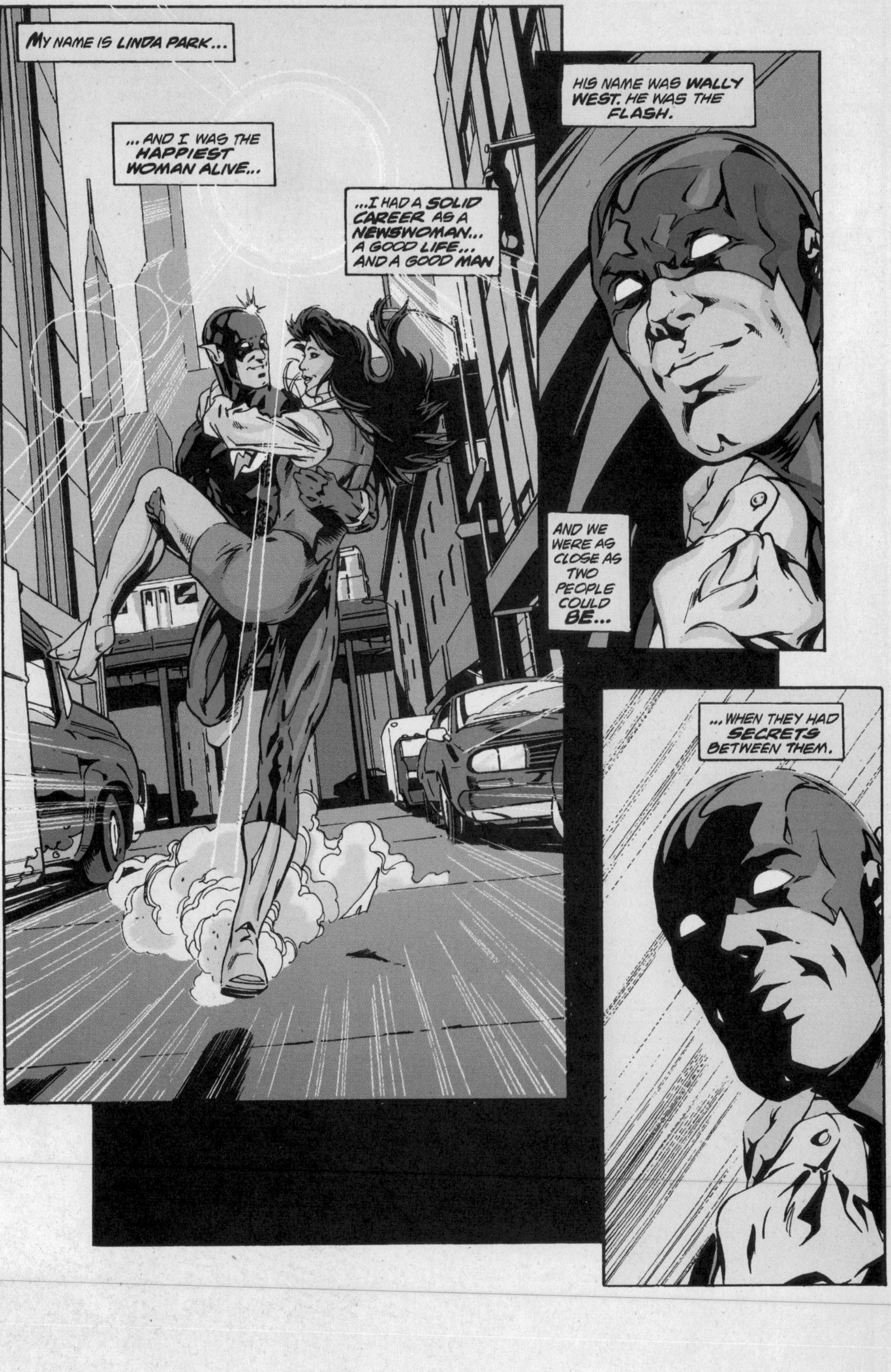

MY NAME IS LINDA PARK...
...AND I WAS THE HAPPIEST WOMAN ALIVE...
...I HAD A SOLID CAREER AS A NEWSWOMAN... A GOOD LIFE... AND A GOOD MAN
HIS NAME WAS WALLY WEST. HE WAS THE FLASH.
AND WE WERE AS CLOSE AS TWO PEOPLE COULD BE...
...WHEN THEY HAD SECRETS BETWEEN THEM.

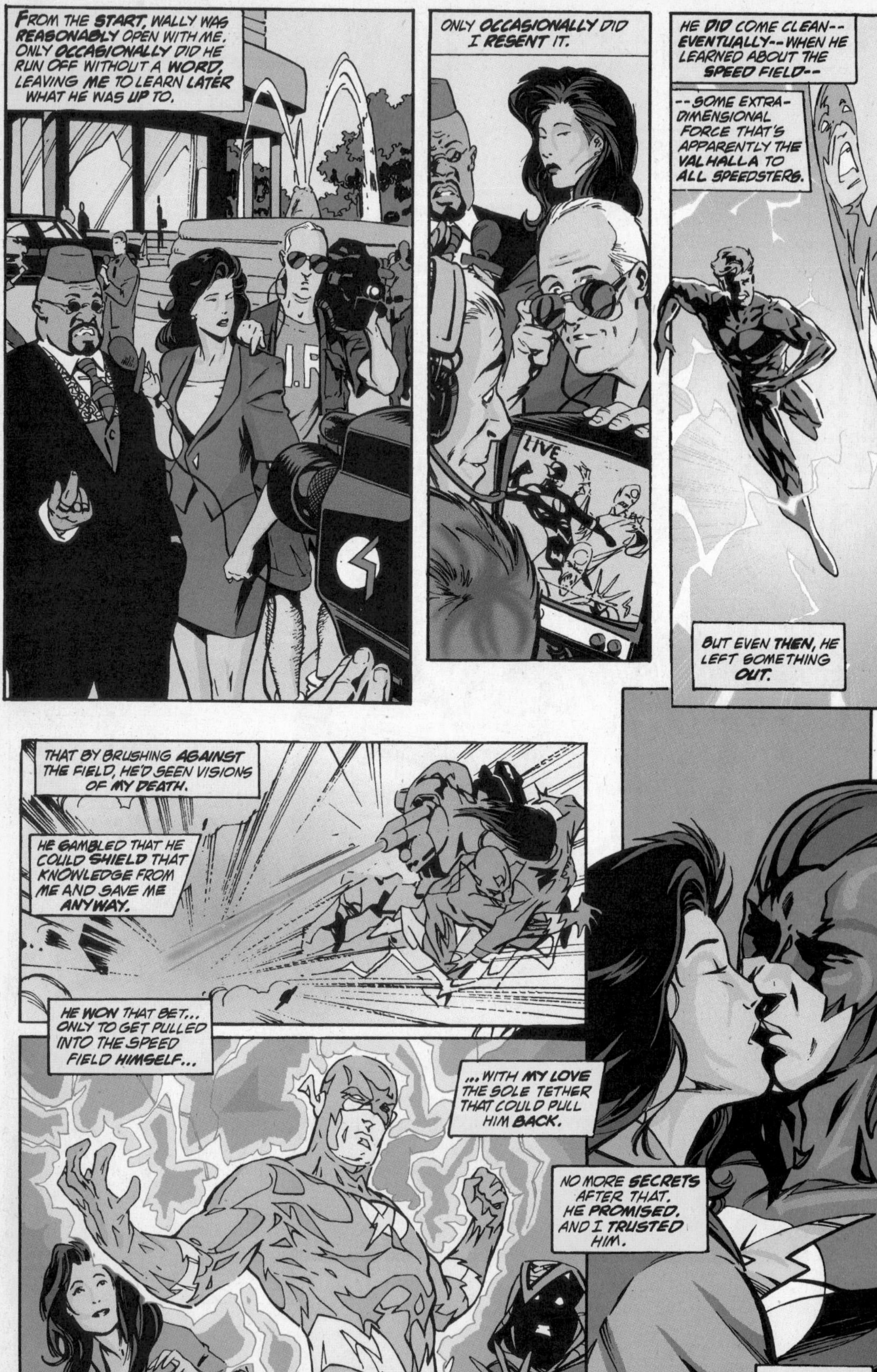
FROM THE START, WALLY WAS REASONABLY OPEN WITH ME. ONLY OCCASIONALLY DID HE RUN OFF WITHOUT A WORD, LEAVING ME TO LEARN LATER WHAT HE WAS UP TO.
ONLY OCCASIONALLY DID I RESENT IT.
LIVE
HE DID COME CLEAN-- EVENTUALLY-- WHEN HE LEARNED ABOUT THE SPEED FIELD--
--SOME EXTRA-DIMENSIONAL FORCE THAT'S APPARENTLY THE VALHALLA TO ALL SPEEDSTERS.
BUT EVEN THEN, HE LEFT SOMETHING OUT.
THAT BY BRUSHING AGAINST THE FIELD, HE'D SEEN VISIONS OF MY DEATH.
HE GAMBLED THAT HE COULD SHIELD THAT KNOWLEDGE FROM ME AND SAVE ME ANYWAY.
HE WON THAT BET... ONLY TO GET PULLED INTO THE SPEED FIELD HIMSELF...
...WITH MY LOVE THE SOLE TETHER THAT COULD PULL HIM BACK.
NO MORE SECRETS AFTER THAT. HE PROMISED. AND I TRUSTED HIM.
I THOUGHT.
2

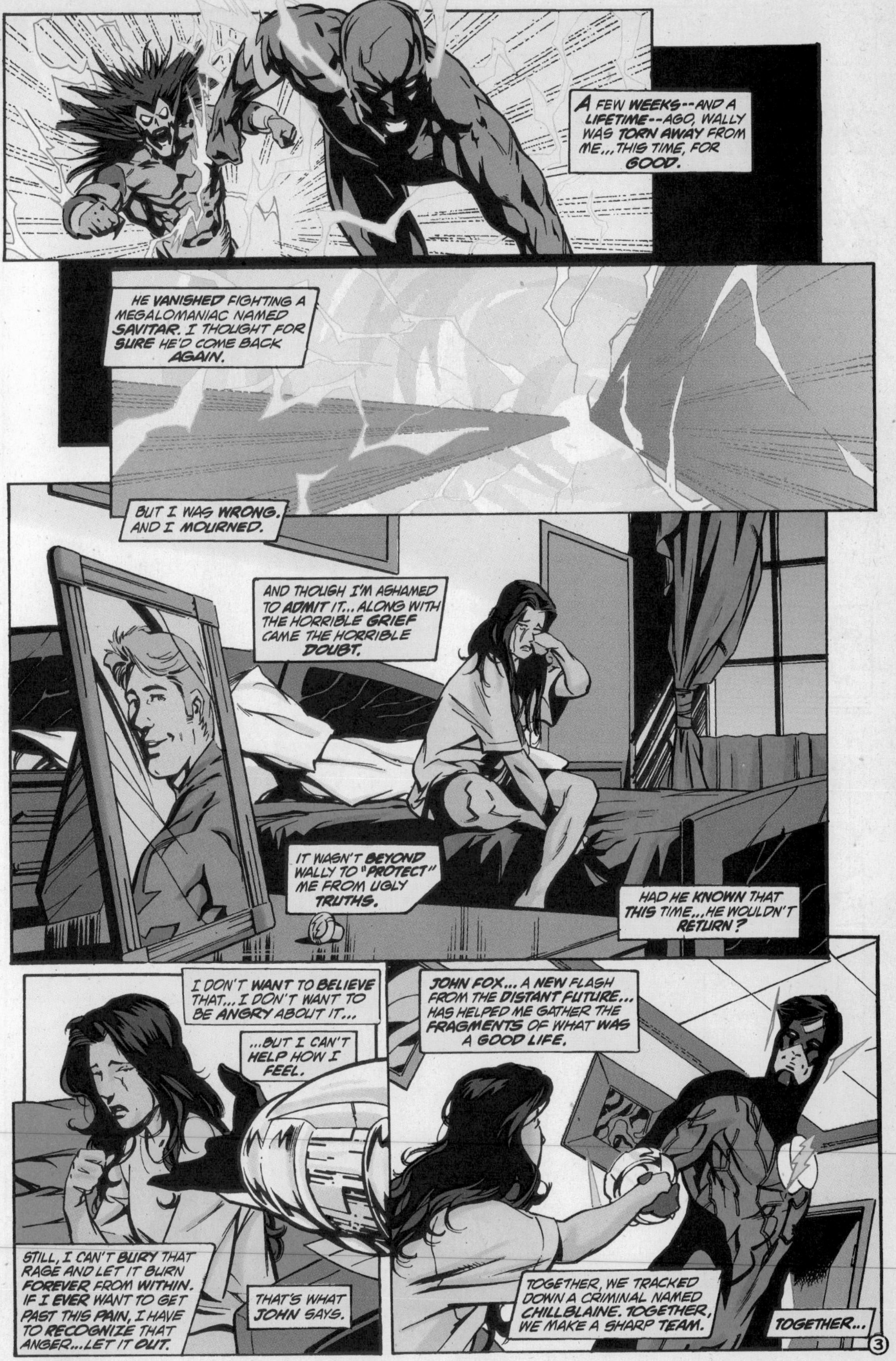
A FEW WEEKS--AND A LIFETIME--AGO, WALLY WAS TORN AWAY FROM ME... THIS TIME, FOR GOOD.
HE VANISHED FIGHTING A MEGALOMANIAC NAMED SAVITAR. I THOUGHT FOR SURE HE'D COME BACK AGAIN.
BUT I WAS WRONG. AND I MOURNED.
AND THOUGH I'M ASHAMED TO ADMIT IT... ALONG WITH THE HORRIBLE GRIEF CAME THE HORRIBLE DOUBT.
IT WASN'T BEYOND WALLY TO "PROTECT" ME FROM UGLY TRUTHS.
HAD HE KNOWN THAT THIS TIME... HE WOULDN'T RETURN?
I DON'T WANT TO BELIEVE THAT... I DON'T WANT TO BE ANGRY ABOUT IT...
...BUT I CAN'T HELP HOW I FEEL.
STILL, I CAN'T BURY THAT RAGE AND LET IT BURN FOREVER FROM WITHIN. IF I EVER WANT TO GET PAST THIS PAIN, I HAVE TO RECOGNIZE THAT ANGER... LET IT OUT.
THAT'S WHAT JOHN SAYS.
JOHN FOX... A NEW FLASH FROM THE DISTANT FUTURE... HAS HELPED ME GATHER THE FRAGMENTS OF WHAT WAS A GOOD LIFE.
TOGETHER, WE TRACKED DOWN A CRIMINAL NAMED CHILLBLAINE. TOGETHER, WE MAKE A SHARP TEAM.
TOGETHER...
3

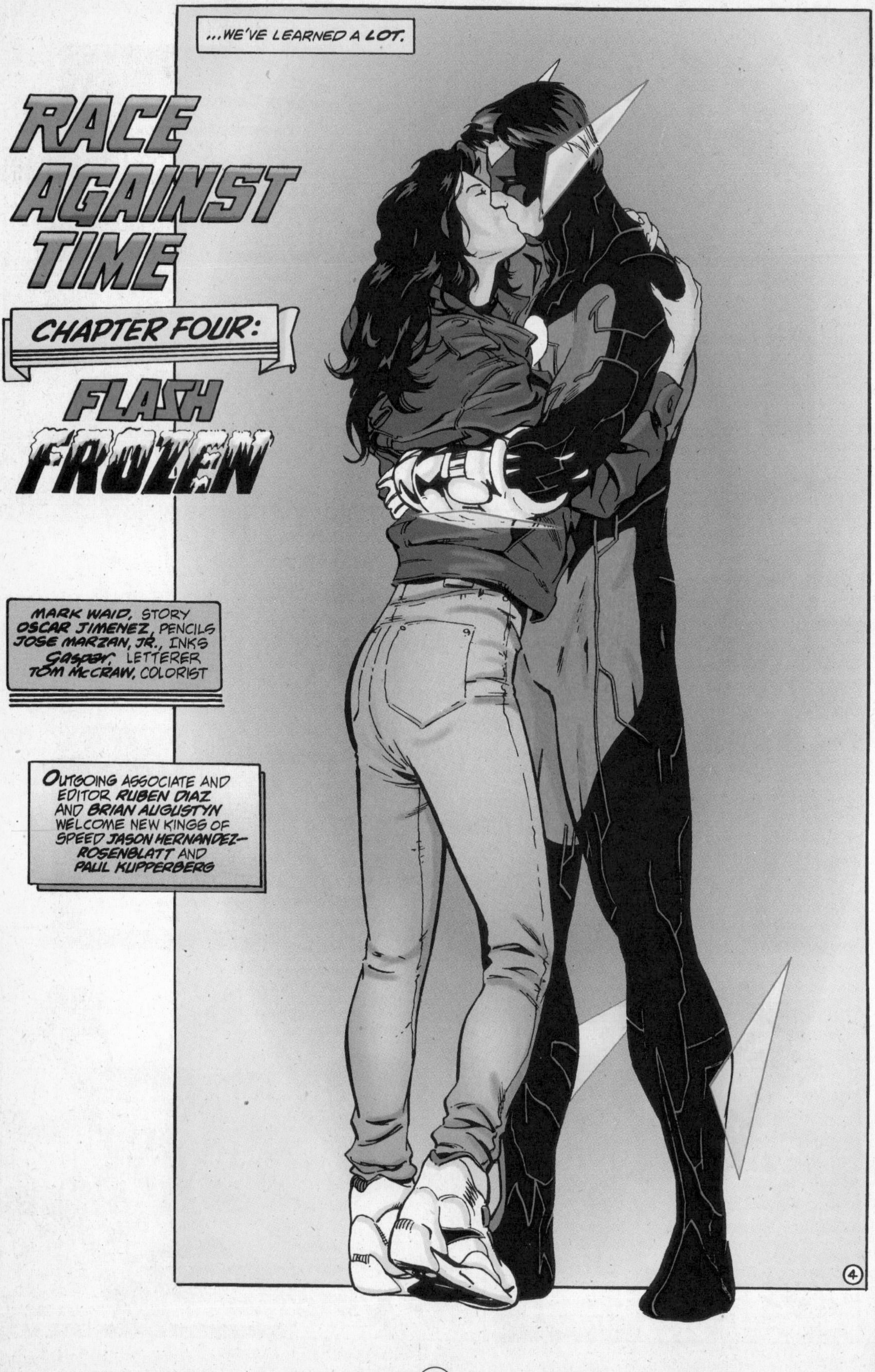
...WE'VE LEARNED A LOT.
RACE AGAINST TIME
CHAPTER FOUR:
FLASH FROZEN
MARK WAID, STORY
OSCAR JIMENEZ, PENCILS
JOSE MARZAN, JR., INKS
Gaspar, LETTERER
TOM McCRAW, COLORIST
OUTGOING ASSOCIATE AND EDITOR RUBEN DIAZ AND BRIAN AUGUSTYN WELCOME NEW KINGS OF SPEED JASON HERNANDEZ-ROSENBLATT AND PAUL KUPPERBERG
4

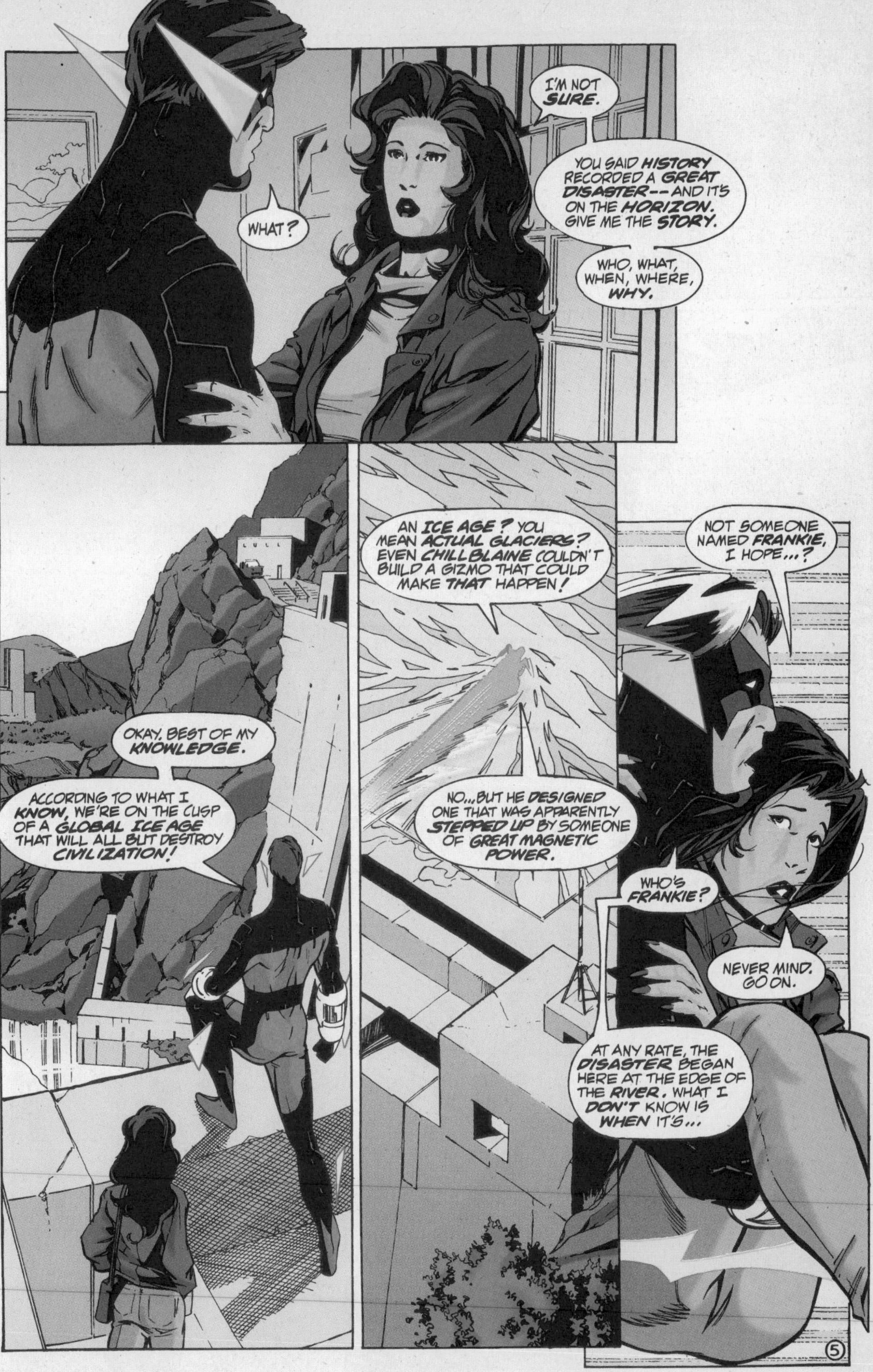

I'M NOT SURE.
WHAT?
YOU SAID HISTORY RECORDED A GREAT DISASTER-- AND IT'S ON THE HORIZON. GIVE ME THE STORY.
WHO, WHAT, WHEN, WHERE, WHY.
OKAY. BEST OF MY KNOWLEDGE.
ACCORDING TO WHAT I KNOW, WE'RE ON THE CUSP OF A GLOBAL ICE AGE THAT WILL ALL BUT DESTROY CIVILIZATION!
AN ICE AGE? YOU MEAN ACTUAL GLACIERS? EVEN CHILLBLAINE COULDN'T BUILD A GIZMO THAT COULD MAKE THAT HAPPEN!
NO...BUT HE DESIGNED ONE THAT WAS APPARENTLY STEPPED UP BY SOMEONE OF GREAT MAGNETIC POWER.
NOT SOMEONE NAMED FRANKIE, I HOPE...?
WHO'S FRANKIE?
NEVER MIND. GO ON.
AT ANY RATE, THE DISASTER BEGAN HERE AT THE EDGE OF THE RIVER. WHAT I DON'T KNOW IS WHEN IT'S...
5

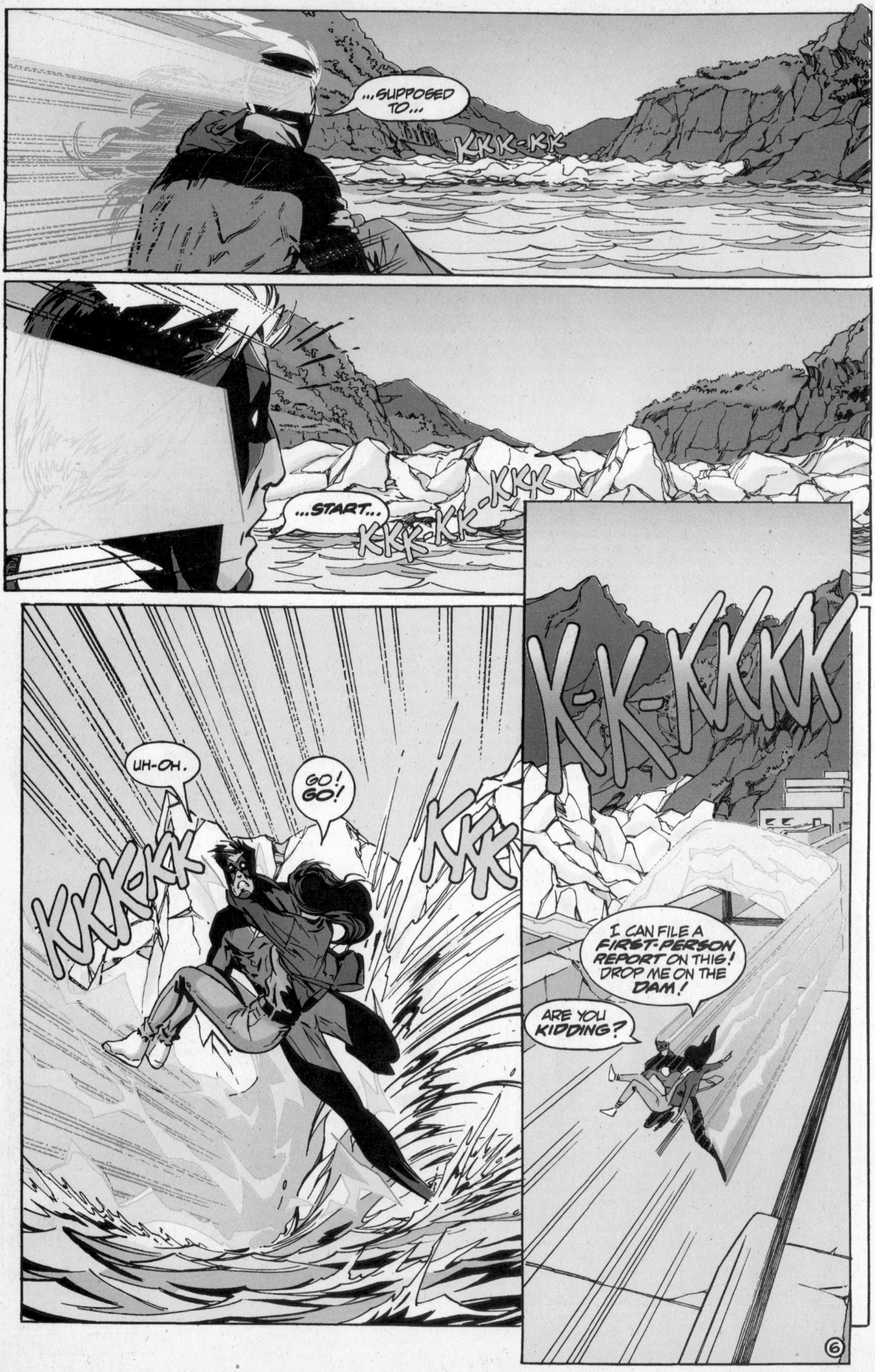
...SUPPOSED TO...
KKK-KK
...START...
KKK-KK-KKK
UH-OH.
GO! GO!
KKK-KK
KKK
K-K-KKKK
I CAN FILE A FIRST-PERSON REPORT ON THIS! DROP ME ON THE DAM!
ARE YOU KIDDING?
6

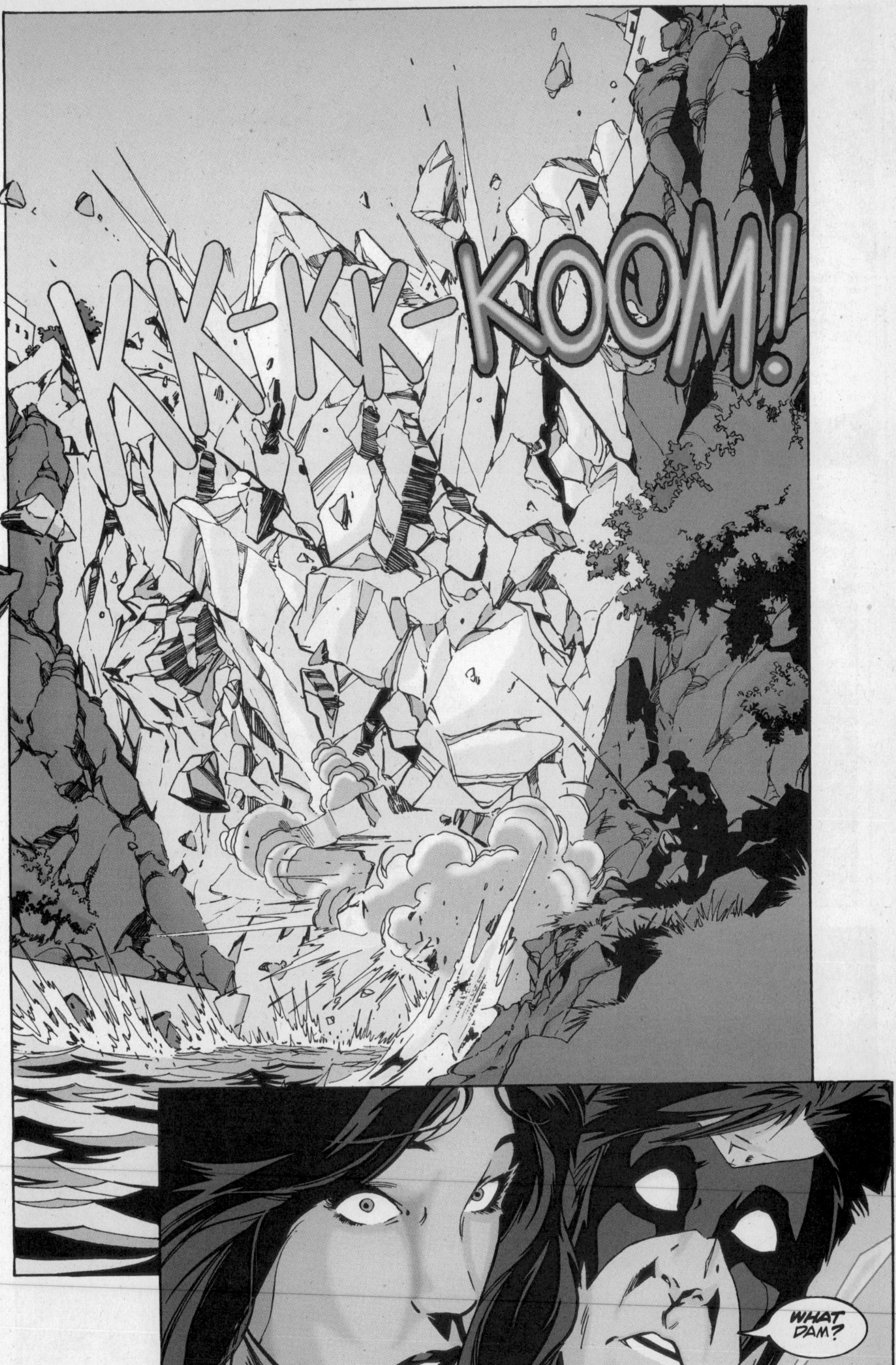
KK-KK-KOOM!
WHAT DAM?
7

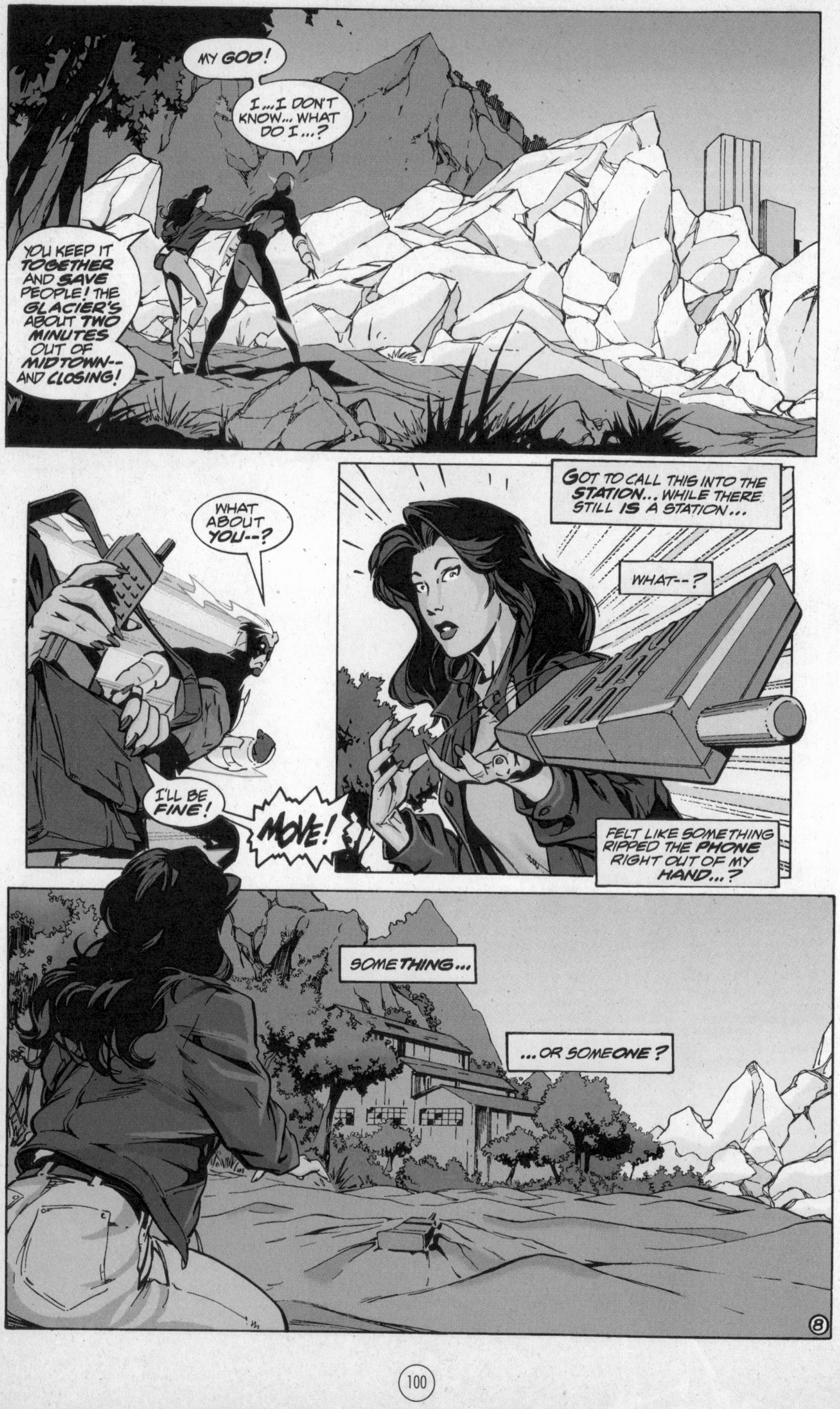
MY GOD!
I...I DON'T KNOW... WHAT DO I...?
YOU KEEP IT TOGETHER AND SAVE PEOPLE! THE GLACIER'S ABOUT TWO MINUTES OUT OF MIDTOWN-- AND CLOSING!
WHAT ABOUT YOU--?
I'LL BE FINE!
MOVE!
GOT TO CALL THIS INTO THE STATION... WHILE THERE STILL IS A STATION...
WHAT--?
FELT LIKE SOMETHING RIPPED THE PHONE RIGHT OUT OF MY HAND...?
SOMETHING...
...OR SOMEONE?
8

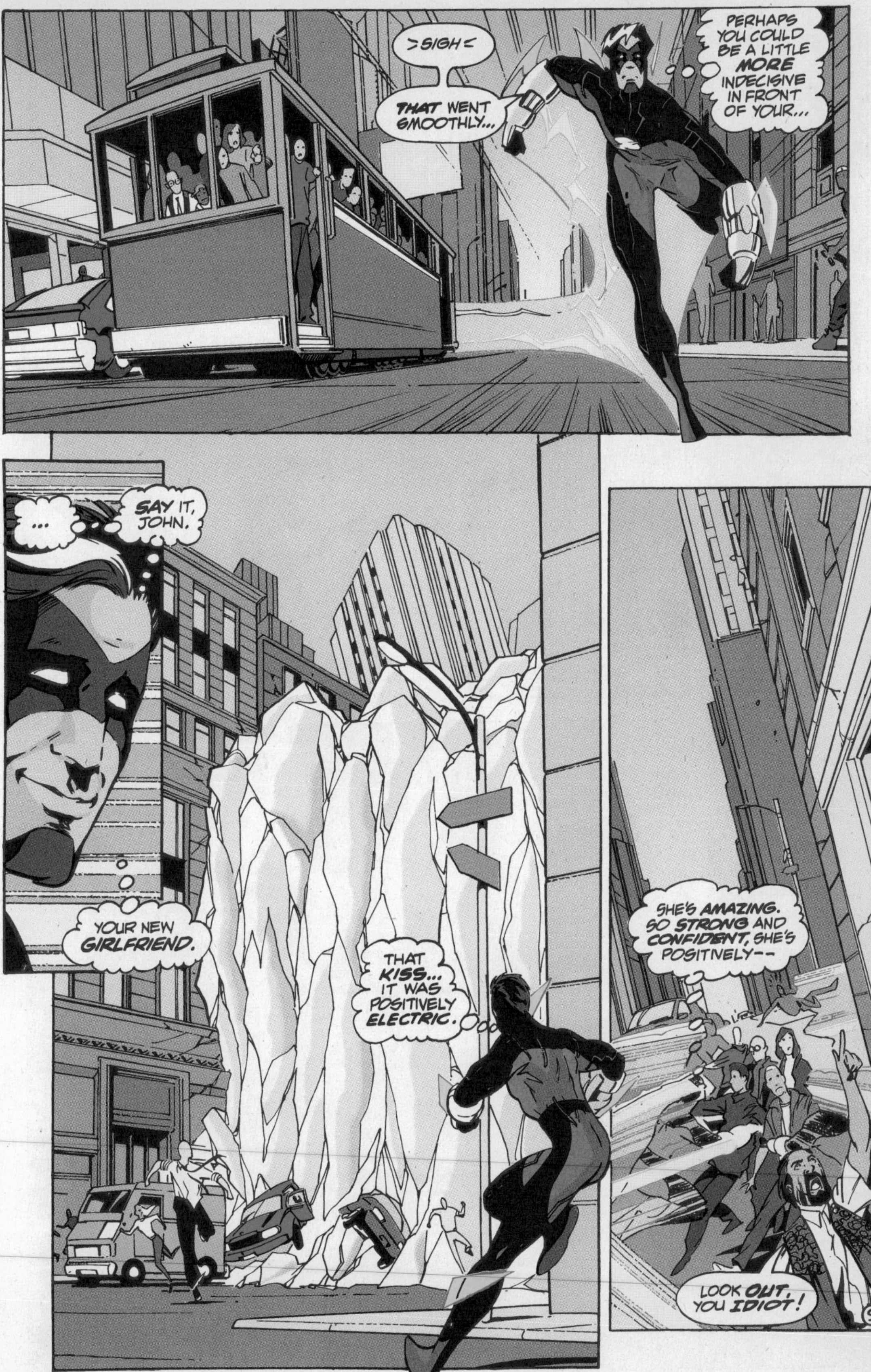
>SIGH<
THAT WENT SMOOTHLY...
PERHAPS YOU COULD BE A LITTLE MORE INDECISIVE IN FRONT OF YOUR...
...
SAY IT, JOHN.
YOUR NEW GIRLFRIEND.
THAT KISS... IT WAS POSITIVELY ELECTRIC.
SHE'S AMAZING. SO STRONG AND CONFIDENT, SHE'S POSITIVELY--
LOOK OUT, YOU IDIOT!
9

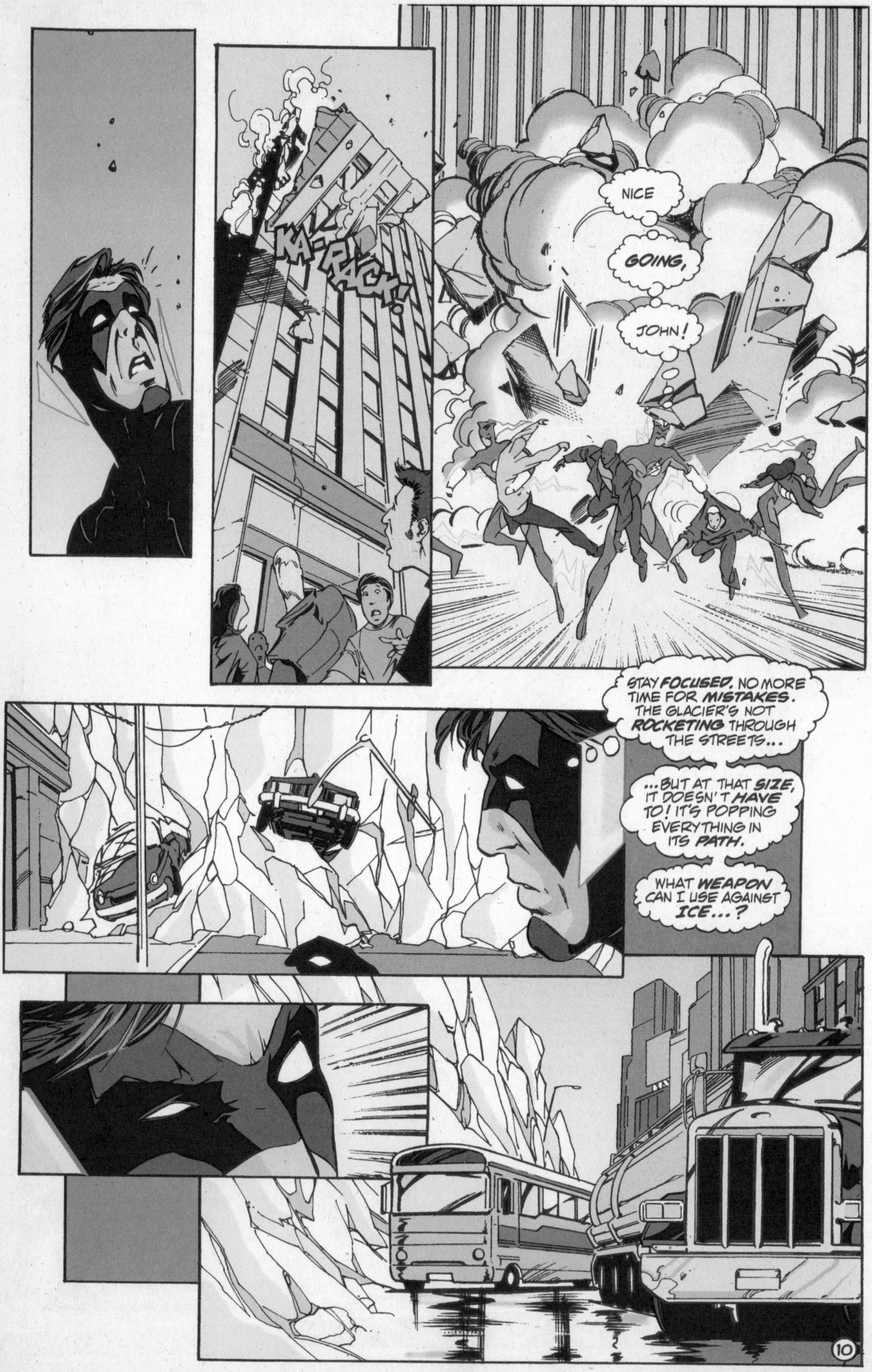
KA-RACK!
NICE
GOING,
JOHN!
STAY FOCUSED. NO MORE TIME FOR MISTAKES. THE GLACIER'S NOT ROCKETING THROUGH THE STREETS...
...BUT AT THAT SIZE, IT DOESN'T HAVE TO! IT'S POPPING EVERYTHING IN ITS PATH.
WHAT WEAPON CAN I USE AGAINST ICE...?
10

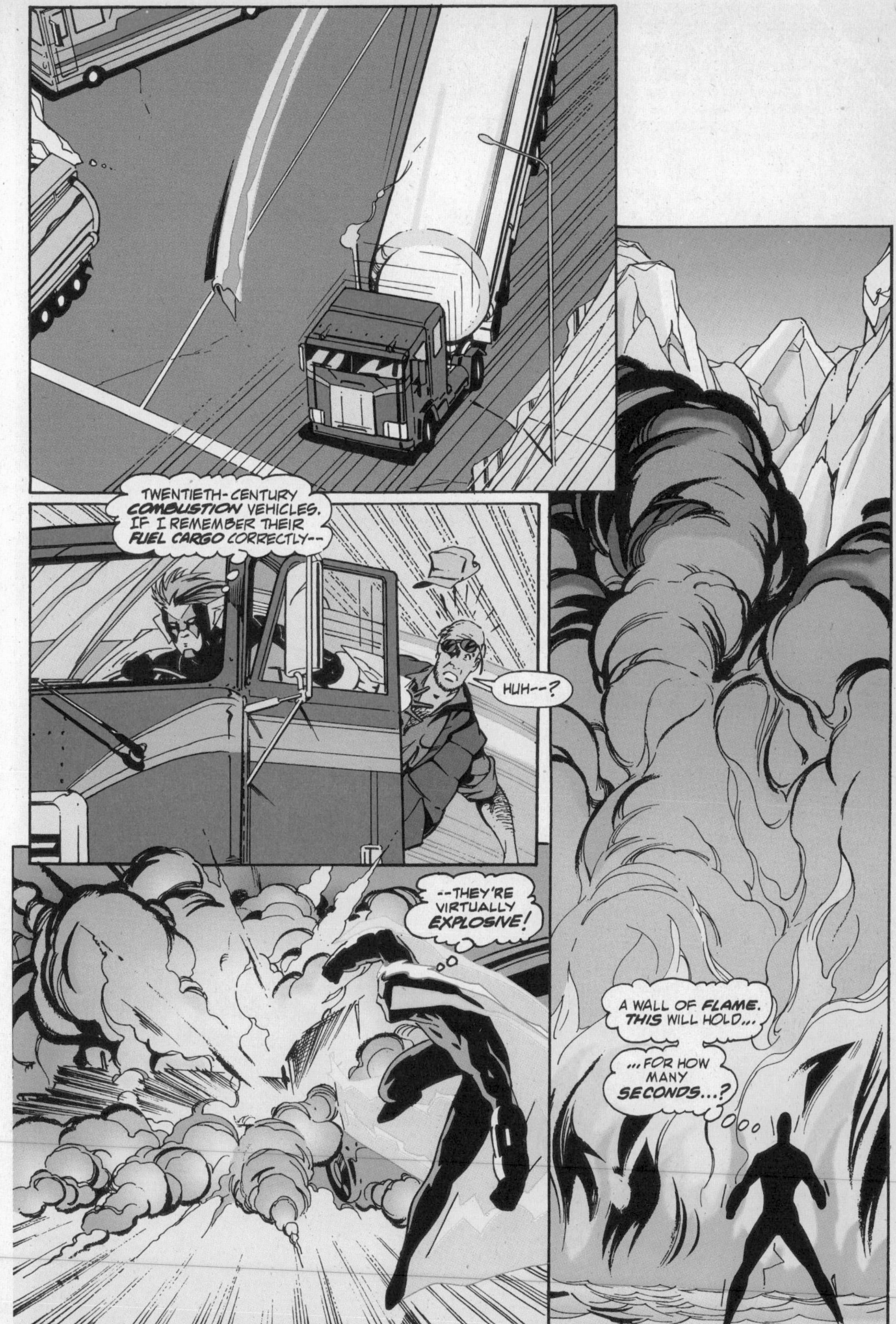
TWENTIETH-CENTURY COMBUSTION VEHICLES. IF I REMEMBER THEIR FUEL CARGO CORRECTLY--
HUH--?
--THEY'RE VIRTUALLY EXPLOSIVE!
A WALL OF FLAME. THIS WILL HOLD...
...FOR HOW MANY SECONDS...?
11

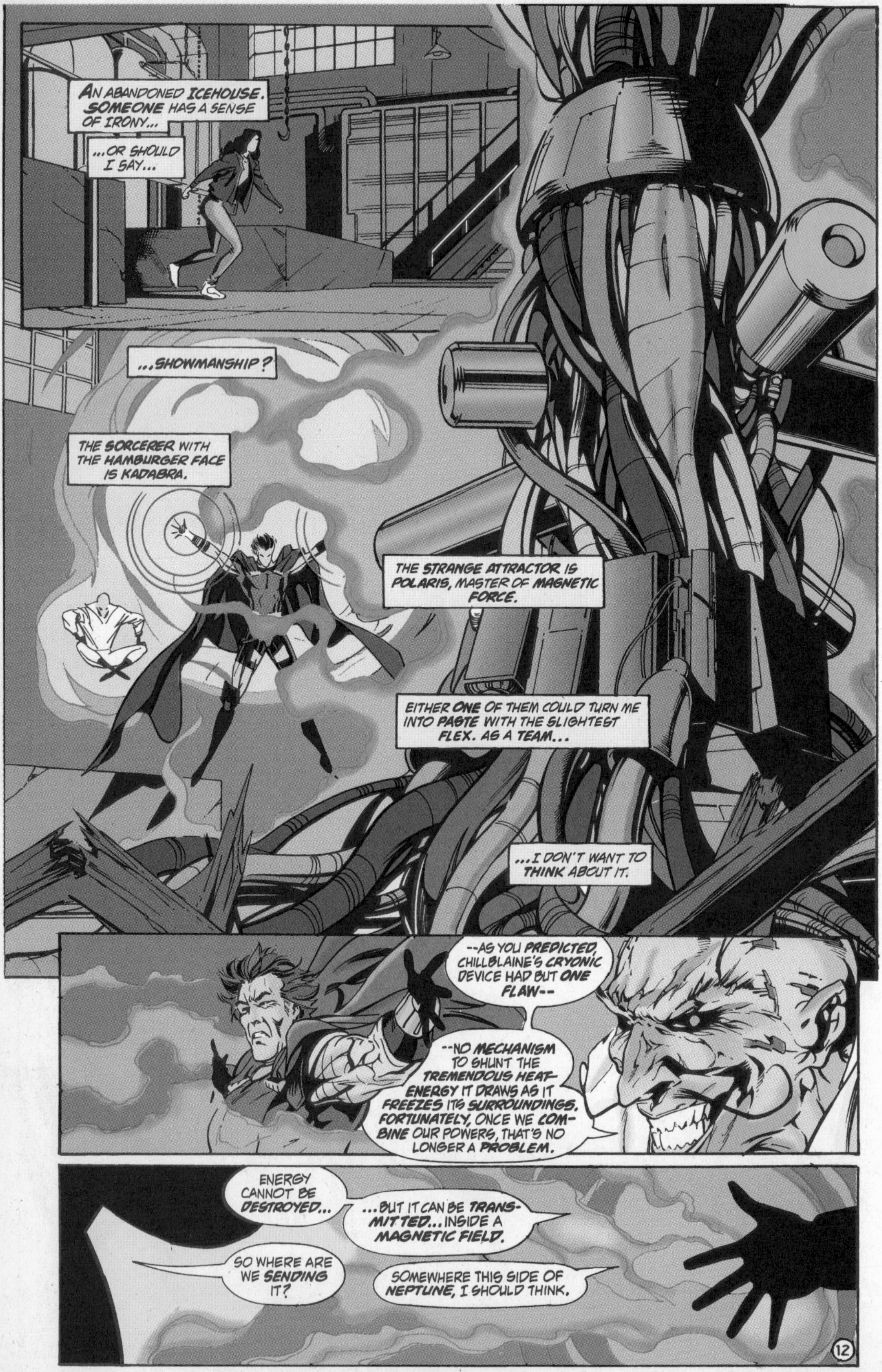
AN ABANDONED ICEHOUSE. SOMEONE HAS A SENSE OF IRONY...
...OR SHOULD I SAY...
...SHOWMANSHIP?
THE SORCERER WITH THE HAMBURGER FACE IS KADABRA.
THE STRANGE ATTRACTOR IS POLARIS, MASTER OF MAGNETIC FORCE.
EITHER ONE OF THEM COULD TURN ME INTO PASTE WITH THE SLIGHTEST FLEX. AS A TEAM...
...I DON'T WANT TO THINK ABOUT IT.
--AS YOU PREDICTED, CHILLBLAINE'S CRYONIC DEVICE HAD BUT ONE FLAW--
--NO MECHANISM TO SHUNT THE TREMENDOUS HEAT-ENERGY IT DRAWS AS IT FREEZES ITS SURROUNDINGS. FORTUNATELY, ONCE WE COMBINE OUR POWERS, THAT'S NO LONGER A PROBLEM.
ENERGY CANNOT BE DESTROYED...
...BUT IT CAN BE TRANSMITTED... INSIDE A MAGNETIC FIELD.
SO WHERE ARE WE SENDING IT?
SOMEWHERE THIS SIDE OF NEPTUNE, I SHOULD THINK.
12

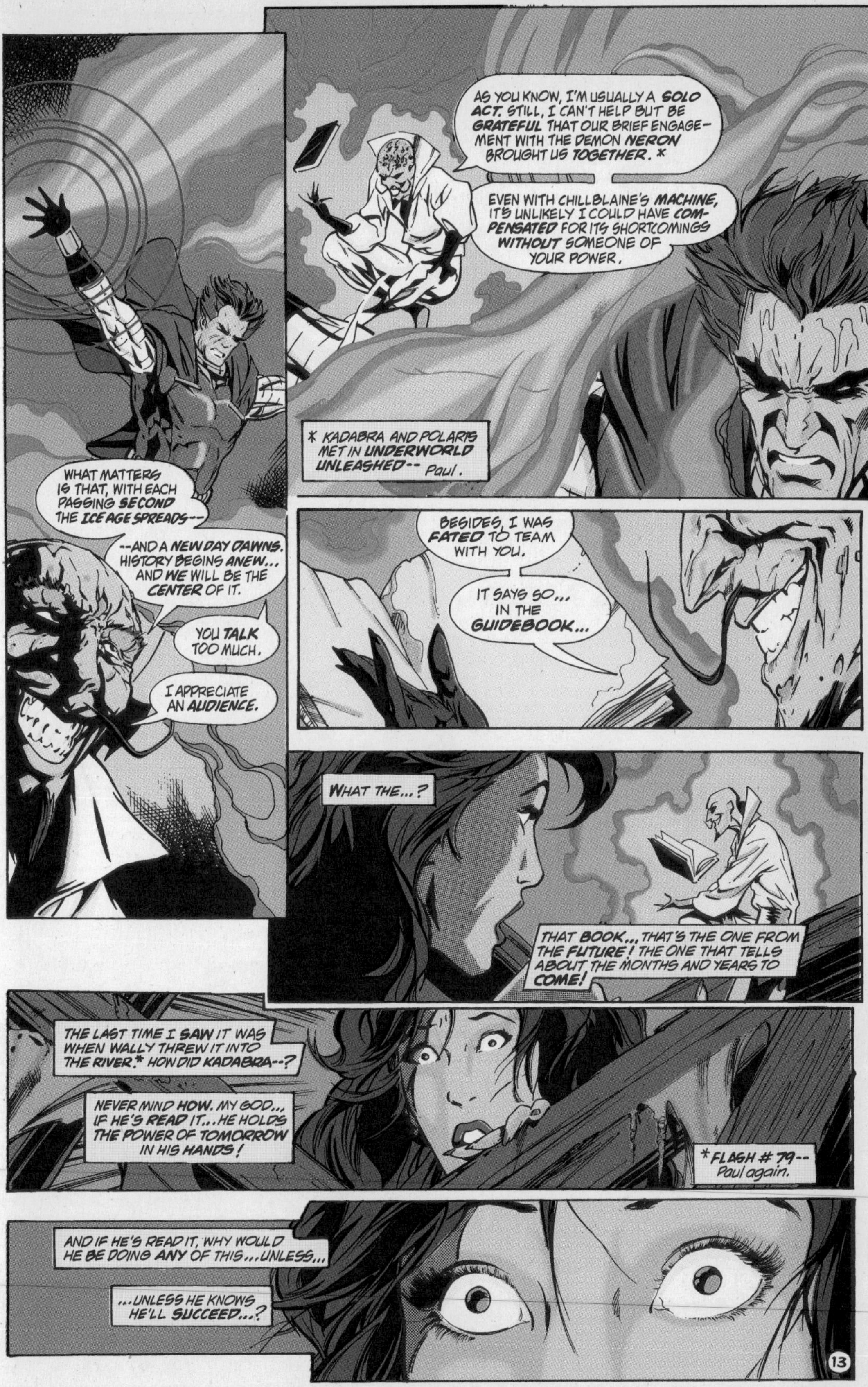
AS YOU KNOW, I'M USUALLY A SOLO ACT. STILL, I CAN'T HELP BUT BE GRATEFUL THAT OUR BRIEF ENGAGEMENT WITH THE DEMON NERON BROUGHT US TOGETHER.*
EVEN WITH CHILLBLAINE'S MACHINE, IT'S UNLIKELY I COULD HAVE COMPENSATED FOR ITS SHORTCOMINGS WITHOUT SOMEONE OF YOUR POWER.
* KADABRA AND POLARIS MET IN UNDERWORLD UNLEASHED-- Paul.
WHAT MATTERS IS THAT, WITH EACH PASSING SECOND THE ICE AGE SPREADS--
--AND A NEW DAY DAWNS. HISTORY BEGINS ANEW... AND WE WILL BE THE CENTER OF IT.
YOU TALK TOO MUCH.
I APPRECIATE AN AUDIENCE.
BESIDES, I WAS FATED TO TEAM WITH YOU.
IT SAYS SO... IN THE GUIDEBOOK...
WHAT THE...?
THAT BOOK... THAT'S THE ONE FROM THE FUTURE! THE ONE THAT TELLS ABOUT THE MONTHS AND YEARS TO COME!
THE LAST TIME I SAW IT WAS WHEN WALLY THREW IT INTO THE RIVER.* HOW DID KADABRA--?
NEVER MIND HOW. MY GOD... IF HE'S READ IT... HE HOLDS THE POWER OF TOMORROW IN HIS HANDS!
*FLASH #79-- Paul again.
AND IF HE'S READ IT, WHY WOULD HE BE DOING ANY OF THIS... UNLESS...
...UNLESS HE KNOWS HE'LL SUCCEED...?
13

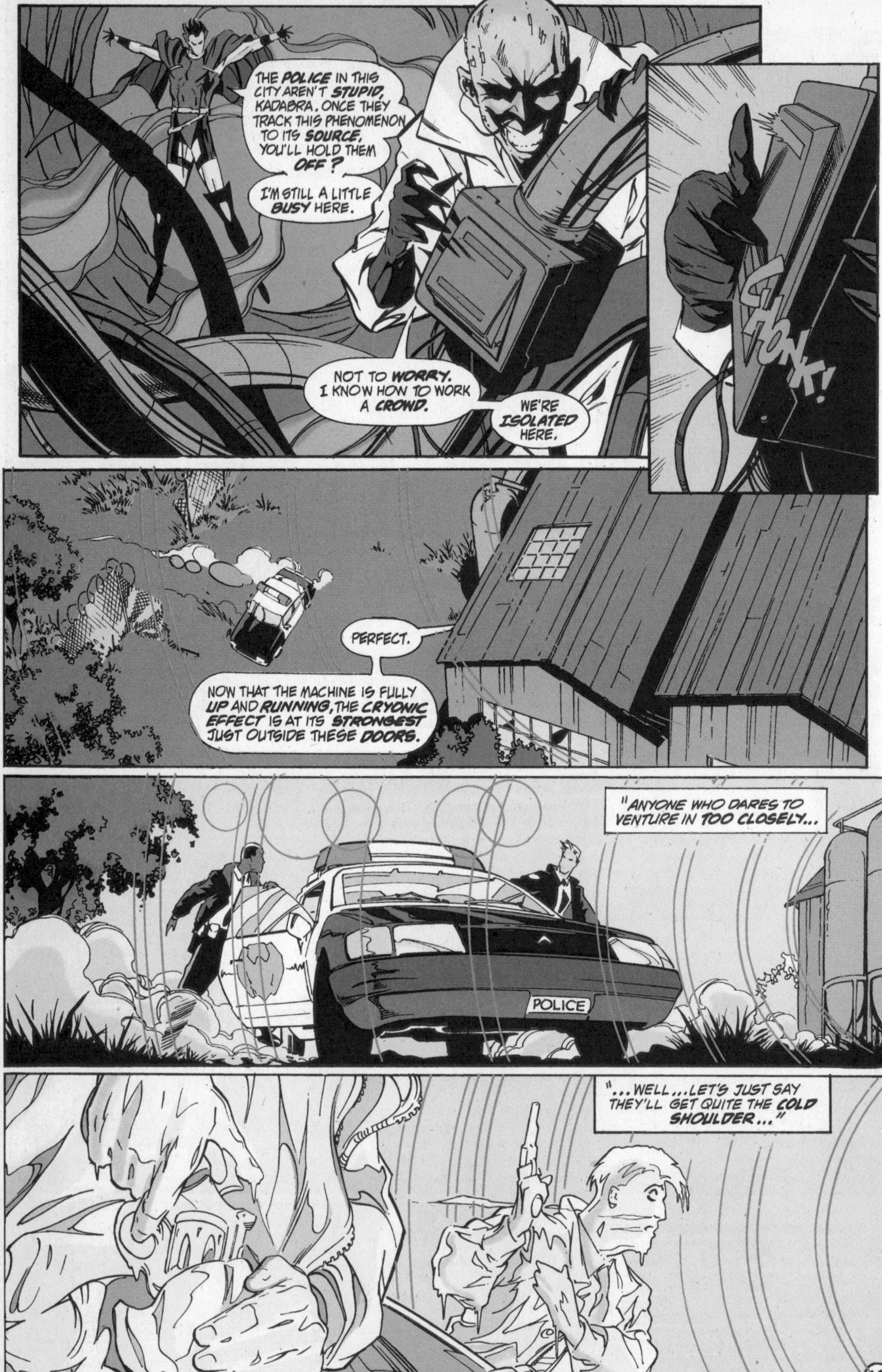
THE POLICE IN THIS CITY AREN'T STUPID, KADABRA. ONCE THEY TRACK THIS PHENOMENON TO ITS SOURCE, YOU'LL HOLD THEM OFF?
I'M STILL A LITTLE BUSY HERE.
NOT TO WORRY. I KNOW HOW TO WORK A CROWD.
WE'RE ISOLATED HERE.
CHONK!
PERFECT.
NOW THAT THE MACHINE IS FULLY UP AND RUNNING, THE CRYONIC EFFECT IS AT ITS STRONGEST JUST OUTSIDE THESE DOORS.
"ANYONE WHO DARES TO VENTURE IN TOO CLOSELY...
POLICE
"...WELL...LET'S JUST SAY THEY'LL GET QUITE THE COLD SHOULDER..."
14

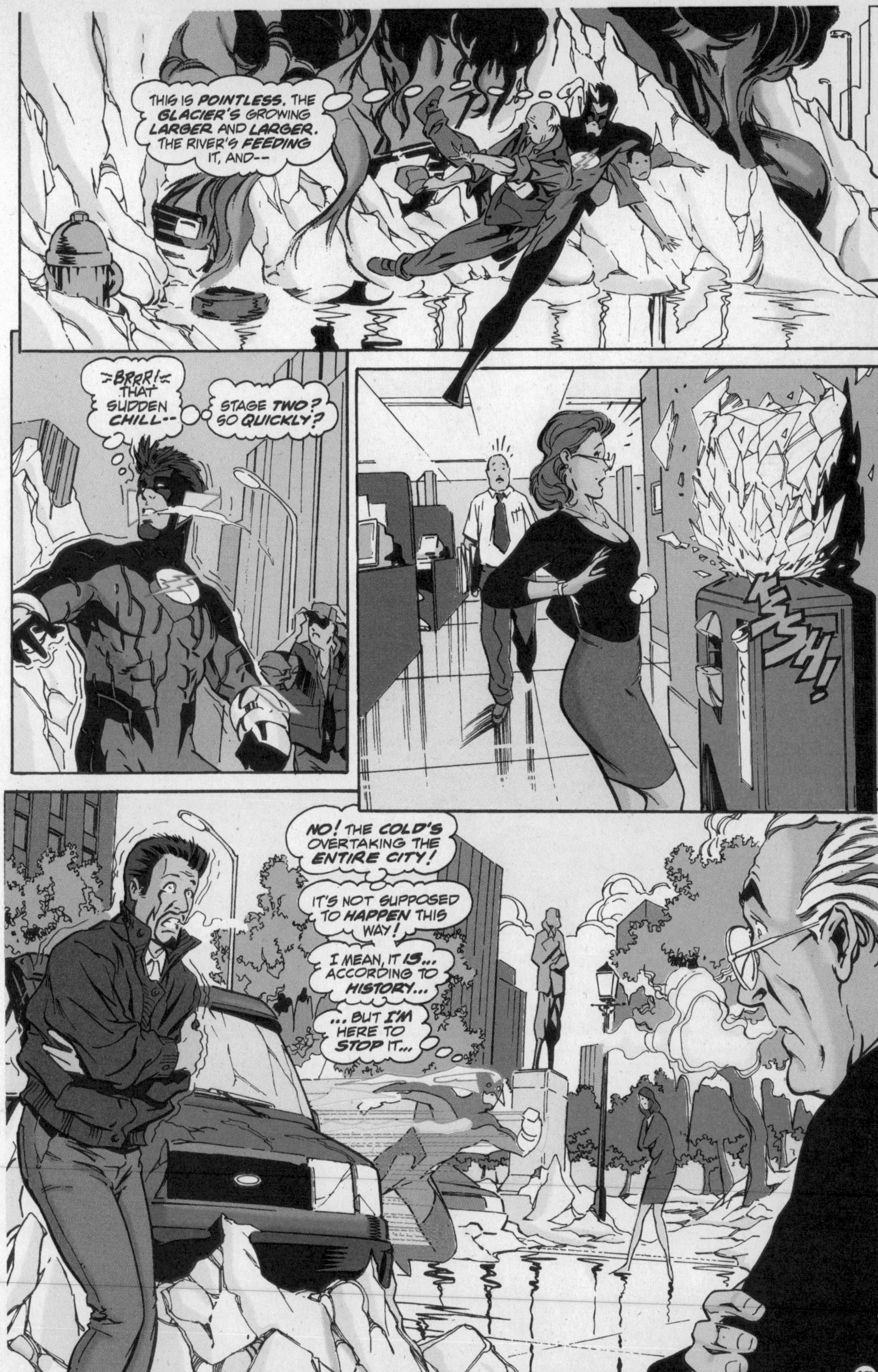
THIS IS POINTLESS. THE GLACIER'S GROWING LARGER AND LARGER. THE RIVER'S FEEDING IT, AND--
BRRR! THAT SUDDEN CHILL--
STAGE TWO? SO QUICKLY?
KESH!
NO! THE COLD'S OVERTAKING THE ENTIRE CITY!
IT'S NOT SUPPOSED TO HAPPEN THIS WAY!
I MEAN, IT IS... ACCORDING TO HISTORY...
...BUT I'M HERE TO STOP IT...
15

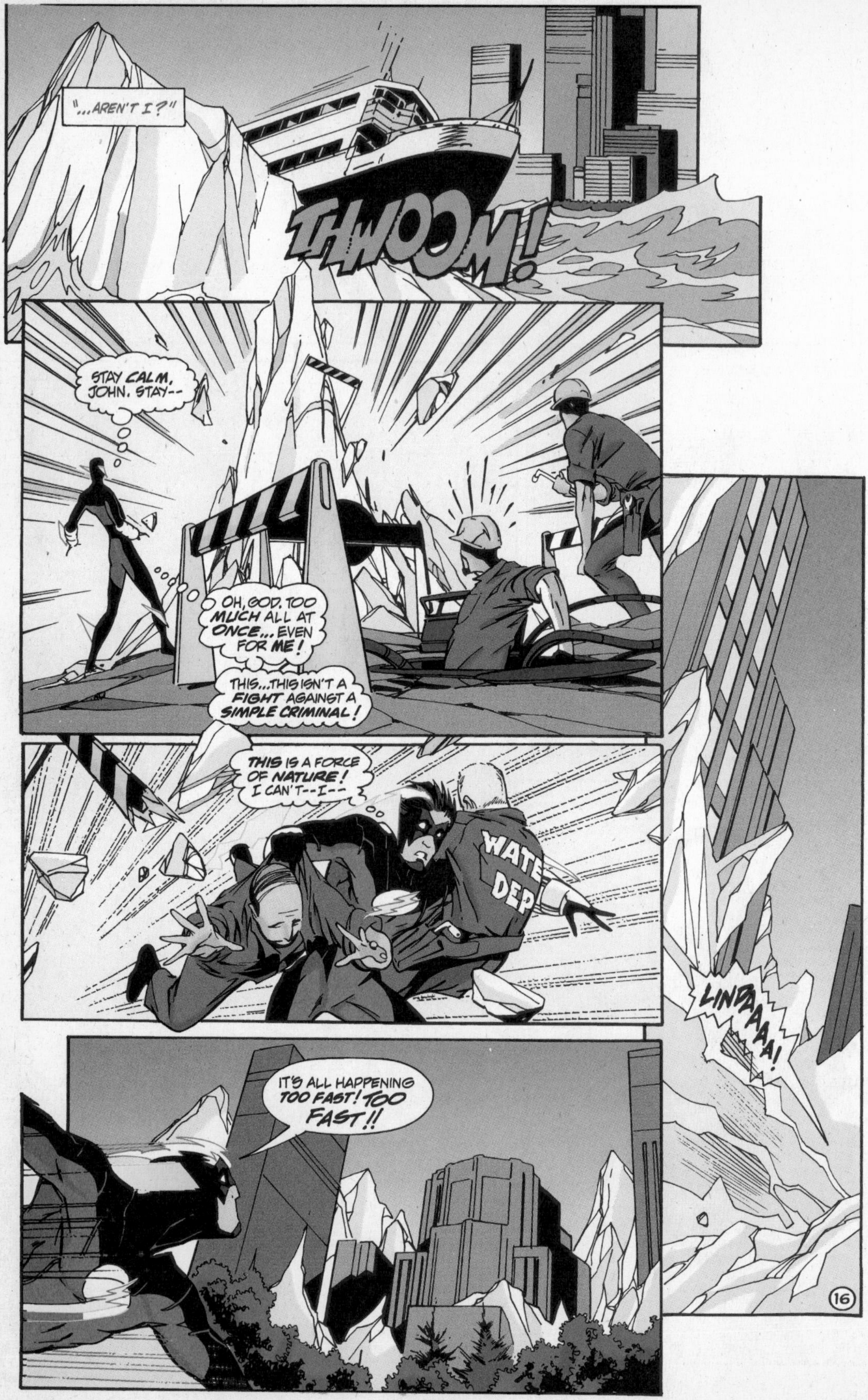
"...AREN'T I?"
THWOOM!
STAY CALM, JOHN. STAY--
OH, GOD. TOO MUCH ALL AT ONCE... EVEN FOR ME!
THIS...THIS ISN'T A FIGHT AGAINST A SIMPLE CRIMINAL!
THIS IS A FORCE OF NATURE! I CAN'T--I--
WATE DEP
LINDAAAA!
IT'S ALL HAPPENING TOO FAST! TOO FAST!!
16

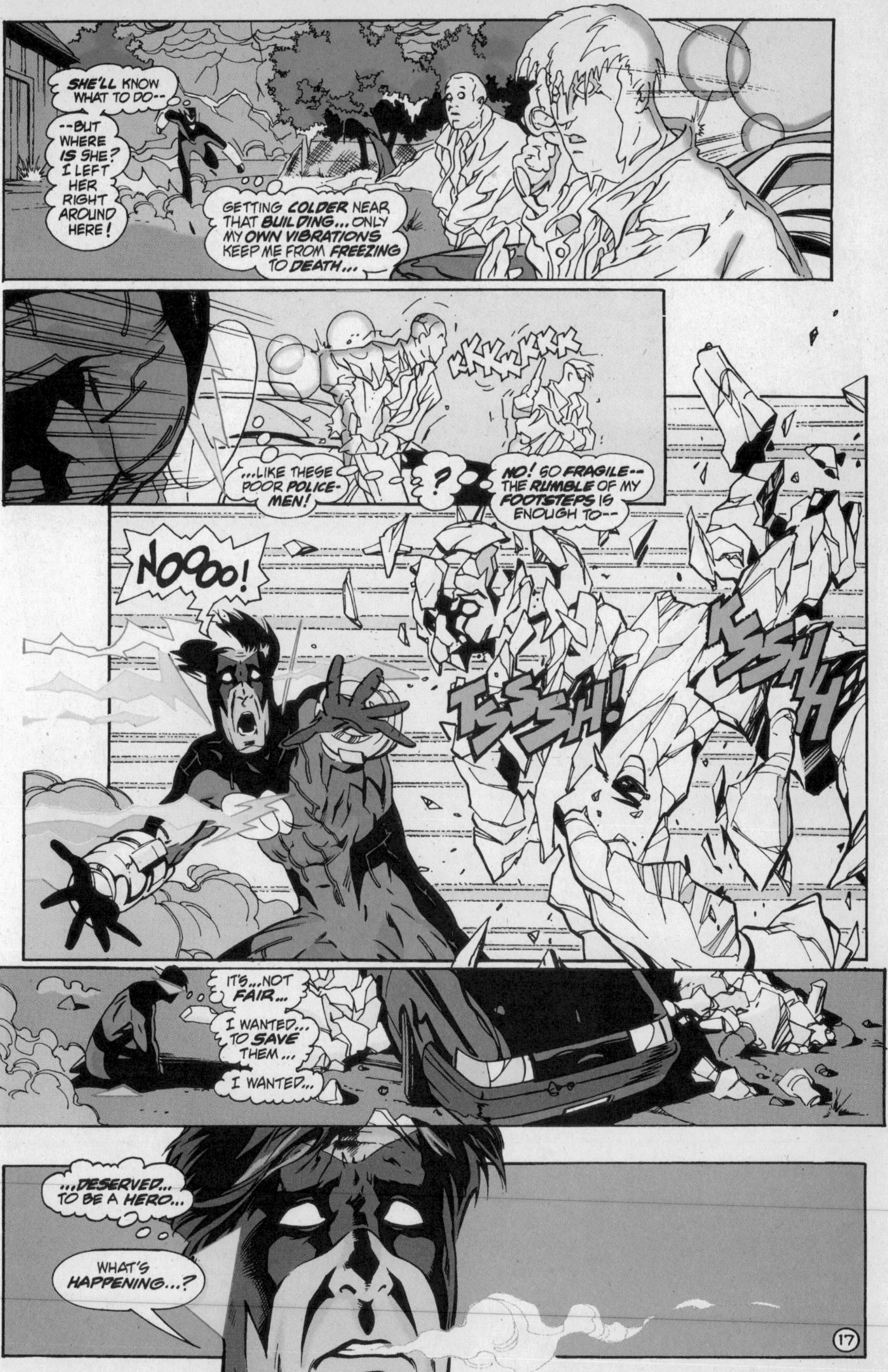
SHE'LL KNOW WHAT TO DO--
--BUT WHERE IS SHE? I LEFT HER RIGHT AROUND HERE!
GETTING COLDER NEAR THAT BUILDING... ONLY MY OWN VIBRATIONS KEEP ME FROM FREEZING TO DEATH...
KKKKKKK
...LIKE THESE POOR POLICE-MEN!
?
NO! SO FRAGILE-- THE RUMBLE OF MY FOOTSTEPS IS ENOUGH TO--
NOOOO!
TSSSH!
KSSHH
IT'S...NOT FAIR...
I WANTED... TO SAVE THEM...
I WANTED...
...DESERVED... TO BE A HERO...
WHAT'S HAPPENING...?
17

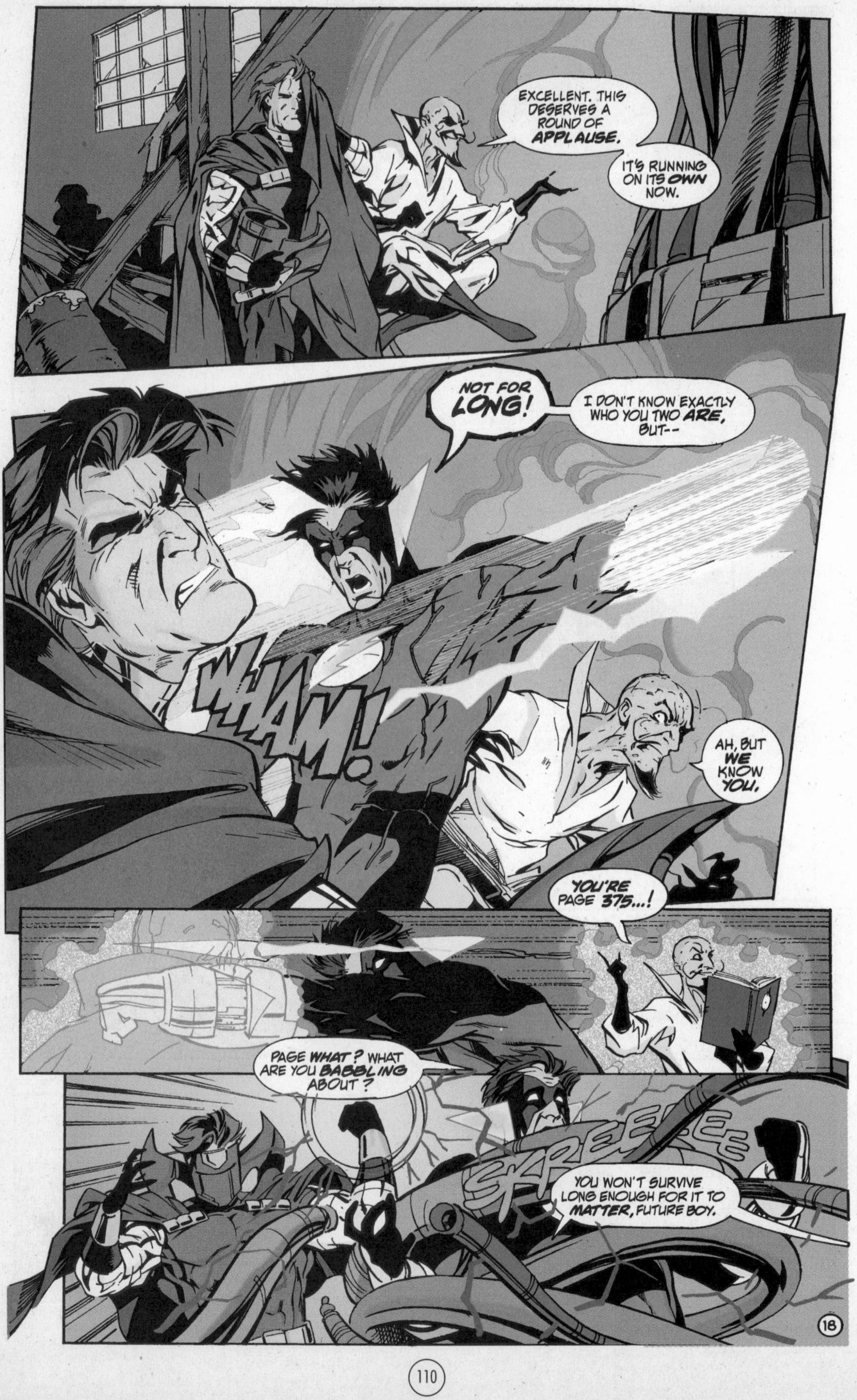

EXCELLENT. THIS DESERVES A ROUND OF APPLAUSE.
IT'S RUNNING ON ITS OWN NOW.
NOT FOR LONG!
I DON'T KNOW EXACTLY WHO YOU TWO ARE, BUT--
WHAM!
AH, BUT WE KNOW YOU.
YOU'RE PAGE 375...!
PAGE WHAT? WHAT ARE YOU BABBLING ABOUT?
SKREEEEEEE
YOU WON'T SURVIVE LONG ENOUGH FOR IT TO MATTER, FUTURE BOY.
18

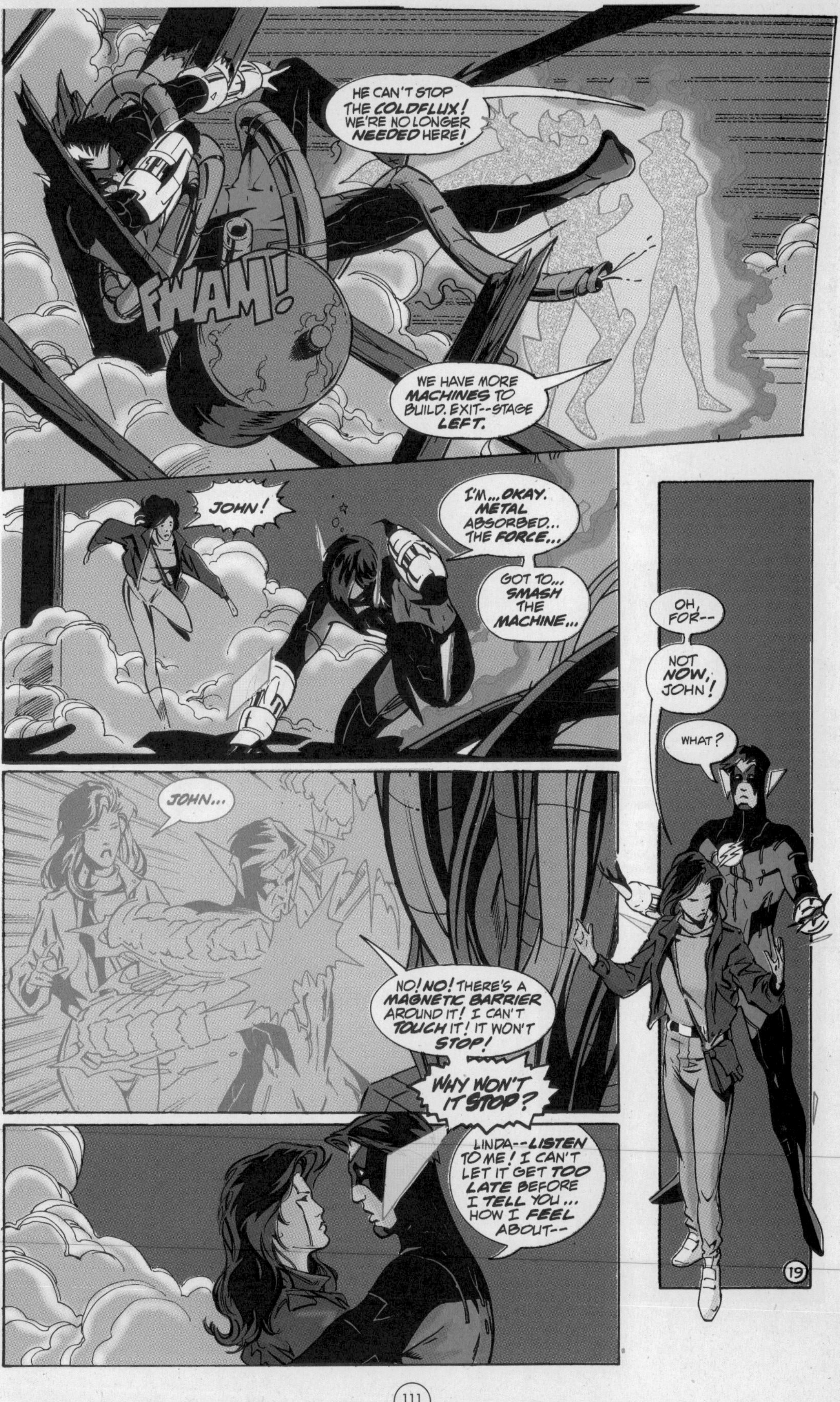
HE CAN'T STOP THE COLDFLUX! WE'RE NO LONGER NEEDED HERE!
FWAM!
WE HAVE MORE MACHINES TO BUILD. EXIT--STAGE LEFT.
JOHN!
I'M... OKAY. METAL ABSORBED... THE FORCE...
GOT TO... SMASH THE MACHINE...
JOHN...
NO! NO! THERE'S A MAGNETIC BARRIER AROUND IT! I CAN'T TOUCH IT! IT WON'T STOP!
WHY WON'T IT STOP?
LINDA--LISTEN TO ME! I CAN'T LET IT GET TOO LATE BEFORE I TELL YOU... HOW I FEEL ABOUT--
OH, FOR--
NOT NOW, JOHN!
WHAT?
19

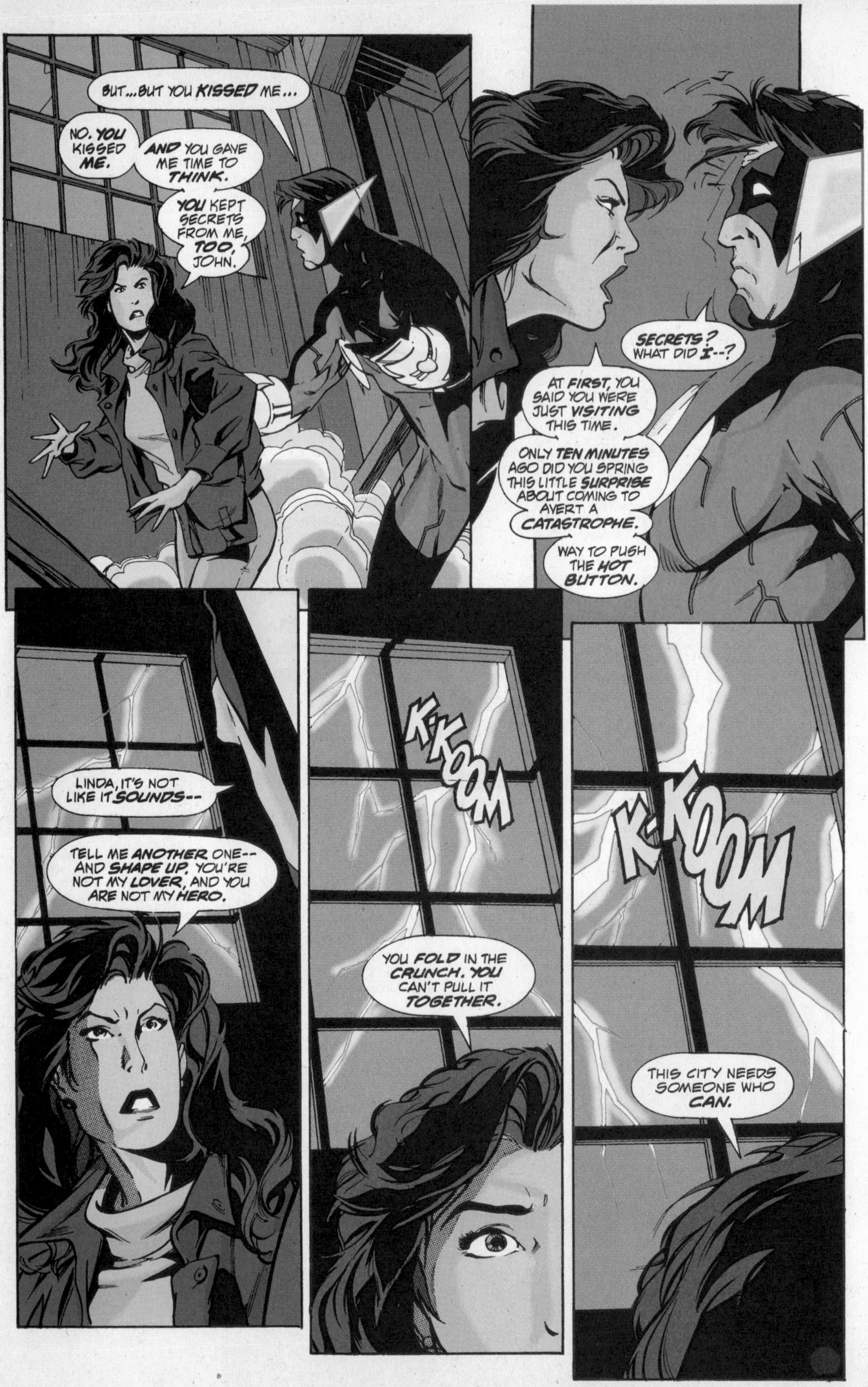
BUT...BUT YOU KISSED ME...
NO. YOU KISSED ME.
AND YOU GAVE ME TIME TO THINK.
YOU KEPT SECRETS FROM ME, TOO, JOHN.
SECRETS? WHAT DID I--?
AT FIRST, YOU SAID YOU WERE JUST VISITING THIS TIME.
ONLY TEN MINUTES AGO DID YOU SPRING THIS LITTLE SURPRISE ABOUT COMING TO AVERT A CATASTROPHE.
WAY TO PUSH THE HOT BUTTON.
LINDA, IT'S NOT LIKE IT SOUNDS--
TELL ME ANOTHER ONE-- AND SHAPE UP. YOU'RE NOT MY LOVER, AND YOU ARE NOT MY HERO.
K-KOOOM
YOU FOLD IN THE CRUNCH. YOU CAN'T PULL IT TOGETHER.
K-KOOOM
THIS CITY NEEDS SOMEONE WHO CAN.

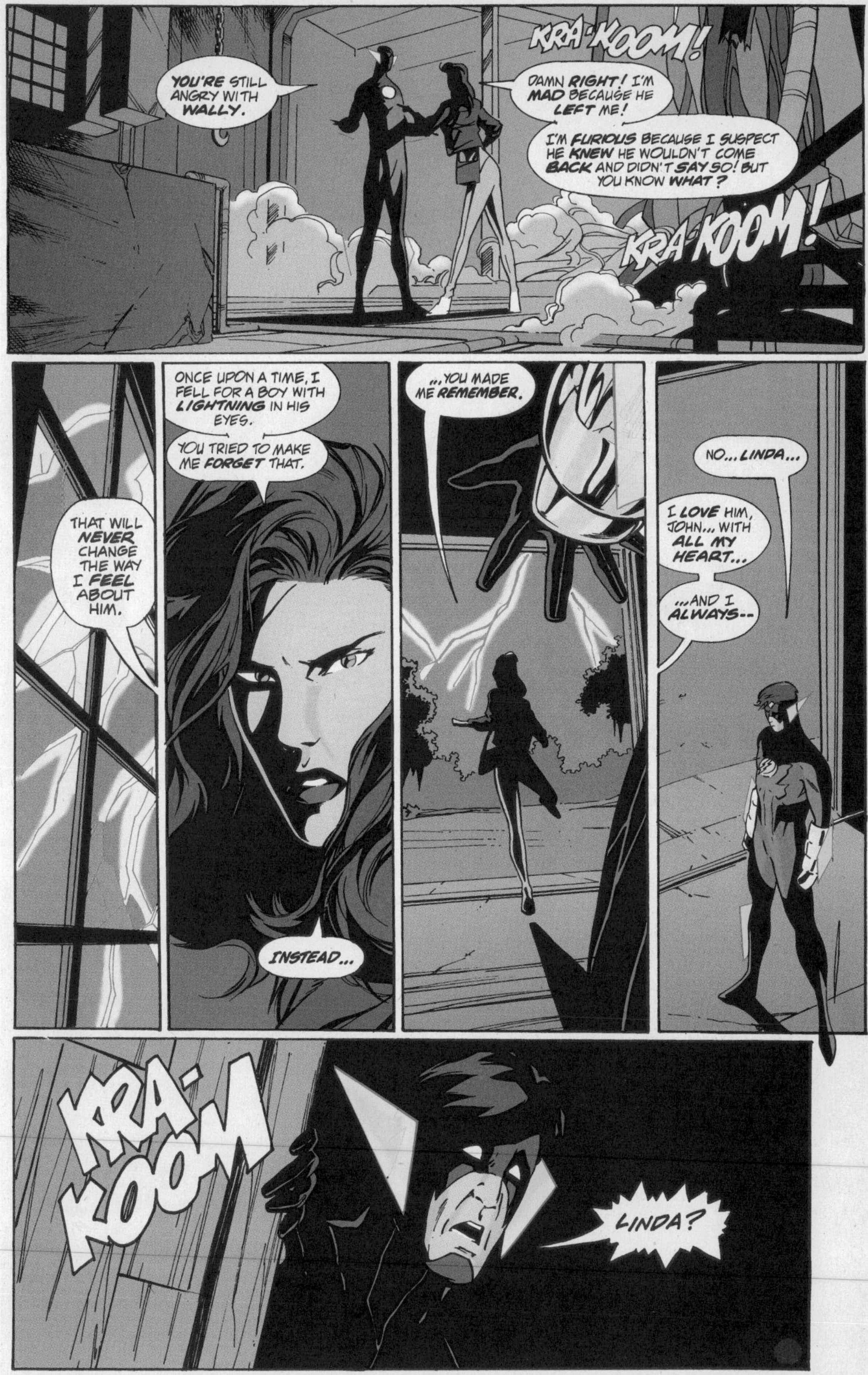
KRA-KOOM!
YOU'RE STILL ANGRY WITH WALLY.
DAMN RIGHT! I'M MAD BECAUSE HE LEFT ME!
I'M FURIOUS BECAUSE I SUSPECT HE KNEW HE WOULDN'T COME BACK AND DIDN'T SAY SO! BUT YOU KNOW WHAT?
KRA-KOOM!
THAT WILL NEVER CHANGE THE WAY I FEEL ABOUT HIM.
ONCE UPON A TIME, I FELL FOR A BOY WITH LIGHTNING IN HIS EYES.
YOU TRIED TO MAKE ME FORGET THAT.
INSTEAD...
...YOU MADE ME REMEMBER.
NO...LINDA...
I LOVE HIM, JOHN... WITH ALL MY HEART...
...AND I ALWAYS--
KRA-KOOM
LINDA?

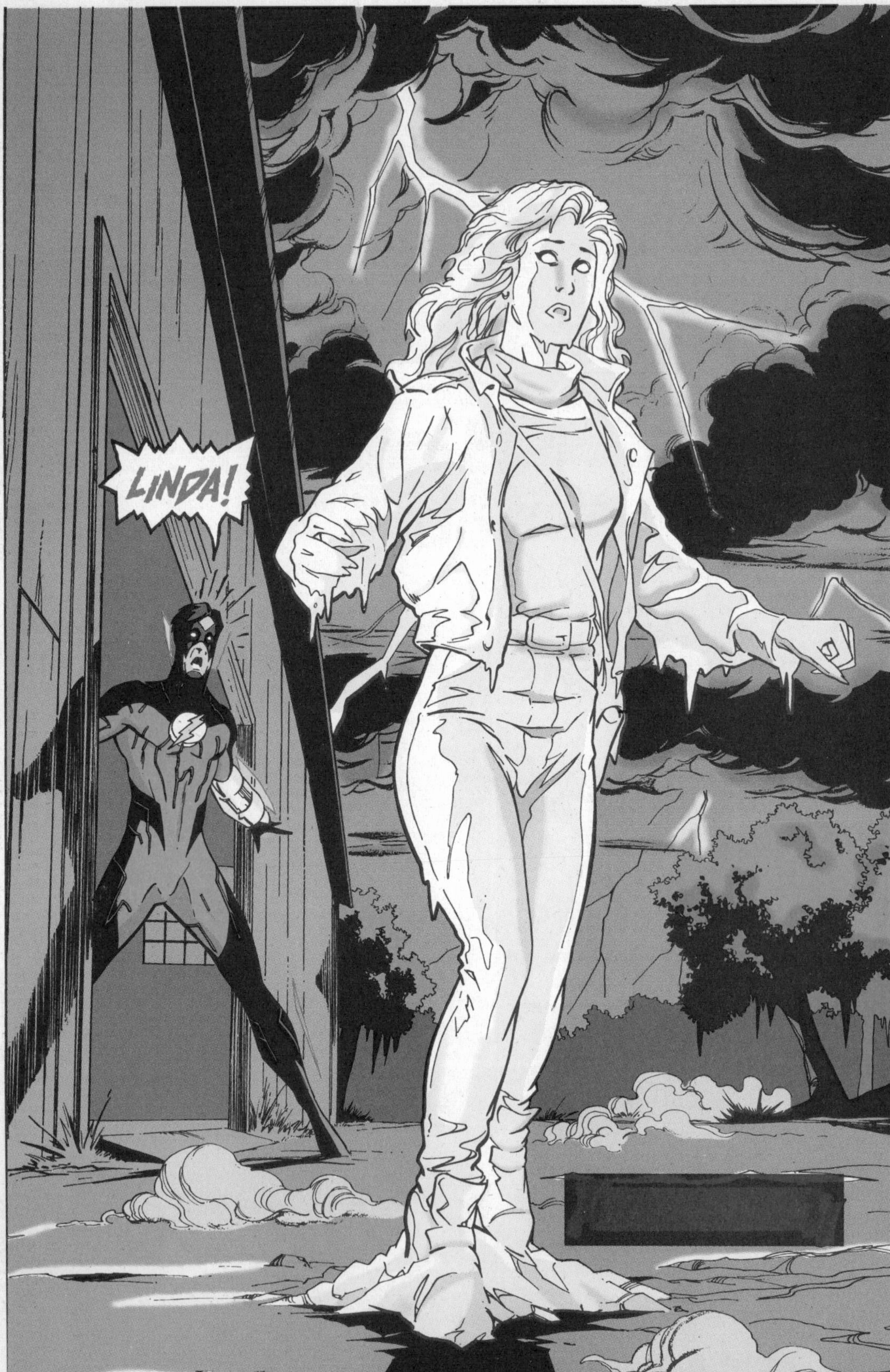
LINDA!

I'll never run away from the BLAME.

My name is JOHN FOX. I'm a FLASH from the FAR FUTURE.

I came back in TIME to avert a LEGENDARY CATASTROPHE...

...and FAILED...

...on EVERY LEVEL.

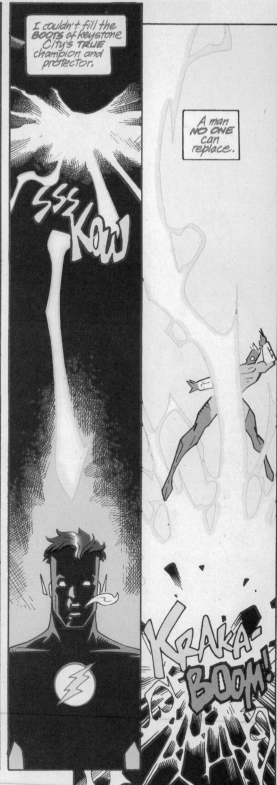

I couldn't fill the BOOTS of keystone City's TRUE champion and protector.

SSS-KOW

A man NO ONE can replace.

KRAKA-BOOM!

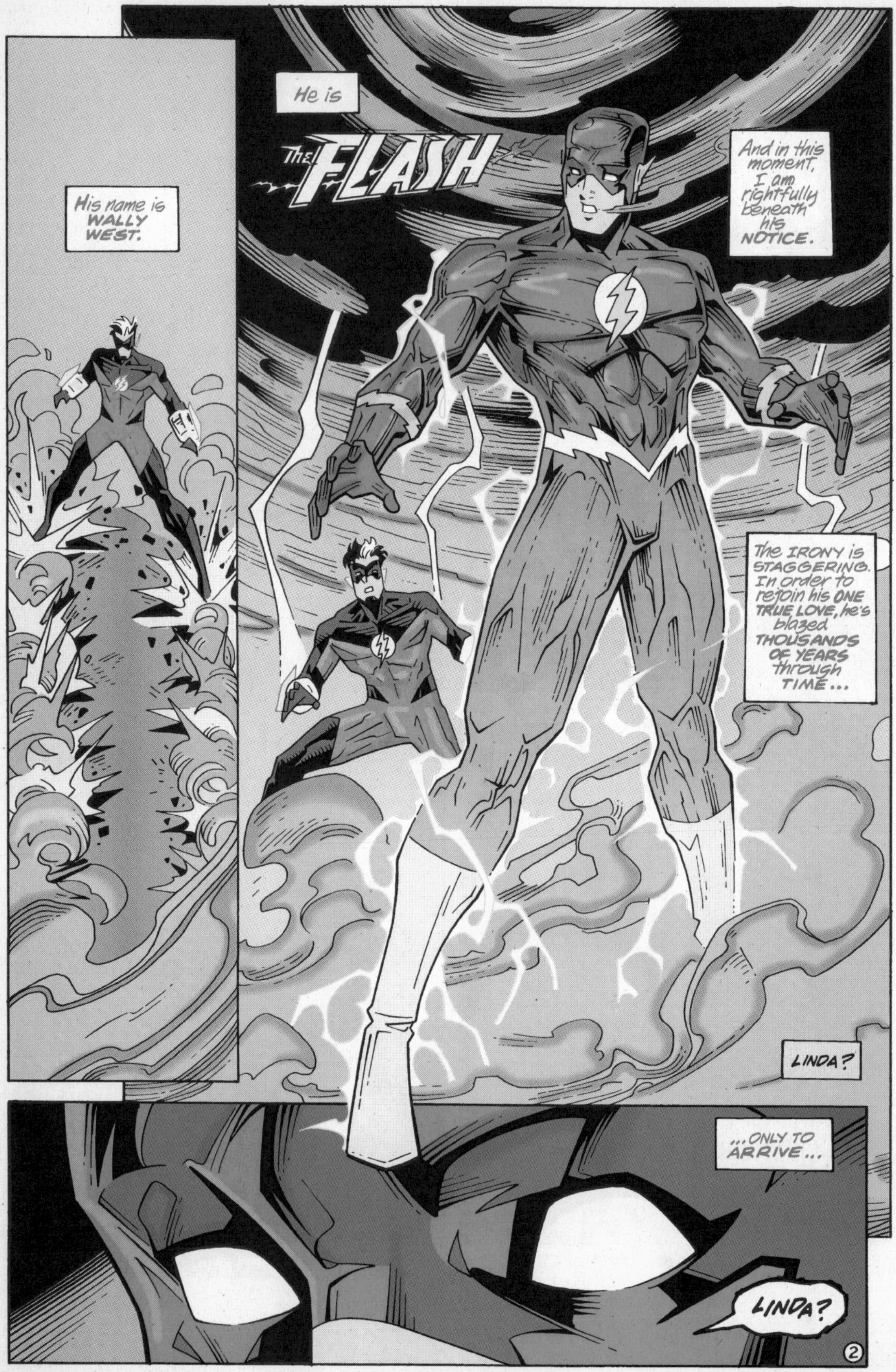

His name is WALLY WEST.
He is
THE FLASH
And in this moment, I am rightfully beneath his NOTICE.
The IRONY is STAGGERING. In order to rejoin his ONE TRUE LOVE, he's blazed THOUSANDS OF YEARS through TIME...
LINDA?
...ONLY TO ARRIVE...
LINDA?
2

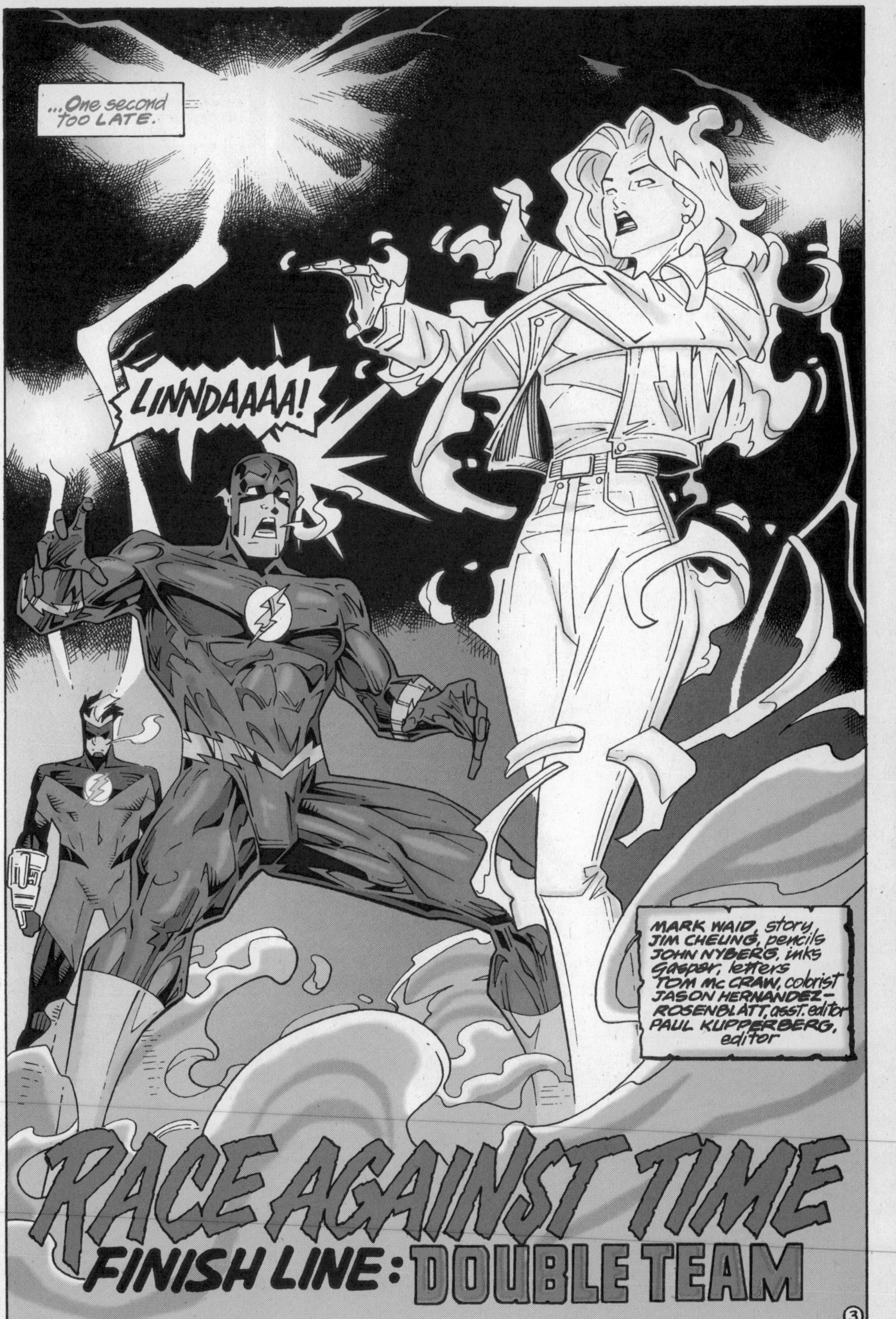
...One second too LATE.
LINNDAAAA!
MARK WAID, story
JIM CHEUNG, pencils
JOHN NYBERG, inks
Gaspar, letters
TOM McCRAW, colorist
JASON HERNANDEZ-ROSENBLATT, asst. editor
PAUL KUPPERBERG, editor
RACE AGAINST TIME
FINISH LINE: DOUBLE TEAM
3

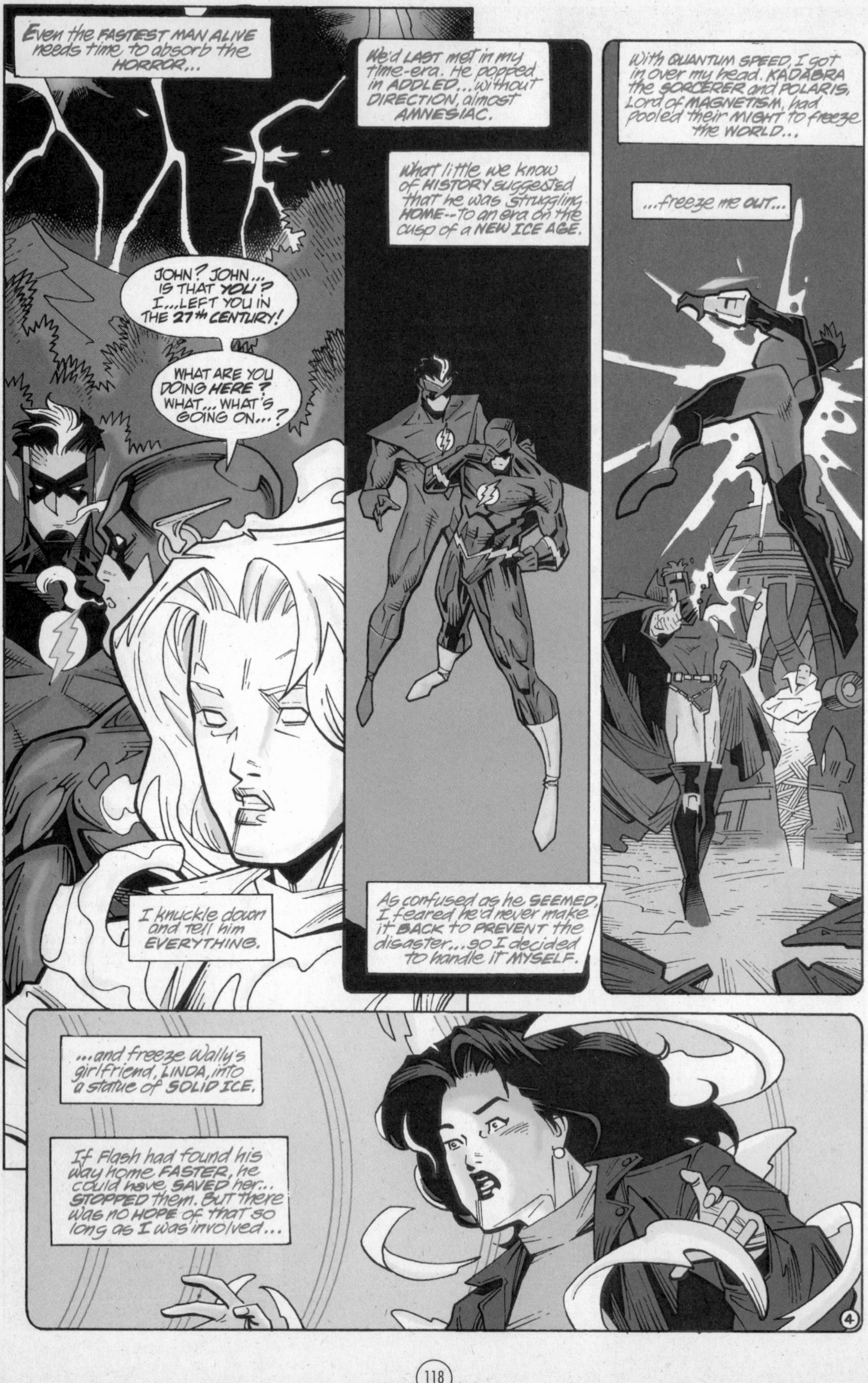

Even the FASTEST MAN ALIVE needs time to absorb the HORROR...
JOHN? JOHN... IS THAT YOU? I...LEFT YOU IN THE 27th CENTURY!
WHAT ARE YOU DOING HERE? WHAT... WHAT'S GOING ON...?
I knuckle down and tell him EVERYTHING.
We'd LAST met in my time-era. He popped in ADDLED... without DIRECTION, almost AMNESIAC.
What little we know of HISTORY suggested that he was struggling HOME--to an era on the cusp of a NEW ICE AGE.
As confused as he SEEMED, I feared he'd never make it BACK to PREVENT the disaster... so I decided to handle it MYSELF.
With QUANTUM SPEED, I got in over my head. KADABRA the SORCERER and POLARIS, Lord of MAGNETISM, had pooled their MIGHT to freeze the WORLD...
...freeze me OUT...
...and freeze Wally's girlfriend, LINDA, into a statue of SOLID ICE.
If Flash had found his way home FASTER, he could have SAVED her... STOPPED them. But there was no HOPE of that so long as I was involved...
4

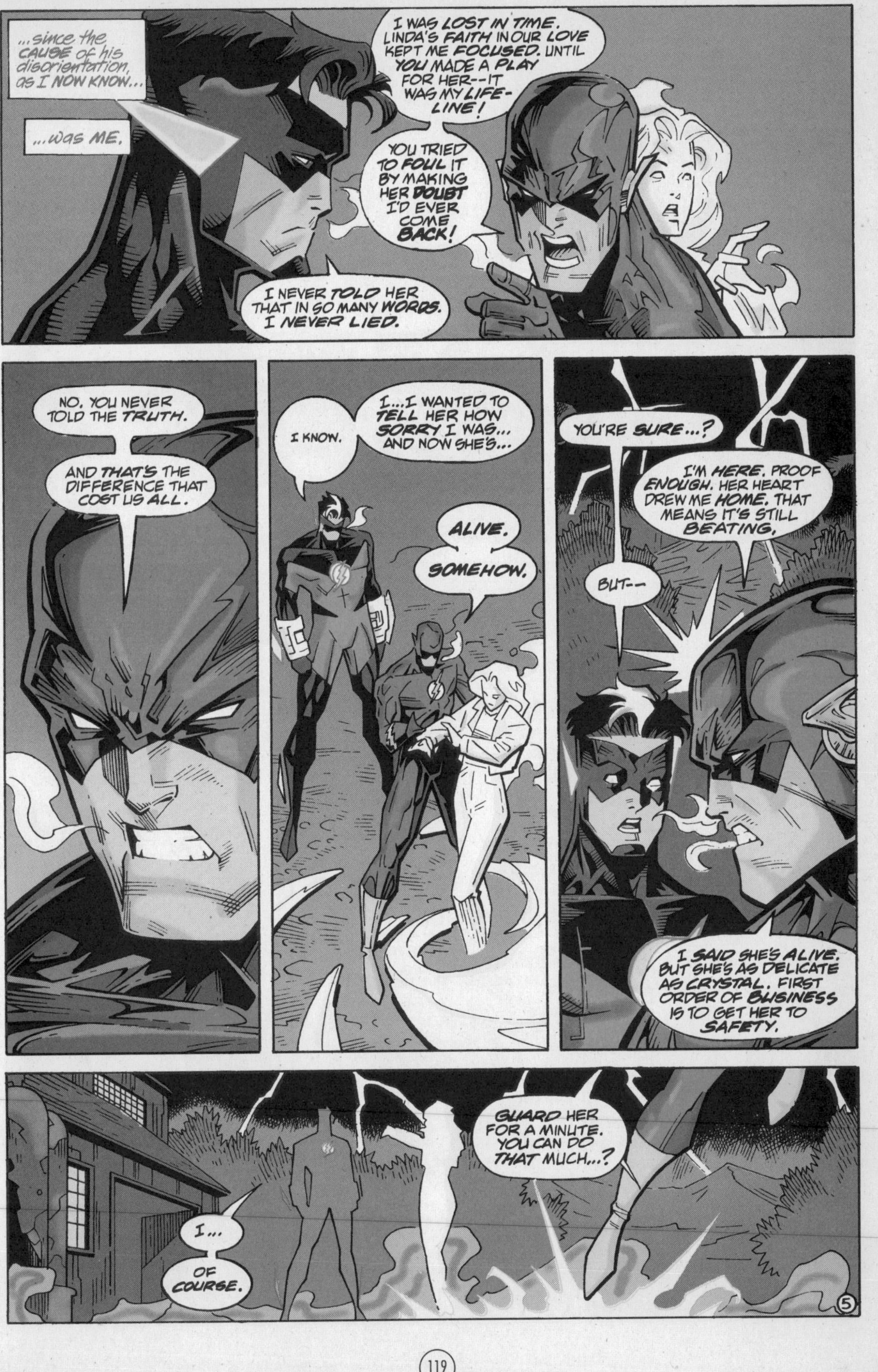
...since the CAUSE of his disorientation, as I NOW KNOW...
...was ME.
I WAS LOST IN TIME. LINDA'S FAITH IN OUR LOVE KEPT ME FOCUSED. UNTIL YOU MADE A PLAY FOR HER--IT WAS MY LIFE-LINE!
YOU TRIED TO FOUL IT BY MAKING HER DOUBT I'D EVER COME BACK!
I NEVER TOLD HER THAT IN SO MANY WORDS. I NEVER LIED.
NO, YOU NEVER TOLD THE TRUTH.
AND THAT'S THE DIFFERENCE THAT COST US ALL.
I KNOW.
I...I WANTED TO TELL HER HOW SORRY I WAS... AND NOW SHE'S...
ALIVE.
SOMEHOW.
YOU'RE SURE...?
I'M HERE. PROOF ENOUGH. HER HEART DREW ME HOME. THAT MEANS IT'S STILL BEATING.
BUT--
I SAID SHE'S ALIVE. BUT SHE'S AS DELICATE AS CRYSTAL. FIRST ORDER OF BUSINESS IS TO GET HER TO SAFETY.
GUARD HER FOR A MINUTE. YOU CAN DO THAT MUCH...?
I...
OF COURSE.
5

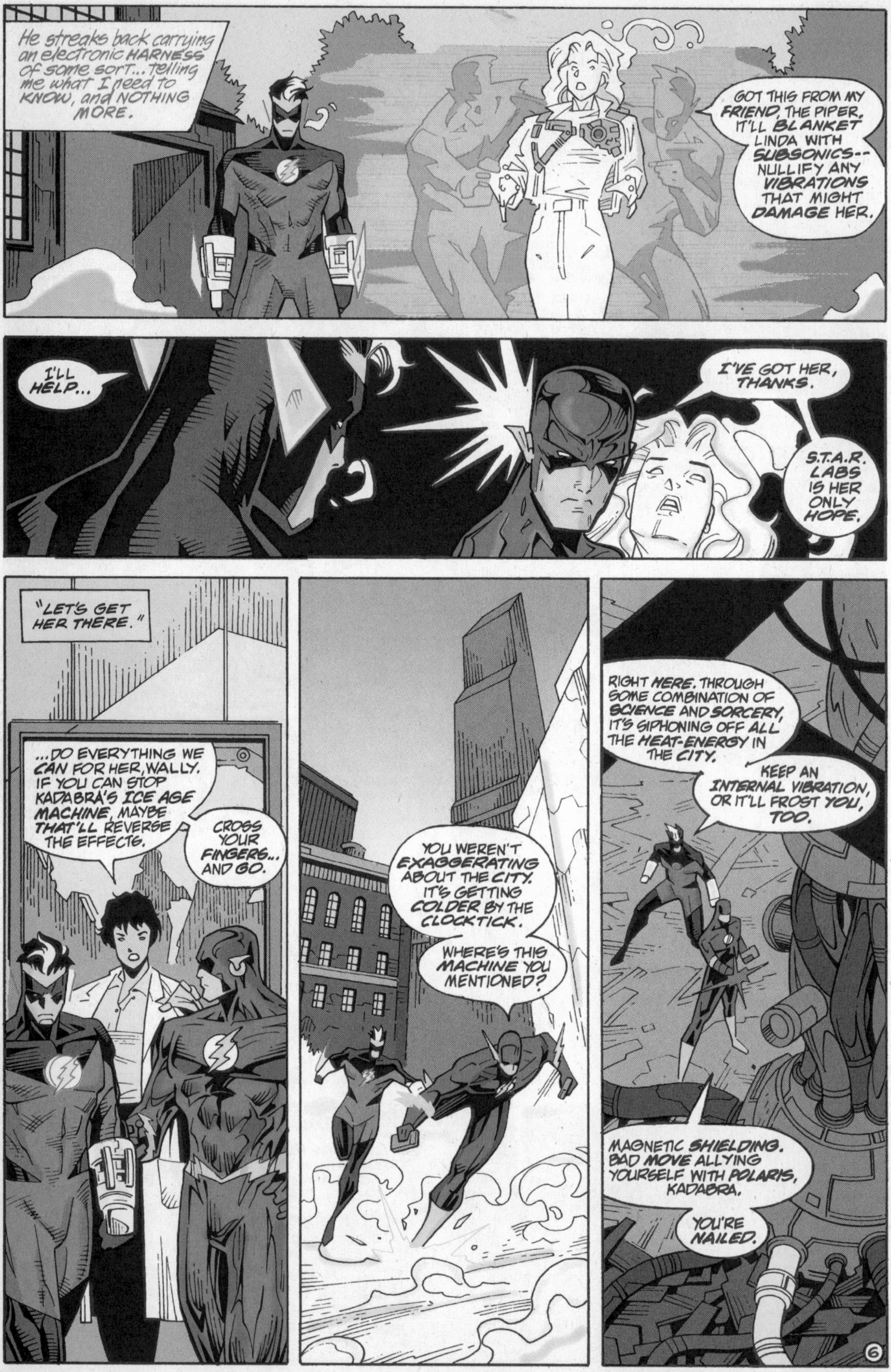
He streaks back carrying an electronic HARNESS of some sort... telling me what I need to KNOW, and NOTHING MORE.
GOT THIS FROM MY FRIEND, THE PIPER. IT'LL BLANKET LINDA WITH SUBSONICS-- NULLIFY ANY VIBRATIONS THAT MIGHT DAMAGE HER.
I'LL HELP...
I'VE GOT HER, THANKS.
S.T.A.R. LABS IS HER ONLY HOPE.
"LET'S GET HER THERE."
...DO EVERYTHING WE CAN FOR HER, WALLY. IF YOU CAN STOP KADABRA'S ICE AGE MACHINE, MAYBE THAT'LL REVERSE THE EFFECTS.
CROSS YOUR FINGERS... AND GO.
YOU WEREN'T EXAGGERATING ABOUT THE CITY. IT'S GETTING COLDER BY THE CLOCKTICK.
WHERE'S THIS MACHINE YOU MENTIONED?
RIGHT HERE. THROUGH SOME COMBINATION OF SCIENCE AND SORCERY, IT'S SIPHONING OFF ALL THE HEAT-ENERGY IN THE CITY.
KEEP AN INTERNAL VIBRATION, OR IT'LL FROST YOU, TOO.
MAGNETIC SHIELDING. BAD MOVE ALLYING YOURSELF WITH POLARIS, KADABRA.
YOU'RE NAILED.
6

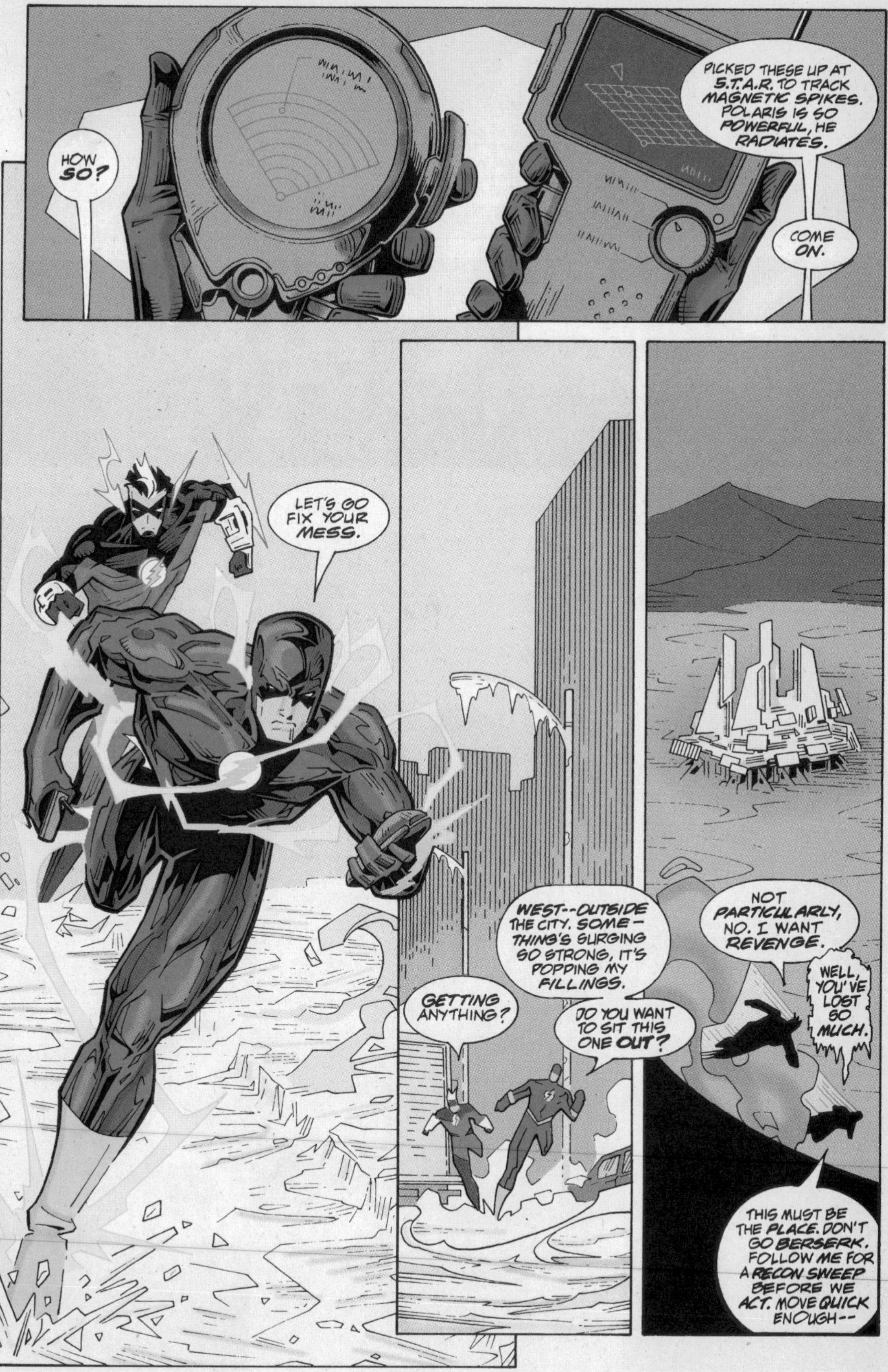

HOW SO?
PICKED THESE UP AT S.T.A.R. TO TRACK MAGNETIC SPIKES. POLARIS IS SO POWERFUL, HE RADIATES.
COME ON.
LET'S GO FIX YOUR MESS.
WEST--OUTSIDE THE CITY. SOME-THING'S SURGING SO STRONG, IT'S POPPING MY FILLINGS.
GETTING ANYTHING?
DO YOU WANT TO SIT THIS ONE OUT?
NOT PARTICULARLY, NO. I WANT REVENGE.
WELL, YOU'VE LOST SO MUCH.
THIS MUST BE THE PLACE. DON'T GO BERSERK. FOLLOW ME FOR A RECON SWEEP BEFORE WE ACT. MOVE QUICK ENOUGH--

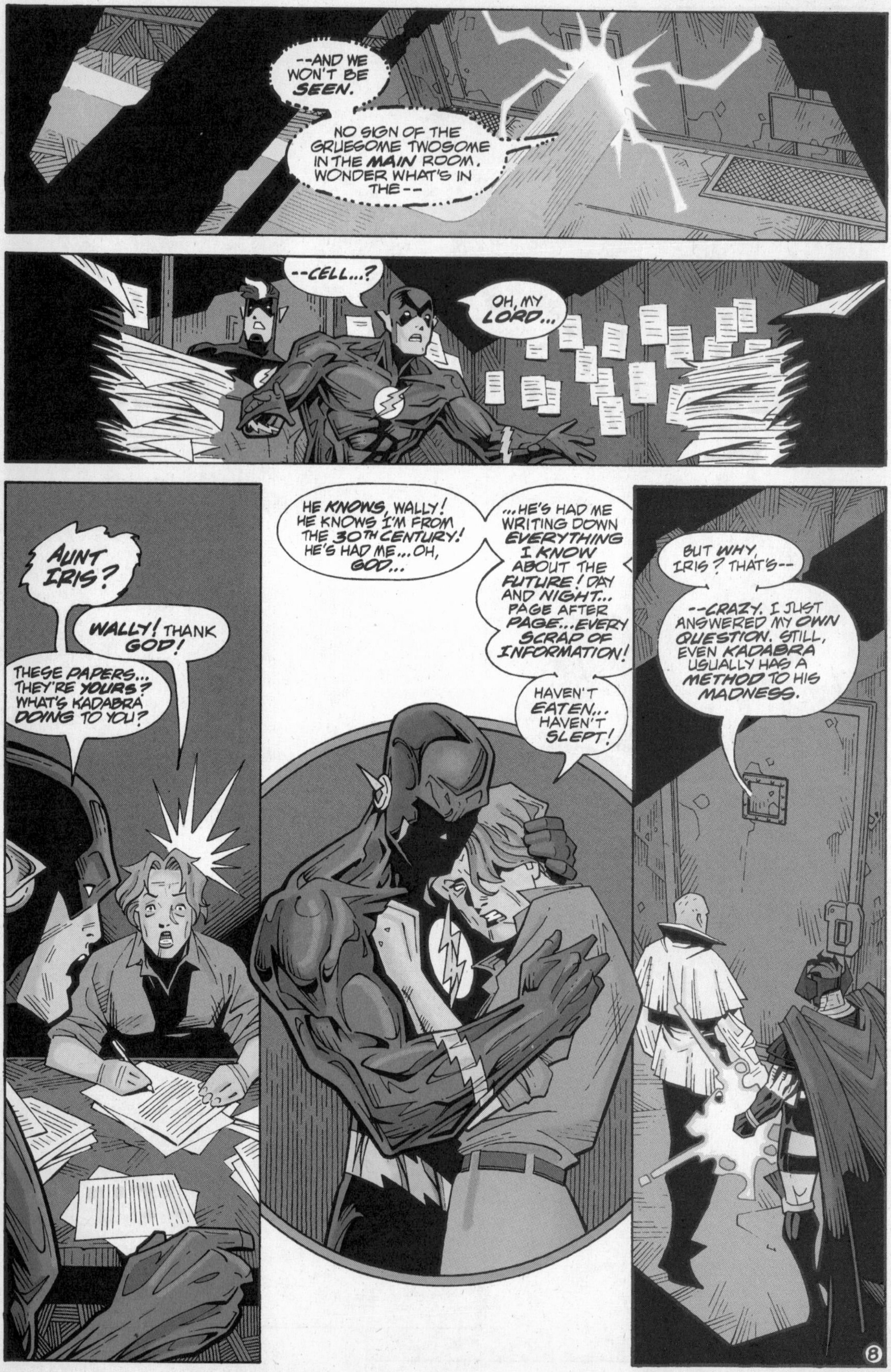
--AND WE WON'T BE SEEN.
NO SIGN OF THE GRUESOME TWOSOME IN THE MAIN ROOM. WONDER WHAT'S IN THE--
--CELL...?
OH, MY LORD...
AUNT IRIS?
WALLY! THANK GOD!
THESE PAPERS... THEY'RE YOURS? WHAT'S KADABRA DOING TO YOU?
HE KNOWS, WALLY! HE KNOWS I'M FROM THE 30TH CENTURY! HE'S HAD ME... OH, GOD...
...HE'S HAD ME WRITING DOWN EVERYTHING I KNOW ABOUT THE FUTURE! DAY AND NIGHT... PAGE AFTER PAGE... EVERY SCRAP OF INFORMATION!
HAVEN'T EATEN... HAVEN'T SLEPT!
BUT WHY, IRIS? THAT'S--
--CRAZY. I JUST ANSWERED MY OWN QUESTION. STILL, EVEN KADABRA USUALLY HAS A METHOD TO HIS MADNESS.
8

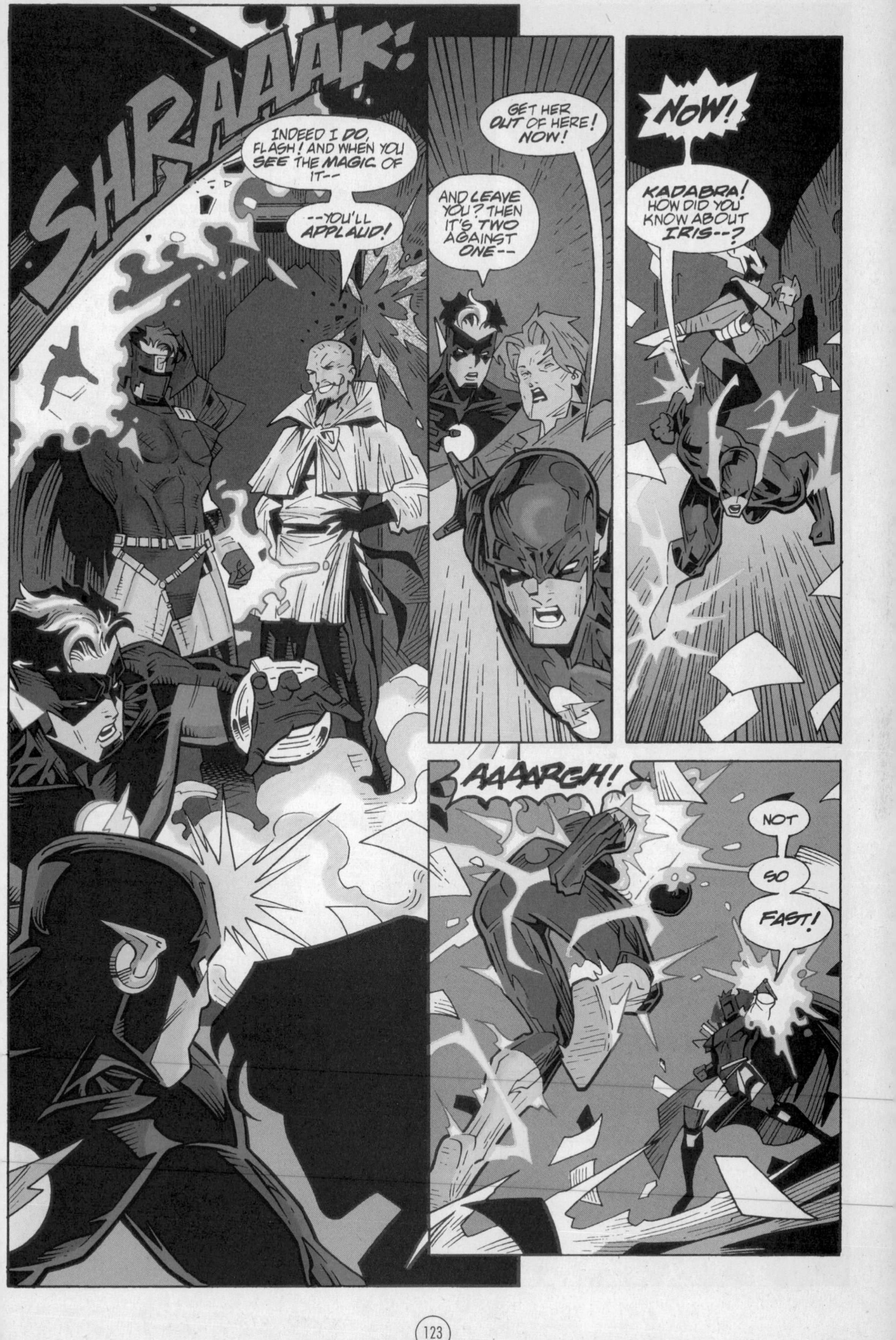

SHRAAAK!
INDEED I DO, FLASH! AND WHEN YOU SEE THE MAGIC OF IT--
--YOU'LL APPLAUD!
GET HER OUT OF HERE! NOW!
AND LEAVE YOU? THEN IT'S TWO AGAINST ONE--
NOW!
KADABRA! HOW DID YOU KNOW ABOUT IRIS--?
AAAARGH!
NOT
SO
FAST!

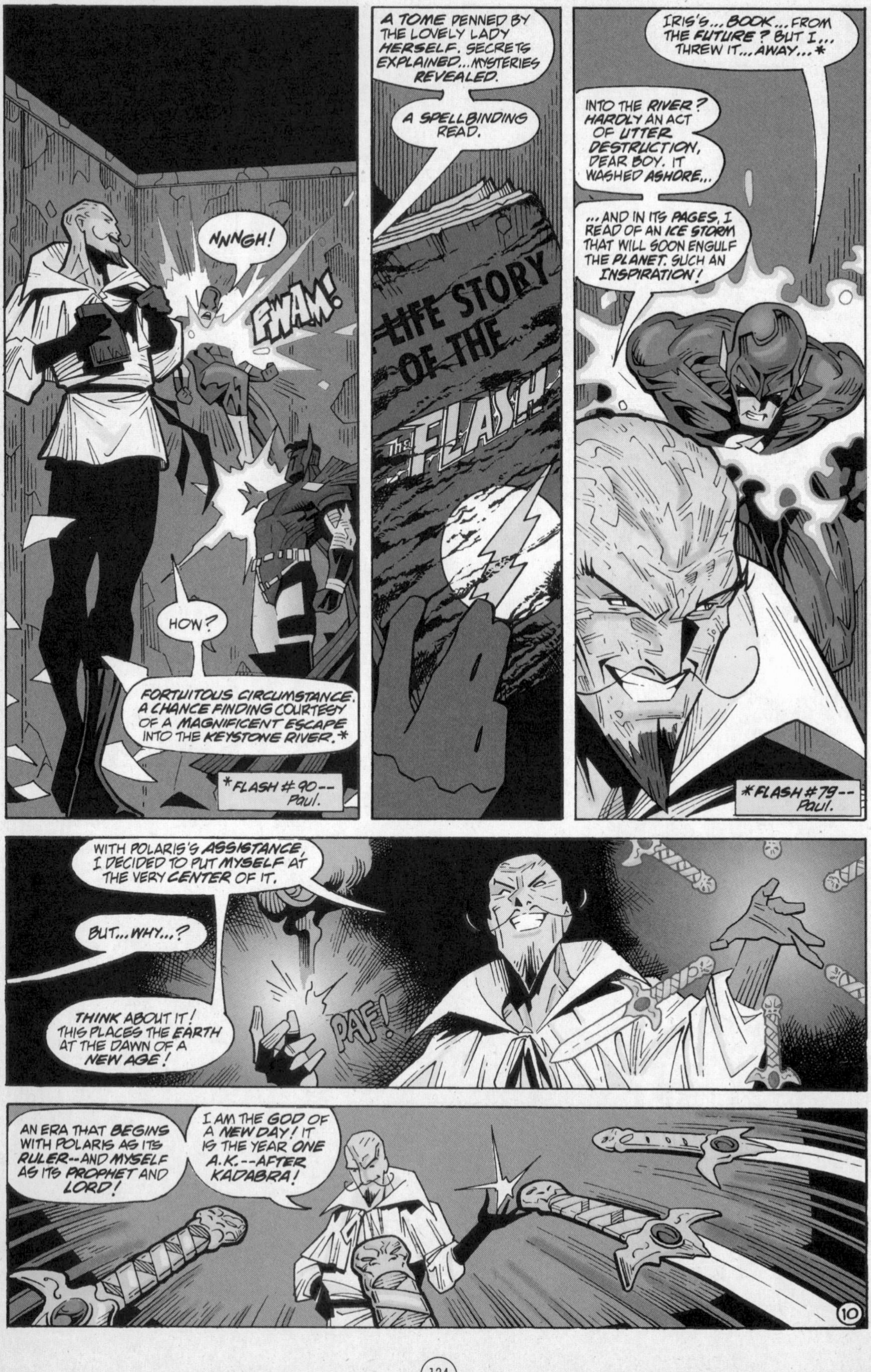
NNNGH!
FWAM!
HOW?
FORTUITOUS CIRCUMSTANCE. A CHANCE FINDING COURTESY OF A MAGNIFICENT ESCAPE INTO THE KEYSTONE RIVER.*
*FLASH #90-- Paul.
A TOME PENNED BY THE LOVELY LADY HERSELF. SECRETS EXPLAINED... MYSTERIES REVEALED.
A SPELLBINDING READ.
LIFE STORY OF THE FLASH
IRIS'S... BOOK... FROM THE FUTURE? BUT I... THREW IT... AWAY...*
INTO THE RIVER? HARDLY AN ACT OF UTTER DESTRUCTION, DEAR BOY. IT WASHED ASHORE...
...AND IN ITS PAGES, I READ OF AN ICE STORM THAT WILL SOON ENGULF THE PLANET. SUCH AN INSPIRATION!
*FLASH #79-- Paul.
WITH POLARIS'S ASSISTANCE, I DECIDED TO PUT MYSELF AT THE VERY CENTER OF IT.
BUT... WHY...?
THINK ABOUT IT! THIS PLACES THE EARTH AT THE DAWN OF A NEW AGE!
PAF!
AN ERA THAT BEGINS WITH POLARIS AS ITS RULER--AND MYSELF AS ITS PROPHET AND LORD!
I AM THE GOD OF A NEW DAY! IT IS THE YEAR ONE A.K.--AFTER KADABRA!
10

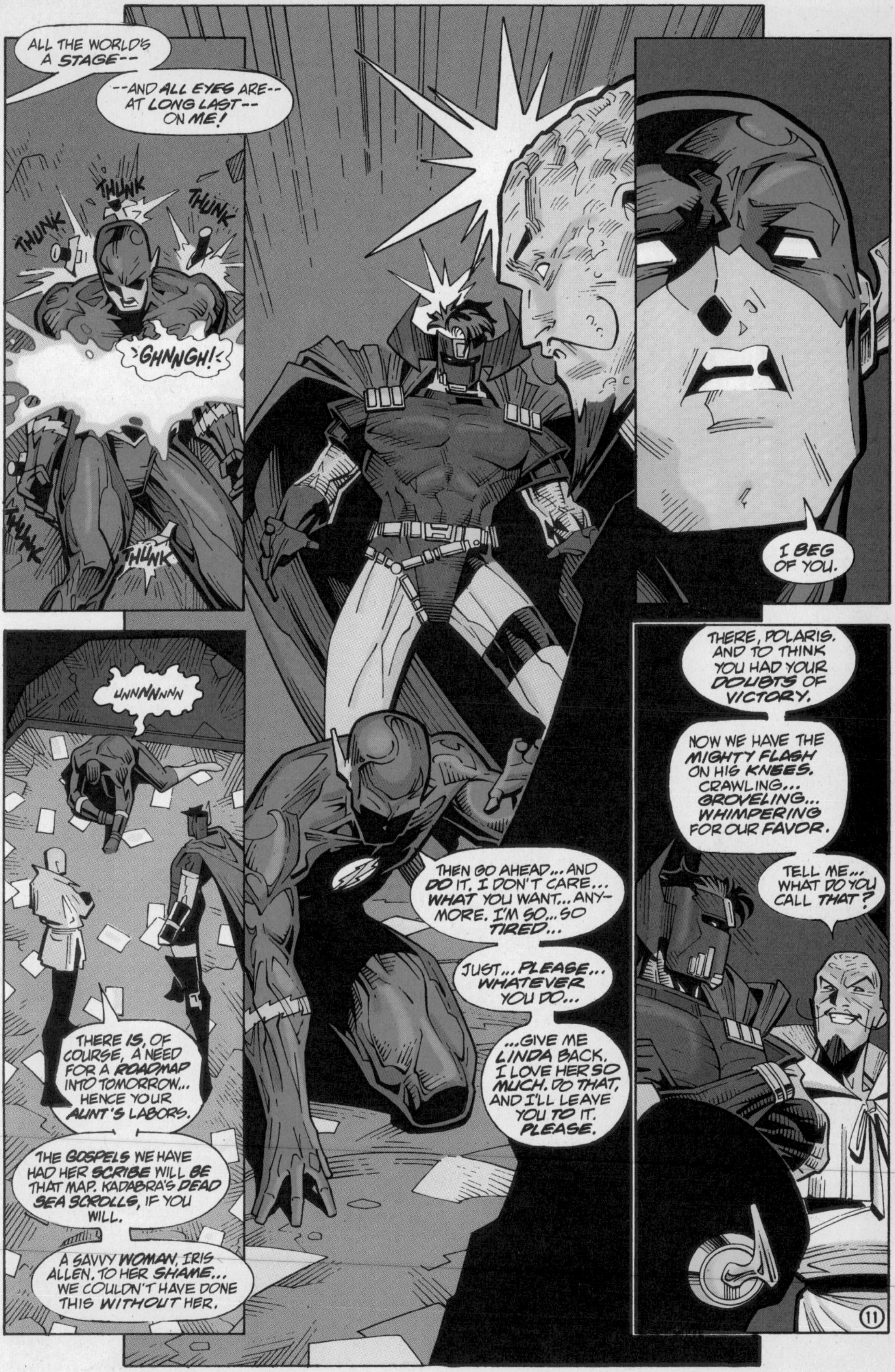
ALL THE WORLD'S A STAGE--
--AND ALL EYES ARE-- AT LONG LAST-- ON ME!
THUNK
THUNK
THUNK
GHNNGH!
THUNK
THUNK
I BEG OF YOU.
UNNNNNNN
THERE IS, OF COURSE, A NEED FOR A ROADMAP INTO TOMORROW... HENCE YOUR AUNT'S LABORS.
THE GOSPELS WE HAVE HAD HER SCRIBE WILL BE THAT MAP. KADABRA'S DEAD SEA SCROLLS, IF YOU WILL.
A SAVVY WOMAN, IRIS ALLEN. TO HER SHAME... WE COULDN'T HAVE DONE THIS WITHOUT HER.
THEN GO AHEAD... AND DO IT. I DON'T CARE... WHAT YOU WANT... ANYMORE. I'M SO... SO TIRED...
JUST... PLEASE... WHATEVER YOU DO...
...GIVE ME LINDA BACK. I LOVE HER SO MUCH. DO THAT, AND I'LL LEAVE YOU TO IT. PLEASE.
THERE, POLARIS. AND TO THINK YOU HAD YOUR DOUBTS OF VICTORY.
NOW WE HAVE THE MIGHTY FLASH ON HIS KNEES. CRAWLING... GROVELING... WHIMPERING FOR OUR FAVOR.
TELL ME... WHAT DO YOU CALL THAT?
11

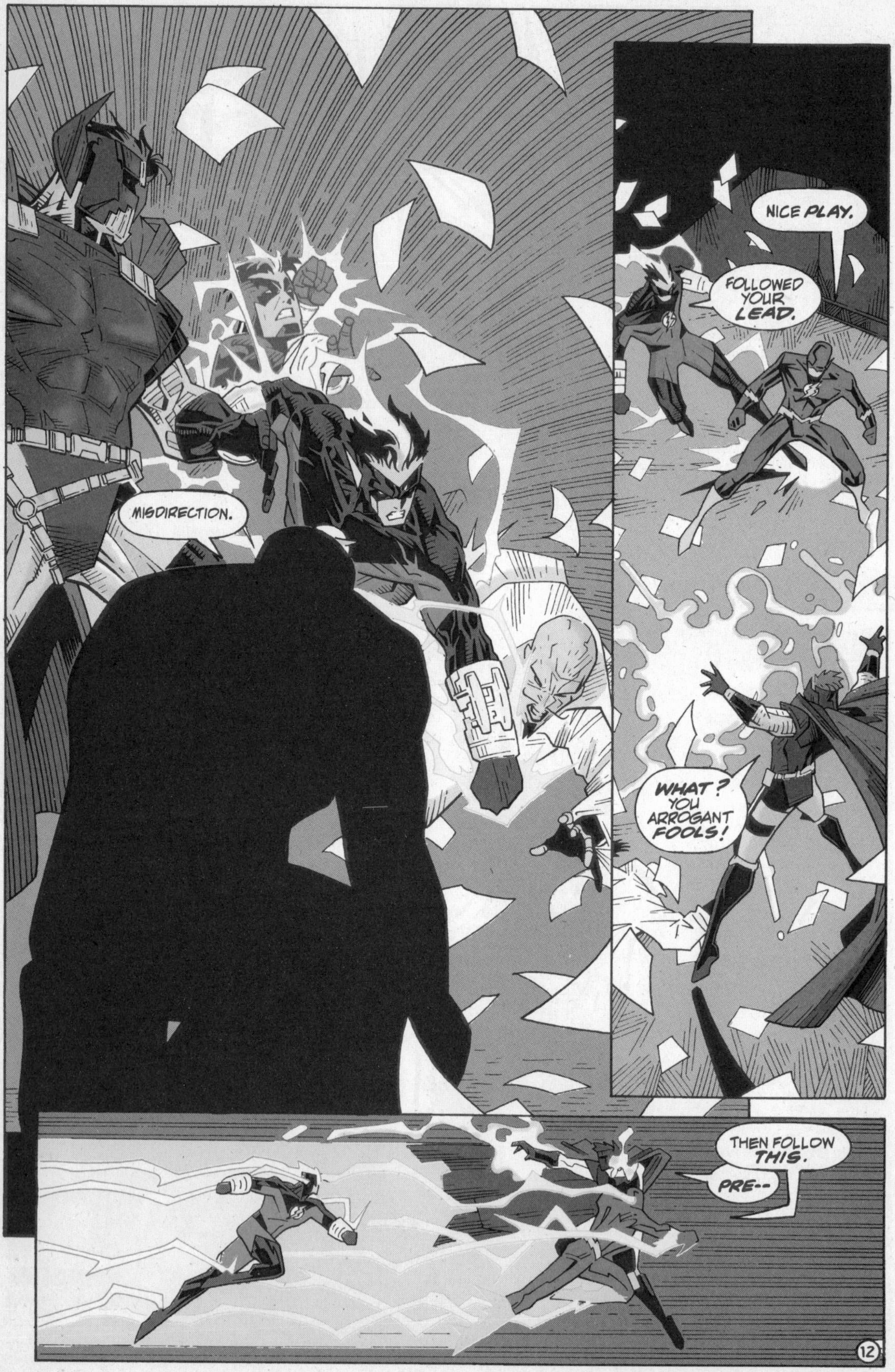
MISDIRECTION.
NICE PLAY.
FOLLOWED YOUR LEAD.
WHAT? YOU ARROGANT FOOLS!
THEN FOLLOW THIS.
PRE--
12

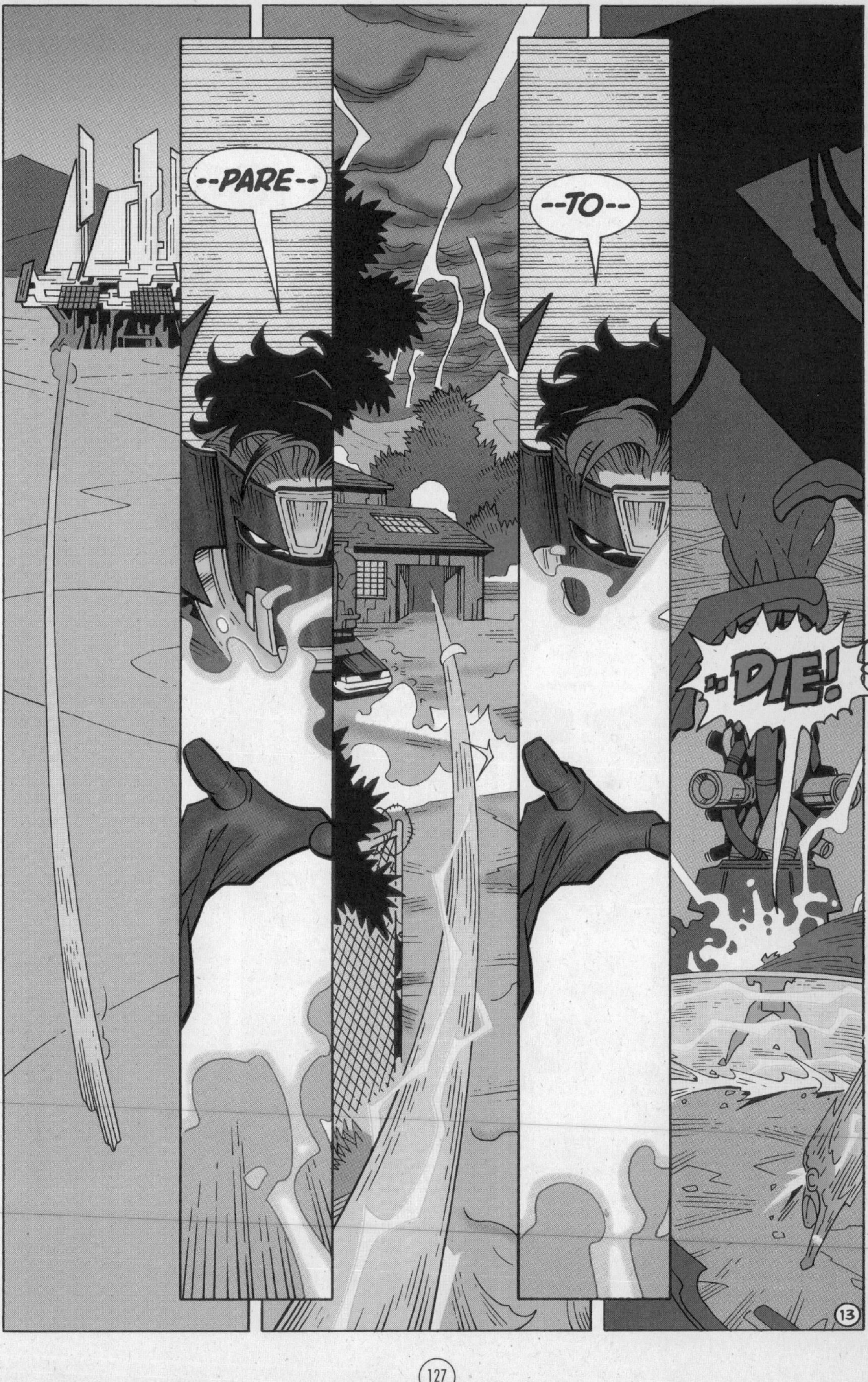
--PARE--
--TO--
--DIE!
13

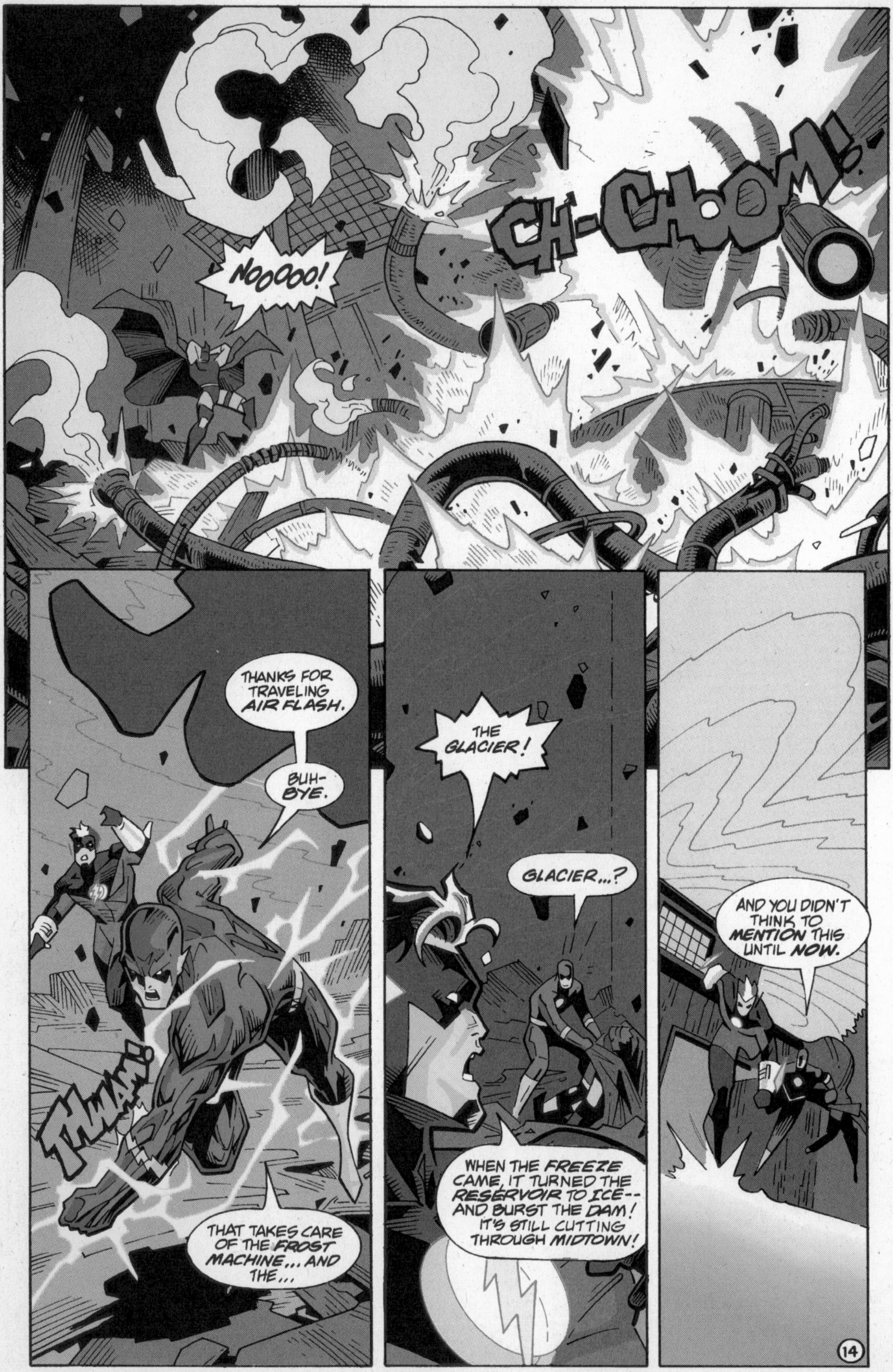
CH-CHOOM!
NOOOOO!
THANKS FOR TRAVELING AIR FLASH.
BUH-BYE.
THWAM!
THAT TAKES CARE OF THE FROST MACHINE... AND THE...
THE GLACIER!
GLACIER...?
WHEN THE FREEZE CAME, IT TURNED THE RESERVOIR TO ICE--AND BURST THE DAM! IT'S STILL CUTTING THROUGH MIDTOWN!
AND YOU DIDN'T THINK TO MENTION THIS UNTIL NOW.
14

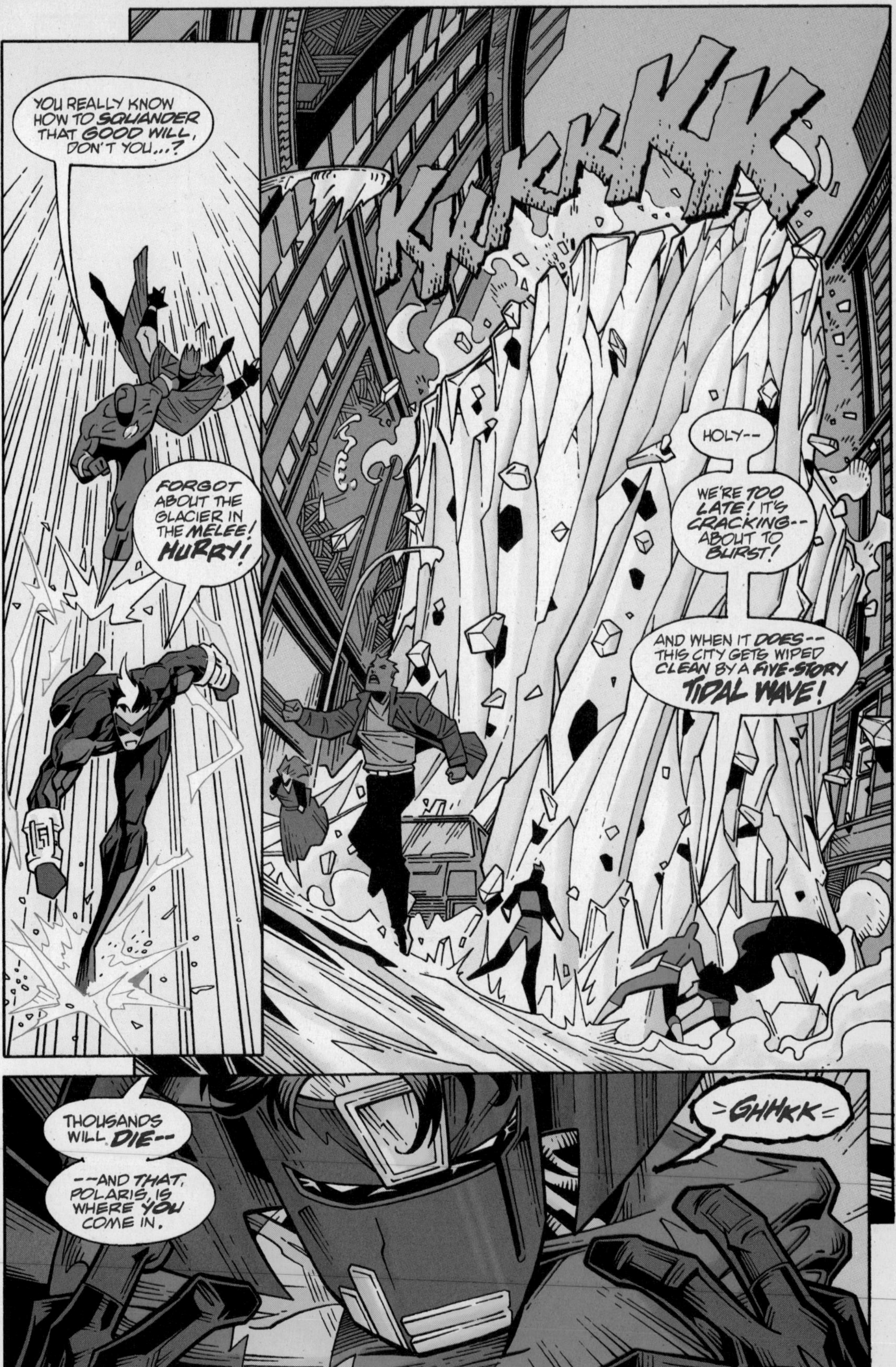

YOU REALLY KNOW HOW TO SQUANDER THAT GOOD WILL, DON'T YOU...?
KKKKKKKK
FORGOT ABOUT THE GLACIER IN THE MELEE! HURRY!
HOLY--
WE'RE TOO LATE! IT'S CRACKING-- ABOUT TO BURST!
AND WHEN IT DOES-- THIS CITY GETS WIPED CLEAN BY A FIVE-STORY TIDAL WAVE!
THOUSANDS WILL DIE--
--AND THAT, POLARIS, IS WHERE YOU COME IN.
=GHHKK=

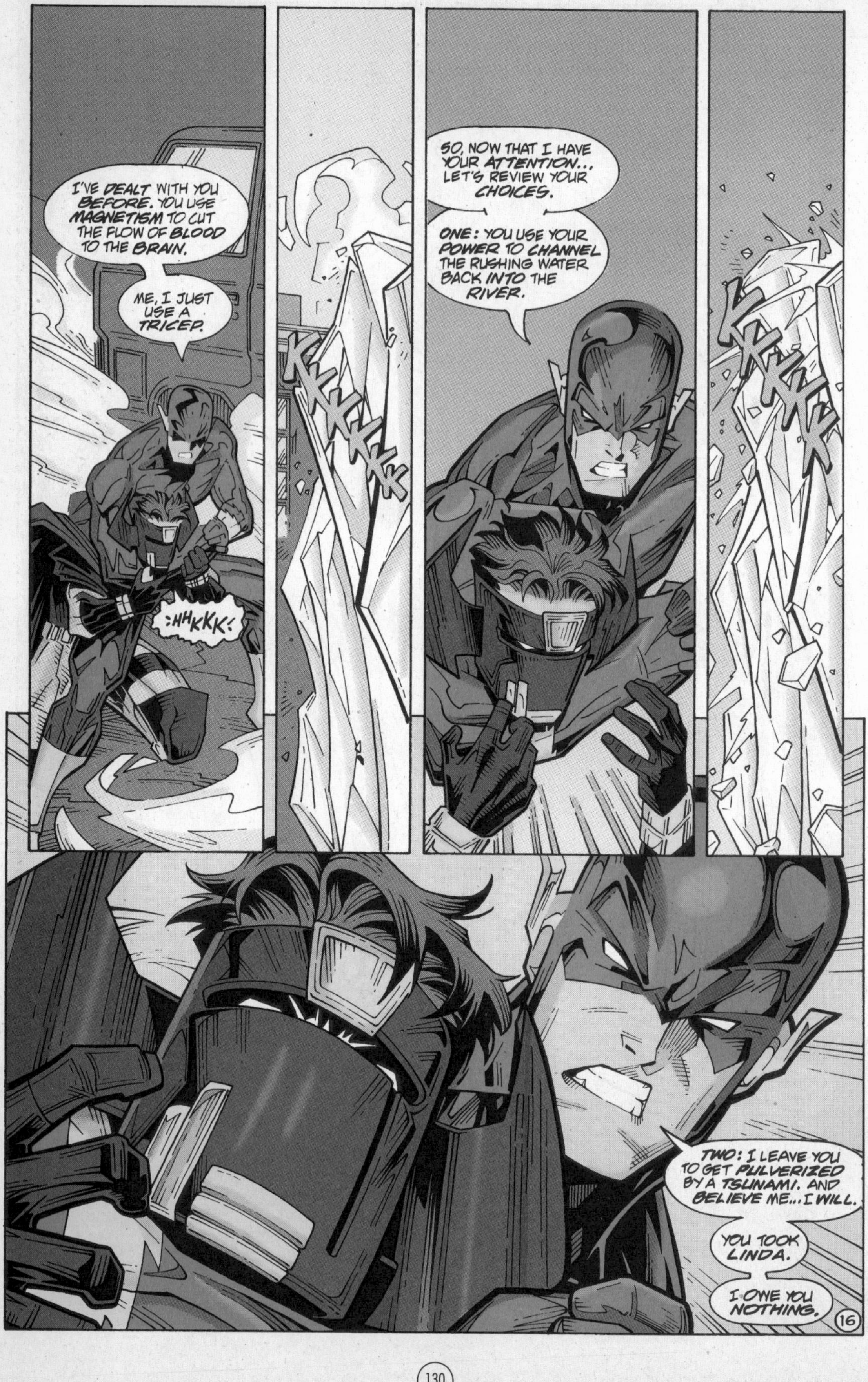
I'VE DEALT WITH YOU BEFORE. YOU USE MAGNETISM TO CUT THE FLOW OF BLOOD TO THE BRAIN.
ME, I JUST USE A TRICEP.
:HHKKK!:
KKKKKK
SO, NOW THAT I HAVE YOUR ATTENTION... LET'S REVIEW YOUR CHOICES.
ONE: YOU USE YOUR POWER TO CHANNEL THE RUSHING WATER BACK INTO THE RIVER.
KKKKKK
TWO: I LEAVE YOU TO GET PULVERIZED BY A TSUNAMI. AND BELIEVE ME... I WILL.
YOU TOOK LINDA.
I OWE YOU NOTHING.
16

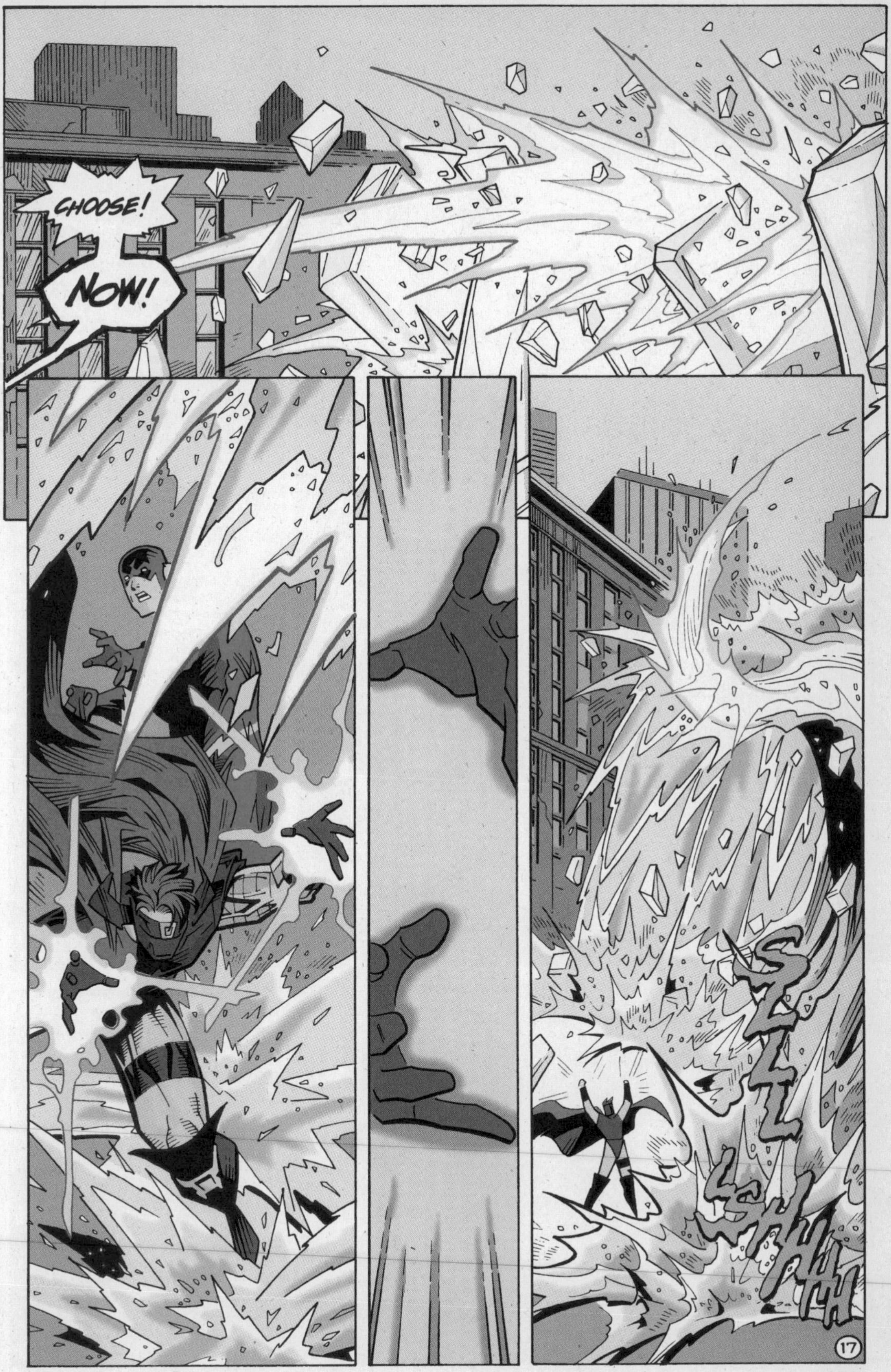
CHOOSE!
NOW!
SSLLLSHHHH
17

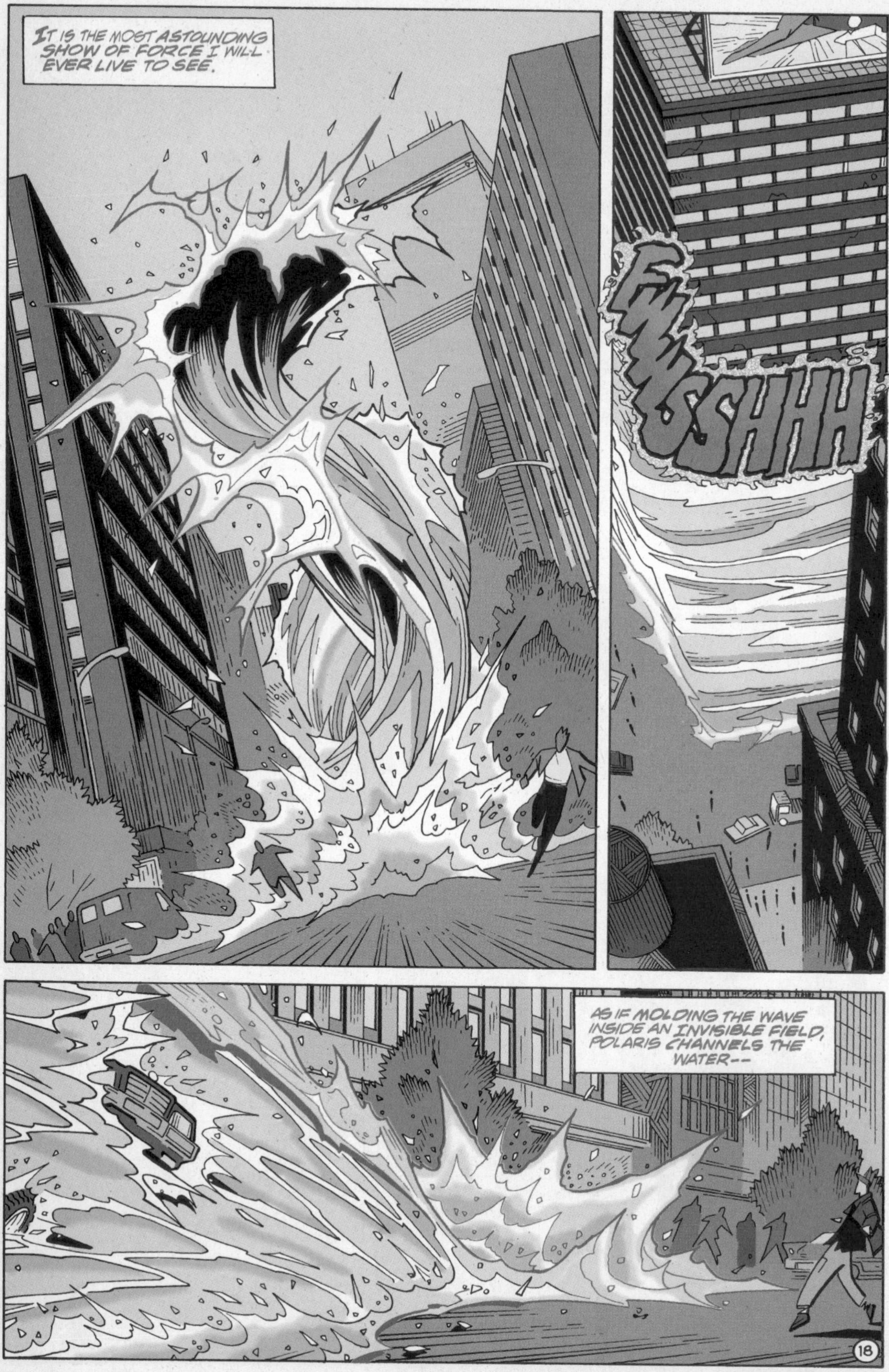
IT IS THE MOST ASTOUNDING SHOW OF FORCE I WILL EVER LIVE TO SEE.
FWWSSHHH
AS IF MOLDING THE WAVE INSIDE AN INVISIBLE FIELD, POLARIS CHANNELS THE WATER--
18

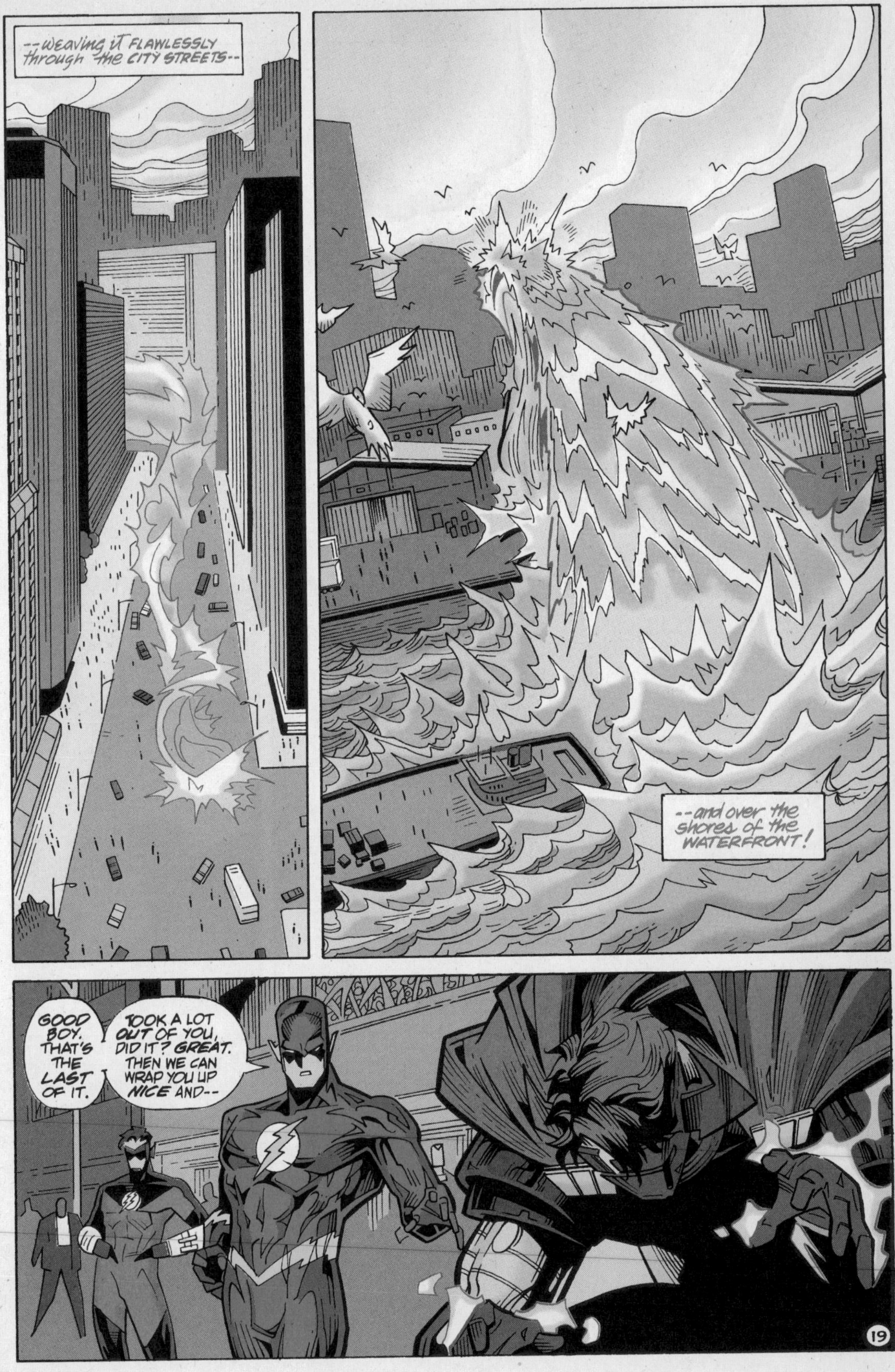
--weaving it FLAWLESSLY through the CITY STREETS--
--and over the shores of the WATERFRONT!
GOOD BOY. THAT'S THE LAST OF IT.
TOOK A LOT OUT OF YOU, DID IT? GREAT. THEN WE CAN WRAP YOU UP NICE AND--
19

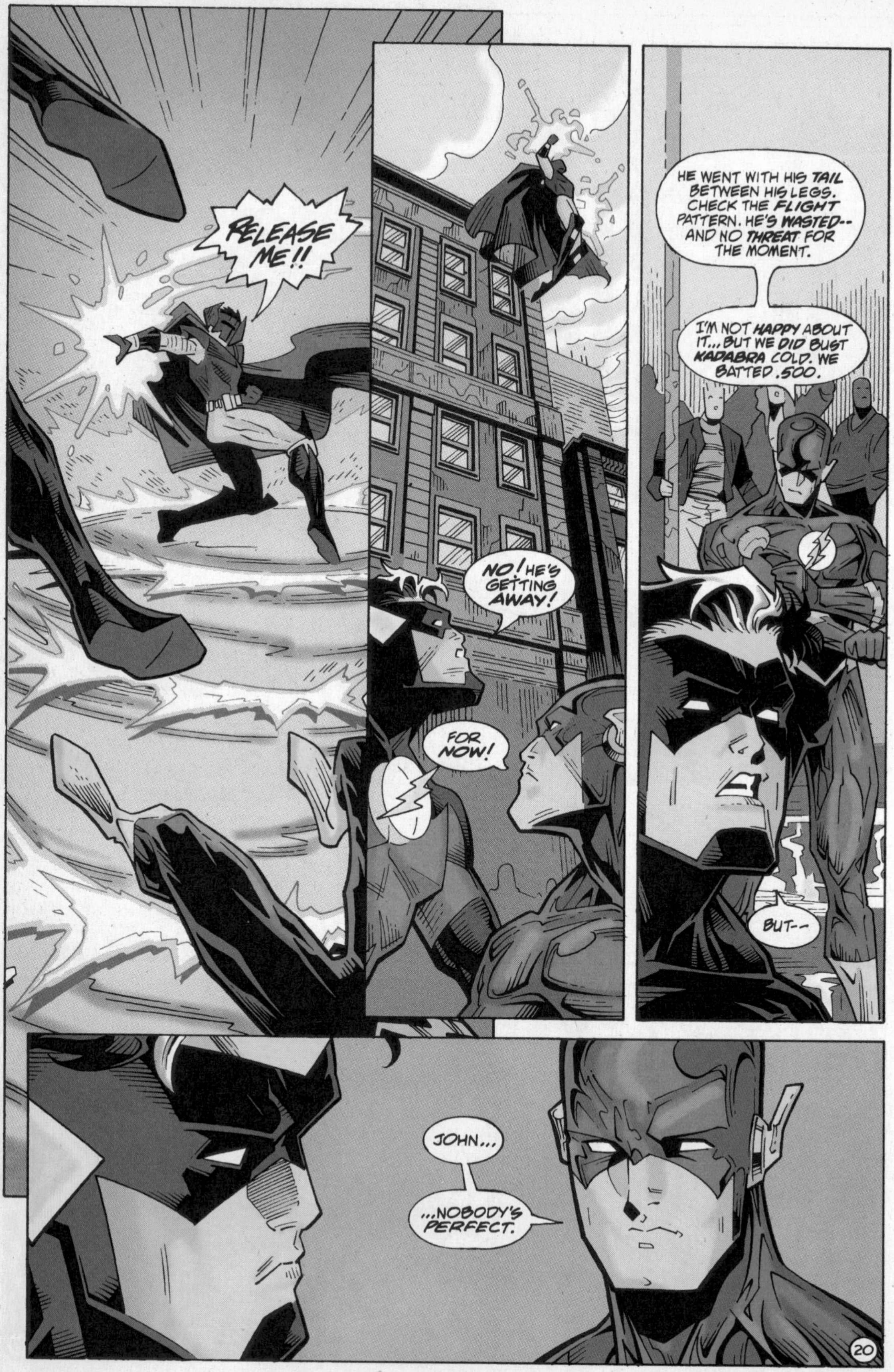
RELEASE ME!!
NO! HE'S GETTING AWAY!
FOR NOW!
HE WENT WITH HIS TAIL BETWEEN HIS LEGS. CHECK THE FLIGHT PATTERN. HE'S WASTED-- AND NO THREAT FOR THE MOMENT.
I'M NOT HAPPY ABOUT IT... BUT WE DID BUST KADABRA COLD. WE BATTED .500.
BUT--
JOHN...
...NOBODY'S PERFECT.
20

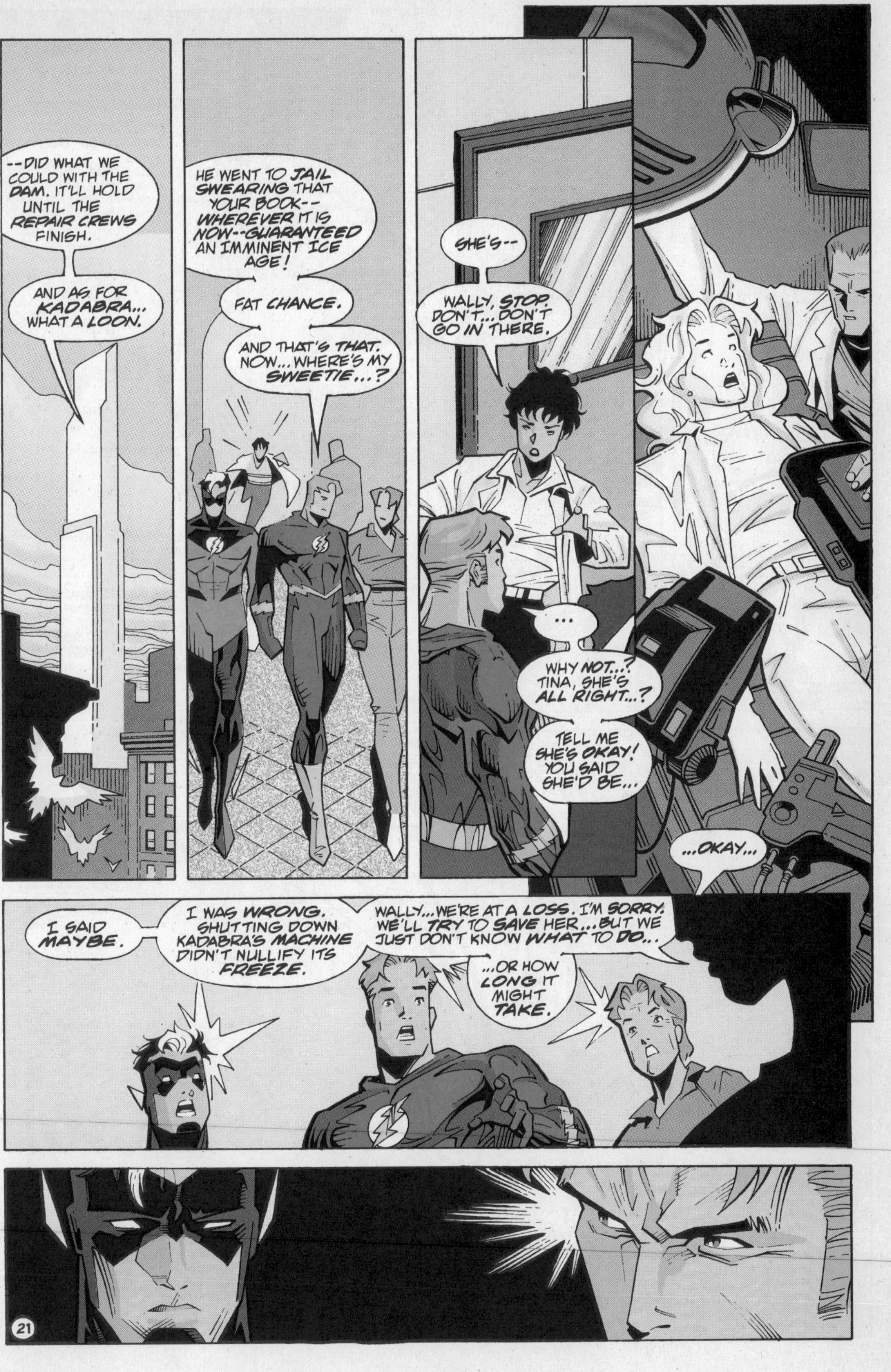

--DID WHAT WE COULD WITH THE DAM. IT'LL HOLD UNTIL THE REPAIR CREWS FINISH.
AND AS FOR KADABRA... WHAT A LOON.
HE WENT TO JAIL SWEARING THAT YOUR BOOK-- WHEREVER IT IS NOW--GUARANTEED AN IMMINENT ICE AGE!
FAT CHANCE.
AND THAT'S THAT. NOW... WHERE'S MY SWEETIE...?
SHE'S--
WALLY, STOP. DON'T... DON'T GO IN THERE.
...
WHY NOT...? TINA, SHE'S ALL RIGHT...?
TELL ME SHE'S OKAY! YOU SAID SHE'D BE...
...OKAY...
I SAID MAYBE.
I WAS WRONG. SHUTTING DOWN KADABRA'S MACHINE DIDN'T NULLIFY ITS FREEZE.
WALLY... WE'RE AT A LOSS. I'M SORRY. WE'LL TRY TO SAVE HER... BUT WE JUST DON'T KNOW WHAT TO DO...
...OR HOW LONG IT MIGHT TAKE.
21

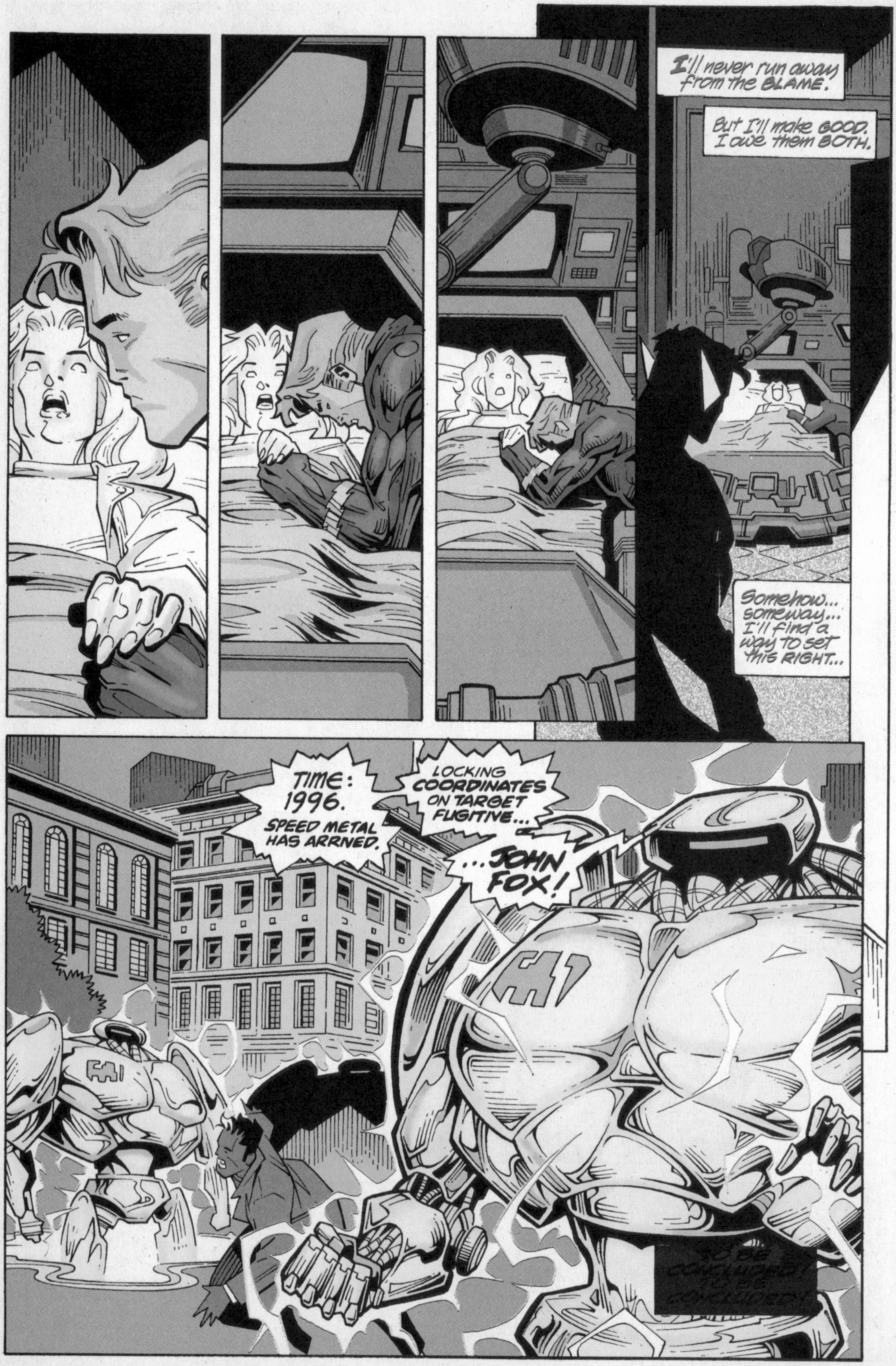
I'll never run away from the BLAME.
But I'll make GOOD. I owe them BOTH.
Somehow... someway... I'll find a way to set this RIGHT...
TIME: 1996. SPEED METAL HAS ARRIVED.
LOCKING COORDINATES ON TARGET FUGITIVE...
...JOHN FOX!
[redacted]

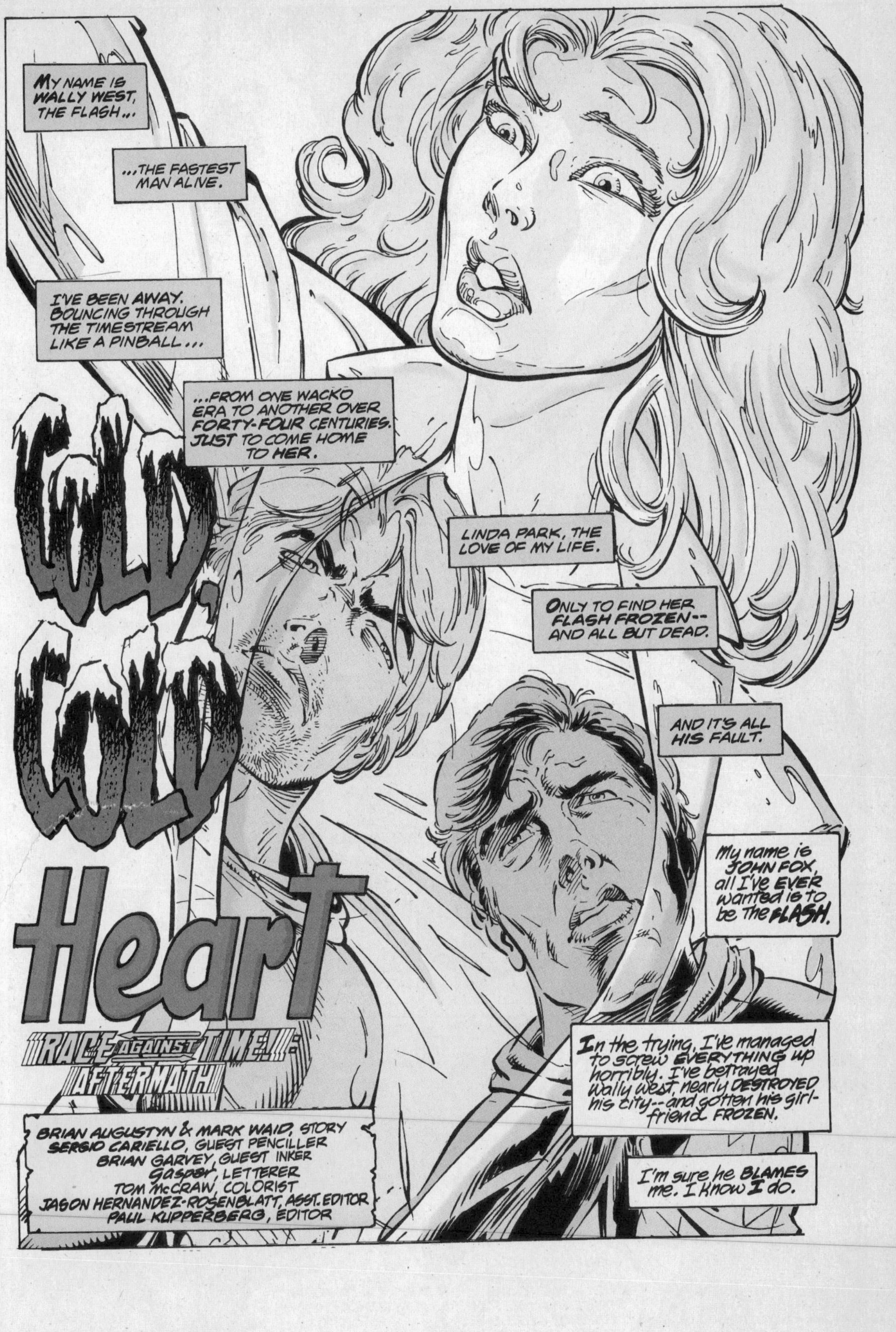

My name is Wally West, the Flash...
...the fastest man alive.
I've been away. Bouncing through the timestream like a pinball...
...from one wacko era to another over forty-four centuries. Just to come home to her.
Cold, Cold Heart
Linda Park, the love of my life.
Only to find her flash frozen--and all but dead.
And it's all his fault.
My name is John Fox, all I've ever wanted is to be the Flash.
Race against Time!: Aftermath
In the trying, I've managed to screw everything up horribly. I've betrayed Wally West, nearly destroyed his city--and gotten his girlfriend frozen.
I'm sure he blames me. I know I do.
Brian Augustyn & Mark Waid, story
Sergio Cariello, guest penciller
Brian Garvey, guest inker
Gaspar, letterer
Tom McCraw, colorist
Jason Hernandez-Rosenblatt, asst. editor
Paul Kupperberg, editor

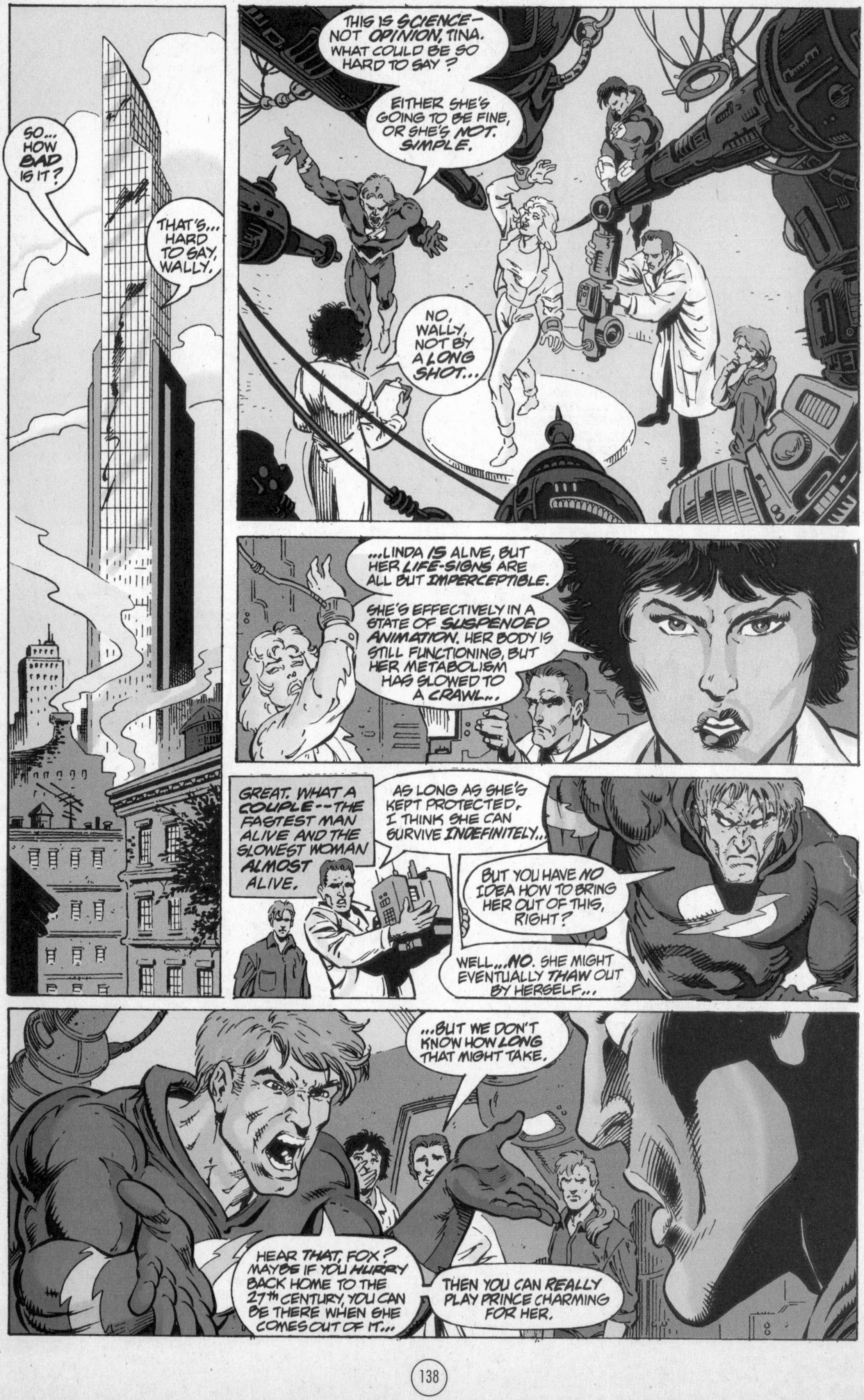
SO... HOW BAD IS IT?
THAT'S... HARD TO SAY, WALLY.
THIS IS SCIENCE-- NOT OPINION, TINA. WHAT COULD BE SO HARD TO SAY?
EITHER SHE'S GOING TO BE FINE, OR SHE'S NOT. SIMPLE.
NO, WALLY, NOT BY A LONG SHOT...
...LINDA IS ALIVE, BUT HER LIFE-SIGNS ARE ALL BUT IMPERCEPTIBLE.
SHE'S EFFECTIVELY IN A STATE OF SUSPENDED ANIMATION. HER BODY IS STILL FUNCTIONING, BUT HER METABOLISM HAS SLOWED TO A CRAWL...
GREAT. WHAT A COUPLE--THE FASTEST MAN ALIVE AND THE SLOWEST WOMAN ALMOST ALIVE.
AS LONG AS SHE'S KEPT PROTECTED, I THINK SHE CAN SURVIVE INDEFINITELY...
BUT YOU HAVE NO IDEA HOW TO BRING HER OUT OF THIS, RIGHT?
WELL...NO. SHE MIGHT EVENTUALLY THAW OUT BY HERSELF...
...BUT WE DON'T KNOW HOW LONG THAT MIGHT TAKE.
HEAR THAT, FOX? MAYBE IF YOU HURRY BACK HOME TO THE 27th CENTURY, YOU CAN BE THERE WHEN SHE COMES OUT OF IT...
THEN YOU CAN REALLY PLAY PRINCE CHARMING FOR HER.

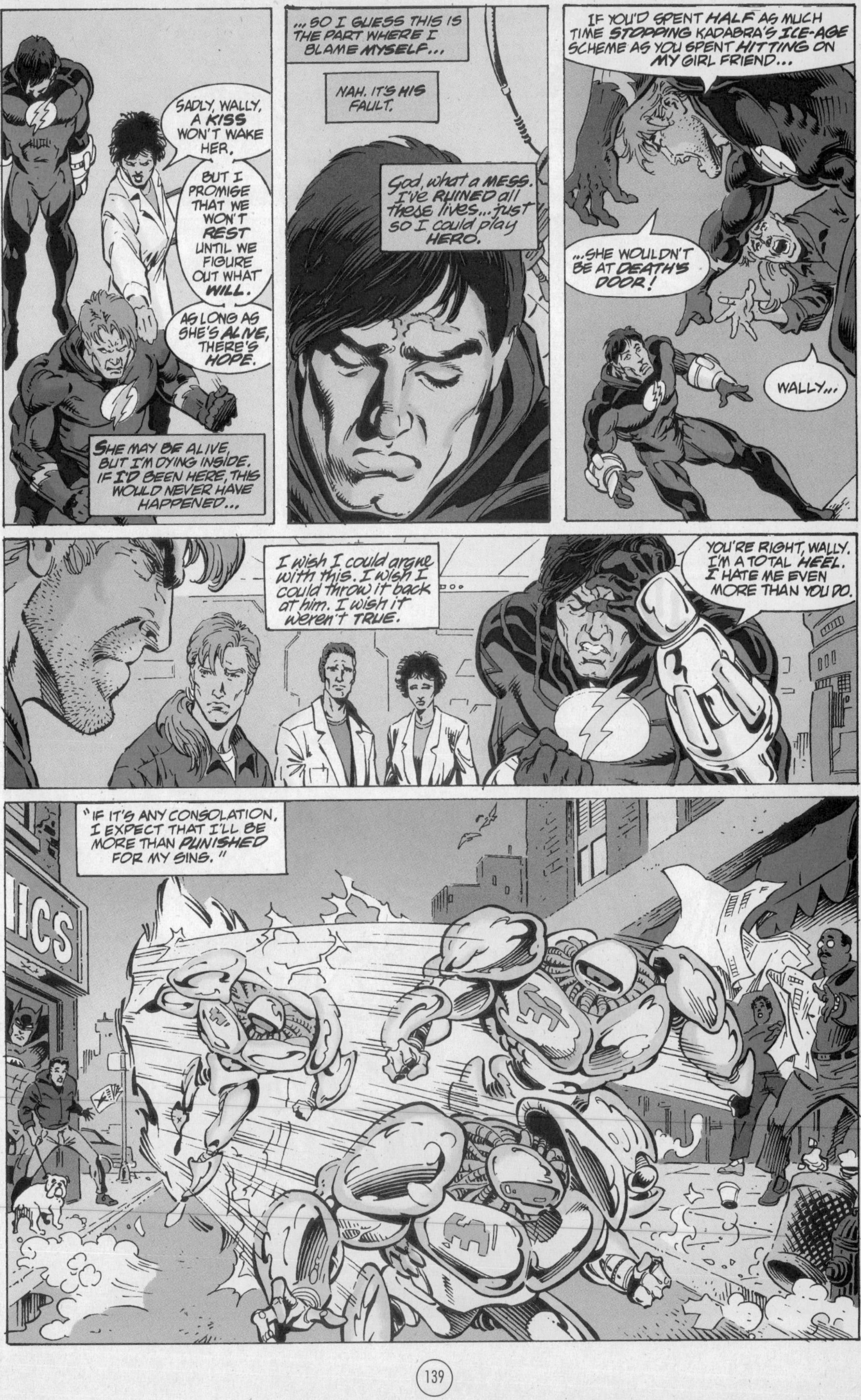
SADLY, WALLY, A KISS WON'T WAKE HER.
BUT I PROMISE THAT WE WON'T REST UNTIL WE FIGURE OUT WHAT WILL.
AS LONG AS SHE'S ALIVE, THERE'S HOPE.
SHE MAY BE ALIVE, BUT I'M DYING INSIDE. IF I'D BEEN HERE, THIS WOULD NEVER HAVE HAPPENED...
...SO I GUESS THIS IS THE PART WHERE I BLAME MYSELF...
NAH. IT'S HIS FAULT.
God, what a MESS. I've RUINED all these lives... just so I could play HERO.
IF YOU'D SPENT HALF AS MUCH TIME STOPPING KADABRA'S ICE-AGE SCHEME AS YOU SPENT HITTING ON MY GIRL FRIEND...
...SHE WOULDN'T BE AT DEATH'S DOOR!
WALLY...
I wish I could argue with this. I wish I could throw it back at him. I wish it weren't TRUE.
YOU'RE RIGHT, WALLY. I'M A TOTAL HEEL. I HATE ME EVEN MORE THAN YOU DO.
"IF IT'S ANY CONSOLATION, I EXPECT THAT I'LL BE MORE THAN PUNISHED FOR MY SINS."
ICS

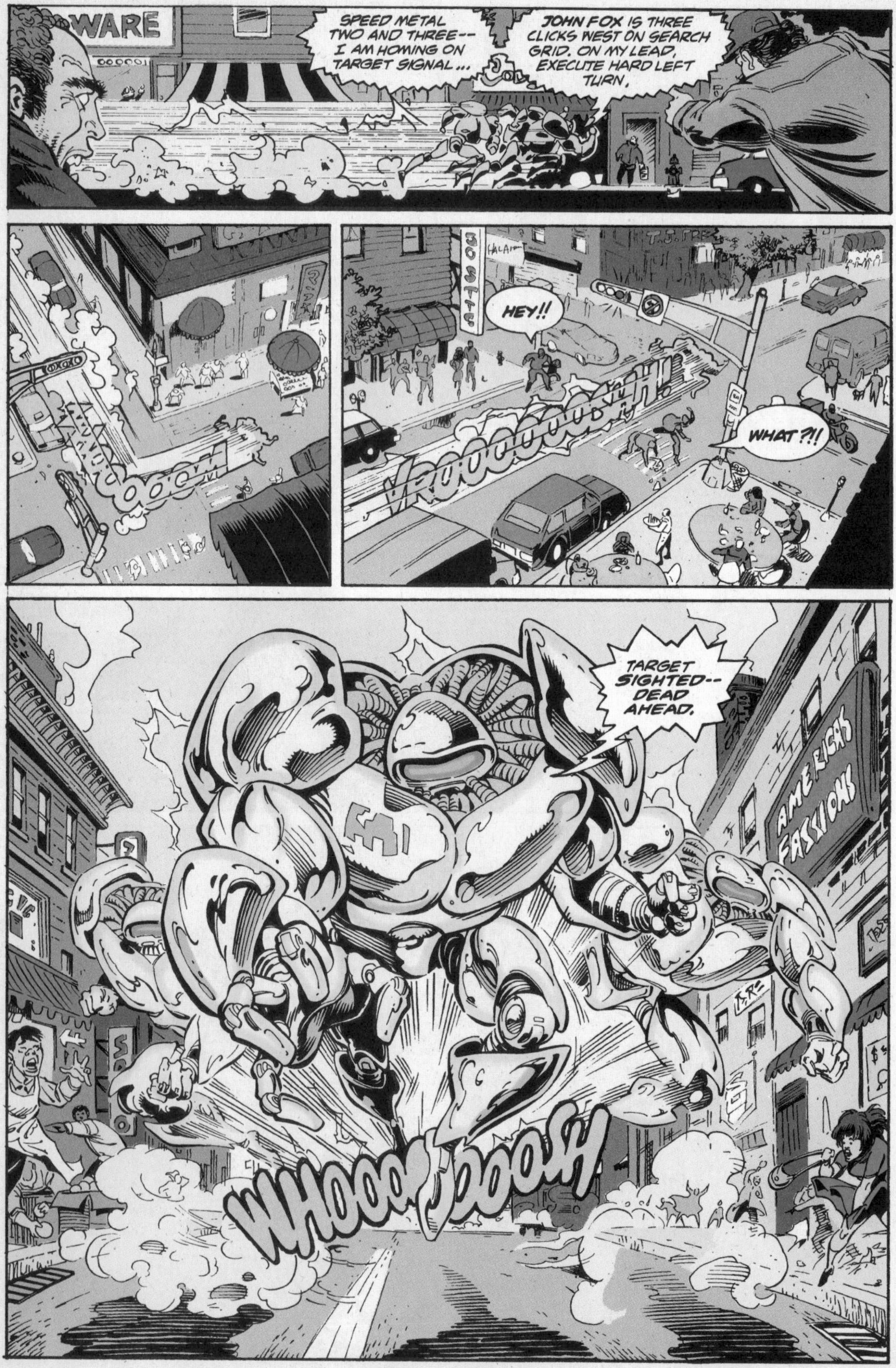
WARE
SPEED METAL TWO AND THREE-- I AM HOMING ON TARGET SIGNAL...
JOHN FOX IS THREE CLICKS WEST ON SEARCH GRID. ON MY LEAD, EXECUTE HARD LEFT TURN.
HEY!!
VROOOOOOOSSH!
WHAT?!!
TARGET SIGHTED-- DEAD AHEAD.
AMERICAS FASSIONS
WHOOOSOOSH

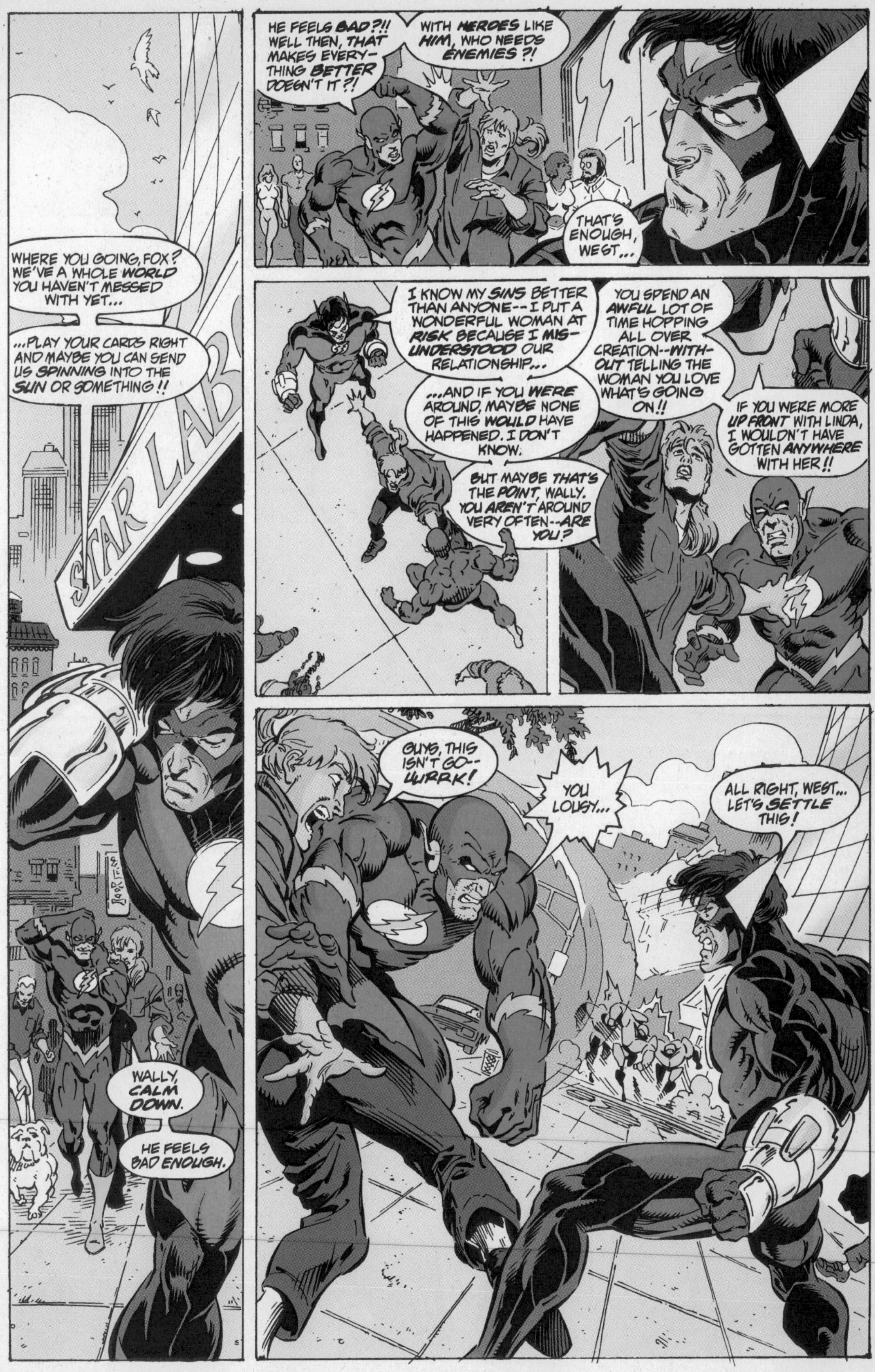
WHERE YOU GOING, FOX? WE'VE A WHOLE WORLD YOU HAVEN'T MESSED WITH YET...
...PLAY YOUR CARDS RIGHT AND MAYBE YOU CAN SEND US SPINNING INTO THE SUN OR SOMETHING!!
STAR LAB
WALLY, CALM DOWN.
HE FEELS BAD ENOUGH.
HE FEELS BAD?!! WELL THEN, THAT MAKES EVERY-THING BETTER DOESN'T IT?!
WITH HEROES LIKE HIM, WHO NEEDS ENEMIES?!
THAT'S ENOUGH, WEST...
I KNOW MY SINS BETTER THAN ANYONE-- I PUT A WONDERFUL WOMAN AT RISK BECAUSE I MIS-UNDERSTOOD OUR RELATIONSHIP...
...AND IF YOU WERE AROUND, MAYBE NONE OF THIS WOULD HAVE HAPPENED. I DON'T KNOW.
BUT MAYBE THAT'S THE POINT, WALLY. YOU AREN'T AROUND VERY OFTEN--ARE YOU?
YOU SPEND AN AWFUL LOT OF TIME HOPPING ALL OVER CREATION--WITH-OUT TELLING THE WOMAN YOU LOVE WHAT'S GOING ON!!
IF YOU WERE MORE UP FRONT WITH LINDA, I WOULDN'T HAVE GOTTEN ANYWHERE WITH HER!!
GUYS, THIS ISN'T GO-- UURRK!
YOU LOUSY...
ALL RIGHT, WEST... LET'S SETTLE THIS!

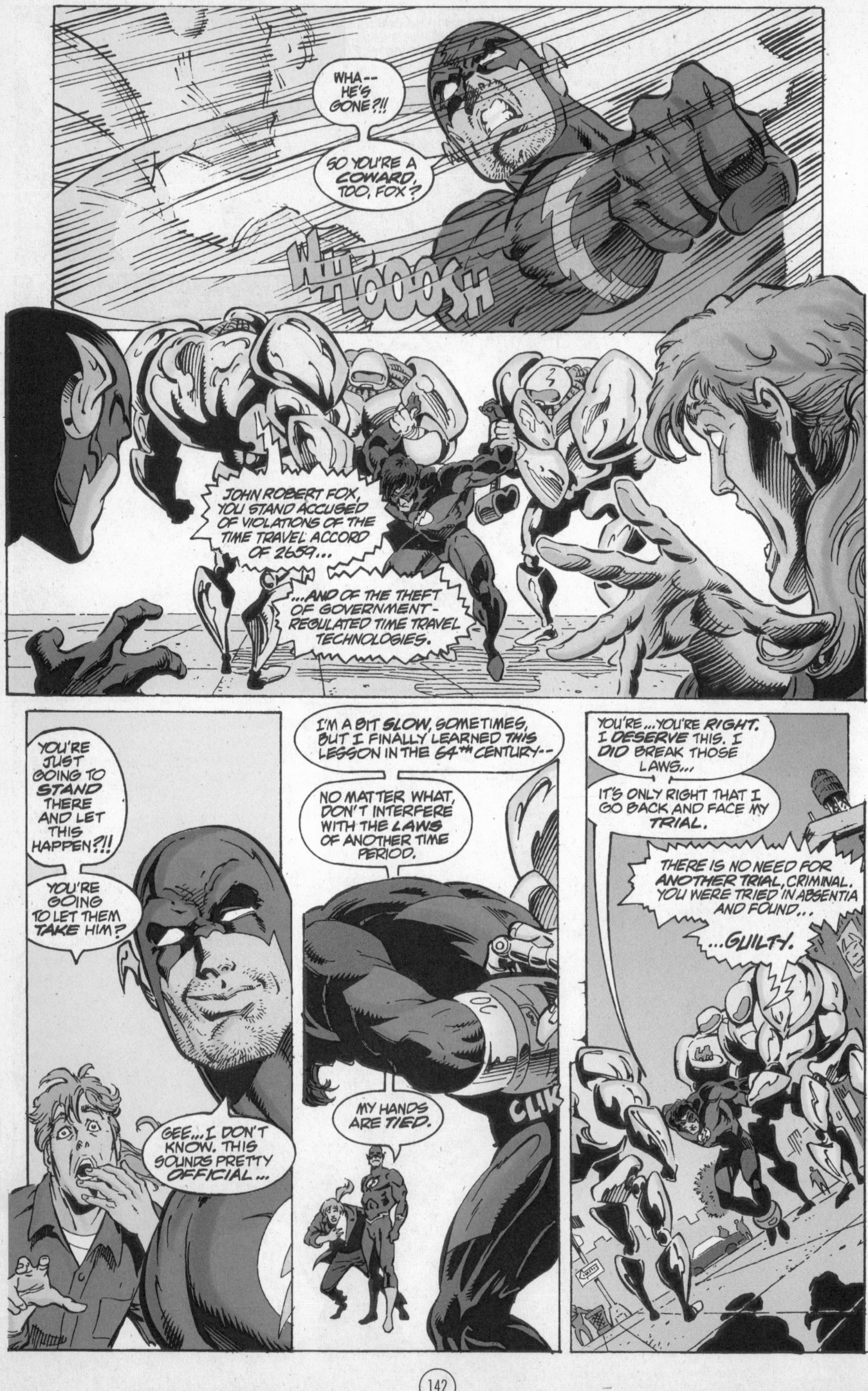

WHA-- HE'S GONE?!!
SO YOU'RE A COWARD, TOO, FOX?
WHHOOOOSH
JOHN ROBERT FOX, YOU STAND ACCUSED OF VIOLATIONS OF THE TIME TRAVEL ACCORD OF 2659...
...AND OF THE THEFT OF GOVERNMENT-REGULATED TIME TRAVEL TECHNOLOGIES.
YOU'RE JUST GOING TO STAND THERE AND LET THIS HAPPEN?!!
YOU'RE GOING TO LET THEM TAKE HIM?
GEE...I DON'T KNOW. THIS SOUNDS PRETTY OFFICIAL...
I'M A BIT SLOW, SOMETIMES, BUT I FINALLY LEARNED THIS LESSON IN THE 64TH CENTURY--
NO MATTER WHAT, DON'T INTERFERE WITH THE LAWS OF ANOTHER TIME PERIOD.
CLIK
MY HANDS ARE TIED.
YOU'RE...YOU'RE RIGHT. I DESERVE THIS. I DID BREAK THOSE LAWS...
IT'S ONLY RIGHT THAT I GO BACK AND FACE MY TRIAL.
THERE IS NO NEED FOR ANOTHER TRIAL, CRIMINAL. YOU WERE TRIED IN ABSENTIA AND FOUND...
...GUILTY.

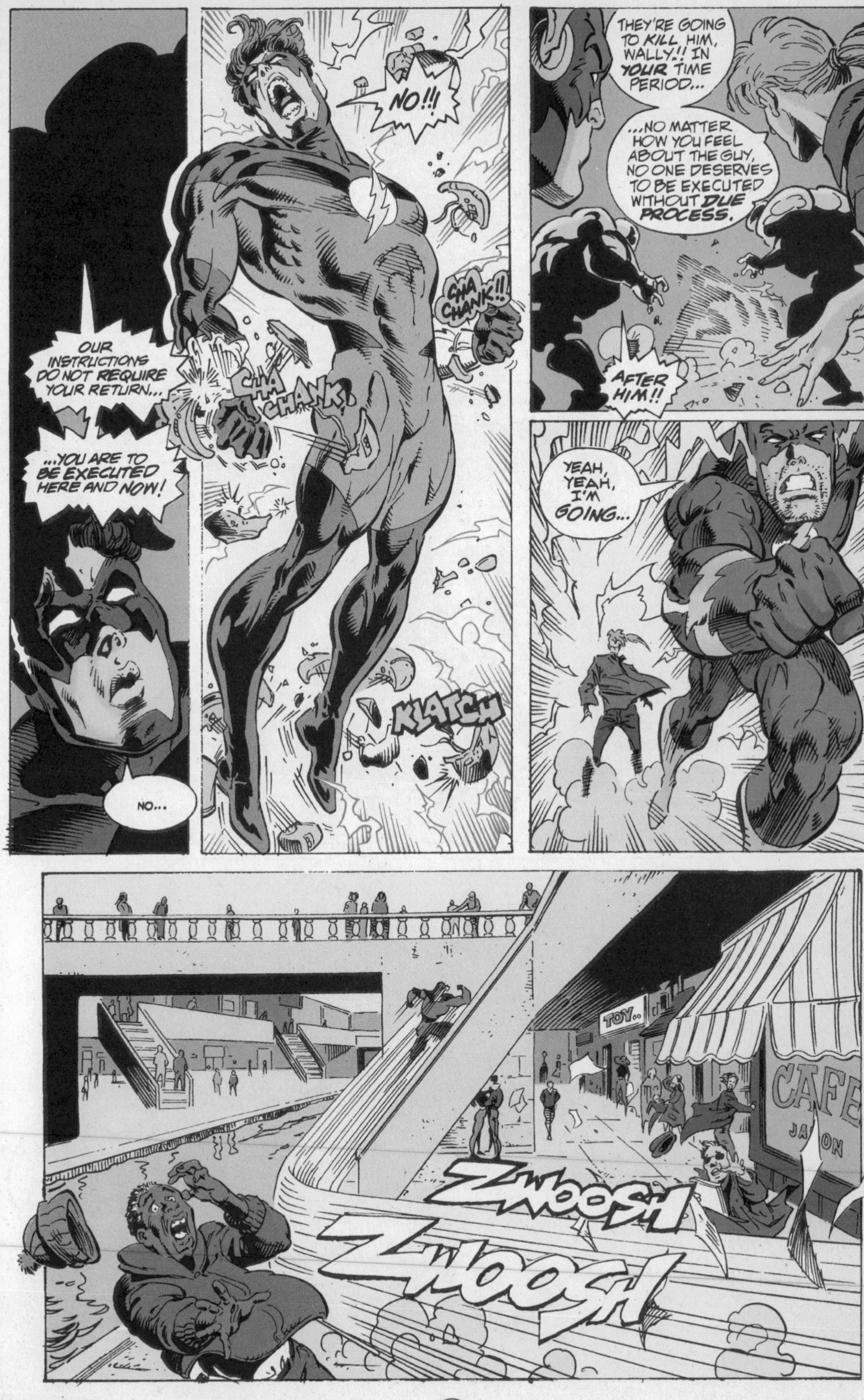
OUR INSTRUCTIONS DO NOT REQUIRE YOUR RETURN...
...YOU ARE TO BE EXECUTED HERE AND NOW!
NO...
NO!!!
CHA CHANK!!
CHA CHANK!
KLATCH
THEY'RE GOING TO KILL HIM, WALLY!! IN YOUR TIME PERIOD...
...NO MATTER HOW YOU FEEL ABOUT THE GUY, NO ONE DESERVES TO BE EXECUTED WITHOUT DUE PROCESS.
AFTER HIM!!
YEAH, YEAH, I'M GOING...
TOY..
CAFE
ZWOOSH
ZWOOSH

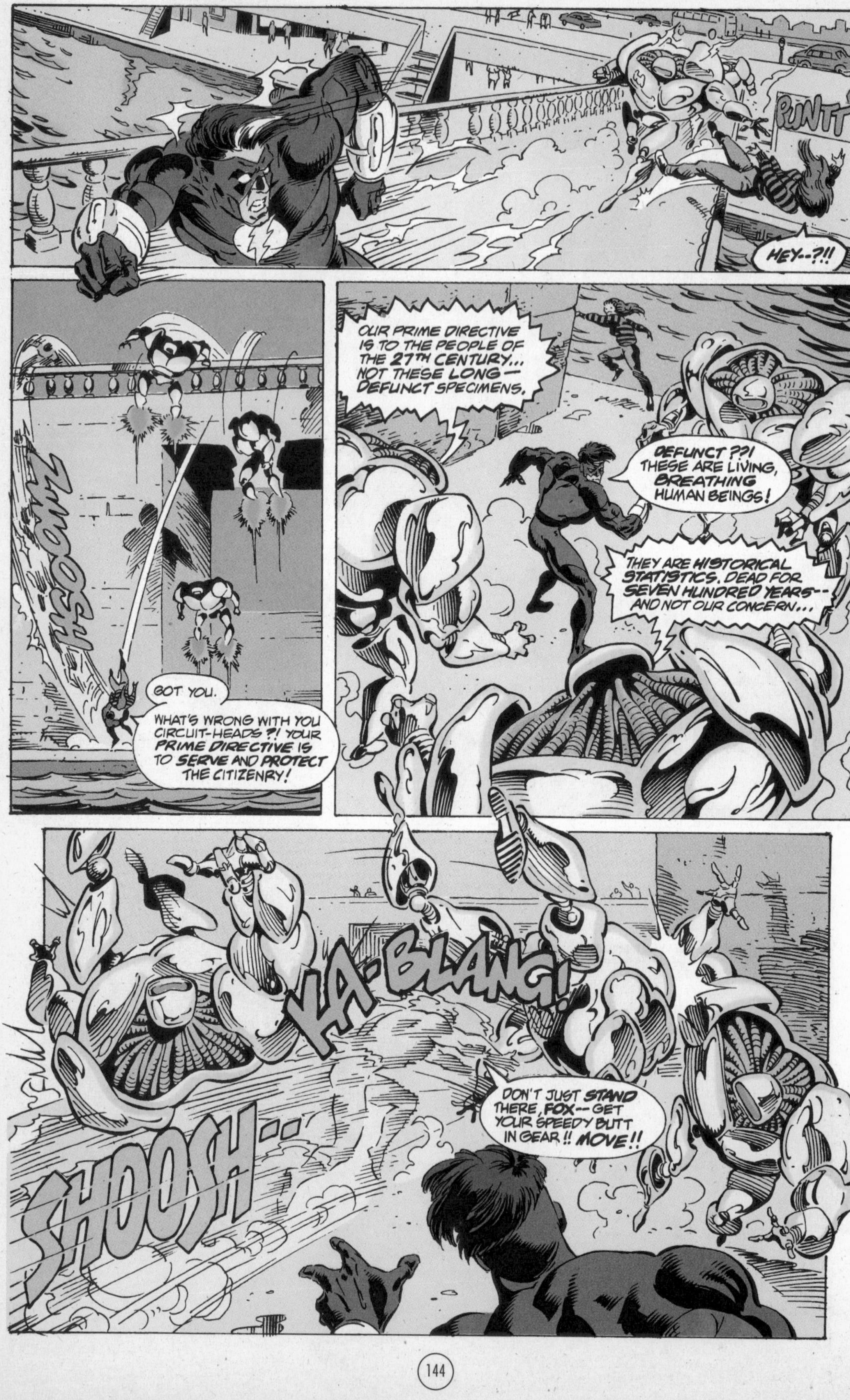
PUNTT
HEY--?!!
ZHOOOSH
GOT YOU.
WHAT'S WRONG WITH YOU CIRCUIT-HEADS?! YOUR PRIME DIRECTIVE IS TO SERVE AND PROTECT THE CITIZENRY!
OUR PRIME DIRECTIVE IS TO THE PEOPLE OF THE 27TH CENTURY... NOT THESE LONG-DEFUNCT SPECIMENS.
DEFUNCT??! THESE ARE LIVING, BREATHING HUMAN BEINGS!
THEY ARE HISTORICAL STATISTICS. DEAD FOR SEVEN HUNDRED YEARS-- AND NOT OUR CONCERN...
KA-BLANG!
DON'T JUST STAND THERE, FOX-- GET YOUR SPEEDY BUTT IN GEAR!! MOVE!!
SHOOSH..

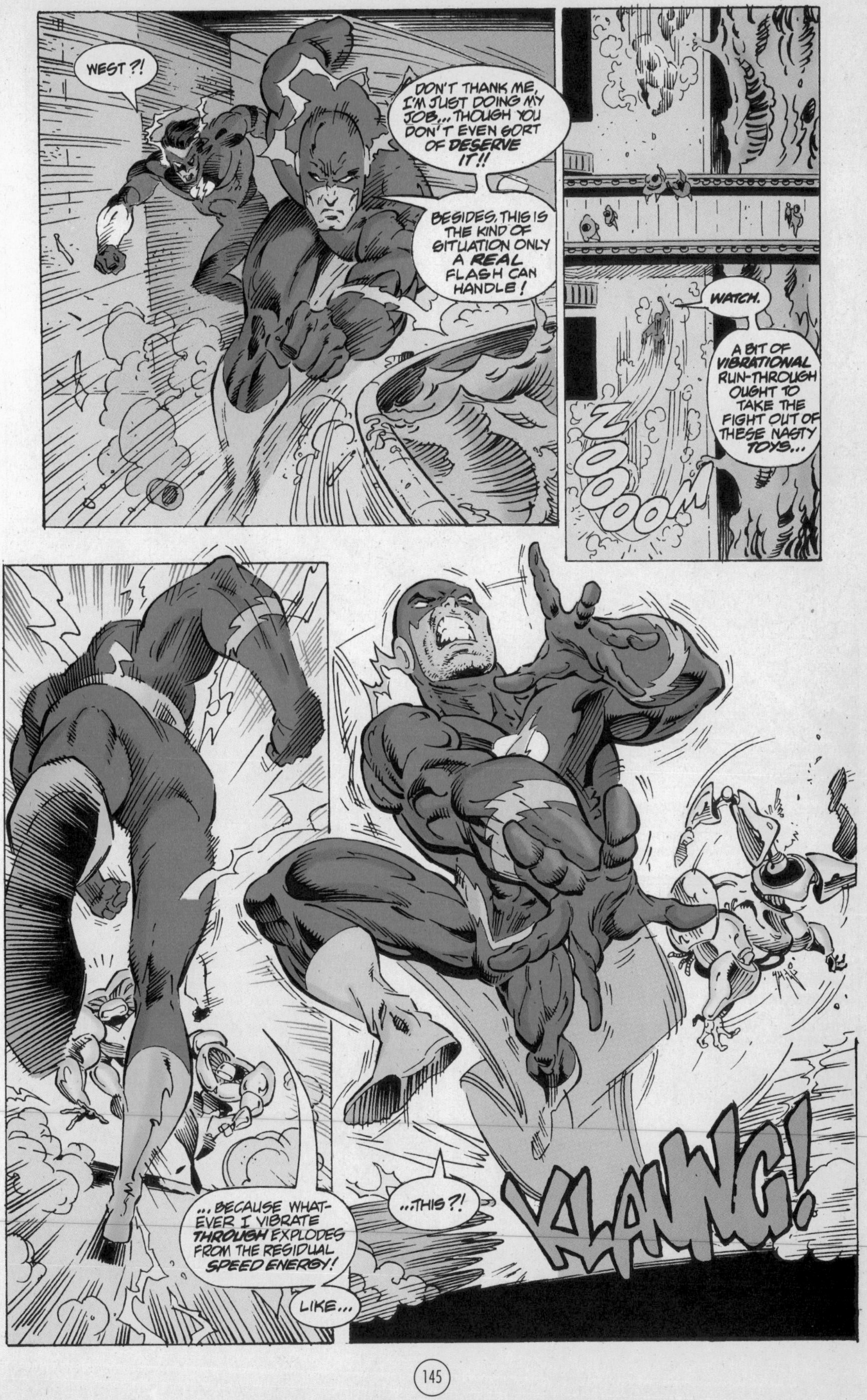
WEST ?!
DON'T THANK ME, I'M JUST DOING MY JOB... THOUGH YOU DON'T EVEN SORT OF DESERVE IT!!
BESIDES, THIS IS THE KIND OF SITUATION ONLY A REAL FLASH CAN HANDLE!
WATCH.
A BIT OF VIBRATIONAL RUN-THROUGH OUGHT TO TAKE THE FIGHT OUT OF THESE NASTY TOYS...
ZOOOOOM
...BECAUSE WHAT-EVER I VIBRATE THROUGH EXPLODES FROM THE RESIDUAL SPEED ENERGY!
LIKE...
...THIS?!
KLANG!

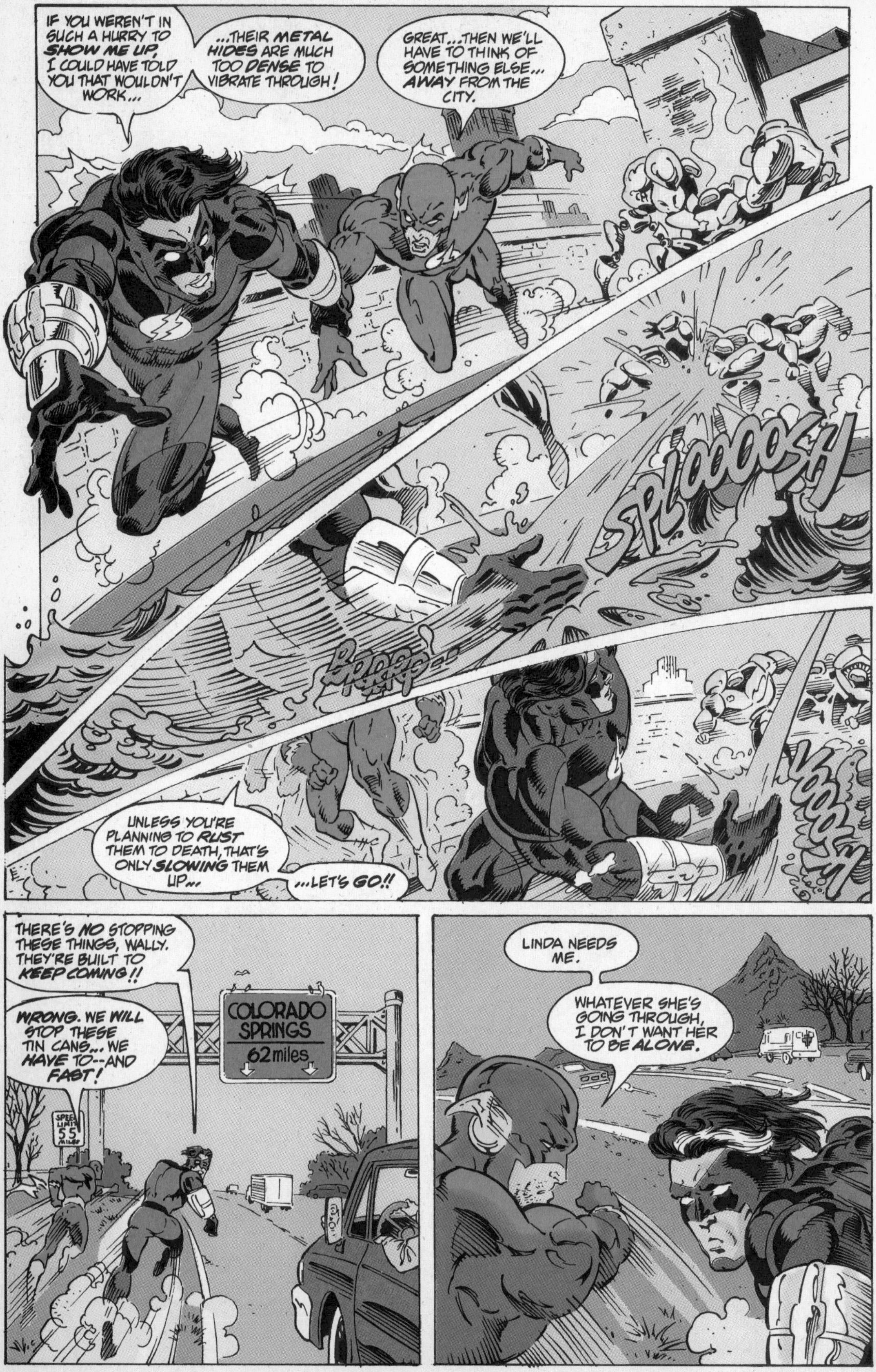

IF YOU WEREN'T IN SUCH A HURRY TO SHOW ME UP, I COULD HAVE TOLD YOU THAT WOULDN'T WORK...
...THEIR METAL HIDES ARE MUCH TOO DENSE TO VIBRATE THROUGH!
GREAT...THEN WE'LL HAVE TO THINK OF SOMETHING ELSE... AWAY FROM THE CITY.
SPLOOOOSH
UNLESS YOU'RE PLANNING TO RUST THEM TO DEATH, THAT'S ONLY SLOWING THEM UP...
...LET'S GO!!
THERE'S NO STOPPING THESE THINGS, WALLY. THEY'RE BUILT TO KEEP COMING!!
WRONG. WE WILL STOP THESE TIN CANS... WE HAVE TO--AND FAST!
COLORADO SPRINGS
62 miles
LINDA NEEDS ME.
WHATEVER SHE'S GOING THROUGH, I DON'T WANT HER TO BE ALONE.

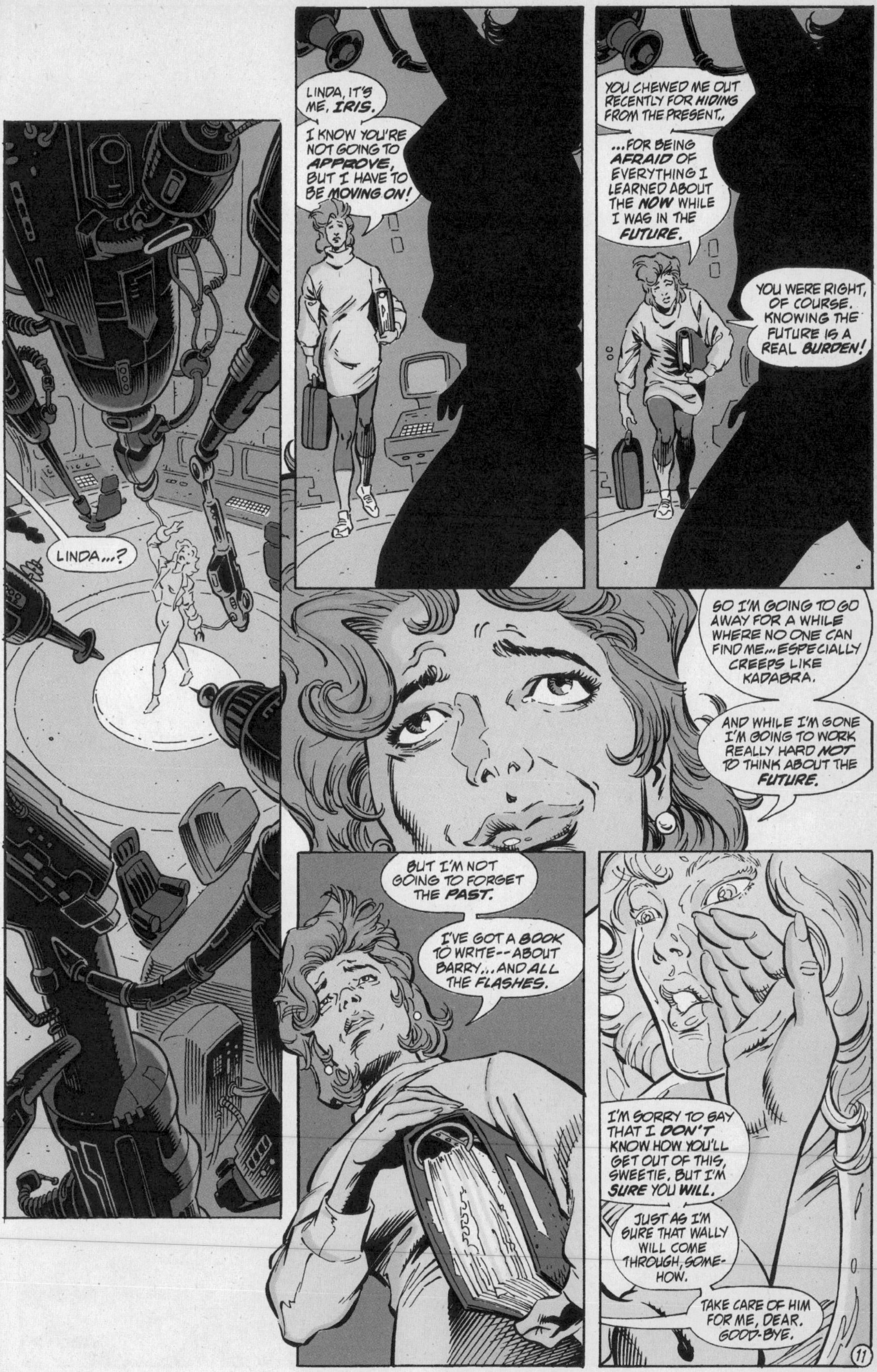
LINDA, IT'S ME, IRIS.
I KNOW YOU'RE NOT GOING TO APPROVE, BUT I HAVE TO BE MOVING ON!
YOU CHEWED ME OUT RECENTLY FOR HIDING FROM THE PRESENT..
...FOR BEING AFRAID OF EVERYTHING I LEARNED ABOUT THE NOW WHILE I WAS IN THE FUTURE.
YOU WERE RIGHT, OF COURSE. KNOWING THE FUTURE IS A REAL BURDEN!
LINDA...?
SO I'M GOING TO GO AWAY FOR A WHILE WHERE NO ONE CAN FIND ME... ESPECIALLY CREEPS LIKE KADABRA.
AND WHILE I'M GONE I'M GOING TO WORK REALLY HARD NOT TO THINK ABOUT THE FUTURE.
BUT I'M NOT GOING TO FORGET THE PAST.
I'VE GOT A BOOK TO WRITE--ABOUT BARRY... AND ALL THE FLASHES.
I'M SORRY TO SAY THAT I DON'T KNOW HOW YOU'LL GET OUT OF THIS, SWEETIE, BUT I'M SURE YOU WILL.
JUST AS I'M SURE THAT WALLY WILL COME THROUGH, SOMEHOW.
TAKE CARE OF HIM FOR ME, DEAR. GOOD-BYE.
11

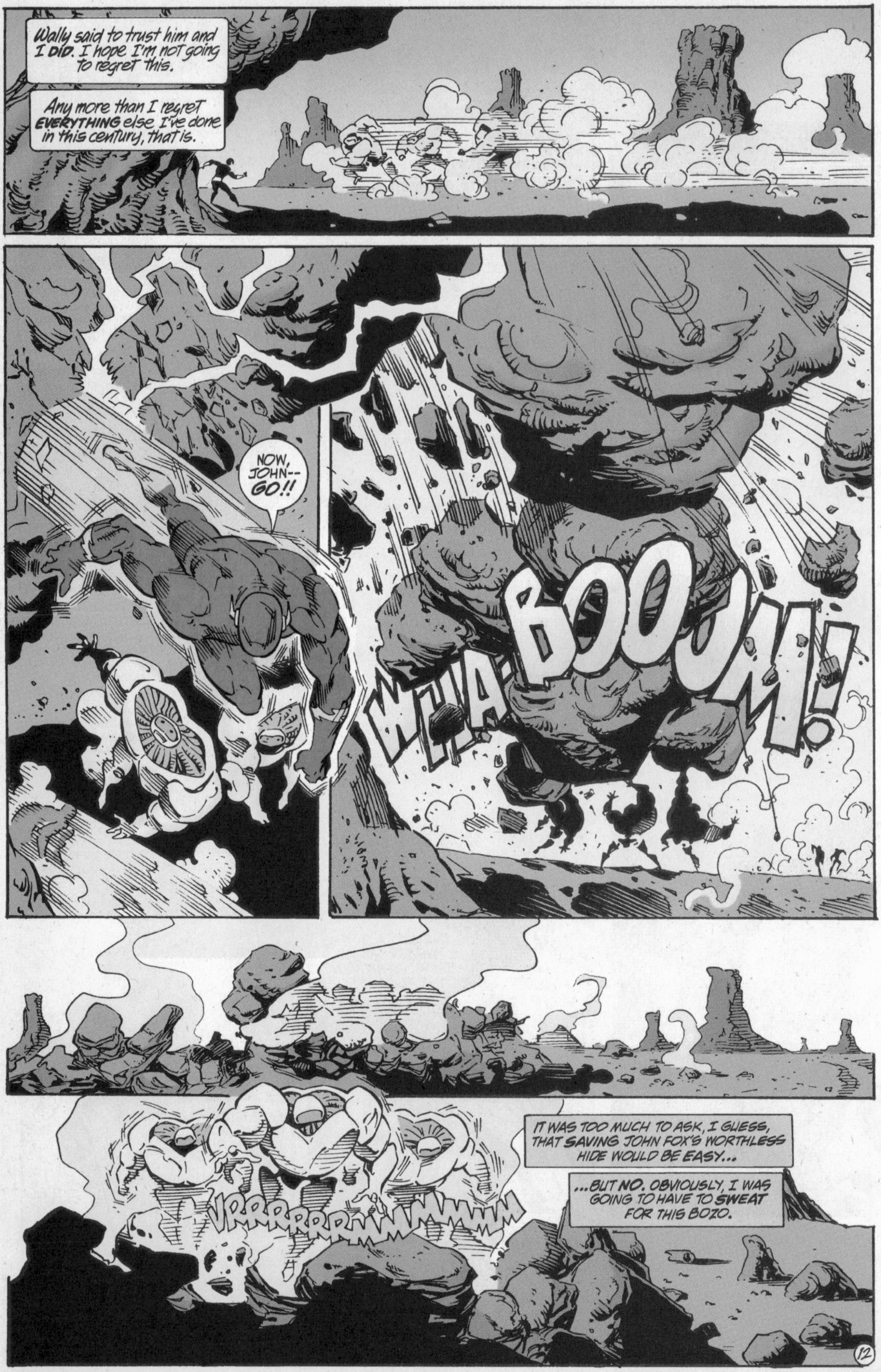
Wally said to trust him and I DID. I hope I'm not going to regret this.
Any more than I regret EVERYTHING else I've done in this century, that is.
NOW, JOHN-- GO!!
WHA-BOOOM!
IT WAS TOO MUCH TO ASK, I GUESS, THAT SAVING JOHN FOX'S WORTHLESS HIDE WOULD BE EASY...
...BUT NO. OBVIOUSLY, I WAS GOING TO HAVE TO SWEAT FOR THIS BOZO.
VRRRRRRRMMMMMM
12

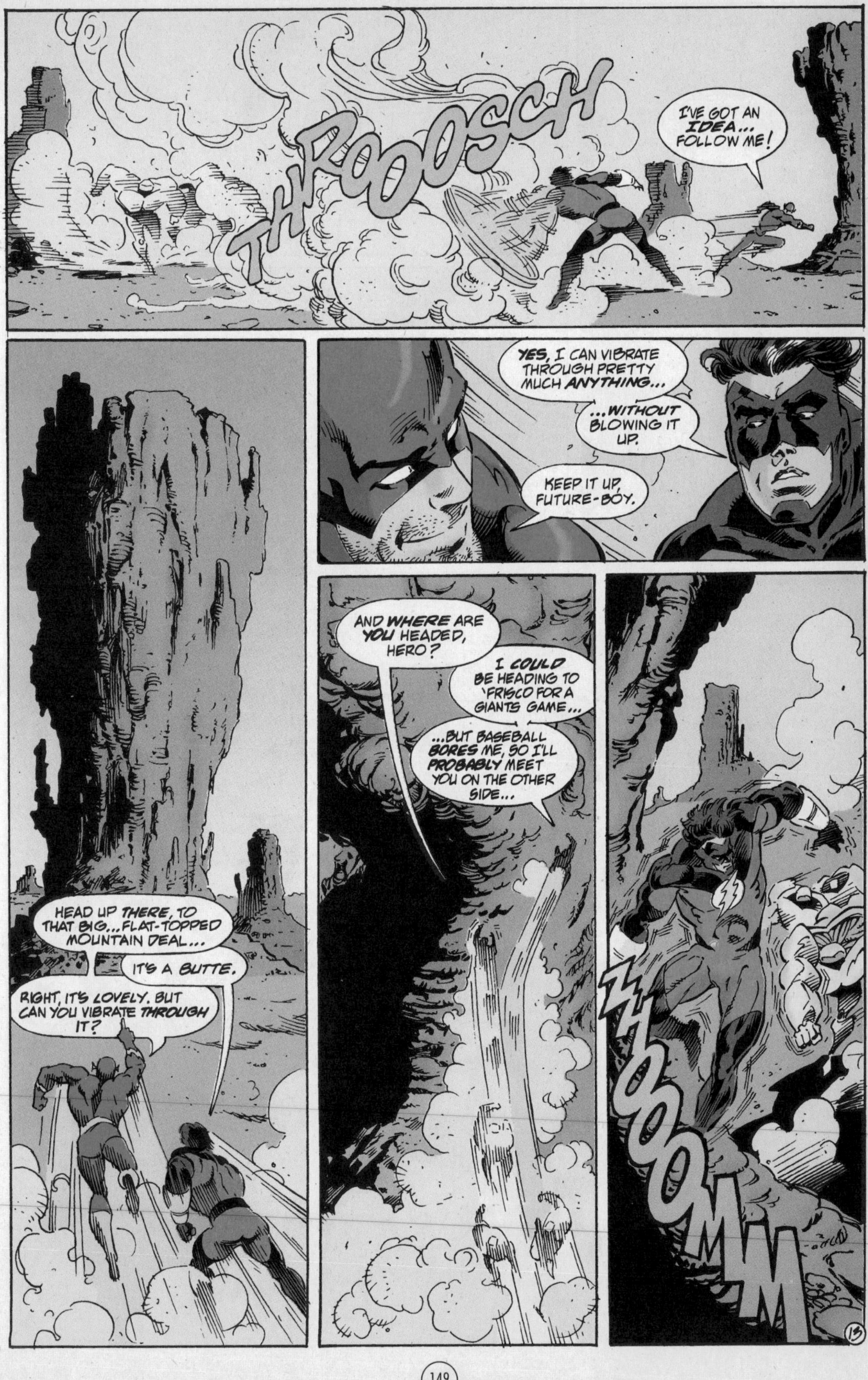
THROOOSCH
I'VE GOT AN IDEA... FOLLOW ME!
HEAD UP THERE, TO THAT BIG...FLAT-TOPPED MOUNTAIN DEAL...
IT'S A BUTTE.
RIGHT, IT'S LOVELY. BUT CAN YOU VIBRATE THROUGH IT?
YES, I CAN VIBRATE THROUGH PRETTY MUCH ANYTHING...
...WITHOUT BLOWING IT UP.
KEEP IT UP, FUTURE-BOY.
AND WHERE ARE YOU HEADED, HERO?
I COULD BE HEADING TO 'FRISCO FOR A GIANTS GAME...
...BUT BASEBALL BORES ME, SO I'LL PROBABLY MEET YOU ON THE OTHER SIDE...
ZHOOOOMMM
13

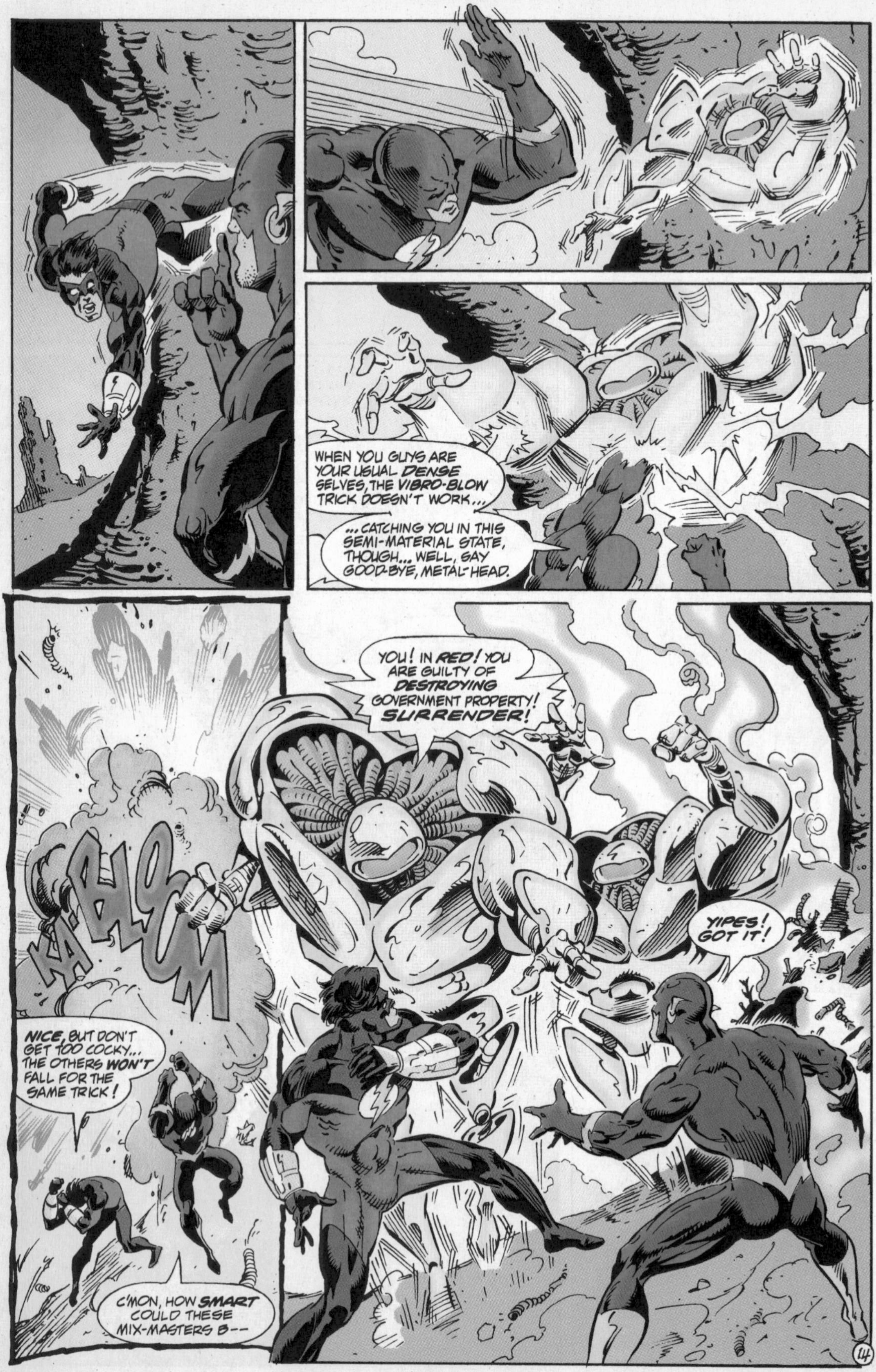

WHEN YOU GUYS ARE YOUR USUAL DENSE SELVES, THE VIBRO-BLOW TRICK DOESN'T WORK...
...CATCHING YOU IN THIS SEMI-MATERIAL STATE, THOUGH... WELL, SAY GOOD-BYE, METAL-HEAD.
YOU! IN RED! YOU ARE GUILTY OF DESTROYING GOVERNMENT PROPERTY! SURRENDER!
KA-BLOOM
YIPES! GOT IT!
NICE, BUT DON'T GET TOO COCKY... THE OTHERS WON'T FALL FOR THE SAME TRICK!
C'MON, HOW SMART COULD THESE MIX-MASTERS B--
14

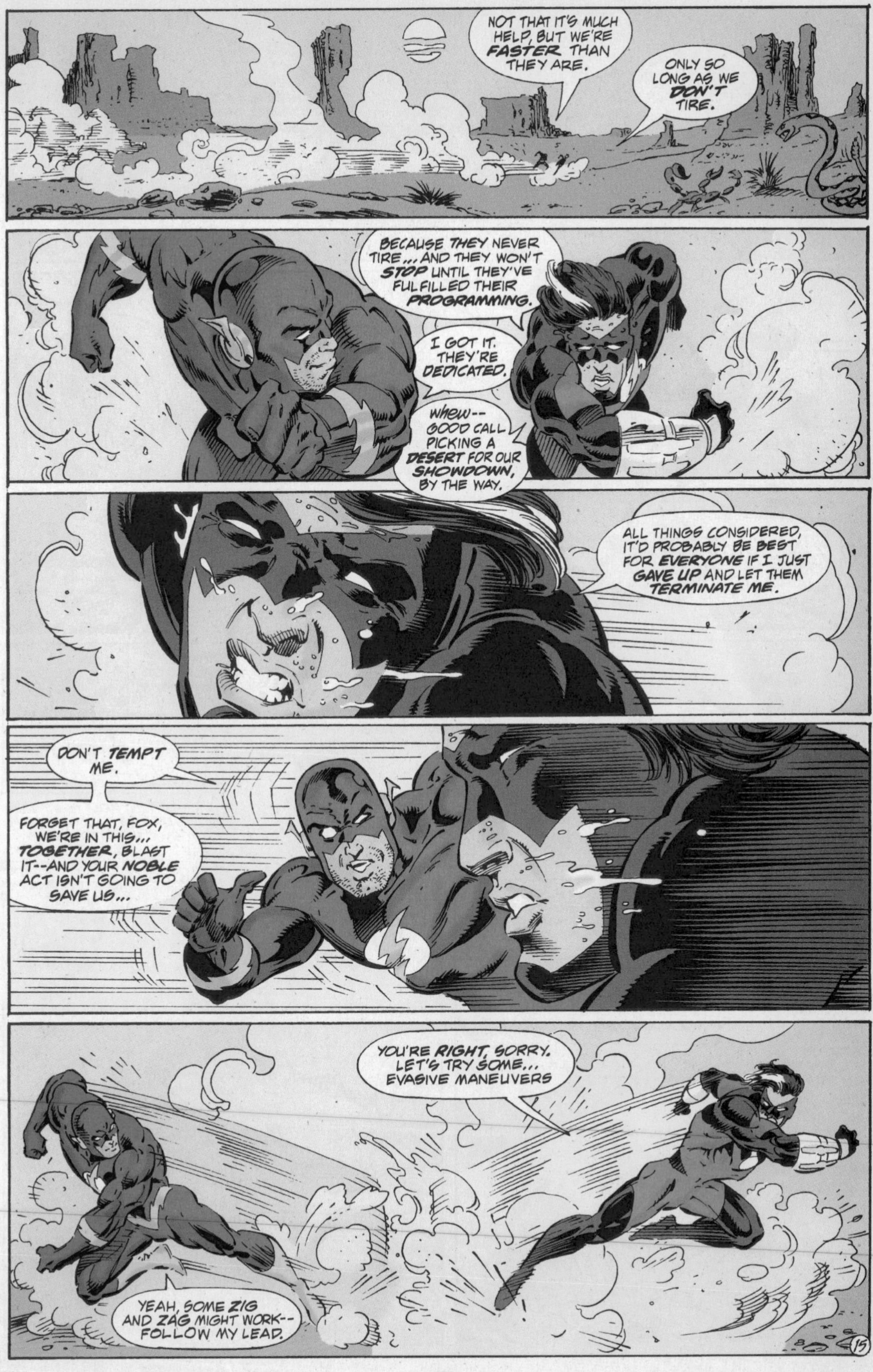
NOT THAT IT'S MUCH HELP, BUT WE'RE FASTER THAN THEY ARE.
ONLY SO LONG AS WE DON'T TIRE.
BECAUSE THEY NEVER TIRE... AND THEY WON'T STOP UNTIL THEY'VE FULFILLED THEIR PROGRAMMING.
I GOT IT. THEY'RE DEDICATED.
whew-- GOOD CALL PICKING A DESERT FOR OUR SHOWDOWN, BY THE WAY.
ALL THINGS CONSIDERED, IT'D PROBABLY BE BEST FOR EVERYONE IF I JUST GAVE UP AND LET THEM TERMINATE ME.
DON'T TEMPT ME.
FORGET THAT, FOX, WE'RE IN THIS... TOGETHER, BLAST IT--AND YOUR NOBLE ACT ISN'T GOING TO SAVE US...
YOU'RE RIGHT, SORRY. LET'S TRY SOME... EVASIVE MANEUVERS
YEAH, SOME ZIG AND ZAG MIGHT WORK-- FOLLOW MY LEAD.
15

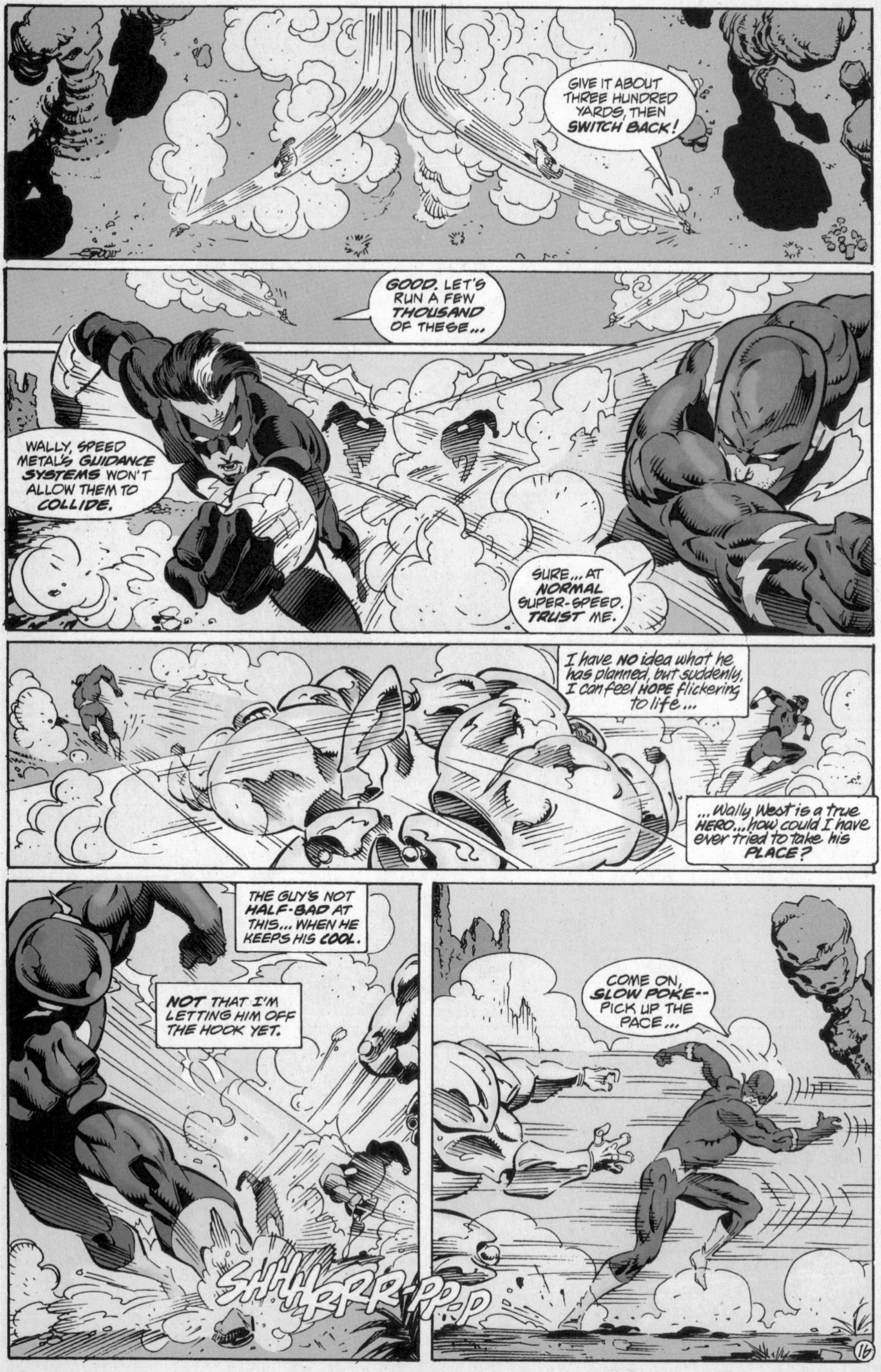
GIVE IT ABOUT THREE HUNDRED YARDS, THEN SWITCH BACK!
GOOD. LET'S RUN A FEW THOUSAND OF THESE...
WALLY, SPEED METAL'S GUIDANCE SYSTEMS WON'T ALLOW THEM TO COLLIDE.
SURE... AT NORMAL SUPER-SPEED. TRUST ME.
I have NO idea what he has planned, but suddenly, I can feel HOPE flickering to life...
...Wally West is a true HERO...how could I have ever tried to take his PLACE?
THE GUY'S NOT HALF-BAD AT THIS... WHEN HE KEEPS HIS COOL.
NOT THAT I'M LETTING HIM OFF THE HOOK YET.
SHHHRRR-PP-P
COME ON, SLOW POKE-- PICK UP THE PACE...
16

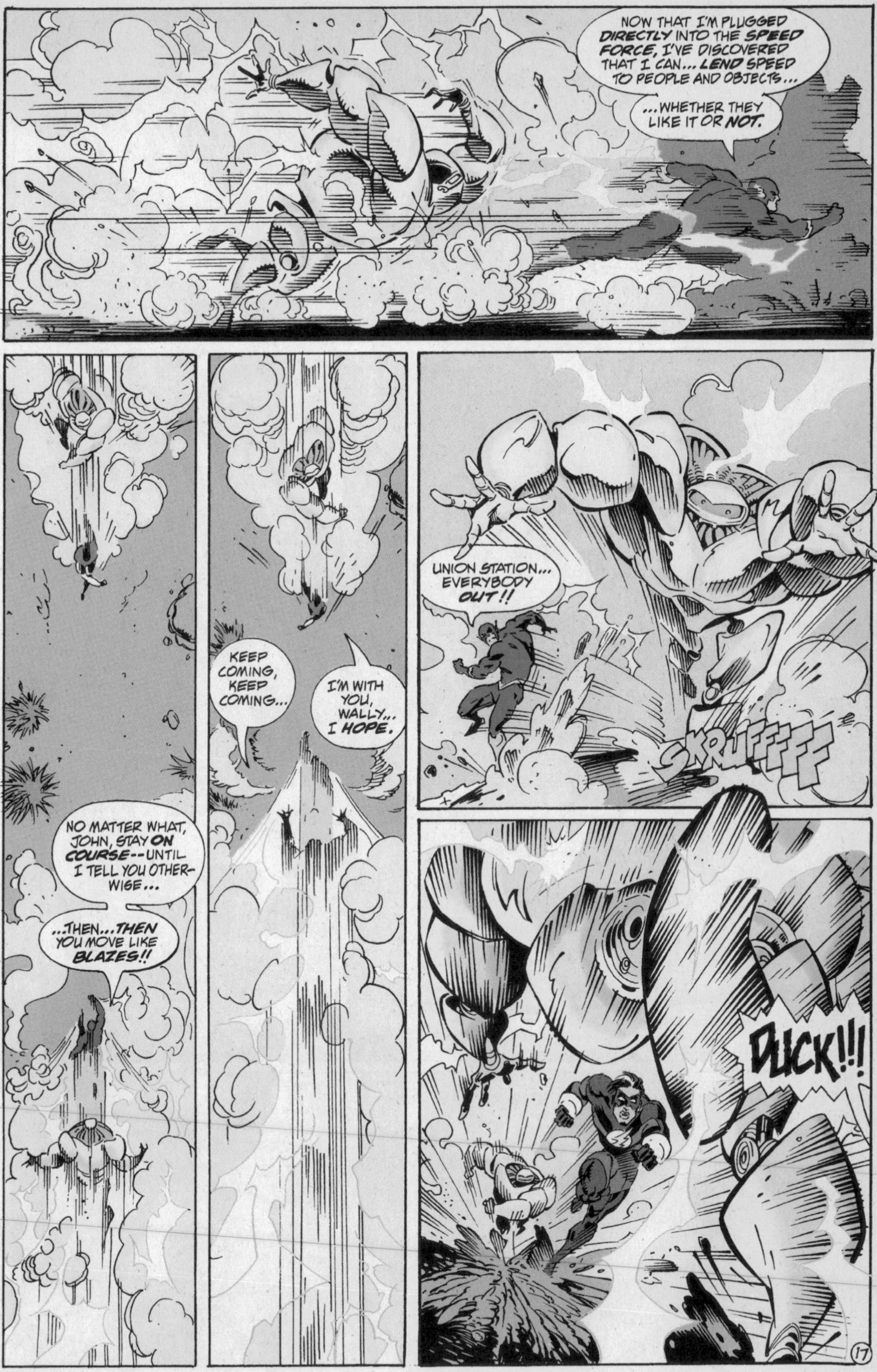
NOW THAT I'M PLUGGED DIRECTLY INTO THE SPEED FORCE, I'VE DISCOVERED THAT I CAN... LEND SPEED TO PEOPLE AND OBJECTS...
...WHETHER THEY LIKE IT OR NOT.
NO MATTER WHAT, JOHN, STAY ON COURSE--UNTIL I TELL YOU OTHER-WISE...
...THEN...THEN YOU MOVE LIKE BLAZES!!
KEEP COMING, KEEP COMING...
I'M WITH YOU, WALLY... I HOPE.
UNION STATION... EVERYBODY OUT!!
SKRUFFFFF
DUCK!!!
17

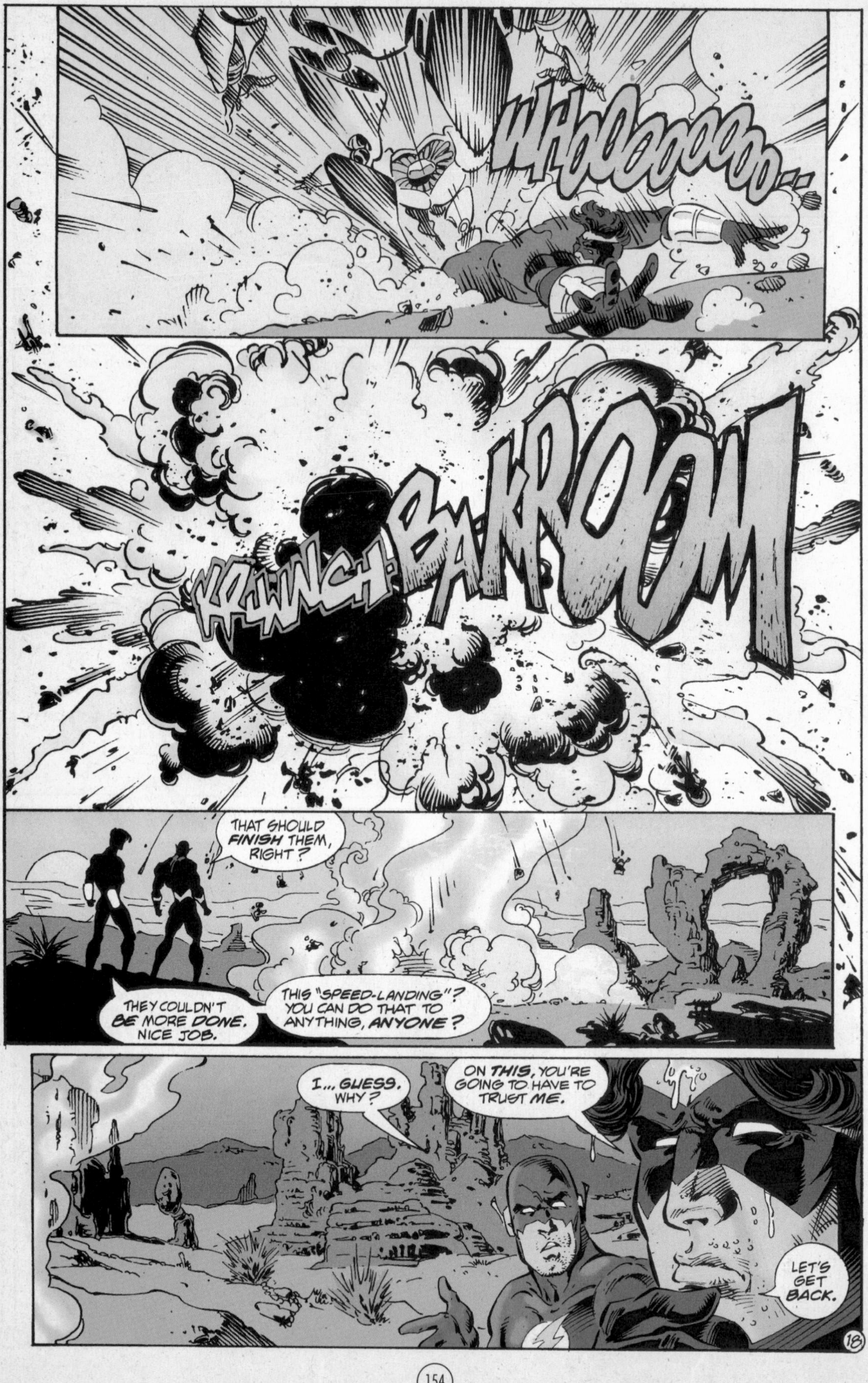
WHOOOOOOOO--
KRUNCH-BAKROOM
THAT SHOULD FINISH THEM, RIGHT?
THEY COULDN'T BE MORE DONE. NICE JOB.
THIS "SPEED-LANDING"? YOU CAN DO THAT TO ANYTHING, ANYONE?
I... GUESS. WHY?
ON THIS, YOU'RE GOING TO HAVE TO TRUST ME.
LET'S GET BACK.
18

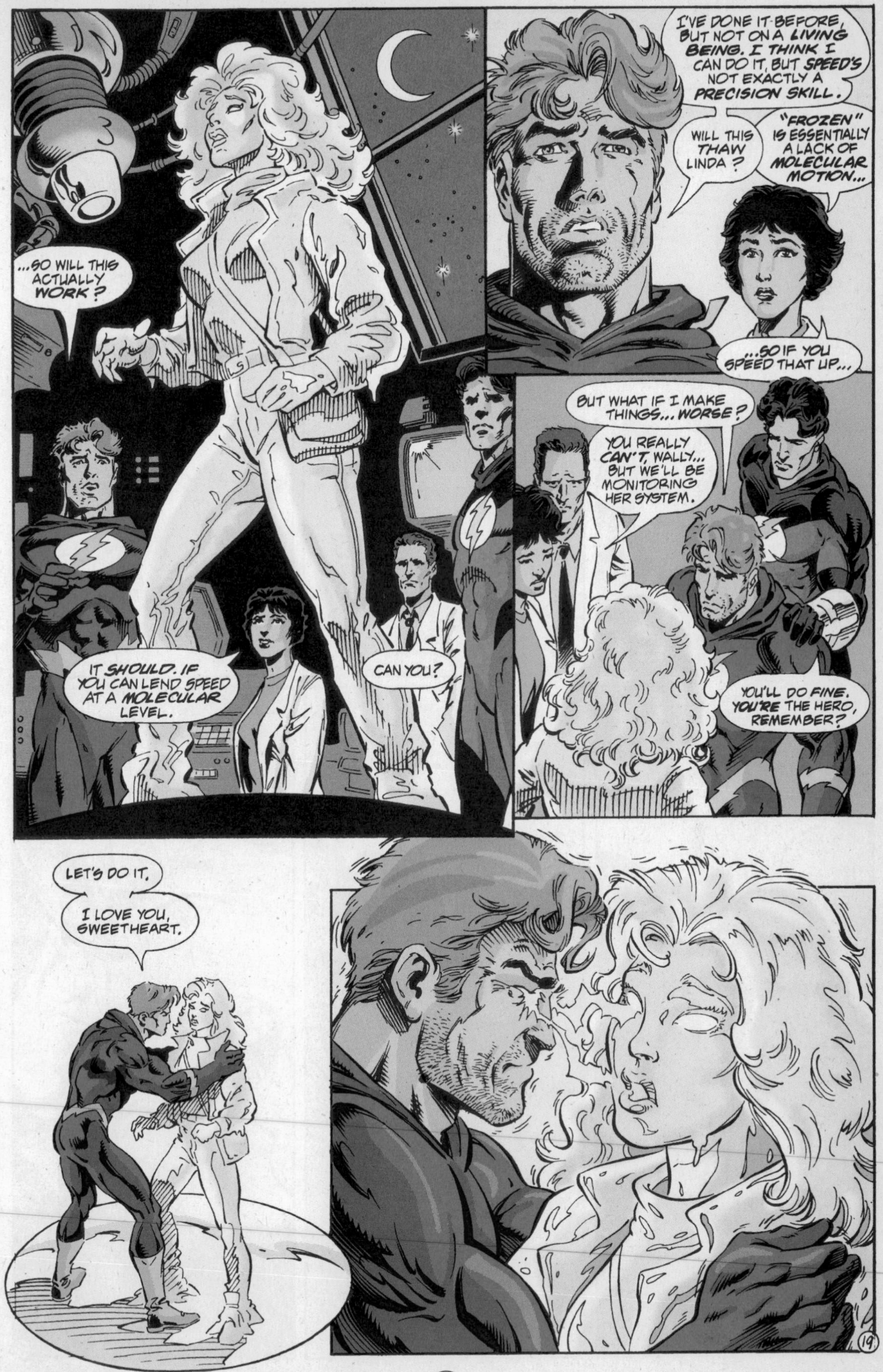
...SO WILL THIS ACTUALLY WORK?
IT SHOULD. IF YOU CAN LEND SPEED AT A MOLECULAR LEVEL.
CAN YOU?
I'VE DONE IT BEFORE, BUT NOT ON A LIVING BEING. I THINK I CAN DO IT, BUT SPEED'S NOT EXACTLY A PRECISION SKILL.
WILL THIS THAW LINDA?
"FROZEN" IS ESSENTIALLY A LACK OF MOLECULAR MOTION...
...SO IF YOU SPEED THAT UP...
BUT WHAT IF I MAKE THINGS... WORSE?
YOU REALLY CAN'T, WALLY... BUT WE'LL BE MONITORING HER SYSTEM.
YOU'LL DO FINE. YOU'RE THE HERO, REMEMBER?
LET'S DO IT.
I LOVE YOU, SWEETHEART.
19

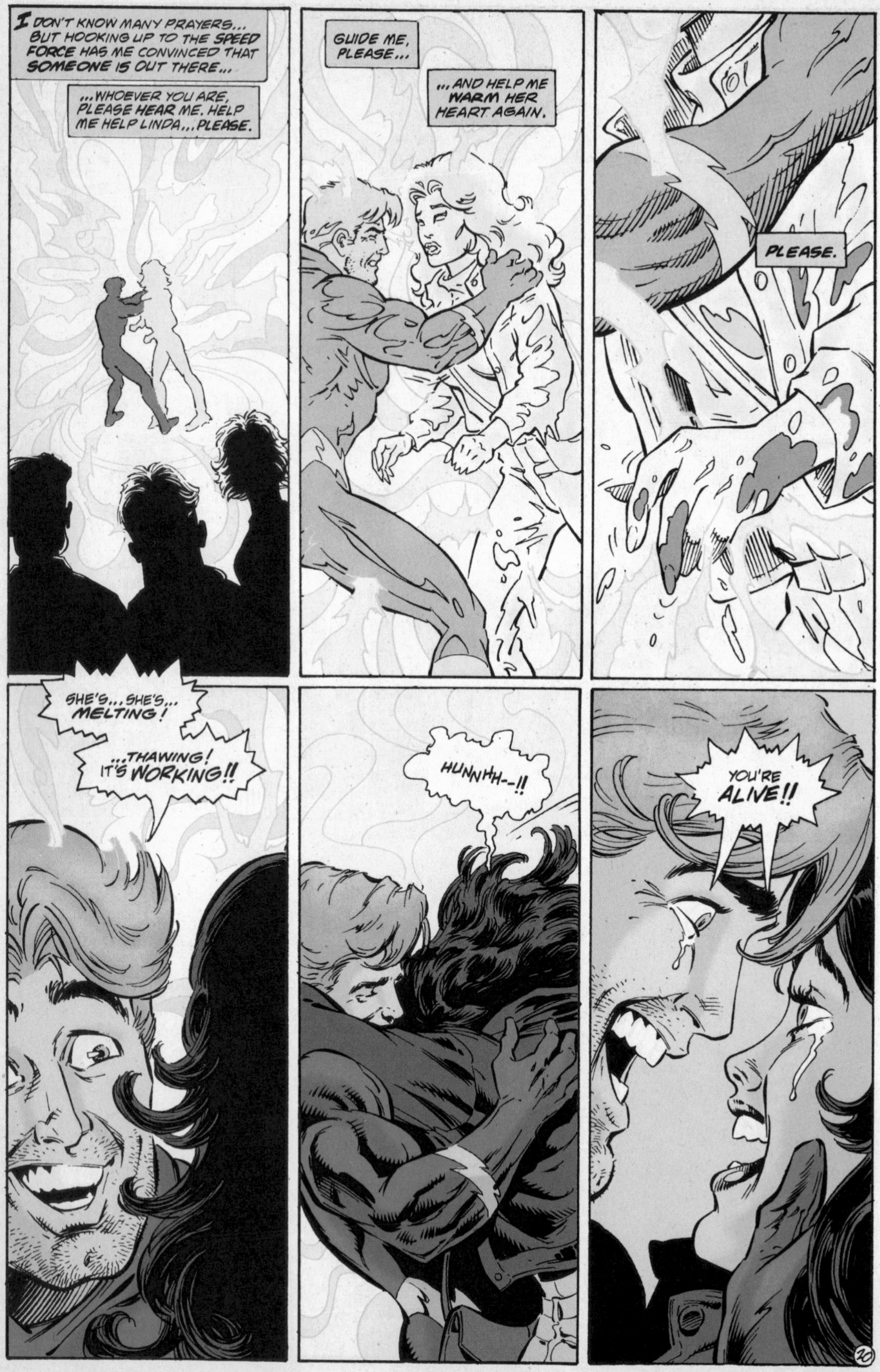
I DON'T KNOW MANY PRAYERS... BUT HOOKING UP TO THE SPEED FORCE HAS ME CONVINCED THAT SOMEONE IS OUT THERE...
...WHOEVER YOU ARE, PLEASE HEAR ME. HELP ME HELP LINDA... PLEASE.
GUIDE ME, PLEASE...
...AND HELP ME WARM HER HEART AGAIN.
PLEASE.
SHE'S... SHE'S... MELTING!
...THAWING! IT'S WORKING!!
HUNNHH--!!
YOU'RE ALIVE!!
20

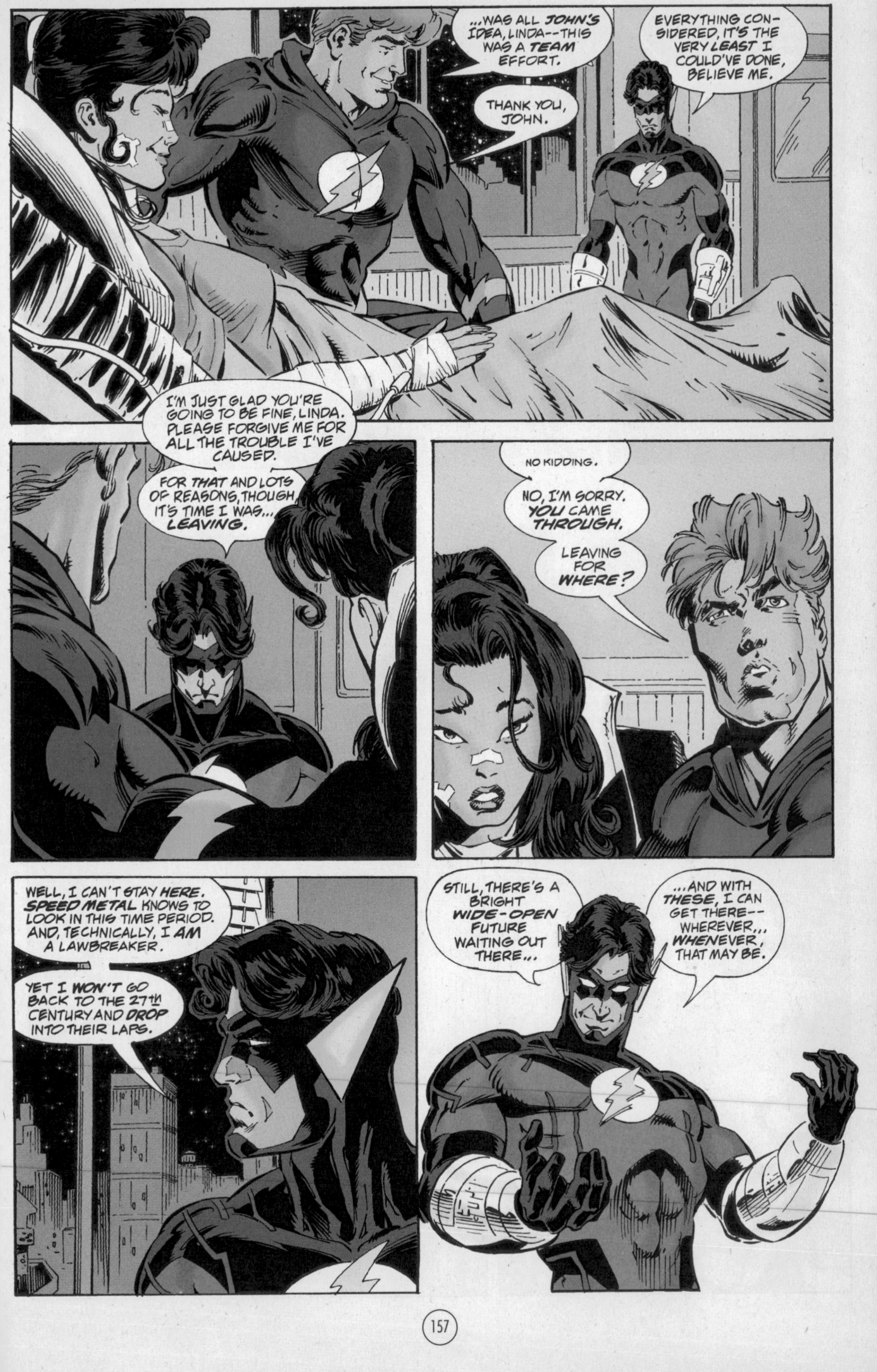
...WAS ALL JOHN'S IDEA, LINDA--THIS WAS A TEAM EFFORT.
THANK YOU, JOHN.
EVERYTHING CONSIDERED, IT'S THE VERY LEAST I COULD'VE DONE, BELIEVE ME.
I'M JUST GLAD YOU'RE GOING TO BE FINE, LINDA. PLEASE FORGIVE ME FOR ALL THE TROUBLE I'VE CAUSED.
FOR THAT AND LOTS OF REASONS, THOUGH IT'S TIME I WAS... LEAVING.
NO KIDDING.
NO, I'M SORRY. YOU CAME THROUGH.
LEAVING FOR WHERE?
WELL, I CAN'T STAY HERE. SPEED METAL KNOWS TO LOOK IN THIS TIME PERIOD. AND, TECHNICALLY, I AM A LAWBREAKER.
YET I WON'T GO BACK TO THE 27TH CENTURY AND DROP INTO THEIR LAPS.
STILL, THERE'S A BRIGHT WIDE-OPEN FUTURE WAITING OUT THERE...
...AND WITH THESE, I CAN GET THERE-- WHEREVER... WHENEVER, THAT MAY BE.

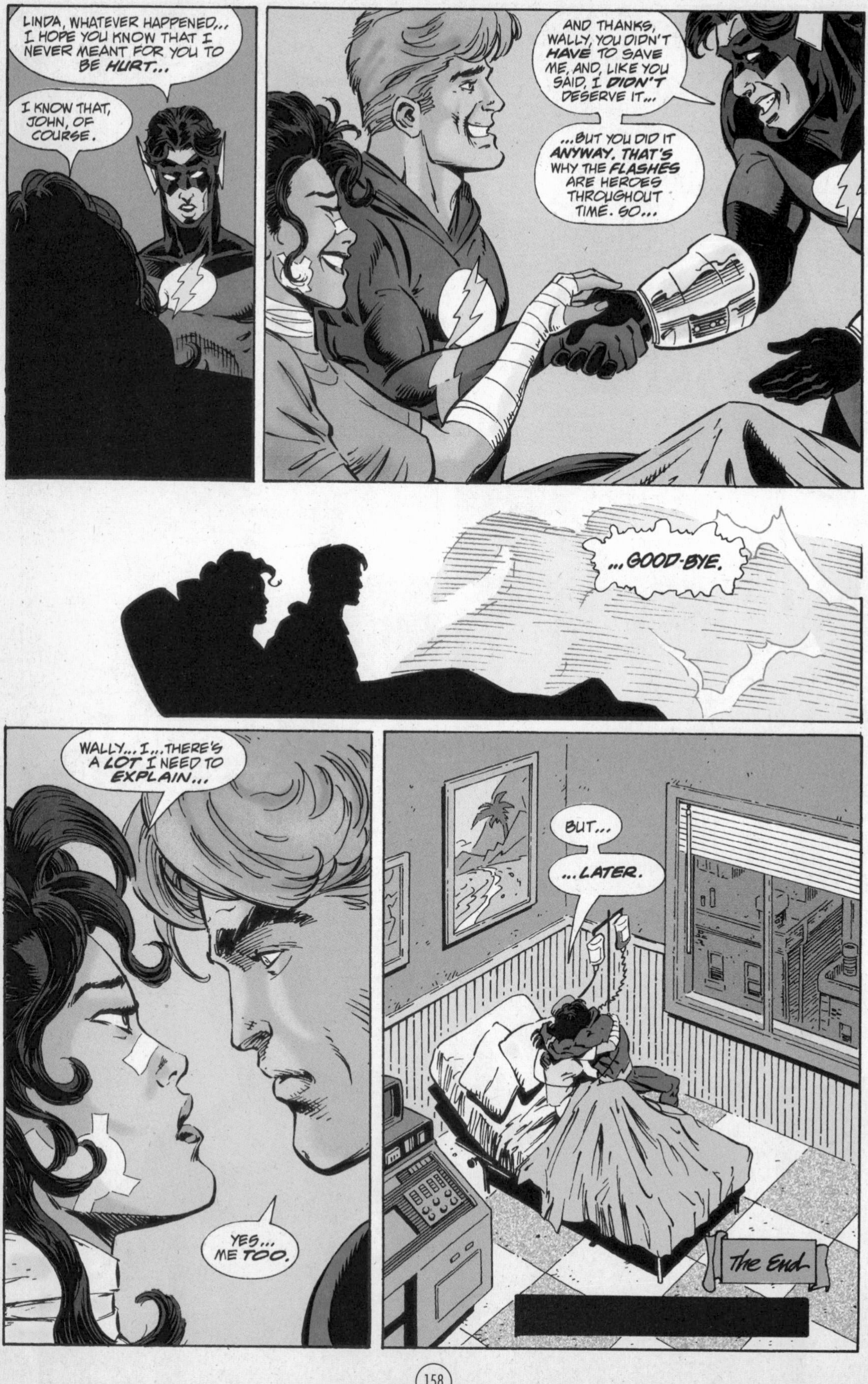
LINDA, WHATEVER HAPPENED... I HOPE YOU KNOW THAT I NEVER MEANT FOR YOU TO BE HURT...
I KNOW THAT, JOHN, OF COURSE.
AND THANKS, WALLY, YOU DIDN'T HAVE TO SAVE ME, AND, LIKE YOU SAID, I DIDN'T DESERVE IT...
...BUT YOU DID IT ANYWAY. THAT'S WHY THE FLASHES ARE HEROES THROUGHOUT TIME. SO...
...GOOD-BYE.
WALLY... I... THERE'S A LOT I NEED TO EXPLAIN...
YES... ME TOO.
BUT...
...LATER.
The End

COVER GALLERY

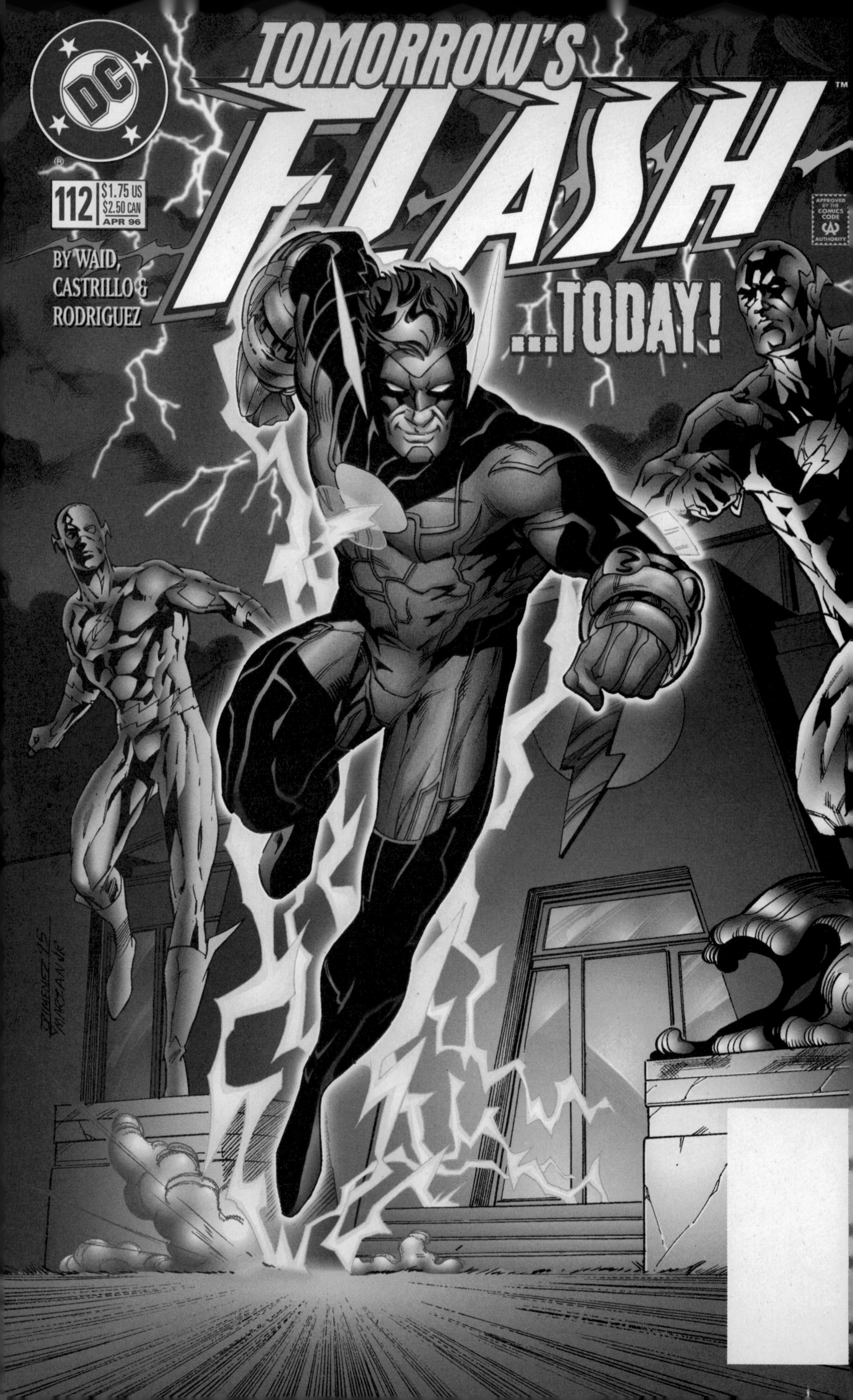

TOMORROW'S
FLASH
...TODAY!
112
$1.75 US
$2.50 CAN
APR 96
BY WAID,
CASTRILLO &
RODRIGUEZ
APPROVED BY THE COMICS CODE AUTHORITY

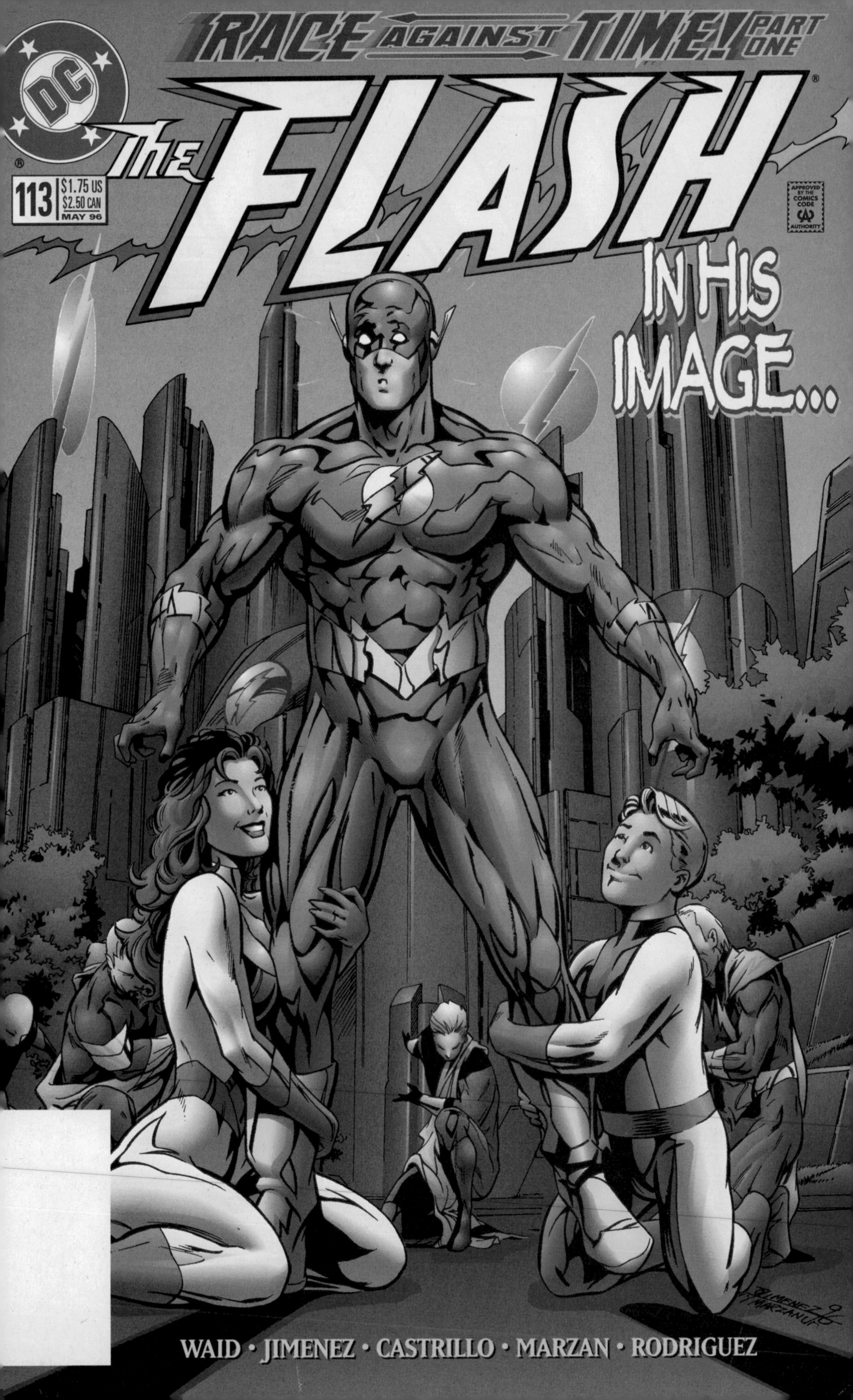
RACE AGAINST TIME! PART ONE
DC
THE FLASH
113
$1.75 US
$2.50 CAN
MAY 96
APPROVED BY THE COMICS CODE AUTHORITY
IN HIS IMAGE...
WAID · JIMENEZ · CASTRILLO · MARZAN · RODRIGUEZ

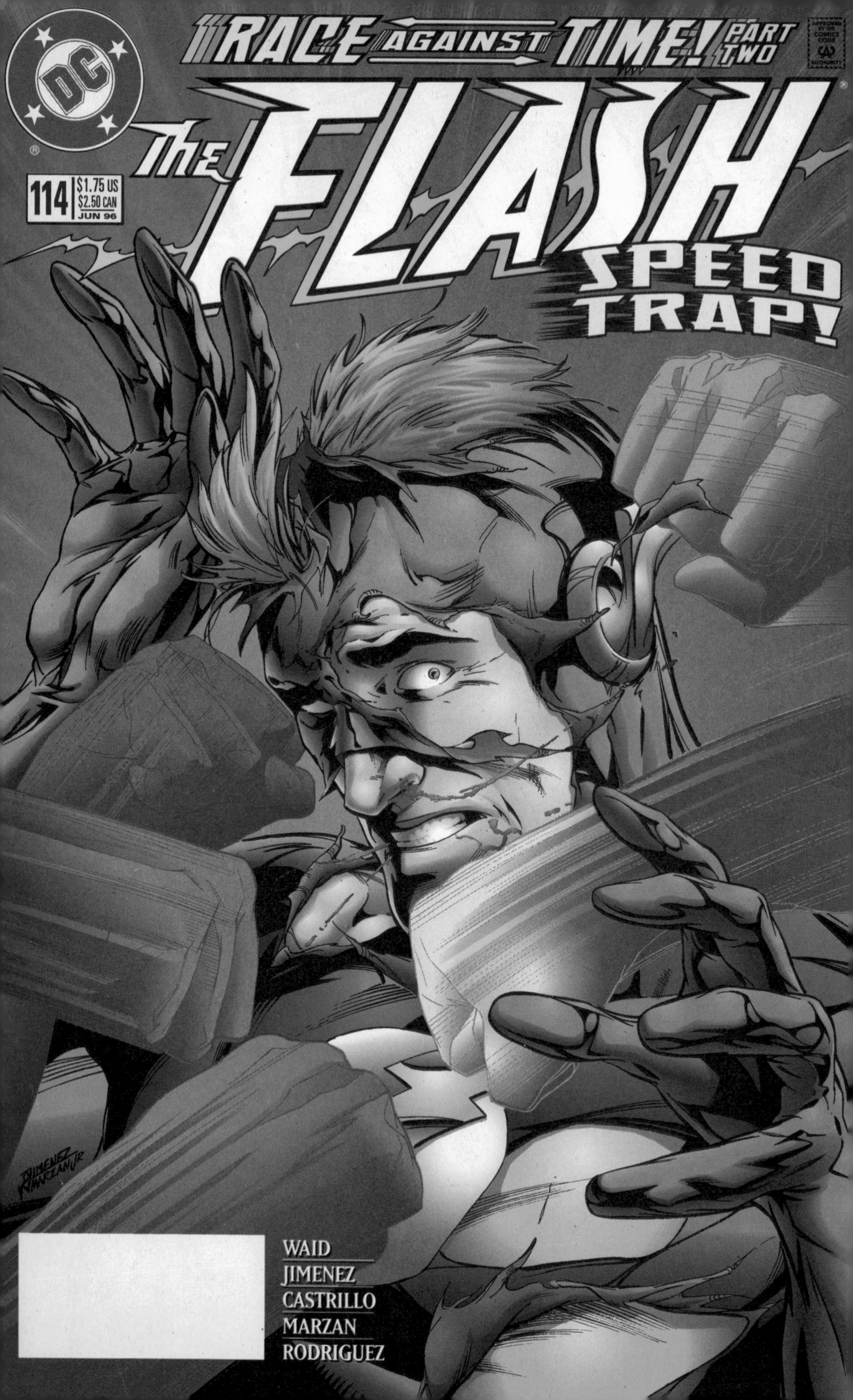
RACE AGAINST TIME! PART TWO
APPROVED BY THE COMICS CODE AUTHORITY
DC
THE FLASH
114 $1.75 US $2.50 CAN JUN 96
SPEED TRAP!
WAID
JIMENEZ
CASTRILLO
MARZAN
RODRIGUEZ

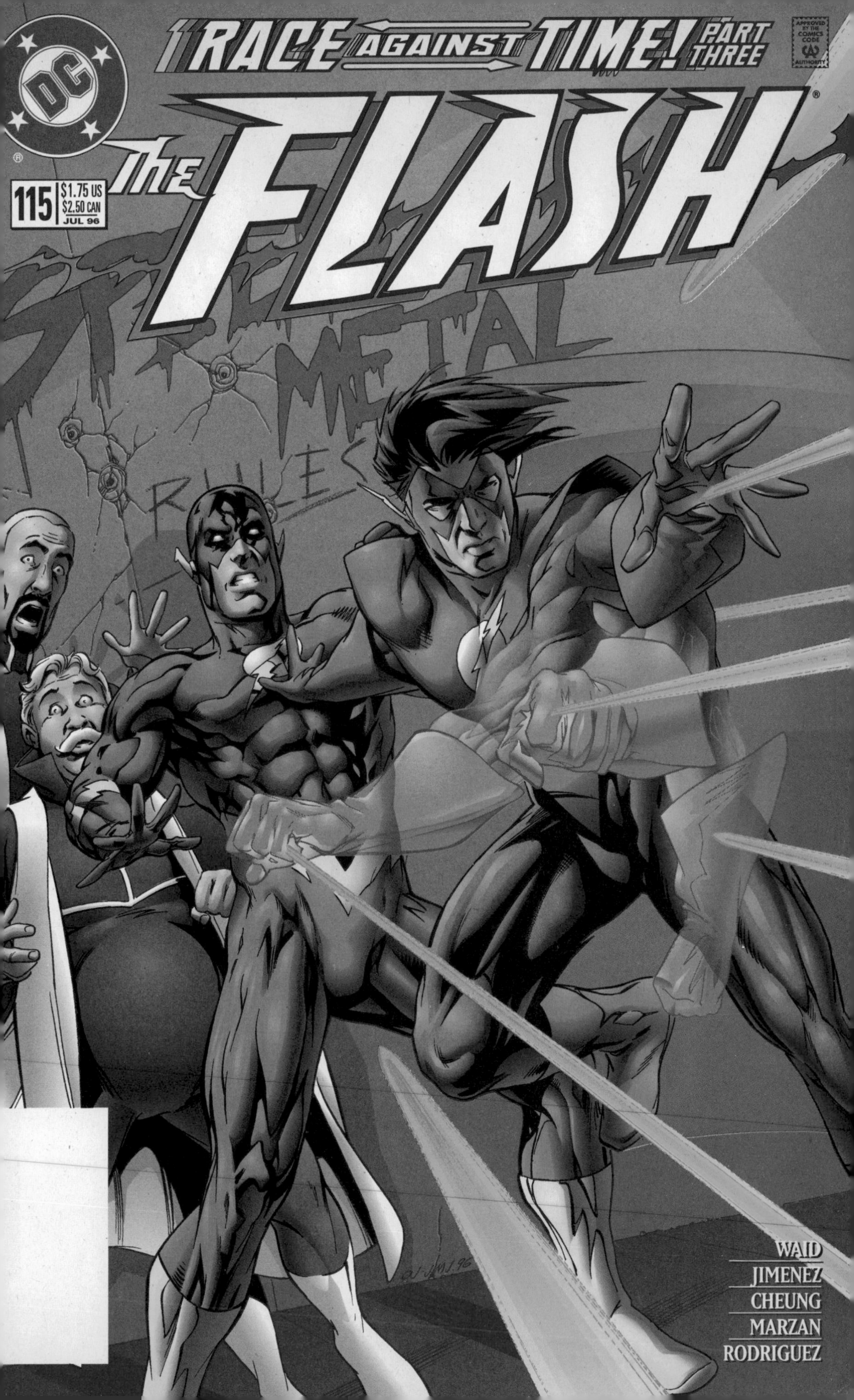
RACE AGAINST TIME! PART THREE
APPROVED BY THE COMICS CODE AUTHORITY
DC
THE FLASH
115
$1.75 US
$2.50 CAN
JUL 96
STEEL METAL
RULES
WAID
JIMENEZ
CHEUNG
MARZAN
RODRIGUEZ

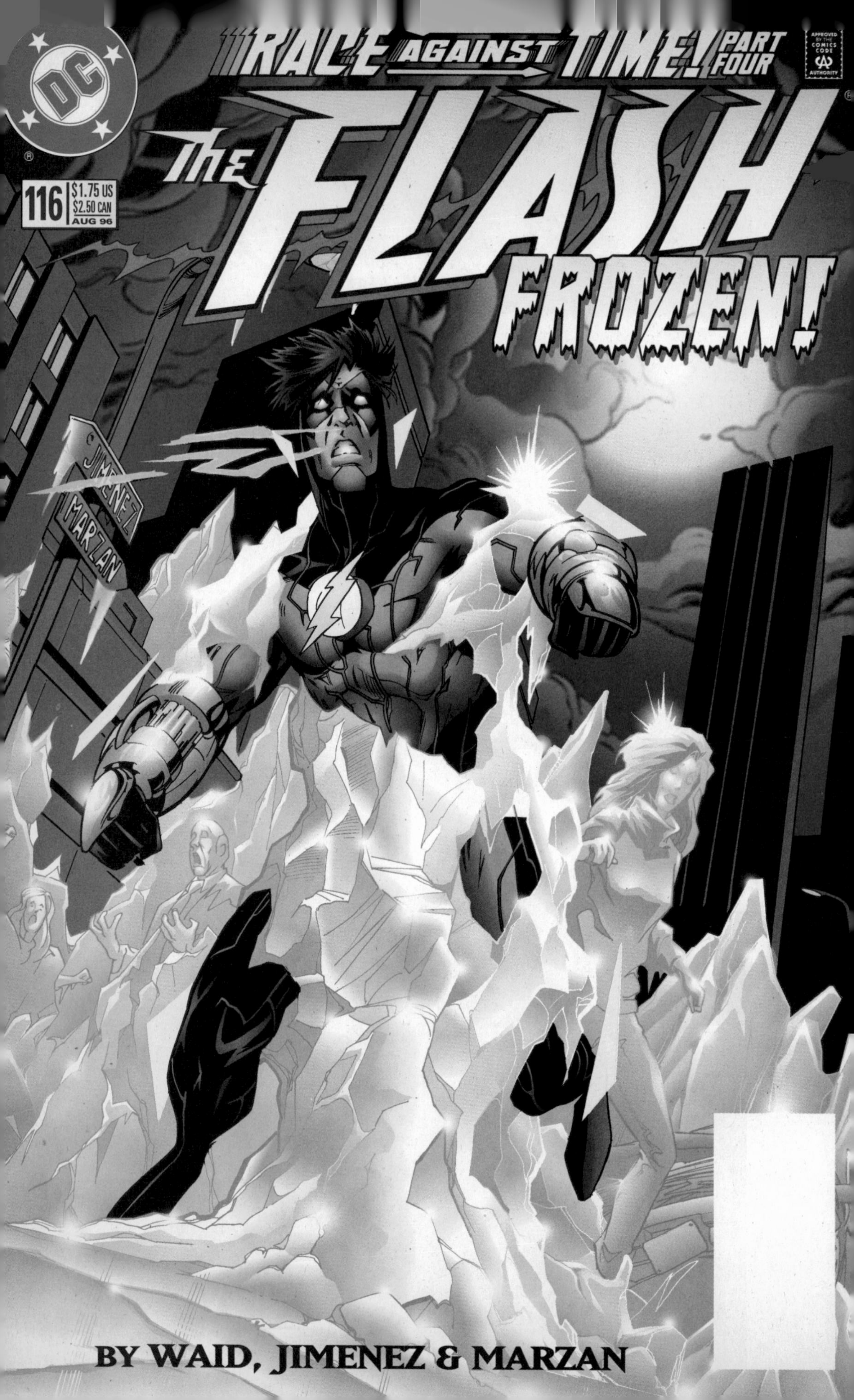
RACE AGAINST TIME! PART FOUR
APPROVED BY THE COMICS CODE AUTHORITY
DC
THE FLASH
116
$1.75 US
$2.50 CAN
AUG 96
FROZEN!
JIMENEZ
MARZAN
BY WAID, JIMENEZ & MARZAN

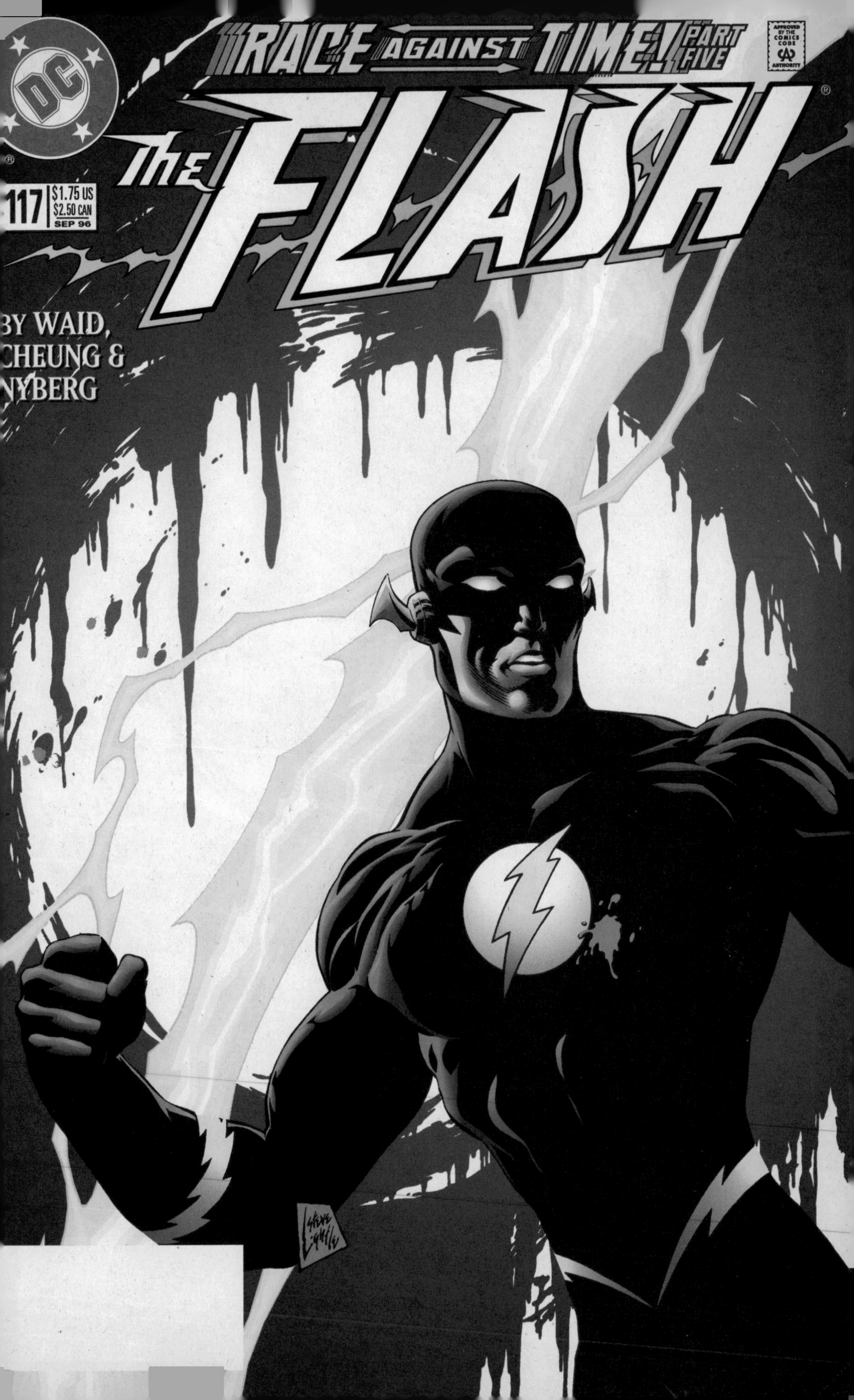
RACE AGAINST TIME! PART FIVE
APPROVED BY THE COMICS CODE AUTHORITY
DC
THE FLASH
117
$1.75 US
$2.50 CAN
SEP 96
BY WAID,
CHEUNG &
NYBERG

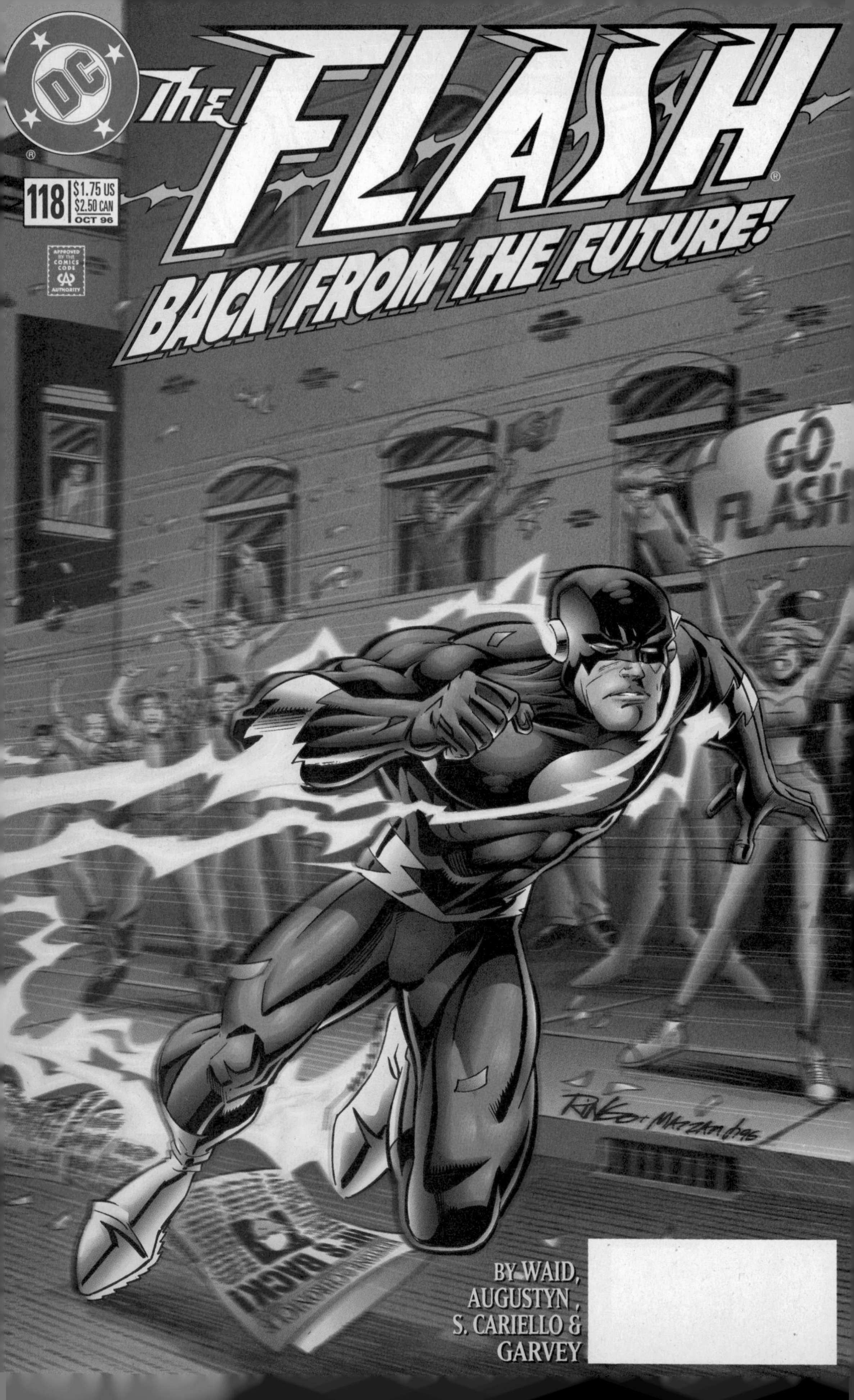
DC
THE FLASH
118
$1.75 US
$2.50 CAN
OCT 96
APPROVED BY THE COMICS CODE AUTHORITY
BACK FROM THE FUTURE!
GO FLASH
BY WAID, AUGUSTYN, S. CARIELLO & GARVEY

THE STARS OF THE
DC UNIVERSE
CAN ALSO BE FOUND IN THESE BOOKS:

DCU0011